JUDGING INEQUALITY

Judging Inequality

STATE SUPREME COURTS AND THE INEQUALITY CRISIS

James L. Gibson and Michael J. Nelson

Russell Sage Foundation   NEW YORK

THE RUSSELL SAGE FOUNDATION

The Russell Sage Foundation, one of the oldest of America's general purpose foundations, was established in 1907 by Mrs. Margaret Olivia Sage for "the improvement of social and living conditions in the United States." The foundation seeks to fulfill this mandate by fostering the development and dissemination of knowledge about the country's political, social, and economic problems. While the foundation endeavors to assure the accuracy and objectivity of each book it publishes, the conclusions and interpretations in Russell Sage Foundation publications are those of the authors and not of the foundation, its trustees, or its staff. Publication by Russell Sage, therefore, does not imply foundation endorsement.

BOARD OF TRUSTEES
Michael Jones-Correa, Chair

Larry M. Bartels	Sheldon Danziger	Nicholas Lemann	Jennifer Richeson
Marianne Bertrand	Kathryn Edin	David Leonhardt	Mario Luis Small
Cathy J. Cohen	Jason Furman	Hazel Rose Markus	
Karen S. Cook	David Laibson	Martha Minow	

LIBRARY OF CONGRESS CATALOGING-IN-PUBLICATION DATA

Names: Gibson, James L., 1951- author. | Nelson, Michael J. (Political scientist), author.
Title: Judging inequality : state supreme courts and the inequality crisis / James L. Gibson, Michael J. Nelson.
Description: New York, New York : Russell Sage Foundation, [2021] | Includes bibliographical references and index. | Summary: "This book investigates the policies made by state high courts that pertain to the seemingly inexorable rise of political, legal, economic, and social inequality in the United States, using data assembled by the authors on the equality-relevant decisions made by the state supreme courts from 1990 to 2015"— Provided by publisher.
Identifiers: LCCN 2021000142 (print) | LCCN 2021000143 (ebook) | ISBN 9780871545039 (paperback) | ISBN 9781610449076 (ebook)
Subjects: LCSH: Equality before the law—United States—States. | Courts of last resort—United States—States. | Equality before the law—United States | United States. Supreme Court.
Classification: LCC KF4764 .G53 2021 (print) | LCC KF4764 (ebook) | DDC 342.7308/5—dc23
LC record available at https://lccn.loc.gov/2021000142
LC ebook record available at https://lccn.loc.gov/2021000143

Copyright © 2021 by Russell Sage Foundation. All rights reserved. Printed in the United States of America. No part of this publication may be reproduced, stored in a retrieval system, or transmitted in any form or by any means, electronic, mechanical, photocopying, recording, or otherwise, without the prior written permission of the publisher. Reproduction by the United States Government in whole or in part is permitted for any purpose.

The paper used in this publication meets the minimum requirements of American National Standard for Information Sciences—Permanence of Paper for Printed Library Materials. ANSI Z39.48-1992.

Text design by Linda Secondari.

RUSSELL SAGE FOUNDATION
112 East 64th Street, New York, New York, 10065
10 9 8 7 6 5 4 3 2 1

JLG: To Cary Patterson and Reggie Whitten, lawyers extraordinaire, who have taught me an enormous amount about how law works in the state courts of the United States—and that law and justice do not have to be enemies of one another.

MJN: To the CERL fellows (plus Keith), who have been an unyielding source of personal and professional support in graduate school and beyond.

CONTENTS

LIST OF ILLUSTRATIONS ix
ABOUT THE AUTHORS xv
PREFACE AND ACKNOWLEDGMENTS xvii

Chapter 1. The Role of State Supreme Courts in Creating Public Policies That Affect Political, Legal, Economic, and Social Inequality *1*

Chapter 2. The Political, Legal, Economic, and Social Inequality State Supreme Court Database *28*

Chapter 3. Do the Haves Come Out Ahead in the State High Courts? *71*

Chapter 4. The Backgrounds and Ideologies of State Supreme Court Justices *97*

Chapter 5. The Institutions *134*

Chapter 6. The Capture of State Supreme Courts by State Political Regimes *159*

Chapter 7. Accounting for the Voting Behavior of State Supreme Court Justices on Cases Pertinent to Inequality *200*

Chapter 8. When Do Courts Advance Equality? *234*

Chapter 9. State Supreme Courts and Political, Legal, Economic, and Social Inequality *260*

NOTES *285*
REFERENCES *319*
INDEX *343*

ILLUSTRATIONS

Figures

Figure 2.1. Pro-Equality Outcomes in State High Courts across Different Policy Subdomains, 1990–2015 *60*

Figure 2.2. Cross-State Variability in State High Court Rulings Favoring Greater Political, Legal, Economic, and Social Equality, 1990–2015 *63*

Figure 2.3. Inter-Justice Variability in the Percentage of State High Court Votes Favoring Greater Equality, 1990–2015 *64*

Figure 3.1. Distribution of Litigant Types across State High Courts, 1990–2015 *79*

Figure 3.2. Distribution of Litigant Power Differential *80*

Figure 3.3. Average Litigant Power Differential, by Issue Domain *81*

Figure 3.4. Percentage of Upperdog Wins in State High Court Cases, by Issue *83*

Figure 3.5. Percentage of Petitioner Wins in State High Courts, by Petitioner Win Advantage *85*

Figure 3.6. Probability of Petitioner Win in State High Courts, by Petitioner Status Differential *87*

Figure 3.7. Seeking Equality in Litigation in State High Courts, by Type of Litigant *89*

Figure 3.8. Interstate Variability in Support for the Upperdog Litigant, Cases in Which the Upperdog Seeks Inequality *94*

Figure 3.9. Interstate Variability in Differential Win Rates by Whether or Not the Upperdog Litigant Seeks Inequality *95*

Figure 4.1. A Simple Model Connecting Backgrounds with Attitudes and Behavior *98*

Figure 4.2. State High Court Justices' Undergraduate Institutions, In-State versus Out-of-State, by State *114*

Figure 4.3. Percentage of State High Court Justices Who Attended Both an Undergraduate School and a Law School in the State Where They Served as a Judge *118*

Figure 4.4. The Previous Career Experiences of State High Court Justices *120*

Figure 4.5. The Distribution of State High Court Justices' Ideologies, by Party Affiliation *124*

Figure 4.6. The Relationship between Justices' Year of Birth and Conservative Ideology *127*

Figure 5.1. Judicial Election Ballot Types *140*

Figure 5.2. Percentage of Appointed Interim State High Court Justices in States with Formal Judicial Elections *150*

Figure 5.3. Percentage of Female State High Court Justices Serving under Different Selection Systems *152*

Figure 5.4. Percentage of Minority State High Court Justices Serving under Different Selection Systems *153*

Figure 6.1. Average Partisan Makeup of State High Courts, 1990–2015 *166*

Figure 6.2. Average Ideological Conservatism Score of State High Courts, 1990–2015 *167*

Figure 6.3. Variability in the Partisan Composition of State High Courts, 1990–2015 *169*

Figure 6.4. Variability in the Ideological Composition of State High Courts, 1990–2015 *170*

ILLUSTRATIONS xi

Figure 6.5. The Relationship between Partisanship and Ideology on State High Courts, 1990–2015 *171*

Figure 6.6. Change in Democratic Party Dominance in the Fifty States, 1990–2015 *174*

Figure 6.7. Governing Coalitions in the States: Party Control of the Branches of Government, 1990–2015 *176*

Figure 6.8. State High Court Alignment with Other State Political Institutions, 1990–2015 *178*

Figure 6.9. Change in Public Opinion, 1990–2015 *182*

Figure 6.10. The Relationship between Public Opinion Liberalism, Democratic Party Dominance, and State High Court Ideology *186*

Figure 6.11. The Marginal Effect of Democratic Dominance, by Retention Method *189*

Figure 6.A.1. The Instrument Used to Impute State-Year Public Opinion *197*

Figure 6.A.2. State Trends in Attitudes toward Equality *198*

Figure 7.1. Rates of Unanimous Decisions by State High Courts in Equality Cases, 1990–2015 *210*

Figure 7.2. Predicted Probability of a State High Court Justice's Pro-Equality Vote, by Judicial Ideology *217*

Figure 7.3. Predicted Probability of a State High Court Justice's Pro-Equality Vote, by Public Opinion *218*

Figure 7.4. Predicted Probabilities of Pro-Equality Votes by State High Court Justices, by Retention Method *221*

Figure 7.5. Marginal Effect of Public Opinion on the Probabilities of Pro-Equality Votes by State High Court Justices, by Retention Method *222*

Figure 7.6. Predicted Probabilities of Pro-Equality Votes by State High Court Justices, by Judicial Compensation *225*

Figure 7.7. Predicted Probabilities of Pro-Equality Votes by State High Court Justices, by Public Opinion Liberalism and Judicial Ideology *227*

xii   Illustrations

Figure 7.8. Predicted Probabilities of Pro-Equality Votes by State High Court Justices, by Retention Method, Public Opinion Liberalism, and Judicial Ideology *229*

Figure 8.1. Predicted Probability of a State High Court Pro-Equality Case Outcome, by Judicial Ideology *242*

Figure 8.2. Predicted Probability of a State High Court Pro-Upperdog Case Outcome, by Judicial Ideology *248*

Figure 8.3. The Marginal Effect of Litigant Motives, by Judicial Ideology *250*

Figure 8.4. Predicted Probability of a State High Court Pro-Upperdog Case Outcome, by Judicial Ideology and Litigant Objectives *251*

Figure 8.5. Predicted Probability of a State High Court Pro-Equality Case Outcome in Four States, 1990–2015 *253*

Figure 8.6. Predicted Probability of a State High Court Pro-Upperdog Case Outcome in Four States, 1990–2015 *254*

Figure 9.1. Governing Coalitions and State High Court Rulings on Political, Legal, Economic, and Social Inequality *268*

Tables

Table 2.1. The Coding of the Dependent Variable—Policy Supporting or Undermining Equality *40*

Table 3.1. Success Rates in State High Courts, by Litigant Status, 1990–2015 *84*

Table 3.2. The Effect of Petitioner Status Differential on Petitioner Success before State High Courts *86*

Table 3.3. The Effect of Litigant Status Differential on Petitioner Success before State High Courts *87*

Table 3.4. Litigant Status and Goals in Litigation before State High Courts *90*

Table 4.1. Predictors of a State High Court Justice's Ideology and Political Party *125*

Table 4.2. Predictors of a State High Court Justice's Ideology, by Political Party *130*

Table 5.1. Methods of Judicial Selection and Retention for State High Courts, 2015 *139*

Table 5.2. Background Characteristics and Attitudes of State High Court Justices, by Initial Selection *151*

Table 6.1. Predictors of Average State High Court Ideology, 1990–2015 *185*

Table 6.2. Predictors of Average State High Court Ideology, by Retention Method, 1990–2015 *188*

Table 6.B.1. Distributions of Variables in Tables 6.1 and 6.2 *199*

Table 6.B.2. Pairwise Comparisons: Marginal Effect of Democratic Dominance *199*

Table 7.1. Random Effects Logistic Regression Results: Pro-Equality State High Court Votes *216*

Table 7.2. Random Effects Logistic Regression Results: Pro-Equality State High Court Votes, with Conditional Effects for Public Opinion *220*

Table 7.3. The Effect of Public Opinion on the Probability of Pro-Equality Votes by State High Court Justices, by Retention Method *223*

Table 7.A.1. Summary Statistics *233*

Table 7.A.2. Pairwise Comparisons: Direct Effect of Retention Method *233*

Table 8.1. Random Effects Logistic Regression Results: Pro-Equality Case Outcome, with Conditional Effects for Public Opinion *241*

Table 8.2. Random Effects Logistic Regression Results: Pro-Upperdog Case Outcome *247*

Table 8.3. Random Effects Logistic Regression Results: Pro-Upperdog Case Outcome, with Conditional Effects for Litigant Objectives *249*

Table 8.A.1. Summary Statistics *259*

Table 8.A.2. Pairwise Comparisons: Direct Effect of Retention Method *259*

ABOUT THE AUTHORS

JAMES L. GIBSON is Sidney W. Souers Professor of Government at Washington University in St. Louis and Professor Extraordinary in Political Science, Stellenbosch University, South Africa.

MICHAEL J. NELSON is Jeffrey L. Hyde and Sharon D. Hyde and Political Science Board of Visitors Early Career Professor in Political Science and associate professor of political science at the Pennsylvania State University.

PREFACE AND ACKNOWLEDGMENTS

AS ANY LARGE project approaches its conclusion, it is natural for the authors to think: How in the world did we get here? That is especially true with this project, which has gone on for a long time and consumed a gigantic amount of blood, sweat, and tears.

We trace the origins of this project to several factors, the first being school finance litigation. We have long been intrigued about this litigation, from two perspectives. First, nearly all state supreme courts have ruled on this issue (some in many rulings), with about half saying yes to equality and the other half saying no. This variability impressed us. Second, school finance litigation has often become protracted and bitter and even involved intense conflict across the branches of state governments (for example, Kansas). Conflict and controversy are the "bread and butter" of judicial politics scholars, so we could not resist paying attention.

Next (at least in our consciousness if not in reality) came the work of Helen Hershkoff. We do not really know Professor Hershkoff, and she is not trained as a social scientist. But her work taught us that virtually every state supreme court has the ammunition—through state constitutions and especially positive rights—to rule in favor of greater political, legal, economic, and social equality. Some have done so; some have not. Again, this variability intrigued us.

Then Ben Page and Marty Gilens entered the scene (via a presentation at the American Political Science Association annual meeting). We were long familiar with Gilens's exceptional treatise on inequality in America, but we were intrigued when Page and Gilens presented the simple argument that greater equality can be fostered by more majoritarianism. We are both judicial scholars, so the idea that giving the majority more power solves problems did not initially sit well with us. After thinking a bit, however, and realizing that there are two kinds of minorities—underprivileged and overprivileged—we began to see how a nineteenth-century theory about judicial elections, put forth by Jed Shugerman, might be tested in the context of the Page and Gilens argument. With our interest whetted by important issues in democratic theory—accountability and independence—we began to think seriously about a project on state supreme courts and political, legal, economic, and social inequality.

And then there is Marc Galanter, who wrote one of the most widely cited law and social sciences articles around, "Why the 'Haves' Come Out Ahead." Perhaps part of the problem of inequality is associated with the fact that "upperdog" parties use the courts to advance their interests, which are inevitably pro-inequality (we presumed). This theory did not turn out to work all that well, but in the early days it seemed to provide a glimpse of the mechanisms undergirding courts and the advancement of inequality.

With all the pieces (sort of) in place, we began to think about how a project might be designed and executed. Inevitably, these thoughts led to the National Science Foundation. As has often been the case, NSF came through with support to fund this research in the form of the following grant:

> Gibson, James L., and Michael J. Nelson. Co-Principal Investigators. "Testing Models of Representation and Institutional Design in State Courts' Consideration of Inequality." National Science Foundation, 2015–2020. Approximately $226,355. [SES-1456568 and SES-1456580].

Moreover, when we finally realized that we might have bitten off more than we could chew, NSF allowed us to alter the completion date of the project. We are eternally grateful for the support NSF has given us and this project.

Collecting the data necessary for this project was demanding, time-consuming, and not all that much fun. And it was expensive. Fortunately, the Russell Sage Foundation came to our rescue. We had already collected nearly all the case-level data with the NSF grant, but then it dawned on us: What good is a dependent variable without a bunch of independent variables? With RSF support, we were able to assemble a host of predictors of court outcomes, the most important of which was a quite substantial judge-based database. The Russell Sage Foundation funded this project through the following grant:

> Gibson, James L., and Michael J. Nelson. Co-Principal Investigators. "Judging Inequality." Russell Sage Foundation, 2018–2021. Approximately $150,000. [G-1962].

We are immensely grateful to both NSF and RSF for their support of this project. Authors always say that "without the support of X, the project could not have been completed," but that is infinitely true in this instance. And of course, any opinions, findings, conclusions, or recommendations expressed in this book and other writings from the project are ours alone and do not necessarily reflect the views of the National Science Foundation or the Russell Sage Foundation.

With these two grants came the "opportunity" to hire and manage nearly fifty research assistants. For answering our seemingly endless stream of questions about managing the grant funds, getting the research assistants on payroll, and gently prompting us to remember to approve time sheets, we thank the hard work of Alana Bame, Kristy Boob, Michelle Ilgen, Gloria Lucy, Carol Mellott, Stephanie Rossman, Melinda Warren, and Rocco Zinoble.

We are deeply grateful to the reviewers of both our grant proposals and this book, as well as conference attendees and discussants at various professional meetings. Ardent believers in peer review, we have profited from the careful and trenchant comments of those who scrutinized our work. We have also been extremely lucky to have one of the best editors ever: Suzanne Nichols. This book and its authors are enormously in her debt.

There are many others to thank. Several of our friends and colleagues helped us to fact-check our data and answered our (seemingly endless) questions about how state courts work. In particular, we thank Alex Bluebond, Tyler Buller, Charlie Geyh, Brandon Harper, Erin Lueker, Kristofer Lyons, Greg Magarian, Neal Schuett, and Anna Smith.

We also profited immensely from the generosity of other scholars. Chris Warshaw provided data on state-level public opinion and public policy; Jason Windett and Matt Hall shared data on judges' dates of service, among sundry other helpful materials; Greg Goelzhauzer kindly shared his data on state supreme court justice characteristics; Bert Kritzer was a generous sounding board as we drafted the book, as well as a limitless fount of knowledge about the state courts; and John Kastellec and Chris Zorn helped us with some key questions about multilevel modeling. In the end, Bert Kritzer read the entire manuscript for us and gave innumerable helpful comments and criticisms. We very much appreciate his help.

And perhaps most importantly, we have benefited unbelievably from the diligent work of our research assistants. Whitney Barr, James Barton, Delaney Battle, L. E. Beck, Andrew Bernstein, Chelsea Betcher, Jarred Boyer, Jonathan Brown, Michael Burnham, Samantha Chestney, Jared Costanzo, Bethany Friedrich, Danny Gerwitz, Anat Gross, Lily Hamer, Carter Hirshborn, Robert Hopkins, Ashley Kennedy, Hannah Kirley, Gwen Klein, Tara Knowlton, Kyle Loraine, Richard Montone, Ashley Moore, Taylor Morthland, Anna Notchick, Katie O'Quinn, Isabella Pantano, Jenna Pedersen, Cooper Powell, Tamara Prevatt, Zachary Rigg, Katharine Ross, Kyle Rush, Dave Rusk, Charles Ryan, Taran Samarth, Steven Saroka, Victor Schleich, Luke Smith, Lee Snodgrass, Paul Spada, Noah Spietel, Caleb Trimm, Jack Wasserman, and Kat Weinstock worked many long hours to produce the data sets we analyze in this book. In particular, we cannot overstate our thanks to Kenny Geisler, Steve Morgan, and Laura Jarasek, who each spent years on this project. Without their assistance, this book definitely would not have come to completion.

Gibson would like to acknowledge several people and institutions that contributed significantly to the completion of this book. The Weidenbaum Center, and especially its director, Steven S. Smith, have long supported his research agenda, and this project is no exception. Most of the writing on this book was accomplished during a 2019–2020 sabbatical that Washington University in St. Louis provided him, for which he is very much indebted. Jim Spriggs and Matt Gabel (chiefs of the Department of Political Science at the time) were also quite helpful in this regard. Finally, the completion of this project was facilitated by the arrival of the Covid-19 virus in both the United States and South Africa. Perhaps perversely, the resulting lockdowns (in the United States) and lockouts (in South Africa) generated a block of time during which the book was finished. So Gibson is indebted, it seems, to whoever gave us the virus.

Nelson would like to thank Jim Spriggs and Heather Sloan-Randick at Washington University in St. Louis for finding him office space for the summers he spent in St. Louis supervising research assistants, and Jim Gibson and Monica Kinsella for generously allowing him to house-sit for them during these summers, especially after Monica learned (the hard way) that he is a much better fish breeder than an orchid caretaker. He also thanks Lee Ann Banaszek and Marie Hojnacki, heads of Penn State's political science department while this project was underway, as well as the McCourtney Institute for Democracy and Penn State and its director, Michael Berkman, for their support of the project. This project was completed during a 2020–2021 release from teaching and sabbatical from Penn State; he is very thankful for the time to push the book past the finish line.

Finally, this book has not been a labor of love—but perhaps no book is when the authors are finally ready to write the preface and acknowledgments. Rather, it has been a labor. After years of working on this project, we still believe that addressing the role of state high courts in the equality crisis in the United States is a vital and important research question. No doubt about that. But while we thought it would be a relatively easy task to create and assemble the relevant data, the project presented a set of formidable and enduring challenges.

We were wrong that this research would be a piece of cake. As an easy example, we had hoped to include the Kagan, Cartwright, Friedman, and Wheeler data from an earlier time period in our analysis. It turns out, however, that their raw data have been swallowed up by history, never to return. (We thank Ariel Dobkin for braving the Yale Law School archives to verify this for us.) As a more difficult example, including school finance cases that predated our 1990–2015 focus increased the amount and complexity of data collection by a factor too large to even try to estimate. And throughout our data collection, we have discovered irksome errors in public data sources, not to mention conflicting public sources of information about the attributes of the justices we study in this book. We have done our best to produce accurate and reliable data for this project, but despite these efforts, errors may well remain. We just hope that twenty years from now, when someone writes a follow-up to our work, the authors will not complain too much about our own errors. Although we accept that there is no realistic chance that this will happen, we did our best.

Part of our difficulty with the data in the project stemmed from serious problems with the sources of the decisional (case) data themselves. We are actually fans of federalism (but wish N were larger than fifty), but the lack of standardization in the way that state supreme courts report their opinions is a serious enough issue that we decided to include some comments on the matter in the final chapter to this book. Simply put, the state supreme courts as a whole do a poor job of reporting their decisions, and an especially poor job of recording how each member of the court voted in those decisions. The state supreme courts are public, policymaking institutions, and they need to be, in our view, much more transparent and accountable for reporting the decisions they make.

Although we sometimes complain about publicly available data, we are indebted to those who have come before us and created public databases. We recognize that data transparency is a movement of the fairly recent past; that funding agencies pay much too little attention to ensuring that accurate, raw data are made available for future use; and that researchers are often overwhelmed by the amount of effort required to produce "certified" data sets. Reconciling our data with existing databases required considerable time and effort. Still, we are very much in the debt (and in awe) of those who have gone into the state supreme court swamp before us.

The analysis we have attempted in this book was difficult, exceedingly time-consuming, and unbelievably complex. In the end, all we can really say is that we have given it our best, doing everything we could to understand and explain these courts and how and why they have ruled on political, legal, economic, and social inequality issues. We hope we have made some contribution to democratic and judicial theory and that future research will delve even more deeply into these vital policymaking institutions that make such important decisions affecting all of the American people.

James L. Gibson
St. Louis, Mo.
August 2020

Michael J. Nelson
State College, Penn.
August 2020

CHAPTER 1

The Role of State Supreme Courts in Creating Public Policies That Affect Political, Legal, Economic, and Social Inequality

SOCIAL SCIENTISTS HAVE recently taught us that at least some portion of the growing political, legal, economic, and social inequality in the United States is a function of the policy decisions made by U.S. political institutions. No one has argued this conclusion more forcefully and persuasively than Martin Gilens, whose research at the federal level stands as a landmark achievement.[1] Gilens argues that political inequality directly translates into economic inequality. More specifically, he shows that policymakers are more responsive to the political preferences of the well-to-do than they are to the preferences of the middle and working classes. Anyone with even a casual awareness of the role of money in contemporary American politics would find the Gilens thesis credible.

As important as policymaking at the federal level may be, a great deal of relevant public policy is made by the states.[2] As the easiest example, most (but not all) states tax income, but few states decide to tax income progressively. States also vary in the benefits they provide to needy residents. An important question is whether state legislation has mitigated, reinforced, or created inequality, and whether the same mechanisms of unequal representation discovered at the federal level apply to state legislatures.

Missing in particular from this research agenda on the ways in which democratic institutions contribute to political, legal, economic, and social inequality is attention to the third branch of government: the courts, and especially state high courts. This may be because courts are not assumed to be important policymakers, or because the type of law courts make (mainly common law precedents) is deemed to be a poor cousin to statutory law. Neither assumption, however, is correct. Because the U.S. Supreme Court has steadily withdrawn from American politics (deciding far fewer than one hundred cases per year, a minority of which deal with state law), the state high courts have become the courts of last resort on a vast array of public policies. Indeed, as has been recognized by interest groups that try to shape the state judiciaries, these institutions are incredibly powerful and efficacious policymakers.[3] And creating judicial precedents is just as valuable to interest groups as getting laws passed through legislation.

The list of policy areas in which state supreme courts have become major policymakers mirrors the list of the most pressing policies confronted by the other branches of state governments. And because each state has its own unique constitution, which often contains provisions dealing *directly* with inequality, the state judicial branch's final say on the meaning of the state constitution makes it impossible to overstate the role these courts play in producing public policies relevant to the political, legal, economic, and social equality of Americans.

Examples of the prominent role of state courts in shaping social and economic policy are easy to find. For instance, many state high courts have ruled on the legality of school funding equalization schemes (shifting tax revenue from wealthy school districts to poorer school districts). In other cases, state supreme courts have set guidelines for the conditions under which employers can dismiss employees without cause ("employment at will" doctrine). Finally, while more than a dozen state constitutions contain provisions dealing with the needs of the poor,[4] many state courts have ruled that these clauses are not judicially enforceable.[5]

These courts have also played a leading role in addressing political inequalities among Americans. For example, some state courts have recently ruled on the constitutionality of restrictions on citizens' ability to vote and the legality of legislative district boundaries. And in the past several years, supreme courts in several states have issued decisions on the collective bargaining rights of unionized workers. Finally, many state supreme courts have directly confronted the matter of same-sex marriage, an issue often framed as one of equality.[6] In sum, there can be little doubt that understanding the politics of inequality in the contemporary United States requires paying considerable attention to the state judicial systems.

The purpose of this book is to investigate the policies made by state high courts that pertain to the seemingly inexorable rise of political, legal, economic, and social inequality in the United States. The project takes advantage of a database we assembled, with support from both the National Science Foundation and the Russell Sage Foundation, on the equality-relevant decisions made by the state supreme courts during the period from 1990 to 2015. To preview our findings, we find that of about six thousand cases coded, half favored greater equality while the other half favored greater inequality. From these cases, we can determine whether the "haves"—the upperdogs in society—come out ahead in the state courts. Our specific analytical objective in this book is to explain why some state supreme courts have been more likely to favor equality than other courts, accounting for differences via these courts' structures, judges, constituents, and time.

This analysis relies heavily on our understanding of democratic theory and of state high courts as minoritarian institutions. In particular, one major contribution of this book is our proposal and adoption of a somewhat unusual twist in democratic theory's understanding of minoritarianism: we address the possibility that state courts are minoritarian institutions, but that they privilege the claims of society's haves rather than its have-nots. Therefore, it is useful to begin this book by going back to basics to review our understanding of democratic theory and the role played by the third branch in that theory.

Courts as Minoritarian Institutions

As every civics class in the United States teaches, the American judiciary is charged with protecting the rights of minorities against abuses by the majority. If democracy is "majority rule, with institutionalized opportunities for the minority to try to become a majority," then courts are minoritarian institutions that are responsible for protecting the minority rights of half of that democratic equation.[7]

Many Americans' socialization into the political process emphasizes this theoretical aspect of the judiciary's role. One of the first court cases many students learn by name is *Brown v. Board of Education*, a case in which the Supreme Court stood for the rights of minority schoolchildren over the powerful opposition of segregationist elites.[8] A new generation of schoolchildren will learn about the Court's *Obergefell v. Hodges* decision, which guaranteed gay and lesbian Americans across the country the right to marry.[9] By this simplistic view of the judiciary, the courts are the primary political institution willing and able to protect minority rights against the steadfast wishes of the majority.

But some have questioned whether courts perform this role at all, suggesting that the U.S. Supreme Court, at least, rarely strays for long from the preferences of the dominant elites, or what Robert Dahl refers to as the "governing coalition": those people (and views) in control of the legislative and executive branches of government.[10] Many legal scholars have adopted this viewpoint, thereby largely dismissing the "countermajoritarian dilemma" in which the unaccountable federal judiciary checks the will of the majority.[11] In some respects, the logic is simple: justices are typically not drawn from the ranks of the revolutionaries; instead, justices serving on the U.S. Supreme Court have historically been members of the dominant elite, sharing the perceptions and values of elected legislators and executives, and they make decisions that do not stray long or far from the preferences of those holding power in the political system.[12]

That judges are not revolutionaries hardly needs much empirical support (Justice William O. Douglas perhaps excepted; see his *Points of Rebellion*).[13] At the federal level, those individuals who sit on the bench are those who have the networks to attract the attention of the legislative and executive branches through their professional or social circles. Given the social class origins—and hence ideological predispositions—of American judges, it would be surprising if the makeup of the federal judiciary were different than it is today.

This selection effect has produced a relatively ideologically homogenous judiciary. As Robert McCloskey puts it, in discussing policy preferences against the regulation of business, the U.S. Supreme Court is "composed of judges who were inevitably drawn largely from the ranks of the 'haves.'" As a result, he argues, the institution "was almost certain to throw its weight against the regulatory movement and on the side of the business community."[14] And it has done so.[15]

More recent data support the assertion that a relatively conservative group of people make up the judiciary. In their comparison of the ideologies of federal judges, their clerks, the law professoriate, and the legal profession, Adam Bonica and his colleagues conclude that judges tend to be more conservative than law professors, who in turn are about 11 percent more liberal than the legal profession as a whole.[16] As Bonica and Maya Sen demonstrate, the bar is more liberal than the general American population, but judges—especially those at higher ranks of the judiciary and those selected through appointive systems—are more conservative than the pool of attorneys in the state.[17]

As a result, there can be little doubt that most judges who have served on appellate courts in the United States have tended to hold "elitist" and conservative political values. That their institutions would, as a result, make conservative public policies should come as no surprise. That their institutions would try to rein in political, legal, economic, and social *inequality* would be surprising.[18]

Some scholars take a step further and resoundingly and directly reject the thesis that courts, as countermajoritarian institutions, have historically protected "underdogs." By these accounts, the Supreme Court's famed rulings in cases like *Brown v. Board of Education* were less the result of a principled institution trying to advance equality proactively than a relatively weak institution ruling in favor of equality for pragmatic, political reasons.[19] For instance, as Michael Klarman notes: "The romantic image of the Court as countermajoritarian savior is shattered by historical reality." As evidence he reminds us:

> The Supreme Court sanctioned rather than attacked slavery, legitimized segregation for much of the Jim Crow era, validated the Japanese-American internment during World War II, sanctioned McCarthyism, and approved sex discrimination until after the emergence of the modern women's movement. The most celebrated examples of the Court's supposed countermajoritarian heroics are less than compelling. The *Brown* decision was the product of a broad array of political, social, economic and ideological forces inaugurated or accelerated by World War II; by the time of the Court's intervention, half the nation no longer supported racial segregation. Similarly, *Roe v. Wade* was decided at the crest of the modern women's movement and was supported by half the nation's population from the day it was handed down. Finally, the Court protected gay rights for the first time in *Romer v. Evans* only after a social and political gay rights movement had made substantial inroads against traditional attitudes toward homosexuality.[20]

By Klarman's account, the Court hardly seems like an institution that has been effective at blocking majoritarian overreach.

The noted constitutional law scholar Erwin Chemerinsky makes a similar argument in *The Case against the Supreme Court*.[21] In addition to noting the marquee cases that Klarman discusses, Chemerinsky emphasizes lesser-known cases with equally tragic consequences. In *Buck v. Bell*, for example, the Court allowed the forced sterilization of a mentally disabled eighteen-year-old because "three generations of imbeciles are enough."[22] Or, in 2010, the justices unanimously dismissed a civil lawsuit from a prisoner's family who sought justice because the prisoner died owing to negligent medical care. In these quieter cases as well, the Court has been apt to side with society's upperdogs.

Of course, a problem with protecting minority rights is that there are two types of minorities: overprivileged and underprivileged. Under the rules of contemporary American politics, the former have little difficulty in protecting their political, legal, economic, and social interests, while the latter have considerably more difficulty. To protect the rights of underprivileged minorities, political institutions must rule against the interests of the privileged elite, who profit so greatly from policies reinforcing inequality and therefore rule in favor of the preferences—or at least the interests—of the majority.

With this distinction in mind, perhaps the Court has indeed protected minorities, but instead of protecting *underprivileged* minorities, it has protected *overprivileged* minorities. This is Klarman's position:

> For much of its history, the Court protected the minority group for which the Framers entertained the greatest sympathy—property owners. Madison candidly revealed his minority rights sympathies in Federalist No. 10, when he identified as a principal virtue of the large republic its capacity to inhibit "a rage for paper money, for an abolition of debts, for an equal division of property, or for any other improper or wicked project." Until the New Deal constitutional revolution, the Court established a track record of protecting certain property-owning minorities from majoritarian redistribution, whether in the form of debtor relief laws, a mildly progressive national income tax, or protective union legislation. In perhaps its most infamous decision, the Court in *Dred Scott* protected the rights of one of American history's classic minority groups, southern slave owners. More recently, the Court in *City of Richmond v. J. A. Croson Co.* secured the equal protection

rights of Richmond's minority white population by invalidating a city council affirmative action plan that awarded racial preferences in construction contracts. The point, to reiterate, is that protecting minority rights is normatively attractive only if the Court protects the "right" minorities. It is unclear why the Court should possess some inherent institutional advantage over legislatures in that enterprise, and the historical record confirms that the Justices have blundered as often as they have succeeded.[23]

Thus, Klarman, at least, is decidedly of the view that the minority rights that are protected by the unaccountable federal courts are the rights of overprivileged minorities, not underprivileged minorities.

It is not difficult to provide additional examples of the legal doctrines with which the federal courts have come to the aid of upperdogs. Take, for example, the U.S. Supreme Court's decision in *Citizens United v. FEC*, a controversial 2010 ruling in which the Court held that legislation that prohibited corporations from participating fully in the electoral process through campaign spending was an unconstitutional violation of the U.S. Constitution's guarantee of free speech.[24]

Another doctrine that often benefits upperdogs is the governmental "taking" of private property for public use, with *Kelo v. City of New London* providing a great example.[25] The takings clause of the Fifth Amendment to the U.S. Constitution has historically been used as a doctrine to advance the public good, with private property taken for the public project. But in *Kelo*, the U.S. Supreme Court allowed the government to take the property of poor people and give it to wealthy developers for their private benefit (developing a shopping mall) because ultimately, the Court reasoned, the city would reap more tax revenue.

As a final example, consider the Roberts Court's 2018 decision in *Janus v. American Federation of State, County, and Municipal Employees* in which the Court struck a blow to public-sector unions and provided a win to those upperdogs opposed to collective bargaining.[26] By ruling that these unions cannot charge an agency fee for union nonmembers in a workplace, even when such workers benefit from union contracts and other services, the Court vastly undermined the work of public-sector unions and advantaged employers nationwide.

This discussion reveals that there is clear evidence for the assertion that courts have contributed to public policies relevant to the maintenance and growth of inequality in the United States. Society's haves—an overprivileged minority—have profited from the formally unaccountable and relatively conservative federal courts in the United States.

The conclusion of this analysis is that even the nominally independent federal courts deviate little and rarely from the preferences of the dominant elites in the country. Consequently, there is little reason to expect them to favor greater political, legal, economic, and social equality. To the extent that the third branch is a minoritarian institution, it seems to be an institution that often protects overprivileged minorities rather than the underprivileged. With a limited handful of exceptions, the minority rights that get protected are the rights of the upperdogs in society.

Elite Capture of Judicial Institutions

As we have noted, one mechanism by which judicial policies favor political, legal, economic, and social inequality is simply that judges are themselves privileged elites who vote their values and interests in rendering judicial decisions. Ran Hirschl has taken an important additional step in his exploration of the influence of elite interests in political institutions by arguing that overprivileged elites use judicial institutions to remove crucial issues of political, legal, economic, and social inequality from majoritarian political arenas in which greater equality might be preferred.[27] His theory is quite useful to our analysis.

Hirschl is interested in the judicialization of politics, but he takes an unusual tack on the subject. Beginning by establishing a paradox—that "judicial empowerment through constitutionalization seems, prima facie, to run counter to the interests of power-holders in legislatures and executives"— Hirschl argues that judicial empowerment is "driven primarily by [the efforts of powerful] political interests to insulate certain policy preferences from popular pressures."[28] More specifically, judicial empowerment takes what he calls an "interest-based hegemonic preservation approach," which "is driven in many cases by attempts to maintain the social and political status quo and to block attempts to seriously challenge it through democratic politics."[29] When threatened by more egalitarian interests, "supporters of dominant but increasingly threatened interests may choose to limit the policy-making authority of majoritarian decision-making arenas by gradually transferring authority to relatively insulated, professional policy-making institutions, such as national high courts, central banks, transnational trade and monetary organizations, and supranational bureaucracies and tribunals."[30] "As political representatives of the established interests started to lose control of [majoritarian] institutions, . . . they started to worry about the 'tyranny of the majority.'"[31] As a consequence, "constitutionalization has more often served as an effective means for shielding the economic sphere from attempts to reduce socio-economic disparities through regulatory and redistributive means."[32]

Hirschl's analysis provides a powerful theoretical foundation for understanding the role that state high courts play in contributing to political, legal, economic, and social inequality in the United States. To the extent that issues can be framed such that they are assigned to minoritarian institutions, upperdog elites are likely to come out ahead. To this segment of society, majoritarian arenas are threatening and dangerous. Courts are not.

Returning to the Elected State High Courts

The same theory can be applied to the state supreme courts. There are several reasons why the struggles between the left and right in state politics have focused on the judiciaries. First, the declining number of cases decided by the U.S. Supreme Court each year empowers the policymaking authority of state supreme courts. The Supreme Court tends to reverse the lower court in the majority of the cases it reviews, effectively negating the policy made by the inferior court (here, the state supreme court). But the Supreme Court has become less active in recent years, reviewing far fewer than one hundred cases—less than 1 percent of those it is asked to review— each year. Therefore, even in those cases in which the Court has the power to review, it is highly unlikely that it will intervene in any given case. And if a decision is neither reviewed by a higher court nor overturned by the present court at a later date, the decision stands. Thus, state supreme courts have broad powers to make policy, even under the federal constitution, in addition to, of course, the authority to interpret state laws.

Second, as American politics has become more polarized, legislatures have become less productive, passing fewer and fewer laws and, as a result, making themselves less active and relevant policymakers.[33] Moreover, it is considerably easier to veto legislation than it is to pass new laws. The state appellate courts, by contrast, continue to decide thousands of cases each year. When they construe the meaning of a statute, that ruling is binding and can generally only be overturned by a state legislature and governor who pass and sign a new law that updates the statute (or by the court itself, in a subsequent decision). In an age of stark elite polarization, the de facto power of courts has increased as the other branches of government are less able to coordinate to overturn courts' statutory rulings.[34]

Third, competing for the state courts is doable because securing majorities on state courts is politically feasible in a way that controlling legislatures or the governorship might not be. Whereas gaining and maintaining control in a legislature is attractive to those who seek to influence policy, it requires capturing a large number of seats. Securing the governorship is attractive, in part, because it requires winning only one seat, but that election is often very expensive. Additionally, executives are quite limited in their ability to affect policy unilaterally. In contrast to legislative and executive seats, state appellate courts are smaller, and their elections have historically been less expensive to influence.

Finally, and quite importantly, in addition to their statutory caseload, state high courts have nearly exclusive access to and control over the meaning of state constitutions. While judges on state supreme courts are bound by the U.S. Supreme Court's interpretations of the U.S. Constitution, each state supreme court has the final say on its interpretation of its own state's constitution. This system of dual constitutions allows state supreme courts to provide broader constitutional protections to their citizens than the U.S. Supreme Court has interpreted the federal constitution as providing (if they are so inclined), per the Supreme Court's 1983 decision in *Michigan v. Long*.[35] According to that opinion, cases decided by state courts of last resort on "adequate and independent state grounds" are shielded from review by federal courts.[36] In other words, if a state supreme court interprets its state constitution more broadly than the federal constitution and grounds its decision on its independent and sovereign interpretation of its state constitution, the U.S. Supreme Court has no jurisdiction to review the decision.[37] This greatly empowers state high courts. If faced with a displeasing ruling by a state supreme court grounded in a state constitution, the only nonjudicial way to nullify the decision is to follow the costly and time-intensive process of amending the state constitution.

State courts in fact try to protect their decisions from federal review. At the beginning of her tenure on the U.S. Supreme Court, Sandra Day O'Connor—a former state judge herself—remarked that, "especially in the constitutional context, state courts have substantial power to grant or withhold jurisdiction to the Supreme Court by the choice and articulation of the grounds for the state court decisions."[38] Indeed, many rulings by state courts of last resort, in the words of prominent scholars of state constitutions, "give the impression of being unprincipled attempts to circumvent the U.S. Supreme Court rather than serious efforts to develop state constitutional law."[39] If state courts choose to ground their decision in their state's constitution instead of the U.S. Constitution—either strategically or because they are interpreting a unique provision of the state constitution—their decisions are not reviewable by a higher court.[40]

These factors—especially the ability to have the last say on the meaning of state constitutions—combine to make state supreme courts especially powerful policymakers on issues relating to inequality. Importantly, the federal constitution has never been thought to be a powerful vehicle for protecting the equality of the downtrodden in the first place. As Helen Hershkoff observes: "Limiting the [federal] constitution to 'negative rights' confines federal courts to the important goal of protecting the individual against government power, but leaves the individual relatively unprotected from private domination in social and economic relationships."[41] Consequently, there are few federal constitutional provisions (outside criminal justice) that offer a means of protecting the have-nots from domination by the haves.

Second, and perhaps more surprising, many of the state constitutions do indeed include references to important "positive rights": "By contrast to the Federal Constitution, every state constitution in the U.S. includes some textual commitment to a social or economic right."[42] For example: "Some state constitutions currently embrace guarantees to decent work and opportunities for livelihood that commentators associate with social citizenship; some states go even further and authorize or guarantee the provision of a safety net during times of financial distress, emergency housing, and protection of the environment as a way to vouchsafe a communal future."[43] These are often referred to as "positive rights clauses." Constitutional protection for these positive rights may enable those who do not have the power to protect themselves to be protected by courts, if the courts are so inclined.[44]

Although we recognize that the literature is far-flung, legal scholars have long been interested in cataloging various constitutional provisions, court rulings, and legislation as they relate to social and economic equality. An interesting early attempt at coding state constitutional protections for the poor was produced by William Rava, who developed an ordinal, categorical indicator of welfare provisions in state constitutions: the degree to which "the [relevant] constitutional section imposes an affirmative obligation on the state to provide economic assistance to those in need."[45] Some constitutions place an affirmative duty on the state to care for indigent residents (for example, Alabama, Kansas, New York, and Oklahoma), and others include a permissive grant of power to care for the needy (for example, Montana, New Mexico, Pennsylvania, and Texas). Other constitutions contain a broad grant of permissive legislative authority to provide public welfare (for example, Alaska, California, Hawaii, and Louisiana). In contrast, some contain only an implied grant of authority to care for the needy (Arizona, Colorado, Idaho, Indiana, Mississippi, Missouri, Nevada, North Carolina, Washington, West Virginia, and Wyoming). According to Rava's analysis, twenty-seven state constitutions contain no express welfare or charity provisions.[46]

State courts certainly vary, however, in how they have dealt with state constitutional mandates. Referring to this as the "underutilization thesis," Hershkoff and Stephen Loffredo observe that "almost every state constitution in the United States explicitly addresses important public goods as education, income assistance, and housing support, and some state courts have even tried to enforce these provisions in the face of legislative indifference or recalcitrance. Other state courts, however, treat socio-economic constitutional provisions as nonjusticiable and so underutilize the authority that the state constitution sets out."[47] The most important conclusion emerging from their analysis is that some state high courts have utilized state constitutional provisions in favor of creating greater political, legal, economic, and social equality, while others have not. Nearly all, however, could have.

There is, however, more to the story when it comes to the state high courts.

Capturing the State Supreme Courts

Hirschl was writing about national high courts in four countries. His theory reflects the fact that these courts are not very accountable to majorities in their countries. Judicial institutions that are insulated from the preferences of the people—such as, obviously, the federal courts in the United States—are unlikely to be responsive to demands from the majority for rulings favoring greater political, legal, economic, and social equality. Indeed, the federal courts were specifically designed to protect privileged interests from demands from the masses for "leveling."[48] But no other judicial institutions in the United States enjoy the extreme insulation of the U.S. Supreme Court.

The state high courts in particular provide a challenge to Hirschl's theory. Unlike their colleagues on the federal bench (and most judges worldwide), the vast majority of state high court judges are accountable in one form or another to the majority via elections.[49] To the extent that the use of popular elections renders state high courts truly accountable to the majority, and under the assumption that the majority generally favors the interests of political, legal, economic, and social underdogs, state high courts pose a direct threat to the generalizability of Hirschl's theory. Moreover, and obviously, different mechanisms for selecting and retaining state high court judges have different consequences for legal policies pertinent to political, legal, economic, and social inequality. Thus, a central hypothesis of this research is that *greater accountability to the majority is associated with the adoption of public policies favoring greater political, legal, economic, and social equality*. Relatedly, systems of accountability could provide a mechanism to overcome the inherent conservative bias among judges and courts.

And indeed, a large literature in state politics research has suggested that greater accountability—as evidenced by greater party competition—could indeed be such a mechanism. Dating back to V. O. Key's 1949 *Southern Politics in State and Nation*, scholars have demonstrated that policy tends to become more favorable to society's have-nots because increased party competition changes the composition of the electorate, bringing more have-nots into the fold.[50] As Thomas Holbrook and Emily Van Dunk sketch the logic, under higher levels of party competition,

> elected officials in competitive areas will be highly responsive to constituency needs, due to the risk of electoral defeat. . . . Due to higher overall levels of voter participation in competitive environments, lower socioeconomic class interests will constitute a greater share of the electorate in competitive states than in non-competitive states. Therefore, in striving to represent the interests of their constituents, elected officials in competitive states will provide benefits to lower socioeconomic interests to a greater degree—and will display a greater propensity to support liberal policies.[51]

Indeed, this conventional wisdom is so strong that Charles Barrilleaux claims that "expectations about the effects of competition on policy-making are unambiguous: existing theory and empirical evidence from the American states consistently links electoral competition to the enactment of more liberal policies."[52]

That most judges in the American states face elections (in one way or the other) and therefore are more directly accountable to majority rule may be good news to those who favor a more (small-*d*) democratic political system. In this vein, Benjamin Page and Gilens believe that one important driver of inequality in America (and other ills as well) is the excessive amount of power held by overprivileged minorities.[53] In partial alignment with Hirschl's theory, they call for a shift to greater majority rule in American politics, arguing that the minority that is so successful in getting its way in contemporary American politics is an overprivileged minority, the upperdogs.

As we have noted, this argument is reminiscent of the type of discourse associated with the implementation of judicial elections in the 1830s and 1840s.[54] The thesis goes like this: Elite dominance of political institutions and public policy produces outputs contrary to the preferences of the majority because overprivileged elites hold policy preferences that are markedly different from those of the majority. Therefore, reducing inequality in the United States requires breaking this minority's stranglehold over American courts. Judicial reformers seeking greater accountability to the majority from their judges would probably have embraced many of the Page and Gilens arguments and proposals.

However, most contemporary judicial scholars would have little difficulty in formulating a rebuttal to Page and Gilens's call for a greater emphasis on majority rule. On occasion, the majority will prefer policies that tread on the rights of political minorities. For example, the political intolerance of the majority has stimulated a robust literature among public opinion specialists on the unwillingness of the majority to "put up with" ideas deemed too "radical" or too "despicable."[55] Even a casual reading of the intent of the American framers reveals a deep and abiding fear that the majority would seek antidemocratic policies that endanger minority rights (especially property rights). That the majority would be complicit in the destruction of democracy is a fear that is as widespread today as it was in the time of Alexander Hamilton. Many judicial scholars would point to unaccountable judicial institutions (as in the federal courts) as essential to block the antidemocratic "passions" of the majority and to secure the rights of all people—including Hillary Clinton's "deplorables"—to participate in the political process.[56]

We are certain that Page and Gilens do not call for unbridled majority tyranny; nor do they eschew the needed qualifier to democracy—"liberal." What Page and Gilens want is to loosen the stranglehold of the overprivileged and monied minority over contemporary American politics. But from our position as scholars of the third branch, Page and Gilens seem to pay insufficient attention to the need to limit the number of policy domains in which the majority in a political system should be allowed to have its way. Thus, the first problem with any theory that seeks to enhance the power of the majority is the need to identify certain policy areas in which majority preferences ought *not* to govern. Virtually all democratic theorists specify at least a minimal basket of contestation rights.[57] All competitors for political power must be able to freely compete, even if the majority would prefer that they not be allowed to compete.[58]

A second problem with majority empowerment is that the preferences of the majority are subject to manipulation. There could be no better illustration of this than in the fight for public opinion on issues of so-called tort reform. William Haltom and Michael McCann have masterfully demonstrated the ways in which misinformation about the "tort crisis" has been successful in swaying public opinion.[59] One need not say much more than "the McDonald's hot coffee case" to bring to many people's minds the lawsuit that is the poster child for successful misinformation campaigns.

While we address this issue in more detail in subsequent chapters, we should note here that the mass public in the United States does not, generally speaking, favor greater economic inequality.[60] Consequently, we agree with Page and Gilens that the majority empowerment thesis provides an avenue for reducing levels of inequality. One also cannot assume that the majority favors greater equality in all instances. But a reasonable hypothesis is that, were public policies to align more closely with majority preferences on issues of political, legal, economic, and social inequality, policy would undermine inequality.

However, it is naive to believe that majority empowerment takes place in a vacuum, with those favoring greater inequality sitting quietly on the sidelines. In a nutshell, this has not happened when it comes to the state judiciaries. More specifically, greater judicial accountability has often resulted in more conservative judges because conservatives learned how to "play the game" much earlier and much better than progressives.[61] It is useful, therefore, to digress to consider how the politics of judicial accountability has played out in the last few decades.

The Politics of Judicial Accountability

State courts contrast significantly with federal courts in the United States in that most are electorally accountable to the majority. In practice, however, state high court judges have not traditionally been realistically accountable to their constituents. The easy and obvious example is retention elections, which of all possible election types are almost certain to return incumbents to the bench.[62] But historically, even partisan and nonpartisan high court elections have been sleepy affairs—sort of like playing checkers by mail, in the words of one journalist—and as such are unlikely to compel much accountability.[63] Courts operating "under the radar" are therefore unlikely to advance the interests of underdogs because the mass public—whose preferences might compel the judges to resist the outcomes preferred by upperdogs—is largely unaware of the policies promulgated by their state court (and are therefore unable to vote retrospectively). If this is so, the interest of the dominant elites is to prevent these courts from becoming salient and useful to the majority.

Until lately. As James Gibson and his colleagues have noted with regard to state supreme court elections:

> Campaigning for state judgeships in America has entered a new era. In the past, campaigns might have been described as decent, docile, and dirt cheap, even if drab and dull. Today, they are said to be "nosier, nastier, and costlier."[64] Whatever the characterization, there can be little doubt that the landscape of judicial elections has changed rather dramatically in the past decade in the United States.[65]

Indeed, the dawn of hypercompetitive judicial elections arguably began in the 1980s.[66] Realizing that courts are smaller policymaking bodies than legislatures and that it is much easier to obtain a majority on a court—where one needs only to capture four seats on a seven-member court, for instance—southern conservatives began to pay close attention to judicial races. At the time, many of these elected southern supreme courts were relatively liberal—especially on workers' rights issues—reflecting the Democratic Party's dominance of the region. Conservatives sought to change that.[67] Karl Rove, who later became famous as an adviser to President George W. Bush, was at the forefront of this movement. As Sam Gwynne, editor of the *Texas Monthly*, described the strategy:

> The kind of cases that would come to the Supreme Court would be, somebody works for an oil refinery down in Corpus Christi or something, and somebody gets hurt or, let's say, claims long-term poisoning by the atmosphere—big case like this, your typical tort case. So a worker for the company would be poisoned or claiming he was poisoned, and then he would sue the company. And of course, the trial lawyers, the tort lawyers, would come in behind this guy, and the corporate defense lawyers would take [on] the major oil company that was being sued. This, then, would go up through the various lower courts, state courts and appellate courts. And some of these cases would get to the [Texas] Supreme Court.
>
> So let's say the Supreme Court sided with the little guy all the time, which they did in the '80s. It became, in effect, a plaintiff's court. The Supreme Court in Texas was ruling almost every time in the favor of plaintiffs. The effect of this . . . is you get higher malpractice rates for doctors; insurance costs a lot more money. Some people perceive it as an ill to society to have too many verdicts in favor of plaintiffs. If a woman gets scalded by McDonald's coffee, maybe she shouldn't get a $5 million award.[68] This is the realm that we're in now.
>
> So Karl comes in and says, "You know, we're going to run [with] tort reform," and he does for a whole decade.[69]

Rove's strategy gained prominence in the 1988 Texas Supreme Court elections, in which he guided Republicans to a historic victory, winning five of the six open seats on the court. That campaign, called "Clean Slate '88," set the stage for a wholesale change in the jurisprudence of the Texas Supreme Court. By 1998, every justice on that court was a Republican.

A few years later, Rove focused his talents on Alabama. As the 1994 election season drew near in that state, no Republican had been elected to the Alabama Supreme Court in more than a century. The Business Council of Alabama asked Rove to manage its slate of Republican candidates, a role in which he was wildly successful, in large part by modernizing the judicial campaign apparatus.

> Rove brought to Alabama a formula, honed in Texas, for winning judicial races. It involved demonizing Democrats as pawns of the plaintiffs' bar and stoking populist resentment with tales of outrageous verdicts. At Rove's behest, Hooper and his fellow Republican candidates focused relentlessly on a single case involving an Alabama doctor from the richest part of the state who had sued BMW after discovering that, prior to delivery, his new car had been damaged by acid rain and repainted, diminishing its value. After a trial revealed this practice to be widespread, a jury slapped the automaker with $4 million in punitive damages. "It was the poster-child case of outrageous verdicts," says Bill Smith, a political consultant who got his start working for Rove on these and other Alabama races. "Karl figured out the vocabulary on the BMW case and others like it that point out not just liberal behavior but outrageous decisions that make you mad as hell."[70]

The conservative successes in Texas and Alabama drew wide notice among conservatives who sought to use courts to entrench their policy preferences in law. The cost of judicial campaigns continued to rise at the dawn of the new millennium, with business and conservative groups funding one set of candidates and plaintiffs' lawyers and unions tending to support liberal candidates. Fundraising in state supreme court elections increased radically, from less than $6 million in 1989–1990 to over $45 million during the 1999–2000 campaign cycle.[71] As campaign fundraising and spending increased, television advertisements became increasingly common and citizen attention to and participation in these elections grew drastically.[72]

These shifts within state judicial politics suggest two important conclusions. The first, which has the greatest implication for the Hirschl theory presented earlier, is that the increasing attention to state high court elections by the political elite was largely driven by conservative Republicans seeking to capture these institutions to advance their political, legal, economic, and social interests. Second, the recognition that the state high courts did not merely "interpret" the law but also crafted binding public policy—especially as it pertained to civil lawsuits—fueled this newfound interest in state supreme courts, especially among upperdogs. It appears that these conservative interests recognized the potential of state high courts to deliver greater political, legal, economic, and social inequality and mobilized accordingly.

Liberal political forces soon joined the fray, with the result that state supreme court elections became more competitive and more polarized. Indeed, in many states struggles to control the state supreme court have become fierce political battles. No one, it seems, wants a truly "independent" state supreme court in their state these days.

Summary

So what explains the rush to control state courts over the past quarter-century? With such a potentially powerful arsenal of positive rights available to them, it was no longer safe to keep state high courts impotent and in the shadows. Instead, they had to be controlled. What is more, instead of attempting to merely neutralize these courts as potential agents of greater equality, dominant political interests sought to mobilize these institutions via doctrines of positive rights that applied with their greatest force to the interests of the haves (for example, damages caps). The state high courts became visible, and their political power widely recognized. It is hardly surprising that both conservatives and liberals have fought to control these institutions. After all, policies regarding political, legal, economic, and social inequality are at stake.

Returning to the Overarching Theory of This Book

We extract a number of theoretically relevant lessons from this recital of the political history of the state supreme courts.

To begin, courts are the object of political conflict, and elites realize the importance of controlling the composition of the court as a mechanism to ensure that their political agenda is enacted and implemented. Because courts are such important players in the policymaking mix of state politics, no political regime can afford to ignore the judiciary. The governing coalitions in state politics therefore typically and inevitably seek to capture the state supreme courts.

Insurgents—those who seek to disrupt the current governing coalition—perceive judicial elections as an important avenue for challenging the dominance of governing elites, just as in the nineteenth century in the

United States.[73] By giving the public the power to control the composition of the court (at least in theory), insurgents hope to break the connection between the state high court and the state's dominant political coalition, instead tying control of the court to the members of their movement.

Challenges to the dominant elite by insurgents have a considerable chance of succeeding if the courts are out of step with majority opinion in a state, as Karl Rove's campaigns illustrate. Courts can become out of step with majority opinion in part because judges on the state supreme court serve very long and multiple terms, especially when elections are not competitive. We refer to these as "hangover" courts and judges. Because of these long tenures, the governor's mansion and the state legislature may trend in one partisan direction while the dominant majority coalition on the state supreme court remains a relic of the past.

But not all courts are at odds with majority preferences in their states. Courts that changed little over the period from 1990 to 2015—such as the Maryland and South Dakota supreme courts, as we demonstrate later in this book—have presumably been continuously in line with both the dominant elites in their states and with public opinion.

Political regimes have different objectives when it comes to capturing their state's high court. In some instances, the regime seeks only to neutralize the court so that it does not block or impede the regime's policy efforts. The last thing a regime wants is to see a hard-won policy victory be scuttled by the state's supreme court. In other instances, the regime seeks the assistance of the state supreme court in implementing its policy preferences. This may mean mobilizing positive rights that have long lain fallow in the state's constitution. And it may be that in some policy domains it is easier for a court to be the leader of policies the regime seeks to perpetuate, whereas in other instances the regime seeks nothing but passive acquiescence to the state's policy initiatives. In some instances, the dominant coalition in a state seeks to advance minority rights—albeit in some contexts the rights of overprivileged minorities.

Regimes under challenge fight back, sometimes by actively contesting judicial elections but also sometimes, as we argue later, by attempting to subvert or manipulate judicial elections. For example, a regime may encourage strategic retirements or tightly regulate campaign activity (which, given the well-known advantages of incumbency, harms challengers far more than it does incumbents). If a regime on the way out of power can fill the court with sympathetic judges, that hungover court can be a headache for the incoming political regime.

A consequence of these political struggles is that state supreme courts are often, if not typically, closely tied to the governing coalition in the state and therefore frequently serve to ratify and legitimize the state's policy preferences, just as Dahl suggested over a half-century ago was a major function of courts. We recognize the existence of both maverick courts and judges, and they may be empowered by hangover processes, but given the importance of these institutions, efforts to capture the judiciary are sustained and determined. In the long term, few state supreme courts can maintain their independence from the governing coalition in their state. Judges have to leave the bench eventually, and elites play a major role in determining who will replace a departing judge.

Courts therefore are unlikely to be successful in pushing legal policies at odds with the governing coalition. If nothing else, the political regime selects the judges, has influence over who is and who is not retained, and therefore has a good chance of getting friendly and like-minded judges on the state supreme courts (and keeping their allies on the court). In this sense, the state supreme courts are essentially majoritarian institutions.

The majority empowerment thesis—which states that the best way to get more equality in the United States is to give more power to the majority—sometimes founders on the rocks of American federalism. It is not necessarily the case that more majoritarianism translates into more equality because majorities do not always favor equality, and even those majorities that do favor equality are not always successful at translating their preferences into policy. That is, while the majority seems to favor greater equality in general, this preference does not necessarily apply to all underdogs in all states. The majorities in some states—or at least the voting majorities—seem to oppose allowing the state's judiciary to act as agents to enhance equality. Of course, this varies by issue area. The majority in most states most likely favors greater equality in school funding (taking from extra-rich school districts to fund those less well off), but this preference does not necessarily extend to empowering unions, granting rights to minority groups like gay Americans, or making it easier to sue businesses, doctors, or even McDonald's.

Therefore, it is unlikely that courts will be active advocates of greater equality in the absence of supportive political institutions. What courts may be able to do is block policy efforts aimed at increasing equality by advancing the rights of overprivileged minorities. But even here, courts cannot block the will of the majority forever. Ultimately, courts become captured, for better or for worse.

Of course, this synopsis of the theory undergirding this research is stylized, and there may well be many important exceptions, qualifications, and even instances in which the theory is turned on its head. Moreover, this theory is perhaps not specific enough in its grandest form to generate a full set of specific hypotheses we can test in this research, although we can certainly test parts of the theory. Nevertheless, these are the broad contours of the reason why we wrote this book.

Our purpose in this book is therefore to investigate the role that state supreme courts have played in the creation and maintenance of public policies regarding political, legal, economic, and social inequality in various issue domains. To do so, we have created a database of state high court rulings in three major types of litigation—rulings pertaining to the rights of minorities, including poor people; rulings pertaining to the rights of workers and employees; and rulings pertaining to access to the state's justice institutions—and coded about six thousand decisions as either favoring or limiting political, legal, economic, and social inequality. The database represents the universe of cases in these three policy domains, in all fifty states, and ranges over time from approximately 1990 to 2015. Very roughly previewing a basic finding of this research, about half of the rulings favor greater equality, and the other half do not.

Our analytical goal in this project is to account for the variability in judicial policies favoring and opposing political, legal, economic, and social equality. We hypothesize that there are numerous sources of the variance in how state high courts fortify political, legal, economic, and social inequality. We focus in particular on three sources of the observed variability: differences across judges, across states and courts, and across time.

An Overview of the Chapters of This Book

We begin our analysis in chapter 2 with a discussion of the data set of nearly six thousand state supreme court cases related to political, legal, economic, and social inequality. We explain how we selected the issue areas included in our data set, how we chose the state supreme court cases that relate to those issues, and the rules under which our research assistants coded each of the cases. We also provide a short doctrinal overview of each of the issue areas we study to provide readers with a taste of the equality issues we consider in our analyses throughout the book.

In chapter 3, we address one of the most venerable and important hypotheses of socio-legal research: whether the haves come out ahead. This is a question with particularly important implications for the study of inequality; if the haves do in fact come out ahead, then perhaps disputes are resolved in our legal system based on litigant resources rather than legal merit. Of particular importance to our analysis in this chapter is our attempt to link litigants' resources to their substantive position in a case. We find that, contrary to an implicit assumption in most previous research, the upperdog party actually seeks to promote *equality* in a substantial number of cases.

Chapter 4 turns to our analysis of state high court judges. Just as we expect that a party's resources affect whether or not they are successful before a state supreme court, we follow a well-trodden tradition in empirical legal studies by suggesting that the background and identity of a judge also affect that judge's decisions on the bench. Of particular importance in this chapter is our attempt to define and measure the social class backgrounds of judges, a topic of considerable importance in studies of elite behavior, but one that has been elusive in studies of judicial behavior. Additionally, we set forth a general theory about the effect of background experiences on judicial behavior, and we test the relationship between judges' educational and professional experiences and their attitudes, as measured by their ideology and partisanship.

One of the best analytical benefits of studying state politics is the opportunity to examine the impact of institutional structures on behavior. No institutional feature of state supreme courts is more noteworthy than the methods by which judges reach the bench and keep their seats. In chapter 5, we explain methods of judicial selection and retention, which, we argue, profit from being treated as separate and discrete. We further differentiate between formal methods of judicial selection: the "on the books" way in which justices in a state reach their high court, and the informal methods of selection (how justices actually reach the bench). Because so many justices die, resign, or retire in the middle of their term, these informal methods of selection are incredibly important. Indeed, our most important conclusion in this chapter is that *nearly a majority of "elected" justices were actually appointed to their position.*

Having described the cases, judges, and institutions that characterize the high courts in the fifty states, we test our theory about the origins of political, legal, economic, and social inequality in chapters 6 and 7. Beginning in chapter 6, we test our elite capture theory—that high court justices are part of the dominant political coalition in a state. We find that the average ideology of a state high court is significantly related to both public opinion liberalism and the level of partisan dominance of the state legislative and executive branches; moreover, "odd man out" high courts—in which the legislative and executive branches are controlled by one party and the judicial branch is controlled by the other—are quite rare. We further find that methods of judicial retention affect this relationship, although in a surprising way: the relationship between partisan dominance of the legislative and executive branches of government and the state high court is actually strongest in states that use *elections* to retain their justices.

Of course, partisan control over a court affects inequality only inasmuch as justices' attitudes affect their behavior on the bench. Testing this proposition, chapter 7 finds that ideology plays a statistically and substantively important role in shaping the votes of state high court justices. Regarding the majority empowerment thesis, public opinion liberalism matters too, although only in states that use partisan or nonpartisan elections to staff their courts. In those states, however, the joint effects of ideology and public opinion are quite substantial.

Although understanding the determinants of individual-level judicial behavior is certainly important, courts ultimately affect inequality through their policies as expressed in the outcomes of cases, not the votes of individual judges. Therefore, in chapter 8 we examine the conditions under which state supreme courts make policies aimed at enhancing, or failing to enhance, equality. We weave together our analyses in the previous chapters to make the argument that courts can contribute to inequality in two ways: by favoring policy outcomes that are pro- or anti-equality, and also by favoring litigants who control greater legal resources than their opponents. In a pair of statistical analyses, we find that the driving force behind judicial policymaking on matters pertaining to political, legal, economic, and social inequality is the overall ideological configuration of the court's justices. In this way, it seems, methods of judicial selection shape the composition of a court, which, by extension, alters the probability that a court will adopt policies through its rulings that seek to advance or retard inequality.

Finally, in chapter 9, we take a step back from our findings to try to lace them together into a coherent account of the role of state supreme courts with regard to the creation of policies relevant to political, legal, economic, and social inequality in the U.S. states. We argue that, regardless of the method of judicial selection or retention, the amount of practical independence enjoyed by these courts is relatively low. As a result, the state supreme courts are unlikely to play the romanticized countermajoritarian role that many ascribe to them.

How This Study Contributes, and Fails to Contribute, to the Literature on Inequality in America

In sum, this book contributes to the literature on inequality in the United States in two ways. First, we add to a broad literature on policymaking in the United States that has paid particular attention to the adoption of policies that might exacerbate or ameliorate the equality of rights and resources in this country. From studies that investigate the adoption of pro-LGBT policies in the states to those that investigate the implementation of Obamacare and the expansion of Medicaid to studies of variation in policies relating to assistance to the poor, scholars of American state politics have long shown a keen interest in understanding the adoption and diffusion of public policies, especially as those policies relate to various aspects of inequality.[74] Indeed, Jack Walker's pioneering study of the diffusion of state policies paid hefty attention to inequality-related policies ranging from right-to-work laws, the presence of a welfare agency, workers' compensation, gender pay equality, and fair housing practices in the U.S. states.[75]

These studies have taught us an enormous amount about the adoption of policies and the dynamics of state policymaking, but they focus almost exclusively on the contributions of the state legislative and executive branches to the creation of pro-equality policies in the United States. Our research, instead, is centered on the important work of state judiciaries with regard to inequality-related policymaking in the United States. Our fundamental argument is that courts set many policies relevant to political, legal, economic, and social inequality, and that to ignore the policymaking role of state high courts is shortsighted.

Second, what are perhaps the best-known studies of inequality in the United States have examined the unequal responsiveness of American political institutions to economically affluent citizens. An outstanding example of this genre, Gilens's 2012 book *Affluence and Influence*, demonstrates that the policy preferences of the affluent sector of the American public have a disproportionate influence on the equality-relevant public policies that Congress makes.[76] Gilens's work at the federal level complements a large literature at the state level that demonstrates a class bias in the adoption of public policies.[77] The American government, it seems, is more responsive to the will of the wealthy than that of the poor.

Curiously, this body of research has developed relatively independently from a major research agenda in the study of law and courts: exploring the possibility that better-resourced litigants tend to win their cases. Based on Marc Galanter's pioneering study, legal scholars and social scientists around the world have sought to examine whether or not affluent litigants tend to be advantaged as they advance their arguments before the courts.[78] Both these studies and the studies of inequality in the Gilens tradition focus on unequal responsiveness, yet these two study streams have flowed separately from one another. Another contribution of this book is to pursue this hypothesis of unequal responsiveness within the context of the policy-making of the state supreme courts on matters pertaining to political, legal, economic, and social inequality.

We should acknowledge here at the beginning an important limitation of this book: like many before us who are concerned with inequality, we focus on the formation of public policies that are likely to have some impact on political, legal, economic, and social equality.[79] Assessing the actual impact of these state supreme court policies is beyond the scope of our analysis. We certainly realize that the gaps between the creation of public policy, the implementation of that policy, and the solution of social problems may be very wide.[80] But we also contend that public policies—whether made by courts or legislators or executives or bureaucrats—are an important component of every model of social change, and therefore that efforts to understand how and why these policies are made contribute to our understanding of political, legal, economic, and social inequality in the contemporary United States.

As will become clear from the various analyses reported in this book, we arrive at two overriding conclusions about the state supreme courts and inequality. First, these courts are largely majoritarian, not minoritarian, institutions in the sense that they are embedded within the dominant governing coalitions in the states. This conclusion stands in sharp contrast to prominent arguments to the effect that electoral methods of judicial selection and retention give state supreme courts an independent base of power that provides them with the independence to reject the policies of the dominant political coalition. Second, because majoritarian institutions can and often do advance greater *inequality*, the solution to inequality in the United States does not necessarily lie in giving the majority greater influence over the making of public policy. Instead, whether one favors greater inequality is closely connected to one's ideology; reducing inequality ultimately depends on the attitudes and values of those recruited to serve on the high courts of the American states. Thus, contrary to the conventional view of courts as uniformly powerful protectors of minority rights, our research suggests that who serves on these high courts has more to do with the judiciary's propensity to ameliorate inequality than any particular institutional arrangements.

CHAPTER 2

The Political, Legal, Economic, and Social Inequality State Supreme Court Database

TO TEST THE hypotheses suggested by our analysis in chapter 1, it is necessary to examine the policy outputs of the state supreme courts. We have done so by creating the Political, Legal, Economic, and Social Inequality State Supreme Court Database, a database comprising the decisions of nearly one thousand justices, in all fifty states, in six thousand equality-relevant cases that were decided from 1990 to 2015, and involving roughly thirty-seven thousand individual justice votes. This database, also known as the State High Court Inequality Database, is the core of this book, although we marshal a large amount of additional data in the service of testing such a broad and complicated set of hypotheses. In the end, we report in this book our analysis of the variability in votes in cases, in case outcomes, across judges, in decisions made in different institutional contexts, and in states with varying sorts of political regimes.

In this chapter, we focus on the case data. In particular, our purpose here is to introduce the State High Court Inequality Database and describe and validate the empirical measures of political, legal, economic, and social inequality used throughout this book. In doing so, we provide the first evidence ever adduced as to how the state high courts have adopted policies that contribute to creating, maintaining, or ameliorating inequality in their states. We begin with a discussion of how we created the database, followed by a review of some of the cases included in our database. After considering some analytical issues, we conclude with some preliminary analysis of the policy outputs of these fifty courts.

Introduction to the State High Court Inequality Database

The fifty-two state supreme courts decide myriad issues of law and policy that arise within their state's boundaries.[1] Our focus is on a slice of that caseload: the policy outputs of the state high courts on issues pertaining to political, legal, economic, and social inequality.

We began our research by deriving overarching policy domains related to political, legal, economic, and social inequality. Because so little is known about the substantive content of the caseloads of the state supreme courts, we began our identification of these issue domains by consulting the available literature. One of the initial sources we reviewed was a study by Theodore Eisenberg and Geoffrey Miller in which they categorized all state supreme court cases decided in the calendar year 2003, using forty-five categories.[2] While their categories were suggestive for our concerns with political, legal, economic, and social inequality, many of their groupings were insufficiently clear as to substantive content—for example, "Const. Law (Rights)"—that we felt it necessary to look elsewhere for guidance on the caseloads of the state supreme courts.[3]

An extremely useful study in Kansas by Stephen Ware of the ways in which the Kansas Supreme Court has made important public policies in recent years turned out to be very helpful.[4] Using rulings on workers' compensation, product liability, parolees, malpractice actions against criminal defense attorneys, negligence per se, and the Uniform Commercial Code as examples, Ware convincingly illustrates two points that stand as bedrocks of this project: state high courts are important policymaking institutions, and many of the policies they make directly implicate political, legal, economic, and social inequality.

Early on, we made the decision to exclude criminal cases. We do *not* contend that criminal justice issues are irrelevant to social, political, legal, and economic inequality in the United States. However, the criminal cases most directly relevant to equality (for example, the political rights of felons) are included in our analysis via other substantive categories of public policy.

For ordinary criminal cases (for instance, those involving procedural due process), the connections to political, legal, economic, and social inequality are more circuitous.

For two reasons, we also decided to exclude workers' compensation cases. First, the states vary in whether these cases are part of the state supreme court's jurisdiction. Second, after examining many of these cases in a pilot study, we concluded that the decisions in a large proportion of these disputes are almost entirely driven by the case facts and often have no clear policy implications. Workers' compensation and criminal cases are the only two substantive case categories that we examined but decided to exclude from our definition of cases relevant to political, legal, economic, and social inequality.

Because we hypothesized that public opinion in the states is an important determinant of state high court policy outputs, our thinking about policy domains was also influenced by earlier research connecting public preferences with policy outputs. For example, Gilens primarily looked at the policies on which pollsters asked the American people for their preferences to identify his policy domains.[5] We were mindful of the need to identify issue domains that fit broadly within the conventional definitions of liberalism and conservatism so as to be able to match up with public opinion data.

We also examined literature on the policy outputs of the state governments, consulting, for example, the State Safety Net Policy data set collected by Sarah Bruch, Marcia Meyers, and Janet Gornick. For nine aspects of the safety net policies, the data set scores each state on the adequacy and inclusiveness of various social welfare policies (for example, cash and food assistance).[6] We incorporated the policy domains relevant to state supreme court litigation into our study.

After developing a rough listing of policy domains relevant to political, legal, economic, and social inequality, we then focused our attention on the task of finding the relevant cases. This took us to the LexisNexis case categorization scheme, which we discuss further later in this chapter. We sharpened our definition of the policy domains in part via the LexisNexis system for categorizing cases decided by the state supreme courts.

In the end, our search for cases in these policy domains (detailed later) resulted in the identification of approximately fourteen thousand state supreme court decisions, about six thousand of which were deemed to be directly relevant to public policy regarding political, legal, economic, and social inequality.

It is perhaps useful to explicate in greater detail each of the issue domains we consider to be relevant to policies pertaining to political, legal, economic, and social inequality. Here we specify the types of litigation we coded and provide examples of the types of outcomes that we judged as ones that advanced greater equality. Note that, later in this chapter, we provide exemplars of actual cases for each of the issue domains.

Rulings Pertaining to the Rights of Minorities, Including Poor People

We postulate that greater political, legal, economic, and social equality is facilitated by court policies that expand the rights of minorities, including poor people. By empowering minorities with rights, rendering them better able to defend their interests against powerful institutions, courts may create a more level playing field.

School Finance Funding Equality: Did the court's decision contribute to greater equality across schools in the support or resources provided by the state? Pro-equality rulings are decisions that:

- Equalize the amount of funding provided to school districts
- Provide increased funding to districts that claim inadequate funding
- Provide additional funding (for special education, facilities, and so on) to parochial schools that claim inadequate funding

Gay Rights: Did the court's decision grant, recognize, or extend rights to gays and lesbians? Pro-equality rulings are decisions that:

- Strike down sodomy bans, as they protect the freedom of sexual choice
- Allow same-sex people to marry, form legally recognized civil unions, adopt children, foster children, and divorce, as they support equal treatment regardless of sexual orientation
- Allow for protection of LGBT individuals against housing and employment discrimination
- Endorse health insurance and other employee benefits for same-sex spouses
- Protect LGBT individuals under hate crime policies

Election Law: Did the court's decision expand opportunities for political participation? Pro-equality rulings are decisions that:

- Endorse access to the ballot for a candidate
- Remove barriers to voting (for example, voter ID laws)
- Reject restrictive qualifications on voting (for example, felon disenfranchisement or property ownership requirements)
- Allow propositions for initiatives or referenda to be placed on the ballot
- Do not allow parties or organizations to regulate ballot access
- Strike down contribution or spending limits
- Require campaign donors to be disclosed
- Do not give rights to organizations (for example, *Citizens United*–type cases)
- Equalize the influence of individual votes (one person, one vote)
- Strike down gerrymandering of districts

Rulings Pertaining to the Rights of Workers and Employees

Like the first issue domain, we posit that court rulings that expand the rights of workers and employees contribute to greater political, legal, economic, and social equality. Empowering workers and employees in their legal disputes helps to create a more equal basis for resolving conflicts.

Collective Bargaining Rights: Did the court's decision endorse the expansion of the rights of workers and unions? Pro-equality rulings are decisions that:

- Strike down restrictions on collective bargaining (for example, by allowing collective bargaining)
- Do not place restrictions on the topics of collective bargaining
- Do not enforce right-to-work policies (since right-to-work policies necessarily weaken individuals' ability to collectively bargain)

Employment-at-Will Policies: Did the court's decision limit the discretion of employers to hire and fire employees at will? Pro-equality rulings are decisions that:

- Restrict the ability of employers to discharge employees
- Provide protections for workers against firings without "just cause"

Rulings Pertaining to Access to a State's Justice Institutions

The privatization of dispute management institutions is one means by which political, legal, economic, and social inequality is reinforced. State-based dispute management institutions provide a more equal basis for resolving conflicts than do private institutions. In many instances, the grievances of less powerful segments of society who lack access to their state's justice institutions will go unheard.

Mandatory Arbitration Policies: Did the court's decision expand the authority of public institutions (rather than private institutions) to adjudicate disputes? Pro-equality rulings are decisions that:

- Do not restrict access to public institutions for private disputes
- Strike down mandatory arbitration clauses
- Impede the privatization of adjudication

Class Action Policies: Did the court's decision make it more likely that a class action lawsuit would be filed or that the plaintiffs in such a suit would prevail? Pro-equality rulings are decisions that:

- Ease restrictions on class certification requirements
- Make it more economically feasible to file a suit (for example, by eliminating caps on quantifications of pain and suffering)
- Require the provision of attorneys' fees and contingency fees
- Reject caps on the total amount of damages
- Reject venue changes to federal courts, thereby keeping class actions in the states (where courts are more accountable to the majority)
- Ease filing requirements (for example, venue)
- Ensure access to jury trials in class action lawsuits

Policies Regarding the Payment of Attorneys' Fees: Were the attorneys' fees paid to the plaintiff undiminished or unrestricted by the court's decision? Pro-equality rulings are decisions that:

- Do not limit the use of contingency fees
- Do not impose a sliding scale (or a scale of any sort) on attorneys' contingency fees

- Do not require an attorney to provide clients with an up-front estimate of what the hourly rate for a case would be versus the applicable contingency fee charge
- Do not require the loser of the lawsuit to pay attorneys' fees (the "English Rule")

Policies Affecting Damage Caps in Civil Litigation: Did the court's decision tend to make plaintiffs' cases more likely to be filed (because it would be economical to do so), or did the court's decision make plaintiffs more likely to prevail? Pro-equality rulings are decisions that:

- Reject placing a cap on damages
- Reject limiting the types of damages a plaintiff can receive (for example, no damages for pain and suffering, or damages for economic losses only)
- Reject restricting the form that "damage" can take (for example, by limiting the ability to receive punitive damages)
- Reject establishing a liability "trigger" that reflects the intentional tort origins and quasi-criminal nature of punitive damages awards (for example, "actual malice")
- Reject raising the standard to establish punitive damages liability (for example, by requiring "clear and convincing evidence")
- Reject requiring proportionality in punitive damages

We spent a considerable amount of energy conceptualizing and exploring empirically possible issue domains for inclusion in our study. Of course, a study like this can never be exhaustive: not every type of state supreme court litigation can be included (too many domains have far too few cases for analysis), and many types of litigation seem to have few implications for political, legal, economic, and social inequality (for example, many contract disputes). Nor do we purport to have selected a random sample of issues. But we do claim to have gone considerably beyond many of the earlier studies of state court policymaking that focus on only a single type of issue, or on a very small number of types of issues (for example, only abortion and the death penalty). Further, we are fairly confident that any sins in our approach to identifying issue domains are sins of omission, not sins of commission.

A Brief Note on the Nature of Judicial Policymaking

On its face, judicial policymaking may seem to differ somewhat from legislatively made law. When the legislature passes a law, a clear statement of policy is set (for example, the minimum wage is $15 an hour), and the law is recorded in either the civil or the criminal code of the state. Of course, the law may or may not be enforced: even in 2020, for example, many states have anti-abortion laws on their books that cannot legally be enforced. Many investigations at both the state and federal levels have considered why some legislatures pass pro-equality laws while others do not.

On the surface, judicial policymaking, especially in the common law systems in place in forty-nine of the fifty states (Louisiana being the partial, and mainly historical, exception), is different because policy is made by judges ruling in individual legal disputes, creating precedents. Some of these disputes are public law controversies (such as school finance), but some lawsuits are largely private causes of action (for example, mandatory arbitration). Nevertheless, in these individual lawsuits, judges often announce a precedent—as, for example, in declaring that punitive damages will not be allowed in certain types of lawsuits. Famous judicial policies include the (federal) definition of incitement: speech likely to produce "imminent unlawful action." Judicial precedents are not necessarily set only in blockbuster cases. Even mere applications of existing precedents—and if it were truly "mere," it would be difficult to understand how the case made its way to a state supreme court—can be highly significant tweaks to public policy (as in abortion litigation through 2020). In the common law systems of the U.S. states, judge-made law has the full force of public policy and, practically speaking, is indistinguishable from legislatively made law.

Having chosen and explicated these broad policy categories, we identified and coded the universe of cases decided by state supreme courts on these issues between 1990 and 2015, creating the State High Court Inequality Database. The details of how we created that database follow.

Creating the State High Court Inequality Database

Case Identification Methodology

Compared to scholars of the U.S. Supreme Court, those who study state supreme courts face a severe disadvantage. Those who research the high court in the U.S. federal judicial system can rely on Harold Spaeth and colleagues' encyclopedic Supreme Court Database,[7] but there is no such systematic data source for state supreme court decisions that covers a substantial period of time, includes the names of the judges who decided each case, and contains information on the issue areas attached to each state supreme court opinion. Neither of the two existing extensive state supreme court databases—Paul Brace and Melinda Gann Hall's State Supreme Court Data Project and Matthew Hall and Jason Windett's State Judicial Database—codes for the substantive policy outcomes in state supreme court decisions.[8] To compound the problem, legal databases like LexisNexis and Westlaw categorize cases on the basis of legal issues rather than policy issues. For example, LexisNexis has no general headnote that encompasses all cases relating to LGBT rights. As a result, obtaining a valid and exhaustive list of cases for analysis within each policy domain is a demanding chore. This makes even the most basic task in the study of judicial decision-making—finding the relevant cases and judicial opinions—difficult and time-consuming.

One way in which scholars have identified cases is through keyword searches in Westlaw or LexisNexis. For example, in their study of environmental law cases, Brandice Canes-Wrone, Tom Clark, and Amy Semet collected a list of keywords related to environmental law, such as "sewage," "natural resources," "pollution," and "endangered species," and identified each case decided by a state supreme court over the time period of interest that contained one or more of these words or phrases.[9] The researchers then read each case carefully, removing cases from the data set that did not actually address issues of environmental law.

Scholars have also relied on the topic codes (such as Lexis's headnote system or Westlaw's keynote system); however, this approach is not foolproof, as it requires cross-referencing for accuracy. For example, Richard Caldarone, Brandice Canes-Wrone, and Tom Clark used a keyword search for "abortion" and "wrongful birth" to compile a list of state supreme court decisions on abortion. Because many states classify abortion and homicide under the same statute, the authors then cross-referenced their list with a topic search for homicide to help them eliminate cases that were erroneously identified in the initial search.[10]

We note that these two approaches are over-inclusive: both cast a broad net to select a long list of cases that may relate to the issue area in question and then cull the cases, leaving only those that pertain to the selected issue area.

Our approach draws on these traditions, following a three-step process to select the cases in each issue area. Because we sought to collect all cases decided by state supreme courts in our issue areas of interest, we cast a wide net and relied on human coders who read each case and eliminated those that did not result in a substantive or procedural ruling on the case's issue area.

The first step in our process was to identify a set of cases in each issue domain that exemplified the legal and policy issues decided by state supreme courts. This research was conducted by a team of law student research assistants who did doctrinal research to identify key cases decided by state supreme courts in each issue area, beginning with lists compiled by interest groups, legal research tools, legal scholars, and law review articles.

Second, after we collected the names of a set of cases that were typical of the litigation we sought to code, our next step was to determine a common feature of these "known" cases that we could use to identify the universe of cases in each issue area. Our tool to select the full set of cases was LexisNexis's headnotes. As LexisNexis explains it: "LexisNexis Headnotes show the key legal points of a case. Each LexisNexis Headnote is written by a LexisNexis® legal editor, drawing directly from the language of the court."[11] The advantage of these headnotes is that they are written by attorney-editors at LexisNexis who provide expert judgments about the issues addressed by the case. These expert judgments therefore form the foundation of our case identification strategy.[12]

For each issue area, we found the LexisNexis headnote that was most common among the known cases (within each policy domain). For example, LexisNexis has an "Employment at Will" headnote under the general "Labor & Employment Law" category, which classifies the employment-at-will cases well. Similarly, we used the "Arbitrations" headnote under "Alternative Dispute Resolution" to provide our listing of possible mandatory arbitration cases. Lexis uses the caret symbol to denote the hierarchical nature of these headnotes; for example, "Alternative Dispute Resolution > Arbitrations" denotes that the "Arbitration" headnote is nested within the broader "Alternate Dispute Resolution" headnote. The headnotes we used for each issue area were:

- *Employment at Will*: Labor & Employment Law > Employment Relationships > Employment at Will

- *Collective Bargaining*: Labor & Employment Law > Collective Bargaining & Labor Relations
- *Mandatory Arbitration*: Civil Procedure > Alternative Dispute Resolution > Arbitrations
- *School Finance*: Education Law > Funding > Allocation of Funds
- *Class Action*: Civil Procedure > Special Proceedings > Class Actions > Certification of Classes
- *Election Law*: Governments > State & Territorial Governments > Elections and Constitutional Law > Elections, Terms & Voting > Poll Taxes[13]
- *Damage Caps*: Torts > Malpractice & Professional Liability > Healthcare Providers > Healthcare Law > Healthcare Litigation > Tort Reform
- *Attorneys' Fees*: Torts . . . > Types of Damages > Costs & Attorney Fees > General Overview
- *Gay Rights*: Because we found that no single headnote adequately characterized the constellation of gay rights issues, we relied on a full-text search using the following keywords: "gay," "gays," "lesbian," "lesbians," "same-sex," "homosexual," or "homosexuals."

Having selected the best headnotes to characterize each issue area, we downloaded the full list of cases decided by each of the state supreme courts from 1990 to 2015 that contained those headnotes. To ensure that our list was as complete as possible, we also added the handful of "known" cases that did not include any of these headnotes to the pool of cases for each issue area. The result was an over-inclusive list containing the approximate universe of potential cases in each issue area decided by a state supreme court during our time period of interest. We know that we identified too many cases, including ones not relevant to our concerns. We reasonably believe that we have not identified too few cases—that all or nearly all relevant cases are included in the universe of decisions we analyze in this book.

To read and code the resulting list of about fourteen thousand cases, our team of law student research assistants used an online coding tool. Appendix 2.A provides further details about the case coding process.

Filtering the Cases

Recall that the initial list of cases for each issue area was significantly over-inclusive. In every issue area, there were many cases on our list that contained the headnote of interest but did not reach a substantive or procedural ruling related to our issue area. Therefore, the first question research assistants answered about each case was whether or not it passed a "filter": "Does the court make a substantive or procedural ruling on an issue related to [THE TYPE OF ISSUE BEING CODED]?" If the coders answered that the case did not rule on the issue, they were told to immediately cease coding the case and move to the next case on their list.[14] In all, we examined approximately fourteen thousand cases and found six thousand that decided relevant issues of political, legal, economic, and social inequality.

Coding Policy Outcomes: Pro- and Anti-Equality Rulings

For each type of case, we conceptualized and coded whether the outcome supported or undermined political, legal, economic, and social equality. Table 2.1 reports the coding rules used to classify the outcome of each case as well as the specific question within each policy type that the coders were asked to answer in order to classify a case's outcome as pro- or anti-equality. The column "Specific Rules" provides detailed illustrations of the types of court policies we regarded as pro- or anti-equality.

This approach to measuring pro-equality policy outcomes overlaps considerably with conventional definitions of legal policy liberalism, such as those used in Spaeth's Supreme Court Database. In every instance in our conceptualization, a pro-equality outcome would be considered by most to be a liberal outcome. Liberalism-conservatism is, of course, a broader categorization of cases (and one that includes criminal cases); our equality cases constitute a subset of policies traditionally scored as liberal legal policy outcomes.[15]

We recoded and merged the outcome variables so that a score of 1 indicated a pro-equality decision and a score of 0 indicated an anti-equality decision. For all analytical purposes, we excluded the tiny proportion of cases in which the coder could reach no substantive decision (discussed later). In the end, 51 percent of our six thousand cases were coded as not favoring greater equality and 49 percent as favoring greater equality.

Table 2.1 The Coding of the Dependent Variable—Policy Supporting or Undermining Equality

Domain	Outcome Question	Conceptualization	Specific Rules
Rulings pertaining to the rights of minorities, including poor people			
School finance funding equality	Did the court's decision contribute to greater equality across schools in the support and/or resources provided by the state?	Pro-equality outcomes are decisions that contribute to greater school equality.	• Decisions that equalize the amount of funding provided to school districts are pro-equality. • Decisions that provide increased funding to districts claiming inadequate funding are pro-equality. • Decisions providing additional funding (for example, for special education, facilities, and so on) to parochial schools that claim insufficient funding are pro-equality.
Gay rights	Did the court's decision endorse equal protection for LGBT individuals?	Pro-equality outcomes are decisions that grant, recognize, and/or extend rights to gays and lesbians.	• Decisions that strike down sodomy bans are pro-equality, as they protect the freedom of sexual choice. • Laws that allow same-sex people to marry, form legally recognized civil unions, adopt children, foster children, and divorce are pro-equality, as they support equal treatment regardless of sexual orientation. • Decisions that allow for protection of LGBT individuals against housing and employment discrimination are pro-equality. • Decisions that endorse health insurance and other employee benefits for same-sex spouses are pro-equality. • Decisions that endorse protecting LGBT individuals under hate crime policies are pro-equality.

Election law	Did the court's decision expand or contract opportunities for political participation?	Pro-equality outcomes are decisions that expand opportunities for political participation.

- Decisions that endorse access to the ballot for a candidate are pro-equality.
- Decisions that remove barriers to voting (for example, voter ID laws) are pro-equality.
- Decisions that allow restrictive qualifications on voting (for example, felon disenfranchisement, property ownership requirements) are anti-equality.
- Decisions that allow propositions for initiatives or referenda to be placed on the ballot are pro-equality.
- Decisions allowing parties or organizations to regulate ballot access are anti-equality.
- Decisions that strike down contribution or spending limits are pro-equality.
- Decisions that require campaign donors to be disclosed are pro-equality.
- Decisions that give rights to organizations (for example, *Citizens United*–type cases) are anti-equality.
- Decisions that equalize the influence of individual votes (one person, one vote) are pro-equality.
- Decisions that strike down gerrymandering of districts are pro-equality.

Rulings pertaining to the rights of workers and employees

Collective bargaining rights	Did the court's decision endorse expansive access to collective bargaining?	Pro-equality outcomes are decisions that endorse the expansive rights of workers and unions.

- Decisions that strike down restrictions on collective bargaining (for example, by not allowing collective bargaining) are usually anti-equality.
- Decisions that place restrictions on the topics of collective bargaining are anti-equality.
- Decisions that enforce right-to-work policies are anti-equality, since right-to-work policies necessarily weaken individuals' ability to collectively bargain.

(continued)

Table 2.1 (Continued)

Domain	Outcome Question	Conceptualization	Specific Rules
Employment-at-will policies	Did the court's decision limit the discretion of employers to hire and fire employees at will?	Pro-equality outcomes are decisions that limit employers' discretion to hire and fire employees at will.	• Generally, decisions that restrict the ability of employers to discharge employees are pro-equality decisions. • Any rule that provides protections for workers against firings without "just cause" are pro-equality.
Rulings pertaining to access to the state's justice institutions			
Mandatory arbitration policies	Did the court's decision make mandatory arbitration more or less likely?	Pro-equality outcomes are decisions that expand the authority of public institutions (rather than private institutions) to adjudicate disputes.	• Any rule that restricts access to public institutions for private disputes is anti-equality. • Decisions that uphold mandatory arbitration clauses are anti-equality. • Decisions that result in the privatization of adjudication are anti-equality.
Class action policies	Did the court's decision make it more likely that a class action lawsuit would be filed and/or that the plaintiffs in such a suit would prevail?	Pro-equality outcomes are decisions that endorse plaintiffs' ability to sue as a class.	• Any rule that endorses eased restrictions on class certification requirements is pro-equality. • Any rule that makes it more economically feasible to file a suit (for example, by eliminating caps on quantifications of pain and suffering) is pro-equality. • Any rule that requires the provision of attorneys' fees and contingency fees—a growing issue—is pro-equality. • Any rule that restricts caps on the total amount of damages (as the Class Action Fairness Act did) is pro-equality. • Any rule that rejects a venue change to a federal court, thereby keeping the class action in the state (where courts are more accountable to the majority) is pro-equality. • Any rule that eases filing requirements (for example, venue) is pro-equality. • Any rule that ensures access to jury trials in class action lawsuits is pro-equality.

Policies regarding the payment of attorneys' fees	Did the court's decision diminish or restrict the attorneys' fees paid by the plaintiff?	Pro-equality outcomes are rulings that diminish or restrict the attorneys' fees the plaintiff must pay.	• Any rule that limits the use of contingency fees is anti-equality. • Any rule that imposes a sliding scale (or a scale of any sort) for attorneys' contingency fees is anti-equality. • Any rule that requires an attorney to provide clients with an up-front estimate of what the hourly rate for a case will be versus the applicable contingency fee charge is anti-equality. • Any rule that requires the loser of the lawsuit to pay attorneys' fees (the "English Rule") is anti-equality.
Policies affecting damage caps in civil litigation	Did the court's decision tend to make plaintiffs' cases less likely to be filed (because it would not be economical to do so), or did the court's decision make plaintiffs less likely to prevail?	Pro-equality outcomes are rules that tend to make plaintiffs' cases more likely to be filed (because it would be economical to do so), or rules that make plaintiffs more likely to prevail.	• Any rule that places a cap on damages is anti-equality. • Any rule that limits the types of damages a plaintiff can receive (for example, no damages for pain and suffering, or damages for economic losses only) is anti-equality. • Any rule that restricts the form that "damage" can take (for example, by limiting the ability to receive punitive damages) is anti-equality. • Any rule that establishes a liability "trigger" that reflects the intentional tort origins and quasi-criminal nature of punitive damages awards (for example, "actual malice") is anti-equality. • Any rule that raises the standard to establish punitive damages liability (for example, by requiring "clear and convincing evidence") is anti-equality. • Any rule that requires proportionality in punitive damages is anti-equality.

Source: Authors' compilation.

Having described the database in considerable detail, we next provide some background on the various issue areas represented in our data set and examples of the types of policies adopted by the state high courts on these issues.

Rulings Pertaining to the Rights of Minorities, Including Poor People

School Finance Funding Equality

The education of children has traditionally been a matter left to the states. While the U.S. Constitution contains no right to education, every state constitution has some provision that mentions public education.[16] Over the past fifty years, these state constitutional clauses have provided a battleground between state legislators, who write a state's budget, and state judges, who often strike down state budgets that fail to live up to a constitutional requirement of an adequate educational experience for residents of the state.

State supreme courts have varied widely in their level of intervention in this matter: some have deferred to the legislature regarding school funding issues, while others have intervened by declaring a specific funding measure unconstitutional. In *Marrero v. Commonwealth*, a group of Philadelphia parents and teachers sued Pennsylvania on the ground that the state budget provided an unconstitutionally low level of funding to the Philadelphia School District.[17] The Pennsylvania Supreme Court declined to intervene by finding that the determination of what constituted an "adequate" education or "adequate" funds raised questions that were exclusively for the legislature to resolve, not the courts.[18]

The South Carolina Supreme Court took the opposite position in *Abbeville County School District v. State*.[19] A group of school districts sued the state on the grounds that the current school funding scheme resulted in the denial of each student's opportunity to receive at least a minimally adequate education, as required by the state constitution.[20] Here the South Carolina Supreme Court clearly found that the state's current school funding scheme was not working, and it declared a constitutional violation.[21] According to the court, the state legislature had failed in its constitutional duty to ensure that students receive the requisite educational opportunity.[22]

Other types of school finance cases have involved particular types or methods of funding public schools. For instance, the North Dakota Supreme Court in *Bismarck Public School District #1 v. State* held that the overall impact of the state's entire statutory method for distributing funding to public schools was unconstitutional in part because it did not bear a close correspondence to the goals of providing an equal educational opportunity to all pupils and supporting public schools from state funds based on the educational cost per pupil.[23] Rather, it was argued, the state's method was based predominantly on each school district's property tax base, which resulted in pupils receiving fewer educational resources in "property-poor" school districts.[24] Another example of judicial intervention is *McCleary v. State*, in which the Washington Supreme Court held that the state failed to meet its duty to public schools because it failed to fund transportation, staff salaries, and benefits at appropriate levels.[25] As these examples suggest, the state supreme courts are badly and often bitterly divided on various aspects of school funding equality.

And then there is Kansas. In a series of state supreme court rulings, beginning in 2014 with *Gannon* I and extending (at least) through *Gannon* VI, the Kansas Supreme Court, dominated by Democratic judges, has been at odds with the Republican legislature and governor (Sam Brownback for much of the litigation period) on whether state funding for Kansas's schools satisfies constitutional requirements of adequacy and equality.[26] We will have more to say about this Kansas litigation later, but no better example than Kansas can be found to serve as the "poster child" for an instance in which a supreme court battles for greater equality against majoritarian institutions (the governor and the legislature) that are steadfastly resisting pro-equality rulings.

Gay Rights

Throughout American history, courts have played an important role in defining and regulating the rights of underrepresented minority groups. Over the past few decades, the rights of LGBT Americans have been a frequently litigated issue in state and federal courts. Importantly, many of the issues related to LGBT rights—marriage, divorce, adoption, and child custody—fall squarely in the domain of family law, a domain typically left to state law. For this reason, state courts have been at the forefront of these matters over the past quarter-century.

Included in our data set are well-known cases in which state supreme courts looked to their state constitutions to grant gay and lesbian couples the right to marry. The Massachusetts Supreme Court in *Goodridge v. Department of Public Health* extended this right to its constituents.[27] Several years later, the Iowa Supreme Court did the same in *Varnum v. Brien*.[28] Included too are two notable California cases. In *Lockyer v. City and County of San Francisco*, the California Supreme Court ruled in 2004 that civil servants in San Francisco could not provide marriage licenses to gay and lesbian couples.[29] That court backtracked in *In re Marriage Cases* in 2008, when it ruled that the California constitution did in fact guarantee gays and lesbians the right to marry.[30]

Still, these well-known cases are only a sliver of the types of cases that state courts have considered over the past few decades. In many instances, particularly in the first half of our time period, state supreme courts were called upon to rule on the custody of children in cases in which one or both parents were members of the LGBT community. In one such case, *Ex parte D.W.W.*, the Alabama Supreme Court ruled in 1998 that the trial court did not abuse its discretion in considering the effects on the children of their mother's ongoing lesbian relationship. As the Court stated in that case:

> Both women are active in the homosexual community. They frequent gay bars and have discussed taking the children to a homosexual church. Although they do not engage in intimate sexual contact in front of the children, they openly display affection in the children's presence. . . . Even without this evidence that the children have been adversely affected by their mother's relationship, the trial court would have been justified in restricting R.W.'s visitation, in order to limit the children's exposure to their mother's lesbian lifestyle. When a noncustodial parent is involved in a continuing homosexual relationship, restrictions on that parent's visitation rights have been widely held to be proper.[31]

In other words, the Alabama court ruled that restrictions on a lesbian parent's visitation rights were legal and appropriate.

In another case, *Robert C. Ozer, P.C. v. Borquez*, the Colorado Supreme Court considered a wrongful termination action that involved an attorney whose HIV status was disclosed to coworkers at the firm, despite a request that it be kept confidential. The attorney sued for wrongful discharge and invasion of privacy; the Colorado Supreme Court allowed the invasion of privacy claim to go forward.[32]

Equal Access to the Electoral Process

The U.S. Constitution gives the states a broad grant of power to regulate "The Times, Places and Manner of holding Elections," and the states have used these powers in wide-ranging and varying ways.[33] Throughout American history, state laws have altered the composition of state electorates by gender, race, age, and class (for example, property ownership). States have used legislation to manipulate the timing of elections in ways that advantage some groups and disadvantage other groups, gerrymandered legislative districts to benefit political candidates on the basis of race or partisanship, and moved polling places in an attempt to alter the set of voters who are likely to turn out on election day.[34] To be sure, significant federal actions, like the post–Civil War constitutional amendments and the 1965 Voting Rights Act, have played an important role in shaping election law in the United States. But the Constitution's broad grant of authority to the states regarding the conduct of federal elections, coupled with the numerous state and local political offices filled by elections in each state, has given state legislatures nearly unfettered discretion to shape elections in this country. As the Federal Election Commission puts it: "The states have the authority and responsibility for setting minimum standards for voting in local, state, and federal elections and for ensuring that individuals seeking to vote comply with the state qualifications."[35]

When regulating elections, the state legislatures are aided (or perhaps restrained) by their state constitutions. According to the National Council on State Legislatures, thirty state constitutions have a constitutional requirement that their elections be "free," eighteen states require that their elections be "open" or "equal," and fifteen state constitutions protect citizens' right to vote against interference by "civil or military" powers.[36] For example, the constitutions of Delaware, Illinois, Indiana, Kentucky, and Oregon provide their states with the same succinct command: "All elections shall be free and equal."[37]

Determining what makes an election "free" or "open" or "equal" falls to state supreme courts, and the types of cases included under this umbrella are varied. State supreme courts have been called on to determine whether states can require voters to show a state-issued identification card in order to cast a vote on election day. In *Gentges v. Oklahoma State Election Board* (2014), for example, the Oklahoma Supreme Court overruled a challenge brought by a voter against that state's adoption of a voter identification law, ruling that the state had validly enacted the law through a referendum.[38] Also included are challenges about legislative districting, as, for example, when litigants have called upon a state supreme court to rule on the constitutionality of a purported gerrymander. In *Holt v. 2011 Legislative Reapportionment Commission* (2013), for example, the Pennsylvania Supreme Court decided one of these challenges by upholding the constitutionality of the state's legislative districts.[39] Other types of prominent challenges regarding state election law have involved ballot access for candidates (for example, did the candidate comply with the requirements to be listed on the ballot?) and the state initiative and referenda process (for example, is the ballot language for the proposed provision biased?).

Rulings Pertaining to the Rights of Workers and Employees

Collective Bargaining Rights

Collective bargaining is the negotiation process between an employer and a group of workers (often a union) over the conditions of workers' employment, such as their schedule, their salary, and their benefits. The states vary in the extent to which the ability to bargain collectively is a function of statutory or case law; a few states have no statutes or case law that clearly establish or prohibit collective bargaining for public-sector employees.[40] Some states have constitutional provisions that guarantee employees the opportunity to bargain collectively. The New Jersey constitution grants private employees a right to "organize and bargain collectively."[41] According to one prominent scholar of state constitutions, that provision has been interpreted as creating a "valid, self-executing, legal basis for a cause of action alleging interference with the rights to organize and bargain collectively even in the absence of statutory law authorizing such suits."[42]

The history of collective bargaining dates back decades. In 1959, Wisconsin became the first state to pass legislation authorizing public employee collective bargaining. In the early 1960s, legislation passed in Ohio allowing public employers to check off dues "led to the evolution of a common-law right to collective bargaining."[43] A 1979 Virginia statute that barred public-sector collective bargaining was preceded by a 1977 Virginia Supreme Court decision, *Commonwealth v. County Board of*

Arlington County, in which the "court held that units of local government lacked authority to enter into collective bargaining agreements."[44] As another example, in 1975 Indiana passed the Public Employee Labor Relations Act, and the Indiana Supreme Court decided on the act's constitutionality in 1977.[45] As these examples show, state supreme courts, generally speaking, began to turn their attention to public-sector collective bargaining in the 1960s and 1970s—the same period in which "public sector collective bargaining in the United States greatly increased."[46]

Across the twenty-six-year time period covered by our study, perhaps the most common issue decided by state supreme courts involved the ability of certain types of employees to bargain collectively. The jurisprudence of the Missouri Supreme Court provides a flavor of the sorts of issues implicated under the umbrella of collective bargaining. That court decided in *Parkway School District v. Parkway Association of Education, etc., Local 902/ MNEA* (1991) that school secretaries were not prohibited as "confidential employees" from entering into a collective bargaining agreement, thereby expanding access to collective bargaining.[47] Then, in *Independence-National Education Association v. Independence School District* (2007), the Independence School District in Missouri argued before the Missouri Supreme Court that it was not required to bargain collectively with its employees and was not bound by any prior agreements that the court had reached with district employees.[48] The state supreme court disagreed, writing: "[The Missouri Constitution's] guarantee that employees have 'the right to bargain collectively' is clear and means what it says. Therefore, agreements that the school district made with employee groups are to be afforded the same legal respect as contracts made between the district and individuals"[49] The court later extended its ruling in this case, deciding in *Eastern Missouri Coalition of Police v. City of Chesterfield* (2012) that school districts have an affirmative duty to meet and confer with employee groups, and again in *American Federation of Teachers v. Ledbetter* (2012) that this bargaining must be carried out in good faith.[50]

Of course, not all the cases in our data set resulted in expanded access to collective bargaining. For example, the New Hampshire Supreme Court in *Appeal of East Derry Fire Precinct* (1993) refused to certify a bargaining unit composed of ten firefighters because state law required a minimum of ten employees in a bargaining unit and three of the ten firefighters were "supervisory employees" who could not legally be included in a bargaining unit.[51]

Employment-at-Will Policies

Employees are considered "at will" if they can be dismissed from employment by their employer for any reason. At-will employment relationships differ from other types of employer-employee arrangements in that the employer is not required to provide some type of "just cause" before removing employees from their position. Because they can be fired without notice and for nearly any reason, employees who have at-will employment relationships typically have no legal recourse to challenge their dismissal in a court of law unless the reason for their firing violates some other state law (for example, a state provision guaranteeing that someone cannot be fired on the basis of their race, gender, or sexual orientation). Such protections, however, are sparse and often ineffective.

At-will employment relationships are common in the United States today. This differs from the early 1900s, when courts viewed employers and employees as bargaining on an equal playing field over their terms at work. The employment-at-will doctrine arose from the idea that, just as employees should easily be able to leave a job they dislike, employers should be able to remove employees to adjust their workforce and its composition as they see fit.[52] As unions became more common, however, courts generally began to realize that employers had a structural advantage when bargaining over terms of employment and gradually began to recognize exceptions to at-will employment relationships that provided employees with a legal recourse to challenge their termination under certain conditions.[53]

Today there are three major exceptions to the employment-at-will doctrine, the presence of which varies from state to state. First, under the "public policy exception," which has been adopted by more than forty states, employees cannot lose their jobs because they took an action inconsistent with "an explicit, well-established public policy of the State."[54] For example, an employee would have a recourse to challenge a dismissal if he or she had refused to perform a task that was illegal, or had sought workers' compensation for an injury suffered while working. Second, under the "implied contract extension," adopted by thirty-eight states, employers and employees can move from an at-will relationship to a more stable relationship based on oral or written statements (perhaps in an employee handbook) about topics like job security or the process for dismissal from employment. If employers do not follow these procedures, employees can challenge their dismissal in court. Third, the "covenant of good faith exception," which is recognized by only eleven states, raises the standard for dismissal by "[reading] a covenant of good faith and fair dealing in *every* employment relationship."[55] The covenant of good faith exception is intentionally broad and has taken on two common interpretations—"either that employer personnel decisions are subject to a 'just cause' standard or that terminations made in bad faith or motivated by malice are prohibited."[56]

Most of the cases that courts consider in this area require the court to rule on whether or not an employee has been wrongfully terminated, which often requires determining whether one of the exceptions to the employment-at-will doctrine applies to the case. The circumstances under which these terminations arise vary as widely as the courts' responses. Consider, for example, *Rooney v. Tyson* (1998), a New York Court of Appeals case in which the court was called on to determine whether or not Mike Tyson, the famous boxer, had wrongfully terminated his trainer after promising the trainer that he would keep the job "for as long as the boxer fights professionally." Ultimately, the court ruled that the oral contract was for a definite duration; therefore, the trainer was not an at-will employee.[57] In another case, *Talley v. Flathead Valley Community College* (1993), the Montana Supreme Court found that a nontenured professor was an at-will employee and therefore could be terminated without reason.[58] Furthermore, consider the Nebraska Supreme Court's decision in *White v. State* (1995).[59] A caseworker was asked to take a polygraph to disprove two inmates' claims that the caseworker had brought marijuana into a jail; the caseworker refused the polygraph and was fired.[60] The court ruled that the termination was wrongful because the caseworker was not a law enforcement employee, and therefore state law prohibited termination for such a refusal.[61] Finally, in *Ryan v. Dan's Food Stores, Inc.* (1998), a pharmacist who had questioned the validity of some prescriptions filled at his place of work had at-will status, in part, because he was given a handbook containing an acknowledgment form indicating that he was an at-will employee when he was hired.[62] The Supreme Court of Utah held in favor of the employer, reasoning, first, that the handbook was not substantively or procedurally unconscionable because the pharmacist had a reasonable opportunity to understand the terms of the handbook and ask questions regarding the at-will clauses.[63] The court also determined that the termination did not violate public policy, regardless of whether the pharmacist was a whistleblower, because the pharmacist could not show that his contacting public authorities was the cause of his termination. In addition, the court found it likely that the pharmacist could have been fired because of a history of customer complaints.[64]

Nelson v. James H. Knight DDS, P.C., *and James Knight*

We pause for a moment to consider in somewhat greater detail one of the employment-at-will cases in our database that received more publicity than most. We digress to outline this case because it illustrates the relevance and salience of the state supreme court to the people of its state.

The Iowa Supreme Court is well known for issuing opinions that attract the attention, and occasionally the ire, of the mass public. One such case is *Nelson v. Knight*, decided in 2013.[65] The facts of the case are relatively simple.

- Dr. James Knight became sexually attracted to his longtime dental assistant, Melissa Nelson.
- They carried on a flirtation of sorts—consensual, but not sexual.
- Dr. Knight's wife was not happy about this. She demanded that Dr. Knight fire Ms. Nelson.
- He did.
- Ms. Nelson sued, claiming that she was the victim of sex discrimination. Discrimination by sex is illegal in Iowa, although discrimination on many other grounds is entirely legal via the state's employment-at-will precedents.
- The Iowa Supreme Court, in a unanimous decision by all seven of the male justices, sided with Dr. Knight (a male).
- Of the three Democrats on the court, three voted for Dr. Knight. Of the four Republicans on the court, four voted for Dr. Knight.
- The justices claimed that the case was not about sex. As the chief justice wrote: "The resolution of the case turns on context: Was Nelson's termination a response by Dr. Knight to a personal relationship or was it his response to Nelson's status as a woman?" All members of the court answered "personal relationship," despite Nelson's argument that the personal relationship occurred because she was a woman. Moreover, the court's ruling, the court itself said, had nothing to do with fairness.

The court's decision attracted a great deal of attention from the media and the people of Iowa, although not as much attention as its same-sex-marriage ruling of a few years earlier.[66]

Admittedly, it is not common for civil decisions to draw the attention of the mass public. (Criminal rulings are more likely to be reported and commented upon.) Nevertheless, rulings such as this one (and the same-sex-marriage decision) caused many Iowans to ask whether their highest court was in tune with the values of its constituents. When people become engaged with the judiciary, they sometimes act to vote the rascals out.

Rulings Pertaining to Access to the State's Justice Institutions

Mandatory Arbitration Policies

When one potential litigant has a grievance with another party, filing a lawsuit seems like a natural option for that person to pursue. However, many contracts increasingly prohibit potential litigants from seeking justice through the public courts. Instead, parties must resolve their disputes through a private and binding process of arbitration outside the judicial branch. The terms of mandatory arbitrations can also be set in contracts, which may specify the state in which the arbitration will be held, how the arbitrator will be chosen, and sometimes even the particular arbitrator that will be engaged.

Legal observers are often quick to point out that jury trials are becoming less and less common in the United States.[67] Mandatory arbitration provides one reason why trials are becoming a rarity; these clauses are ubiquitous in the United States today.[68] When you shop on Amazon, you agree to mandatory arbitration; fifteen of the largest twenty banks that issue credit cards and seven of the eight largest cell phone providers also mandate arbitration in the event of a dispute.[69] As one study showed, an average Los Angeles resident is subject to mandatory arbitration in disputes that relate to over one-third of the major transactions he or she conducts.[70]

These clauses have proliferated in recent decades, and the federal government has supported this increase. Indeed, the U.S. Supreme Court has interpreted Congress's Federal Arbitration Act as preempting many types of legislation that states might pass in order to limit mandatory arbitration within their borders.[71] State supreme courts, then, can do little either to bless mandatory arbitration or block it altogether. Instead, in most of the relevant cases in our data set, the state court must referee whether a dispute can continue to be resolved in the judiciary or whether it must be resolved through non-state-based arbitration.

In one notable case, *State ex rel. Hewitt v. Kerr* (2015), a former employee of the St. Louis Rams football team alleged that his termination was due to age discrimination.[72] The Missouri Supreme Court held that the terms of the employee's contract—which compelled him to resolve his dispute in an arbitration in which the NFL commissioner was the sole arbitrator and had the power to unilaterally set the rules of arbitration—were unconscionable, and that therefore the contract terms were unenforceable.[73] In another high-profile dispute, the New Hampshire Supreme Court held in *State v. Philip Morris USA, Inc.* (2007) that the state of New Hampshire was bound by an arbitration agreement that it made with tobacco companies as part of a multistate lawsuit against those companies.[74] Therefore, the state could not sue the tobacco companies as a result of a dispute about the amount of money the state was entitled to under its settlement with the companies; instead, the dispute needed to be handled through arbitration.

A second set of cases deal with the authority of arbitrators during arbitration. The Montana Supreme Court, in *Paulson v. Flathead Conservation District* (2004), found that Montana would give broad authority to arbitrators to determine issues of fact or law: in fact, the Court explained that arbitrators had broader power in regard to bodies of law than the courts.[75] By contrast, the New Hampshire Supreme Court, in *Appeal of Town of Durham* (2003), decided differently in considering a dispute between a town and a probationary firefighter.[76] The town and the firefighters' union had entered into an agreement requiring all disputes between the town and permanent firefighters to be decided by arbitration. In this case, the court held that the firefighter was not bound by this agreement because he was a probationary, rather than permanent, firefighter. As these cases illustrate, upperdog litigants profit—or believe they profit—from keeping legal disputes out of the state's courts.

Class Action Policies

A class action lawsuit is a legal action in which one of the litigants is a group of similarly situated people who are collectively represented by a member of that "class" of people. In many cases, such as large-scale products liability lawsuits, it is inefficient and unfair for each wronged individual to be required to bring a separate lawsuit.[77] A class action combines the potential legal actions by all similarly situated individuals, resolving the dispute a single time and potentially making the legal process more efficient and cost-effective. But most importantly, class actions allow those with only small damages to get their day in court.

The procedures for these lawsuits are complex, and defining the group of people who make up the class, notifying potential members of the class, and disbursing the eventual damage award to class members are all complicated tasks that may inspire their own bouts of litigation. The typical class action case in our data set deals with one of these procedural issues in class action law; these procedural decisions have huge effects on access to justice for underdogs. If a judge, for example, fails to certify a class (therefore not allowing the lawsuit to go forward), it potentially deprives many of the members of that group—who may not have the means to pursue the legal action on their own—of the ability to achieve compensation for the wrongs they experienced.

Thus, it is not surprising that many of the class action cases in our data set involve the certification of classes. For example, the Alabama Supreme Court decertified several purported classes throughout the time period of our study. In *Ex parte Equity National Life Insurance Company* (1997), the Alabama court withdrew a trial court order certifying a group of insureds as a statewide class, holding that the trial court had not conducted an analysis that was "rigorous" enough for the class to stand.[78] The Alabama court came to similar conclusions in *Ex parte Water Works & Sewer Board* and *Disch v. Hicks*.[79]

In contrast to the Alabama court, the Arkansas Supreme Court has been more lenient in granting class status to litigants.[80] For example, in *American Abstract & Title Co. v. Rice* (2004), a married couple who had purchased a home in Little Rock sued the American Abstract & Title Company, alleging that the company had engaged in deceptive trade practices and was guilty of the unauthorized practice of law.[81] The couple sought to expand their lawsuit to include "all persons who paid document preparation fees for the preparation of legal documents such as deeds, mortgages, and notes; who paid a settlement or closing [fee]; and/or who had money held in escrow by American that earned interest."[82] The Arkansas Supreme Court upheld the class certification.[83]

Another case that stands out is *Wilkes v. Phoenix Home Life Mutual Insurance Company* in Pennsylvania.[84] In this litigation, the appellees had established a trust to purchase $7 million in life insurance.[85] The appellees received notice of a proposed settlement of an out-of-state class action suit against the appellant (the insurance company).[86] Appellees claimed to have contacted an agent who told them that they were not involved in the suit.[87] The trial court barred appellees' complaint against the insurance company, concluding res judicata barred appellees' complaint.[88] On appeal, the superior court reversed and remanded the case, claiming that the class action notice did not contain an adequate description to warn appellees that their policy was affected by the settlement.[89] After granting the appellant's appeal, the Supreme Court of Pennsylvania disagreed with the superior court and held that the notice was sufficient to have allowed appellees to have comprehended their inclusion in the class.[90] Though the legalese in this case is complicated, the outcome was not: the upperdog litigant won.

Policies Regarding the Payment of Attorneys' Fees

In most countries around the world—but not in most of the United States—funds to pay for legal representation are awarded to the winning party to a lawsuit as a matter of right.[91] As one commentator explains: "For generations of American lawyers it has been boldfaced black letter law that in the absence of contrary statutory authority a litigant must, with few exceptions, bear the single greatest cost of asserting his legal rights—his attorney's fees—regardless of the outcome of his action. This so-called 'American Rule' of attorney's fees is almost unique in the jurisprudential world."[92] The rule is so ensconced that the U.S. Supreme Court has summarized this country's jurisprudence in this succinct way: "In the United States, the prevailing litigant is ordinarily not entitled to collect a reasonable attorneys' fee from the loser."[93]

The "American Rule" developed over time. Colonial courts awarded attorneys' fees to the winning litigant; however, perhaps as Americans' distrust in the legal profession grew, this practice dissipated, partly in an attempt to weaken the economic health of the legal profession.[94] Changes to the "English Rule"—in which the loser pays the winner's attorneys' fees—have periodically been put on the agenda, most notably as part of

George H. W. Bush's proposed tort reform legislation and as part of the Republican House of Representatives' famous 1994 "Contract with America."[95] Still, today the American Rule widely prevails.

Today, as the cost of hiring quality counsel has skyrocketed, the ability of litigants to afford counsel plays an important role in access to justice. Under the American Rule, a litigant could prevail in court but owe such substantial attorneys' fees that those fees negate any damage award the litigant is owed. In this way, the high costs of legal services, coupled with the American Rule, make many potential litigants less likely to seek legal remedies for wrongs they have experienced.

The attorneys' fees cases in our data set typically involve a state supreme court determining whether a prevailing litigant in a lawsuit is entitled to receive attorneys' fees as a part of their award. In one notable case, *In re Corral-Lerma* (2014), the Texas Supreme Court held that an appellant's bond was not required to include security for the attorneys' fees because those fees were not compensatory damages, thereby limiting the ability of a litigant to collect attorneys' fees.[96] The Utah Supreme Court held a similarly hard line against attorneys' fees in *Broadwater v. Old Republic Surety* (1993).[97] In that case, the court held that litigants in Utah were not generally entitled to attorneys' fees absent some preexisting contractual or statutory basis.[98] The Wyoming Supreme Court came to a similar conclusion in *Pribble v. State Farm Mutual Automobile Insurance Company* (1997), holding that attorneys' fees were not recoverable in Wyoming unless there was a specific statute, rule, or contract that provided for recovery of those fees.[99]

While common, these rulings are not universal, as not all state supreme court decisions in this issue area prohibit the recovery of attorneys' fees. For example, the Washington Supreme Court, in *Roberts v. Dudley* (2000), ruled that the Washington State Law Against Discrimination allows plaintiffs who are victims of discrimination to recover reasonable attorneys' fees under state law. However, a successful plaintiff in a common law claim for wrongful discharge cannot recover attorneys' fees.[100] Likewise, as the New Jersey Supreme Court ruled in *In re Estate of Lash* (2000): "If a plaintiff has been forced because of the wrongful conduct of a tortfeasor to institute litigation against a third party, the plaintiff can recover the fees incurred in that litigation from the tortfeasor. Those fees are merely a portion of the damages the plaintiff suffered at the hands of the tortfeasor."[101]

Policies Affecting Damage Caps in Civil Litigation

In many lawsuits, prevailing plaintiffs are entitled to a monetary damage award to compensate the litigants for the harm they experienced. In a medical malpractice lawsuit, for example, a patient who is disabled as a result of a botched surgery might receive one amount of money as "economic damages" (to compensate for the medical expenses incurred, wages lost as a result of not being able to work, and lost future income) and another amount for "non-economic damages" (to compensate the plaintiff for nonmonetary harms, such as disability and/or pain and suffering).

Some states have passed legislation that limits the maximum size of the damage awards that litigants are entitled to receive in these types of lawsuits. Part of a broader "tort reform" movement, this type of legislation became common in response to a perceived trend of juries becoming more generous in their damage awards. According to one commentator, "The number of multi-million dollar jury verdicts doubled between 1972 and 1983."[102] The rise in these verdicts was blamed, mistakenly it turns out, for a rise in the cost of insurance for health-care providers, which, in turn, inspired many states to pass laws that limit (or "cap") the damages that litigants can receive.

During the twenty-six-year period of our study, many state supreme court cases dealt with the applicability of state damage cap provisions to particular cases and ruled on the overall constitutionality of these provisions. For example, the Michigan Supreme Court faced this issue in *Jenkens v. Patel* (2004), in which a daughter sued her deceased mother's doctor and clinic for medical malpractice.[103] A jury awarded the plaintiff $10 million in non-economic damages.[104] The Michigan Supreme Court ruled that, because the state's medical malpractice non-economic damages cap applied to wrongful death actions where the underlying claim was medical malpractice, the non-economic damages awarded by the jury had to be reduced to an amount that aligned with state law.[105] Relatedly, in *Mobile Infirmary Medical Center v. Hodgen* (2003), the Alabama Supreme Court considered the legality of a $2,250,000 punitive damage award given to a patient and his wife who sued a hospital for medical malpractice, affirming the judgment only on the condition that the patient file a remittitur of the punitive damages award to $1,500,000.[106]

State courts sometimes do affirm large damage awards. In another Michigan case, *Stone v. Williamson*, the state's high court upheld a $1.9 million damage award on behalf of a plaintiff who argued that a negligent diagnosis had led to an amputation of both of his legs.[107] The court ruled that, because the plaintiff had suffered a substantial loss of opportunity, going from a 95 percent chance of attaining a good result to a 10 percent chance of attaining a good result, and because the jury properly found that the defendant's negligence more probably than not caused the plaintiff's injuries, the award was acceptable.[108]

Summary

The six thousand cases in our database represent six thousand individual stories. Nevertheless, just as is done in the U.S. Supreme Court Database, case outcomes can be categorized as generally favoring equality or inequality. Also like the U.S. Supreme Court Database, however, these assessments of case outcomes are made on the basis of contextualized and specific rules about how outcomes must be scored. Our purpose in this section has been to provide some contextual information for representative cases within each of the issue domains. Just as the liberal-conservative distinction sometimes breaks down when applied to real disputes—the U.S. Supreme Court Database codes *Citizens United* as a liberal decision (because it protects freedom of speech, even if for the wealthy and powerful)—not all cases can be unambiguously coded. At the same time, our coding of the vast majority of these cases is most likely not very controversial.[109]

The Validity and Reliability of the Coders' Judgments

We conducted formal tests of the validity and reliability of the coders' judgments of the outcomes of the six thousand cases, and the results are reported in appendix 2.B. Generally, these tests reveal that the main dependent variable of this book—whether the outcome in the case favored greater political, legal, economic, and social inequality—was coded with a very high degree of both validity and reliability.

Controlling for Case-Level Attributes

Figure 2.1 reports the distribution of pro-equality cases across the nine sub-issue domains.[110] The issue areas vary significantly in the frequency with which pro-equality decisions were made. In later chapters, we develop and test hypotheses to explain this variation.

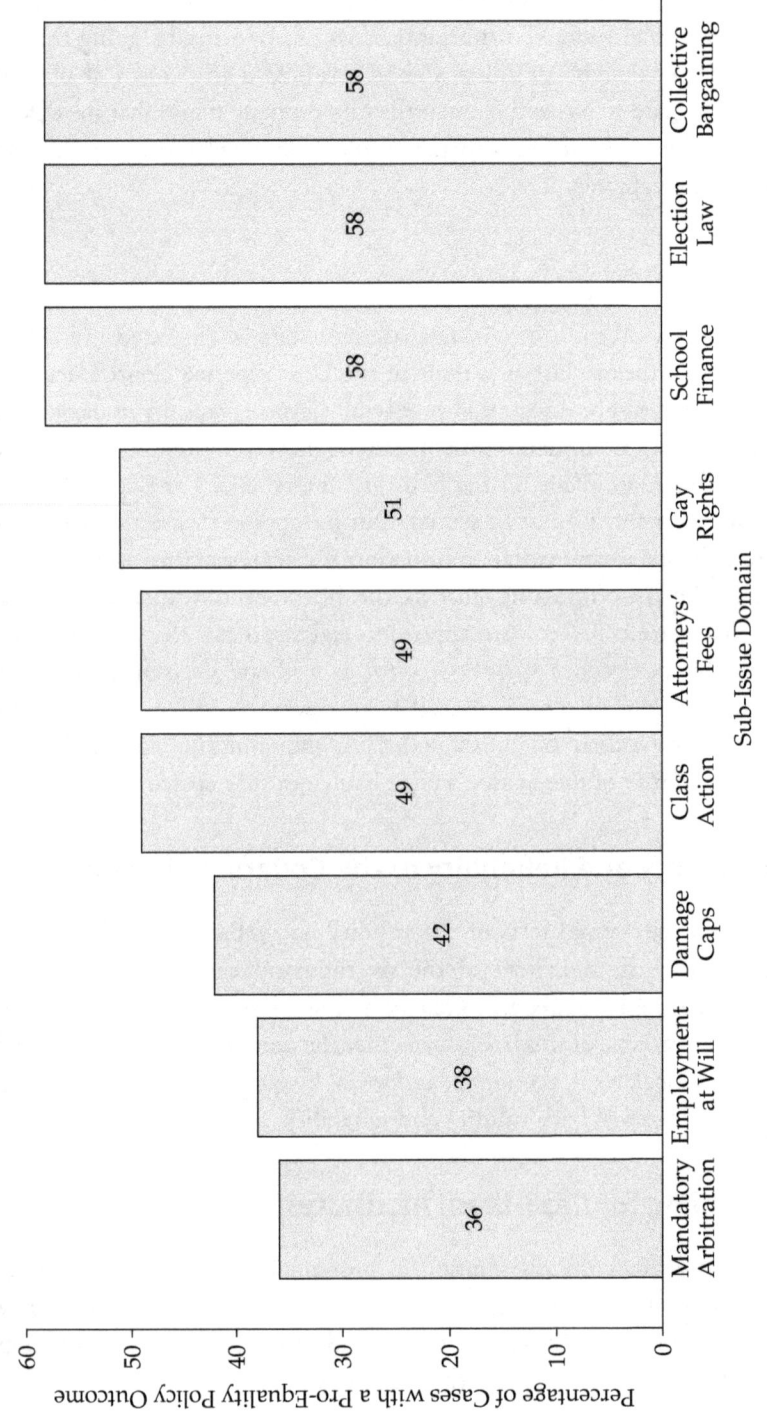

Figure 2.1 Pro-Equality Outcomes in State High Courts across Different Policy Subdomains, 1990–2015

Source: Gibson and Nelson, State High Court Inequality Database, 1990–2015.
Notes: $N = 5,936$. F-test for difference of proportions: $p < .001$; eta = 19. Cases weighted by weights associated with three issue domains.

These six thousand or so cases are spread across three overarching issue domains and therefore represent a variety of different types of litigation. It is therefore useful to consider a set of control variables that can be implemented to render the cases more comparable, both across and within domains.

The control variables we use are:

- Issue-domain fixed effects, with the rights of economic underdogs as the excluded category
- Whether the lower court's decision favored greater equality or inequality
- Whether the court's decision was based on procedural grounds

Some of these variables require further discussion. We asked the coders to indicate whether the decision was made on procedural grounds (standing, mootness, justiciability, and so on) versus substantive grounds, by which we meant whether the court ruled on an issue of direct relevance to the issue they were coding. To the extent possible, however, we allowed the coders to assign a policy outcome to the case even if it was decided on procedural grounds, under the theory that a procedural loss is just as harmful to a litigant seeking greater equality as a substantive loss (although we recognize that the latter may have greater precedential value).[111] About 14 percent of the cases judged to favor greater equality were scored as being based on procedural grounds; the comparable figure for cases judged not to favor greater equality was 17 percent. Of the decisions made mainly on procedural grounds, 45 percent favored equality; of the substantive decisions, 49 percent favored equality.

We can also score whether the decision of the court below favored equality or inequality.[112] In 44 percent of the cases the lower court ruled in favor of equality, and in favor of inequality in 44 percent of the cases.[113] It is perhaps not surprising that the state supreme court decisions tend to agree with lower court decisions when it comes to equality. However, it is perhaps surprising that the relationship is not stronger. In about 55 percent of the cases in which the lower court ruled in favor of inequality, the state supreme court ruled the same; for cases in which the lower court ruled in favor of equality, the state supreme court agreed in 52 percent of the cases. Thus, there was a slight—but far from strong—tendency for the two courts to reach the same conclusion on issues of political, legal, economic, and social inequality.

Intercourt Variability in Support for Greater Equality

To what degree did the state high courts in our database vary in their policy outputs on cases implicating political, legal, economic, and social inequality? Based on our coding of these six thousand cases, we find tremendous intercourt variability in the degree to which the decisions favored greater equality or inequality (see figure 2.2).[114]

The first and most obvious conclusion from these data is that considerable variability exists across the courts in the degree to which their rulings were pro-equality.[115] While most states vary in a band from about 40 percent to 60 percent of their decisions favoring greater equality—a significant range in itself of twenty percentage points—a handful of state supreme courts stand out as outliers. The Arizona, New Jersey, and Kentucky courts issued an unusually high percentage of pro-equality decisions, while the state supreme courts in seven states issued an unusually low percentage of such decisions. The Texas Supreme Court was the most anti-equality court in the country, followed by the Indiana Supreme Court. Although more systematic analysis is certainly required to draw firm conclusions, we can note here that there are quite a few seeming anomalies in this figure, ranging from the rather high percentage of pro-equality decisions in Arizona to the middling scores for the New York and Massachusetts courts, to the fairly low percentage of pro-equality decisions by the Michigan Supreme Court.

Inter-Justice Variability in Support for Greater Equality

It turns out that about 954 judges cast votes in our roughly 6,000 political, legal, economic, and social inequality cases, with an average number of votes cast of 40 cases (standard deviation = 46; median = 27).

About 80 percent of the judges voted in at least ten cases. To investigate judge-level variability, we have focused on this subset of judges, calculating for each judge the percentage of votes favoring greater equality. Obviously, this measure can range from 0 to 100 percent of the cases in which the judge voted. We refer to this as a behavioral *propensity*, and we correlate it with

Figure 2.2 Cross-State Variability in State High Court Rulings Favoring Greater Political, Legal, Economic, and Social Equality, 1990–2015

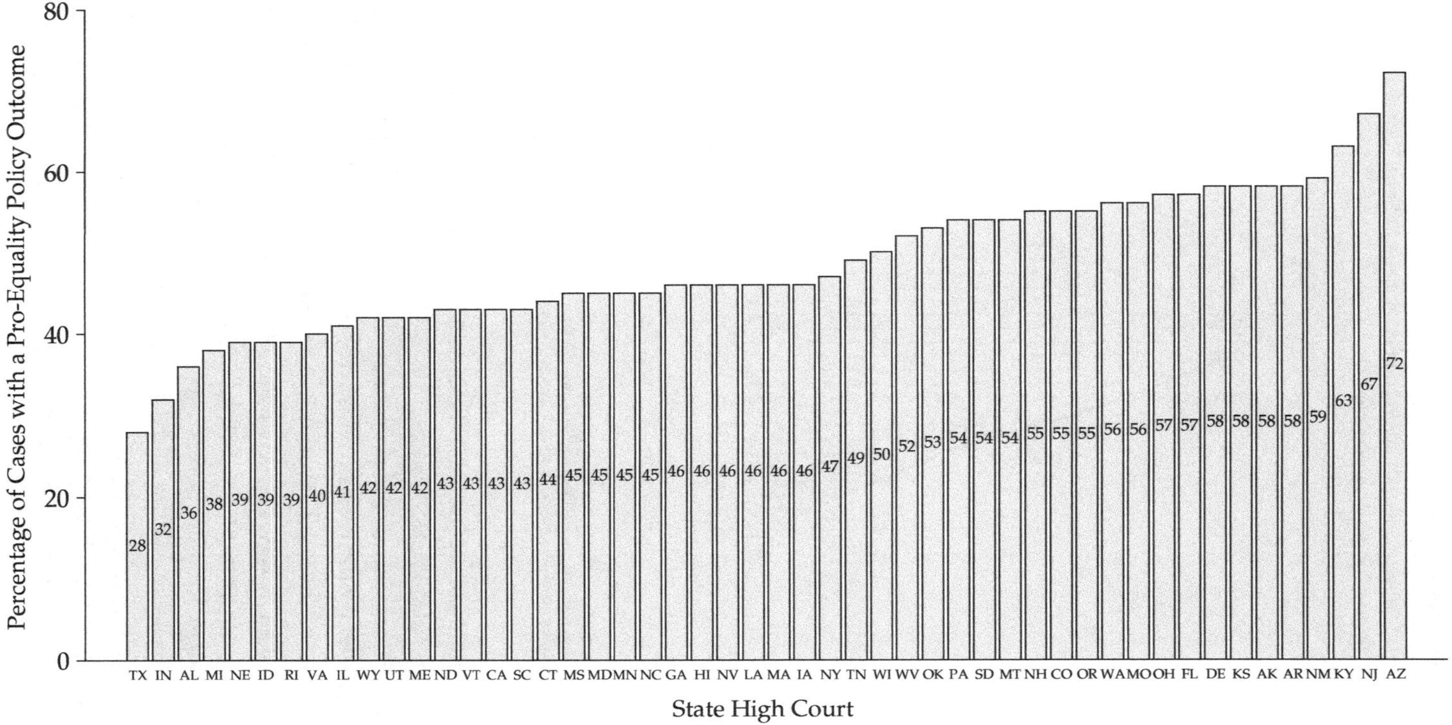

Source: Gibson and Nelson, State High Court Inequality Database, 1990–2015.
Notes: This figure aggregates outcomes in all equality-relevant cases decided between 1990 and 2015.

Figure 2.3 Inter-Justice Variability in the Percentage of State High Court Votes Favoring Greater Equality, 1990–2015

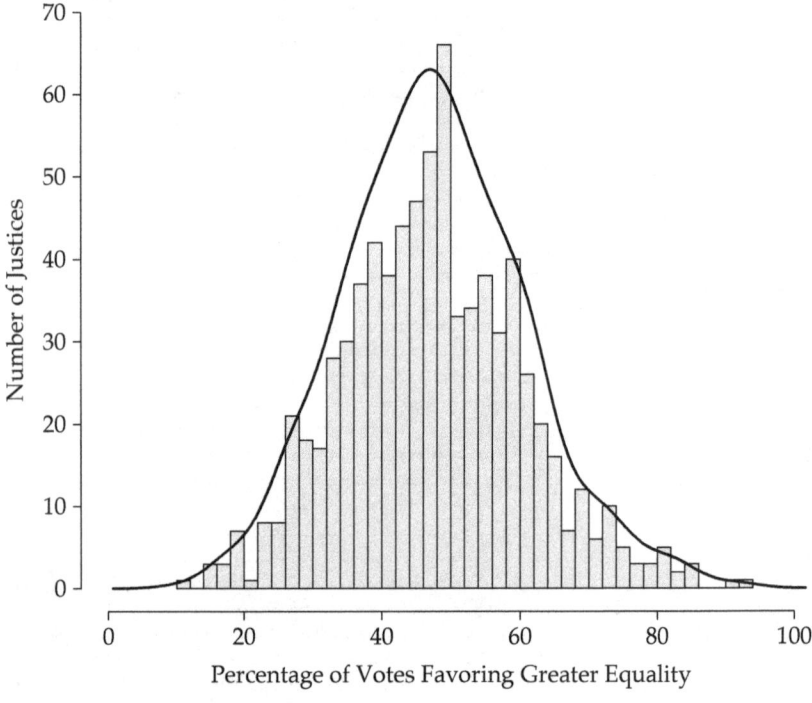

Source: Gibson and Nelson, State High Court Inequality Database, 1990–2015.
Notes: This figure reports the distribution of the percentage of votes favoring greater equality for the 768 justices in our database who voted in at least ten equality-relevant cases.

fixed attributes of the justices.[116] Figure 2.3 reports the frequency distribution of the votes of these 768 justices.

The distribution of the propensity to vote in favor of greater equality very closely approximates a normal distribution, with a mean of about 48 percent of the votes favoring greater equality. Among the 768 justices who voted in at least ten cases, the average percentage of votes favoring equality is 48 percent (standard deviation = 13; median = 47 percent), with a range from 10 percent to 92 percent. According to our data, Justice Charles R. Malone of the Alabama Supreme Court voted in favor of equality in only 10 percent of the ten cases on which he cast votes.[117] Justice Eric S. Rosen of the Kansas Supreme Court voted in favor of greater equality in 92 percent of the thirteen cases in which he voted.[118]

Summary and Concluding Comments

Some earlier research has coded case outcomes on the basis of reading the cases. Most such research, however, has considered a fairly small number of cases, and all within a single issue domain (for example, death penalty cases). Our State High Court Inequality Database is perhaps unique in that it examines multiple issue domains; it analyzes all state supreme court decisions within those domains, over a lengthy period of time; and it codes the outcome variable—whether the decision favored political, legal, economic, and social inequality—with very high degrees of both validity and reliability. Creating, cleaning, and verifying this database has been a herculean job. In the end, our analysis shows that about one-half of these state high court rulings favored equality, and the other half favored inequality. The rest of this book is devoted to accounting for the variation in pro-equality outcomes and focuses on the litigants in the cases, the justices who decided the cases, the courts in which those justices worked, and the larger state political context in which the judiciary was embedded.

Appendix 2.A: The Case Coding Process

Throughout a coding process, ensuring the reliability and validity of the coded data is of the utmost importance. Yet, in perhaps the most common method by which cases are scored—giving research assistants direct access to a spreadsheet that is subsequently analyzed by the researcher—both reliability and validity are endangered when coders make innocent errors. For example, a research assistant might become confused about the coding scheme, entering an incorrect value into a spreadsheet. Or a research assistant might sort the spreadsheet incorrectly or absentmindedly delete rows from a spreadsheet, thereby undermining data validity and reliability.

We attempted to rectify these issues in advance by having our research assistants code the cases using a Qualtrics "questionnaire," a "smart" web form. By coding data through a form/questionnaire rather than a spreadsheet, our coders were limited in the answers they could provide to each question and in their ability to manipulate the raw data. For example, the Supreme Court Database has advanced beyond Spaeth's original notecard-based coding scheme to a sophisticated online coding interface.

Similarly, Brace and Hall's project used a Microsoft Access database, which has many of the advantages of the sophisticated Supreme Court Database approach. However, many coders do not have access to that software program, and they cannot code the cases without such access. Our approach was particularly advantageous because it allowed coders to complete their work from anywhere in the world, so long as they had an internet connection.

There were other advantages to our approach as well:

Data were labeled. Whereas spreadsheet-based coding systems often require coders to memorize a system of numeric response categories for each possible value of a variable, as well as the correct column of a spreadsheet for each variable, the use of an online survey enables researchers to present respondents with a full prompt for each question, including coding notes normally hidden in a codebook. We were then able to ensure that every research assistant had access to the same complete information when coding each case.

Case-level data were "piped" in. Using a Python script, we parsed the text files for metadata about each case, such as the names of the parties, the court that decided the case, the date of the decision, the number of separate opinions in the case, and the names of the dissenting and concurring opinion judges. The script output a .csv file in which the unit of analysis was the case. In the same way that surveys often pipe respondents' previous answers into subsequent questions, we uploaded this spreadsheet to Qualtrics as a contact list and incorporated these data throughout the "survey."

The survey branched. Just as survey respondents might be directed to a page of additional questions based on their answer to an initial question, we provided coders with individual pages keyed to the name of the dissenter for each dissenting opinion. The survey presented the correct number of screens for dissenting opinions and labeled each page with the author of the opinion to ensure that data were correctly assigned to each case.

Recoded cases were saved. Qualtrics saved the original coding for cases that were coded multiple times, enabling us to recover accidental miscodings—something that would never have been possible if coders had entered their data directly into a spreadsheet.

Coders were checked for consistency. Just as survey respondents are often prompted to fill in missing questions or to verify seeming inconsistencies in their answers before advancing to the next page of the questionnaire, researchers can design their coding questionnaire to check the consistency of coders' answers before they move to the next page. By checking the validity of coders' answers on key variables in real time, the survey prompted coders—who had the case fresh in their mind—to verify their answers, thus limiting the number of mistaken entries in their work. For example, coders were not able to move to the next page of our survey if the answers they gave about the parties to a case were logically inconsistent with one another (for example, saying in the answer to one question that an educational institution was a party to a case but neglecting, in a later question, to indicate that an educational institution was a party to that same case).

After creating the coding form and uploading the case-level information to Qualtrics, we created individual survey links for each case, an approach similar to the way in which researchers create individual, identifiable surveys for their respondents. Each link could be taken only once (though new links could be created to allow coders to revise a case's original coding), so each case was coded only one time. These were the links we distributed to our coders.[119]

Appendix 2.B: The Validity and Reliability of the Coders' Judgments

It is crucial to this analysis to assess the validity and reliability of the central dependent variable used throughout nearly all of our analyses. As we see it, the issue of validity is addressed in part by the first question put to our coders: whether the case concerned one of the political, legal, economic, and social inequality issues. We consider the level of guidance provided to the coders for making this decision to be validity-enhancing.

We also provided the coders with ample opportunity to *not* draw a conclusion about the outcome in the case by offering three indeterminant codes associated with the policy outcome variable: "unclear," "not relevant," and "other."[120] A code of "unclear" was often associated with a procedural judgment; a code of "not relevant" essentially meant that the filter question was not accurately coded; and a score of "other" indicated a variety of unusual circumstances, including outcomes that seemed to favor both parties to a considerable degree. In only slightly more than one hundred cases (out of about six thousand) was the coder unable to reach a conclusion about the substantive policy outcome in the case. We have scored "unclear," "not relevant," and "other" codes as missing data on this policy-outcome variable and removed those cases from our analyses.

The reliability of our measures is more complicated and difficult to assess. As an initial approach to reliability, we asked the coders to indicate the degree to which they had confidence in the various scores they recorded for each of the key variables in our analysis. The confidence question was asked regarding most of the key variables in our analysis.

After they coded the policy outcome (see table 2.1), the coders were asked two further questions:

Did the court decide the case on procedural (standing, mootness, justiciability, etc.) rather than on substantive grounds? By "substantive grounds" we mean that the court ruled on an issue of direct relevance to the issue area you are coding.

Looking at your answers to the previous two questions [the policy outcome and the procedural questions], how certain are you of your characterization of the outcome? (*extremely certain, somewhat certain, not very certain, not certain at all*).

The coding in about 81 percent of the cases was scored as "extremely certain," although there was significant variation across issue areas. Only 68 percent of the class action cases received the highest certainty rating, while 97 percent of the employment-at-will cases were rated as "extremely certain." The differences in accuracy certainty across the nine sub-issues are highly statistically significant, as is the level of association (eta = .20). Overall, the coders had the highest level of confidence in their judgments in about four out of every five cases.

To assess the degree to which our coders reliably coded the characteristics of these cases, we conducted an inter-coder reliability (ICR) check. Within each of the nine issue subdomains, we randomly selected twenty-five cases from the population of cases that passed the filtering check. We then had these 225 cases coded afresh. However, during the ordinary data cleaning process, which was not related to the ICR analysis, we determined that six of these cases should not have passed the filter in the primary database. We discarded these from the ICR database, leaving 219 cases for the analysis.[121]

Of the 219 recoded cases, seventeen (8 percent) failed the filter in the ICR coding despite having passed the filter in the primary data set. In two of these seventeen cases, the original coders could not make a determination as to whether the outcome in the case was pro- or anti-inequality, so in some sense disagreement among the coders was limited to fifteen of the 219 cases. Thus, if we focus only on the cases in which the policy outcome could be determined, only fifteen out of 219 cases (about 7 percent) were erroneously filtered out of the ICR database. This left 202 cases for the reliability analysis, although we note that the coders were not able to make a policy outcome determination in all 202 of these cases.

The key variable of interest for the ICR analysis is of course the assessment of the policy outcome in the case. There were at least two ways to think about the reliability of this variable: Was the coder able to make a substantive judgment in the case? And if so, was there agreement on whether the outcome favored or disfavored political, legal, economic, and social inequality? Regarding the former, we found *100 percent* agreement on the seven cases in the two databases that could not be scored on the substantive policy outcome. This left 195 cases on which a policy determination could be made by both the primary database coder and the ICR coder.

The primary database coders and the ICR coders agreed on the substantive policy outcome in 99 percent of these 195 cases. On only three cases was there disagreement on the outcome. Were we to add back the seven cases on which the coders agreed that no clear policy outcome could be coded, inter-coder agreement approaches 100 percent. It appears that our coding guidelines and rules were sufficiently clear to produce a highly reliable dependent variable for this analysis. Consequently, we conclude that the principal dependent variable of this book is measured with a quite high degree of reliability.

Appendix 2.C: Weighting the Case Data

Our equality cases are not a random sample of the cases heard by the state supreme courts. Instead, we identified a number of issue domains and attempted to code *all cases* falling within each domain.

Because we coded the universes of cases, not samples, this strategy resulted in a large disparity in the number of cases per domain. Subdomain sizes range from 138 coded cases in the school finance category to 1,527 cases in the mandatory arbitration group. Without any adjustments, the case data are implicitly weighted by the numbers of cases within the domain. So, without weights, whatever was true of mandatory arbitration cases had a much more disproportionate impact on our conclusions; whatever was true of school finance cases had practically no impact on our conclusions. Of course, this is not true of conventional analyses of state supreme court policymaking in discrete and narrow issue areas such as abortion and search and seizure. Nor is it true when we conduct analyses *within* issue domains. For analyses of the entire database, however, it seems that the appropriate strategy is to try to neutralize these case size differences—that is, to standardize in some way so that each issue domain contributes roughly equally to our overall findings.[122]

As noted earlier, we conceptualize these cases as pertaining to three overarching issue domains: (1) the rights of minorities, including poor people; (2) the rights of workers and employees; and (3) access to the state's justice institutions. These three domains are not equal in size: the first includes 29 percent of the cases, the second 23 percent, and the third 48 percent.

One solution might be to take the actual number of cases—5,886—and divide it by the number of issue domains (3), and then weight within each domain so that the number of cases is equal to 1,962 (5,886/3). This means weighting some cases upward and some cases downward, although none of the adjustments is particularly radical. This is the strategy we have adopted. When we analyze the entire database, we use this weighing factor; however, we use unweighted data when conducting analysis within each issue domain.

Without weights, 53 percent of the case outcomes favor inequality. With weights, the figure declines slightly, to 51 percent. Some variability by issue domain remains, ranging from 43 percent of the minority rights cases not favoring equality to 52 percent of the economic underdog cases, to 59 percent of the access to justice institutions cases. This of course means that differences in the case-type distributions across independent variables (for example, judges, courts, time) may account for some of the differences in the degree to which equality prevails. However, these distributional differences are, in some sense, the nature of reality, leading us not to feel it necessary to implement any corrections for distributional differences.

CHAPTER 3

Do the Haves Come Out Ahead in the State High Courts?

WITH THE ANALYSES in this chapter, we begin our efforts to determine why some court decisions favor greater equality while others favor greater inequality. Here we focus on the role of the litigants in our six thousand or so cases, and in particular on the relative power of the petitioner and respondent in the case. The two overriding hypotheses of this chapter are that upperdog litigants tend to seek greater inequality in the cases they litigate, and that, owing to their superior resources and experiences, they are more successful than underdog litigants in getting the policies from the state supreme courts that they want. In testing these hypotheses, we contribute to a well-established literature concerning bias in court policy decisions in favor of well-resourced litigants.

Do the haves come out ahead in the American legal system?[1] This seemingly simple question is one that has consumed a great many intellectual resources and empirical efforts by scholars ever since Marc Galanter published his pathbreaking article "Why the 'Haves' Come Out Ahead" in 1974.[2] In the United States, Galanter's hypothesis has been aggressively pursued throughout the U.S. federal judicial hierarchy as scholars have investigated it in the U.S. Supreme Court, the U.S. courts of appeals, the U.S. district courts, and the U.S. state supreme courts.[3] Galanter's thesis has also been assessed outside the United States in countries as varied as England, Taiwan, Israel, the Philippines, China, and Australia.[4]

In light of the mixed findings of these numerous research efforts, Galanter's premise—that the haves do indeed come out ahead (and that it is therefore necessary to explain why they do)—must be restated to ask whether, in fact, the haves enjoy a significant advantage in American courts. More precisely, because these varied research efforts on this question have revealed the answer to be "sometimes they do and sometimes they do not," the research question must be refined to ask under what conditions the haves prevail. Investigating that question is the purpose of the research reported in this chapter.

We rely in this analysis on the database of court decisions regarding political, legal, economic, and social inequality (as described in chapter 2). It seems to us that there are no policy domains that are more pertinent to the haves/have-nots hypothesis than cases that directly address issues of equality and inequality.

Our purposes in this chapter are several. Following much earlier research, we provide an answer to the question of whether the haves came out ahead in state high court rulings from 1990 to 2015 in several different policy domains relevant to political, legal, economic, and social inequality. Second—and deviating quite a bit from earlier research—we investigate whether high-status litigants tended to pursue inequality-enhancing policy goals through their litigation. Finally, putting the conventional and the unconventional parts of our analysis together, we determine whether well-resourced litigants were particularly effective when seeking greater inequality through their litigation. Throughout all three parts of our analysis, our findings diverge from conventional wisdom and existing expectations quite a bit.

The Success of the Haves in the State High Courts of America

How is it that state supreme courts could systematically contribute to inequality? One possibility is that these courts—and indeed, courts in general—are conservative institutions that tend to protect the interests of the haves over those of the have-nots. In modern times, this hypothesis was first put forth and empirically supported by Robert Dahl, who showed that the U.S. Supreme Court has historically advanced the interests of minorities.[5] Unfortunately for inequality in America, the minorities benefiting the most from the Court's rulings have been privileged minorities, so-called upperdogs, rather than less privileged minorities (underdogs). Examples are easy to cite, but the one that has remained relevant throughout much of American constitutional history—including to some degree now—is what may be one of the most anti-equality doctrines: substantive due process. Under this policy, the assets of the upperdogs have been protected from regulation, taxation, and expropriation. If judiciaries in the United States equally favored the interests of all social classes, the result would be neutral insofar as inequality is concerned. Unfortunately for those who favor greater equality in the country, that does not seem to be the case.

Dahl's thesis has been the subject of a considerable amount of research by political scientists and legal scholars. One of the most important papers ever published in the law and social sciences literature is Galanter's previously mentioned 1974 article, "Why the 'Haves' Come Out Ahead."[6] Galanter posited that much (if not most) of the litigation in the United States pits relatively privileged and powerful parties (the haves) against relatively underprivileged and powerless parties (the have-nots). He discussed the relative success in courts of the haves and explained their advantage with the concept of the "repeat player"—litigants who litigate often, thereby acquiring extremely valuable experience, and who, perhaps more importantly, focus not just on winning individual cases but on shaping relevant law and the rules of the legal game.

Among the more notable upperdogs that regularly use the U.S. legal system are business interests; the extent to which courts favor business interests has been a topic of intense interest both inside and outside the academy.[7] In particular, a major recent study has investigated the fortunes of business interests at the federal level. In a comprehensive analysis of all U.S. Supreme Court cases in which one or both litigants were businesses, Lee Epstein, William Landes, and Richard Posner found that, perhaps contrary to popular wisdom, business interests generally fared worse than their opponents over the entire 1946–2011 period.[8] Yet this pattern is not invariant; their analysis indicates that the Roberts Court is a much more pro-business court than either the Burger or Rehnquist Courts. With time, the U.S. Supreme Court changed.

At the state level, two widely cited studies have investigated whether the haves do well in litigation in state high courts.[9] In research based on sixteen states from 1870 to 1970, Stanton Wheeler and his colleagues found a relatively small but consistent advantage for privileged parties in cases decided by these courts.[10] As they report, "parties with greater resources—relatively speaking, the 'haves'—generally fared better than those with fewer resources. In match-ups between stronger and weaker parties, the stronger consistently and on a variety of different measures won an advantage averaging 5 percent."[11] The authors go on to explain that, owing to difficulties in determining whether litigants are haves or have-nots, their data most likely systematically underreport the advantage that the haves enjoy in court.[12]

In their investigation of whether the haves come out ahead, using their database for all state high courts in the mid-1990s, Brace and Hall similarly find considerable interstate variability in the proportion of cases in which underdogs win.[13] The most important contribution of this research is its direct focus on explaining interstate variation in bias toward the interests of upperdogs, a question that Wheeler and his colleagues largely ignore. One of Brace and Hall's more intriguing findings is that the "supply of lawyers [in a state], more than any other variable, emerges as critical in accounting for have nots getting to court and how these litigants fare once there."[14] They also discover that state public opinion has a significant influence on court outcomes, with more liberal states producing more decisions favoring the underdogs. Their documentation and explanation of cross-sectional variability in how state high courts treat underdog litigants are among the most valuable contributions of the Brace and Hall research.

The fear that business interests are "buying" judicial rulings through campaign contributions has recently heightened concerns about haves winning in state supreme courts.[15] Indeed, some evidence shows that judges are predisposed to vote in favor of their campaign contributors, although this relationship only seems to exist in partisan election systems.[16] Difficult questions regarding causal structures abound in this research, but all agree that powerful commercial interests are committed to helping pro-business judges ascend to the state high courts.

Wheeler and his colleagues report that the sixteen state high courts included in their analysis became less biased toward the interests of upperdogs in the 1940–1970 period (the end of their database).[17] At the same time, however, the Brace and Hall findings and the Kang and Shepherd findings suggest that underdogs have been less likely to prevail since the mid-1990s than they had been in the last part of the period analyzed by

Wheeler and his colleagues. (We recognize that strict comparison of the databases is difficult given considerable and consequential differences in samples, methodologies, and so on.) Therefore, in addition to interstate variability, earlier research suggests that the degree to which the state high courts have sided with the upperdogs has also been temporally variable. Clearly, the haves do not always come out ahead.

The Policy Objectives of the Haves and Have-Nots

Because litigation so often pits the haves against the have-nots, it is tempting to use the relative status and power of the litigants to treat nearly all state court rulings as affecting levels of inequality. Resisting this temptation, we focus instead on outcomes in several concrete areas of public policy.

To reiterate, we posit that state high courts make public policy in a variety of domains that directly influence levels of inequality in society, including:

- Rulings pertaining to the rights of minorities, including poor people
- Rulings pertaining to the rights of workers and employees
- Rulings pertaining to access to the state's justice institutions

Each of these policy areas has significant implications for political, legal, economic, and social equality in the United States. Thus, our approach to the question of inequality in judicial rulings is two-pronged, in that we consider both litigant status and substantive policy domain outcomes relevant to judicially created and sustained inequality in the American states.

Our purpose in this chapter is to join the litigant resources literature with our case outcome analysis.[18] We begin with the measurement of key concepts for the analysis.

Measurement

In this section, we detail our approach in measuring our key variables of interest: the status and power of the litigants on each side of the cases, the power differential between the litigants in a given case, and the outcomes of the cases.

Measuring Litigant Status

First, we distinguish between the parties on both sides of the case. We refer to these parties as the "petitioners," or "first-listed litigants," and the "respondents," or "second-listed litigants," even though this is not always technically correct owing to a variety of legal conventions and issues.[19] Moreover, a very small number of cases have no second-listed party or even anything close to a conventional "petitioner" and "respondent."[20] These have been excluded from our analysis of the relative status of the litigants.

We are particularly concerned about the "status," "power," or "resources" (as they are variously known in the literature) of the litigants on each side of the case. Our approach to characterizing the parties draws from earlier research, which uses litigant type as a measure of litigant power or resources. For example, Donald Songer and Reginald Sheehan, in their study of litigant status in the U.S. courts of appeals, employ a seven-point scale: "underdog individuals, residual category, other business, big business, local government, state government, federal government."[21] Recent examinations have expanded and refined this scale.

Our own approach follows most closely that taken by Ryan Black and Ryan Owens in their book on the influence of the solicitor general in the Supreme Court; they use a ten-point litigant power scale based on the type of litigants in the case.[22] The parties or party sets are assigned to one (parties) or more (party sets) of the following categories:[23]

1. Indigent or poor natural person (an individual recognized by the court as lacking resources for litigation and/or appearing pro se)
2. Minority or an individual alleging discrimination (for example, a woman alleging sex discrimination, but not all women; only applicable if the individual's minority status is at issue in the case)
3. Other natural person
4. Private organization or association (for example, a union, interest group, or political organization)
5. Small business (a local business that appears to be closely held or to have an individual owner-operator)
6. Other business (either a medium-sized business or one for which classification as a "small" or "big" business is ambiguous)

7 Big business (an airline, railroad, multistate financial institution, insurance company, oil company, or other large business entity)
8 City, county, local government, or educational institution
9 State government

For analytical purposes, we have collapsed educational institutions with city, county, and local governments. We have also chosen to exclude the tiny number of cases in which the U.S. government was a party, for two reasons: First, because our analysis is of state-court litigation, the U.S. government rarely appeared as a party. And second, the few cases in which the U.S. government was involved were convoluted. To reiterate, the categories are considered to be an ordinal scale of the power of the parties, with "power" conceptualized mainly as having the benefits associated with being a "repeat player"—one who frequently litigates the same sorts of cases and therefore not only develops great legal expertise but also seeks to shape the law through litigation (not just win cases) and other means.[24] Our scale of litigant status ranges from 1 to 9, with higher values indicating higher status.

Using the nominal type of litigant as an indicator of "power" is fraught with potential measurement error. Consider the recent case of the attorney general of Oklahoma suing several opioid manufacturers.[25] Comparing the legal resources of the Oklahoma attorney general and, for example, Johnson & Johnson, does not at first lead to the conclusion that Attorney General Mike Hunter's office was the upperdog. But the issue is even more complicated: the Oklahoma attorney general engaged outside legal counsel for this lawsuit, including at least two powerful plaintiffs' firms. Still, these firms were small and had far from unlimited resources. Especially when comparisons are made between city, county, local, and even state governments and corporate behemoths such as Johnson & Johnson, resource inequality may be turned on its head.[26]

Coding the status of *all* listed parties on both sides of the case is an innovation of our measurement approach.[27] While extant explorations of litigant status are common, most research is unclear about exactly *which* party's status they use when there are multiple litigant types on the same side of the case. Therefore, for both the first-listed and second-listed litigant sets, we code both the first-named party and all parties listed on that side of the case.[28] We then identify the listed litigant on each side of the case with the greatest power.

One natural question to ask is how often the first-named party on one side of the case is also the most powerful litigant on that side of the case. Perhaps luckily, the answer is "nearly always." The two are the same in about 96 percent of cases for first-listed parties and 92 percent of cases for second-listed parties. For the first-listed parties, the correlation between the status of the first-named party and the most powerful party on that side of the case is $r = .95$. On the other side of the case, the correlation is $r = .91$.

Even though the two are similar, the most powerful party on each side of the case is the one measured to have superior facial validity. When multiple litigants with different levels of resources band together, their ability to battle the lawsuit depends less on how they are listed in the litigation than it does on the resources they are able to contribute. Our measures of litigant status take as the measure of status the highest value of any of the first-named parties and the highest value of any of the second-named parties.

Figure 3.1 shows the distribution of party types on both sides of the case. The modal category on both sides is "other natural person" (46 percent for petitioners, 29 percent for respondents). The second-most-common party on the petitioner side of the case is medium-sized businesses (16 percent of petitioners); for respondents, the second-most-common party type is state government (23 percent of respondents).

Measuring Power Differentials

Of course, the theory from which our hypotheses derive speaks to the "relative power" of the parties in a lawsuit.[29] We created a measure of relative power by subtracting the score for the most powerful party on the petitioner side of the case from the score for the most powerful party on the other side of the case. We followed common practice in this respect.[30]

Because each side of the case has a value ranging from 1 to 9, our measure of the litigant power differential has a theoretical range of −8 to +8; in practice, the variable's range is from −6 to +6.[31] Positive values of the measure indicate that the petitioner is more powerful, while negative values indicate that the respondent is more powerful. The variable has a mean of −1.1 (meaning respondents are somewhat more powerful on average) and a standard deviation of 3.8.

Figure 3.2 shows the distribution of the power differential variable. In 33 percent of cases, petitioners are more powerful than respondents; the

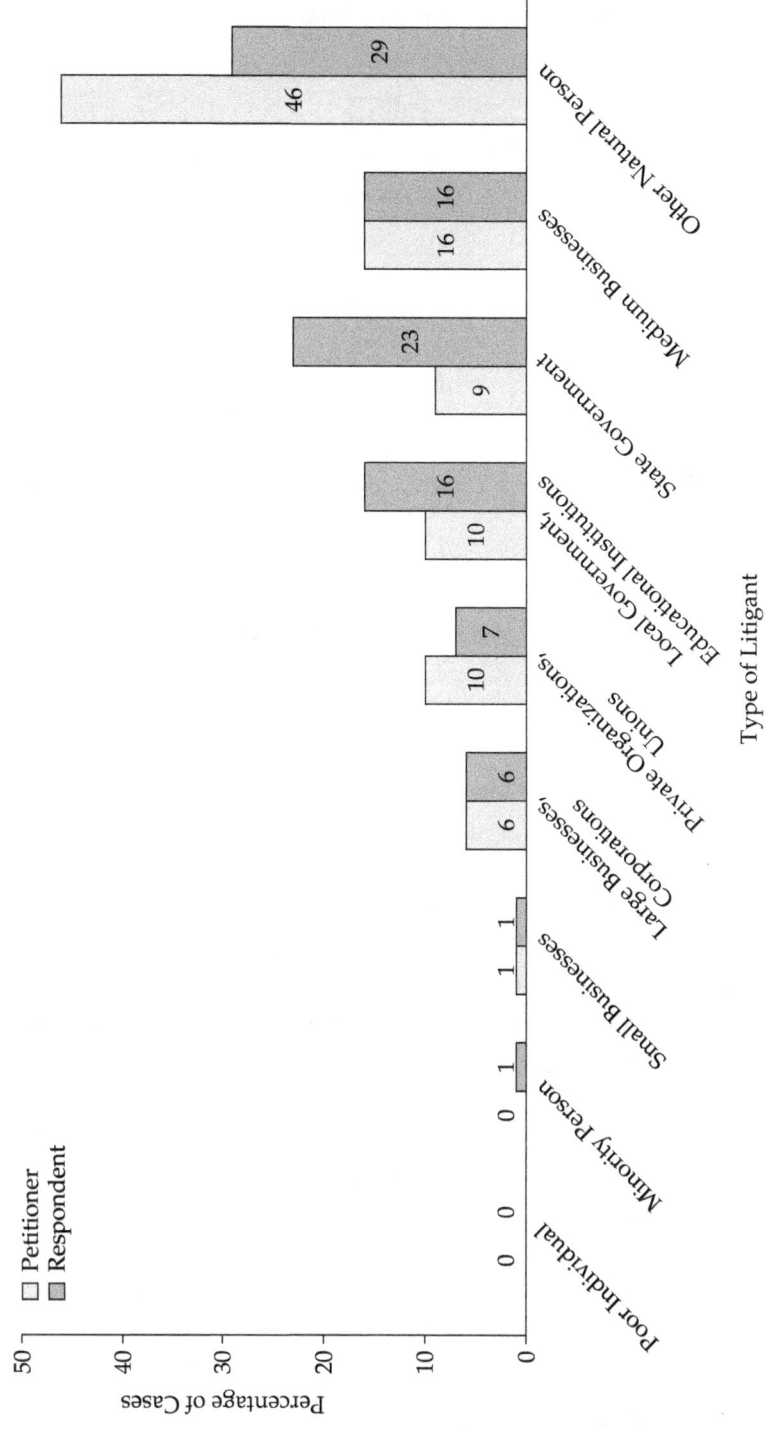

Figure 3.1 Distribution of Litigant Types across State High Courts, 1990–2015

Source: Gibson and Nelson, State High Court Inequality Database, 1990–2015.
Notes: $N \approx 5{,}849$. The percentages reported sum to 100 percent across the different types of litigant status (except for rounding errors), within petitioners and within respondents. Cases are weighted by weights associated with the three issue domains.

Figure 3.2 Distribution of Litigant Power Differential

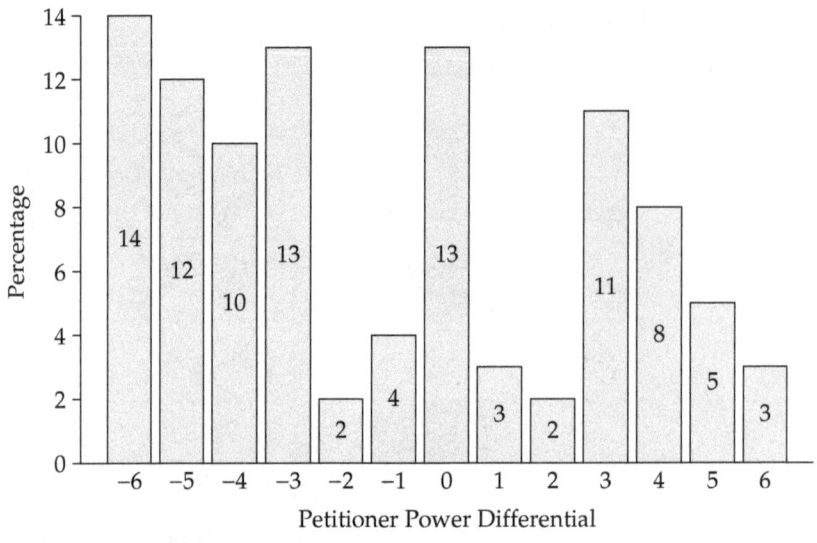

Source: Gibson and Nelson, State High Court Inequality Database, 1990–2015.
Notes: N ≈ 5,839. The percentages reported sum to 100 percent across the different levels of the relative power of the petitioner versus the respondent (except for rounding errors). Positive values of the *x*-axis mean that the petitioner is more powerful than the respondent, negative values indicate the converse, and an *x*-axis value of 0 indicates that the parties are of equal power. Cases are weighted by weights associated with the three issue domains.

converse is true in 54 percent of cases (data not shown). In the remaining 13 percent of cases, the two parties are equally matched.

That average value masks a significant amount of cross-issue variation. Figure 3.3 plots the average litigant power differential by issue. As expected, respondents in the minority rights issue area—in which individuals are particularly likely to sue the government (election law, gay rights, and school finance)—tend to be considerably more powerful. This is also true, but to a lesser degree, in cases involving the rights of workers and employees. Conversely, petitioners tend to be slightly more powerful in cases involving issues around access to justice institutions.

Measuring the Outcome of a Case

We are interested in two aspects of the case outcomes. First, we need to know whether the petitioner or the respondent won a case. This concept is

Figure 3.3 Average Litigant Power Differential, by Issue Domain

Source: Gibson and Nelson, State High Court Inequality Database, 1990–2015.
Notes: $N \approx 5{,}839$. Difference of means, relative power of petitioners and respondents: $p < .001$, eta = .32. Cases are weighted by weights associated with the three issue domains.

the traditional outcome in studies seeking to test Galanter's hypothesis, and it follows fairly straightforwardly from a court's disposition of a case: cases that overturned a lower court ruling are "wins" for the petitioner, while those that affirmed a lower court ruling are "wins" for the respondent. Respondents are somewhat more likely to prevail in our cases, winning in 53 percent of cases compared to petitioners' success rate of 47 percent.

Second, our analysis requires that we determine whether the cases' outcomes were pro- or anti-equality. We identify decisional outcomes within each policy domain that tend to contribute to or subtract from equality, in very much the same way that scholars of court policymaking code whether decisional outcomes are liberal or conservative.[32] Based on the coding form we use to analyze these supreme court opinions, table 2.1 provides specific definitions and rules by which we code pro-equality or anti-equality court decisions.

Results

We structure our analysis in a series of steps. First, following much earlier research, we provide an answer to the question of whether the haves came out ahead in state high court rulings from 1990 to 2015 in the various policy domains relevant to political, legal, economic, and social inequality. Second—and deviating quite a bit from earlier research—we investigate whether high-status litigants tended to pursue inequality-enhancing policy goals through their litigation. Then, putting together the conventional and the unconventional parts of our analysis, we determine whether well-resourced litigants were particularly effective when seeking greater inequality through their litigation.

Do the Haves Come Out Ahead?

We begin our analysis by addressing Galanter's canonical question: do the haves come out ahead? Our answer is a mild "yes." On the whole, the haves tend to win slightly more often (56 percent of cases) than the have-nots (44 percent of cases).[33] However, as figure 3.4 shows, there is considerable variability in win rates by issue, with upperdogs prevailing in about 58 percent of the minority rights cases but in only 53 percent of the cases concerning access to justice institutions. These basic findings generally echo those of earlier research: the haves do come out ahead in the state high courts, but not by a great deal; and as our analysis demonstrates, the type of litigation matters at least a little.

We begin our more systematic analyses by examining the net advantage of each litigant: that is, the difference between the litigant's win rate as a petitioner and its loss rate as a respondent, just as previous studies have done.[34] Overall, petitioners win in 53 percent of the cases in which they are the stronger party; they lose in 43 percent of the cases in which they are the weaker party. This gives them an overall net advantage of about 9.8 percentage points, which is much lower than the 28.6 percent reported by Songer and Sheehan in their analysis of cases before the U.S. courts of appeals.[35] One tentative conclusion from this analysis is that the haves do come out slightly ahead in these state court cases, but not to the same degree as they do in federal appeals courts. We note, however, that the state court average undoubtedly masks considerable variation across the individual state high courts, a dynamic that we address in our later analysis.

Figure 3.4 Percentage of Upperdog Wins in State High Court Cases, by Issue

Source: Gibson and Nelson, State High Court Inequality Database, 1990–2015.
Notes: N = 5,029. Difference of percentages across issue domain: p = .011; eta = .04. Cases are weighted by weights associated with the three issue domains.

Another way to assess the party differential is to examine the net advantage enjoyed by a litigant based on its party type. To this end, table 3.1 displays the net advantage for each party type. If the haves do in fact come out ahead, we should see the party's net advantage (the third column of the table) get progressively larger as the party becomes more powerful. This is generally the pattern shown in table 3.1. The net advantage for poor individuals and natural persons is negative, indicating that their opponent's success rate is greater than their own success rate. On the other hand, governmental parties and businesses have positive net advantages. Though the relationship is not perfect (as with parties who are minority persons), the net advantage does increase as we move down the rows of the table. As Galanter expected, the net advantage tends to grow with the increasing status of the party.

Table 3.1 Success Rates in State High Courts, by Litigant Status, 1990–2015

Type of Party	Success Rate as Petitioner	When Respondent, Opponents' Success Rate	Net Advantage	Combined Success Rate as Petitioner and Respondent
Poor individual	19.1%	60.0%	−41.0%	23.1%
	(21)	(5)		
Minority person	45.5	37.5	8.0	54.3
	(22)	(24)		
Other natural person	44.0	53.5	−9.4	45.1
	(2,601)	(1,910)		
Private organizations, unions	46.5	43.2	3.3	50.9
	(501)	(370)		
Small businesses	50.9	42.3	8.6	54.6
	(59)	(71)		
Medium businesses	49.8	44.9	5.0	52.4
	(1,144)	(1,048)		
Large businesses, corporations	56.2	54.1	2.1	51.3
	(461)	(420)		
Local government, educational institutions	51.8	45.9	5.9	53.2
	(512)	(780)		
State government	50.0	41.0	9.0	56.4
	(468)	(1,150)		

Source: Gibson and Nelson, State High Court Inequality Database, 1990–2015.

Notes: This table is analogous to table 1 in Songer and Sheehan 1992. The net advantage is the difference between the first two columns. Numbers of cases are reported in parentheses.

Finally, perhaps the most obvious way to consider whether the haves come out ahead in state supreme courts is to investigate variation in petitioner success—the percentage of cases in which the petitioner prevails—as the petitioner's power advantage varies. Figure 3.5 plots this relationship. If Galanter's hypothesis holds, we should see a steep, positive "stairstep" effect with each subsequent bar higher than the next. This is the general pattern depicted in the figure; however, while there is some overall upward movement in the bars, it is not particularly strong.

We also consider this relationship in multivariate contexts. Tables 3.2 and 3.3 report the results of two logistic regressions. The dependent variable in those regressions, following Songer and Sheehan, is whether the petitioner

Figure 3.5 Percentage of Petitioner Wins in State High Courts, by Petitioner Win Advantage

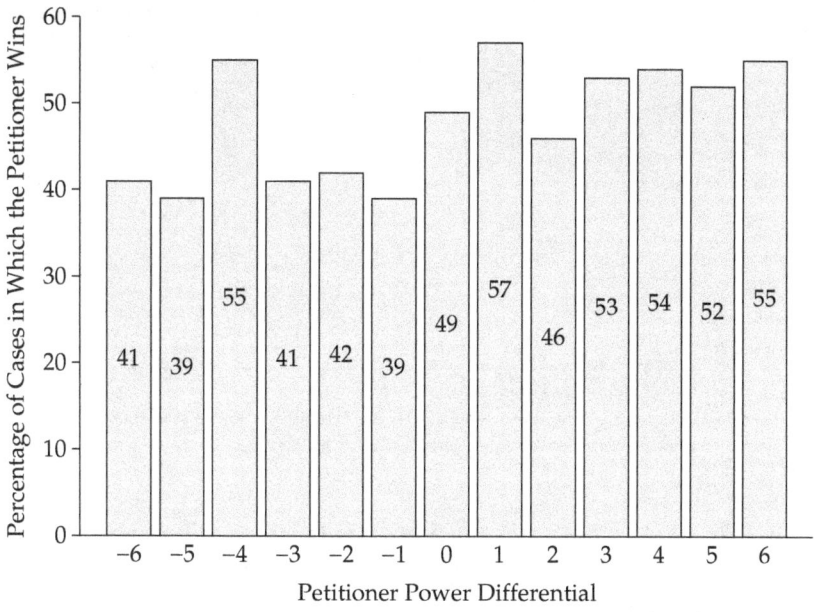

Source: Gibson and Nelson, State High Court Inequality Database, 1990–2015.
Notes: $N \approx 5{,}755$. Differences in percentages across relative power of the petitioner: $p < .001$; eta = .13. The bars plot the percentage of cases within each score on the power status differential index in which the petitioner won the case. Cases are weighted by weights associated with the three issue domains. Positive values of the x-axis mean that the petitioner was more powerful than the respondent, negative values indicate the converse, and an x-axis value of 0 indicates that the two parties were of equal power. The overall positive trend in the bars ($r = .09$) indicates that the petitioner is generally more likely to win as it becomes more powerful relative to the respondent. In other words, the haves (slightly) tend to come out ahead.

prevailed in the case.[36] The variable is coded 1 if the petitioner won, and 0 if not. Table 3.2 uses our measure of litigant status differential (as shown in figure 3.5) as a key independent variable. Recall that this variable ranges from –6 to +6 and takes on positive values when the petitioner is more powerful and negative values when the respondent is more powerful. Drawing again from Songer and Sheehan, table 3.3 uses separate variables for petitioner and respondent status. Recall that these are nine-point scales, with higher values indicating more power. Both models control for issue area.

Table 3.2 The Effect of Petitioner Status Differential on Petitioner Success before State High Courts

	Logistic Regression Results		
	b	s.e.	p-value
Petitioner status differential	.04	.01	**.001**
Rights of workers and employees	.13	.07	**.046**
Access to justice institutions	.18	.07	**.008**
Equation			
Intercept	−.18	.05	**.001**
Log likelihood	7,901.9		
Nagelkerke R^2	.01		
Weighted N	5,771		

Source: Gibson and Nelson, State High Court Inequality Database, 1990–2015.

Notes: The omitted issue area is minority rights cases. Probabilities less than .05 are shown in bold. b = unstandardized logit regression coefficient; s.e. = standard error of unstandardized logit regression coefficient; Nagelkerke R^2 = coefficient of determination.

In both models, the status variable is statistically significant and signed in the hypothesized direction. In table 3.2, the probability of a petitioner win increases from .38 when petitioners are completely outmatched to .48 when the petitioner and respondent have equal power to .57 when the petitioner's power is at its greatest and the respondent's power is at its nadir. This is a significant relationship. The more powerful party comes out ahead.

Table 3.3 supports the same conclusions; note that the coefficients for petitioner power and respondent power are identical, though signed in different directions to account for their different directional effects on a petitioner's win probability. When both parties have equal status—for example, when both are natural persons—the petitioner wins about half of the time (.48). But when the petitioner's status is much greater than the respondent's (setting them at their maximum and minimum, respectively), the petitioner's win rate increases to .59. When those positions are reversed, the petitioner's fate suffers, garnering a predicted win probability of a mere .38. This strong, positive relationship is shown visually in figure 3.6.

This analysis, consistent with Galanter's hypothesis, demonstrates important but limited substantive differences in win rates based on party status. Overall, while the haves win only a slightly higher percentage of cases, the predicted probability of a petitioner winning varies heavily based on litigant status, just as Galanter taught us. Of course, there are *many*

Table 3.3 The Effect of Litigant Status Differential on Petitioner Success before State High Courts

	Logistic Regression Results		
	b	s.e.	*p*-value
Petitioner power	.05	.01	**.001**
Respondent power	−.03	.01	**.016**
Rights of workers and employees	.14	.07	**.037**
Access to justice institutions	.19	.07	**.005**
Equation			
Intercept	−.31	.14	**.002**
Log likelihood	7,900.3		
Nagelkerke R^2	.01		
Weighted *N*	5,771		

Source: Gibson and Nelson, State High Court Inequality Database, 1990–2015.

Notes: The omitted issue area is minority rights cases. Probabilities less than .05 are shown in bold. *b* = unstandardized logit regression coefficient; s.e. = standard error of unstandardized logit regression coefficient; Nagelkerke R^2 = coefficient of determination.

Figure 3.6 Probability of Petitioner Win in State High Courts, by Petitioner Status Differential

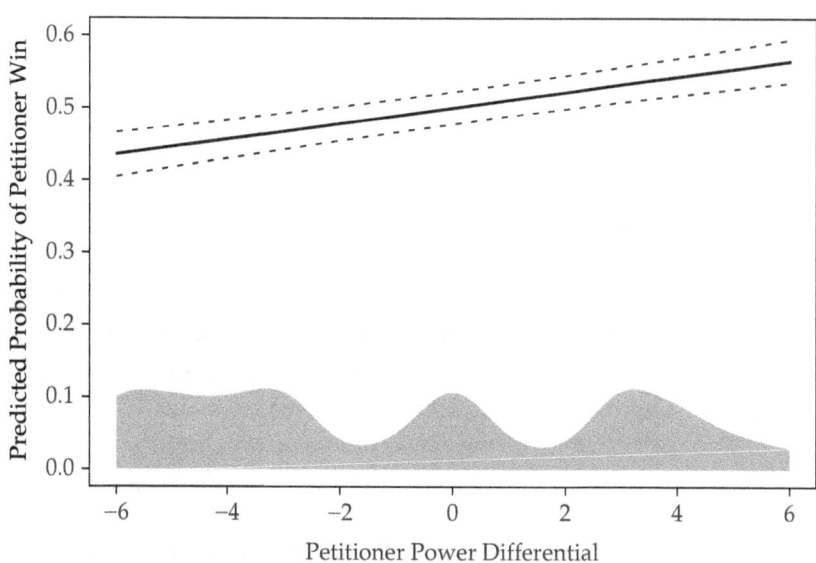

Source: Authors' compilation.
Notes: The solid line in the figure plots the predicted probabilities of a petitioner win, holding issue area at its modal (mandatory arbitration) category. Positive values of the *x*-axis indicate that the petitioner was more powerful than the respondent, negative values indicate the converse, and an *x*-axis value of 0 indicates that the two parties were of equal power. The dotted lines provide a 95 percent confidence interval around the estimated predicted probability. These estimates are derived from the model in table 3.2. The "rug" above the *x*-axis shows the frequency distribution of the petitioner power differential.

88 Judging Inequality

other factors that could affect the probability that petitioners will win their case besides litigant status. In later chapters of this book, we test explanations as diverse as the court's institutional characteristics, the political and sociodemographic characteristics of the state, the composition (both ideological and partisan) of the state supreme court, and public opinion on the issues before the court.

Do Upperdog Litigants Seek Inequality in Their Litigation?

Unlike earlier research, we have coded both the status of the parties in the litigation *and* whether the outcome in the case tends to favor equality or inequality. A natural and conventional hypothesis is that upperdogs seek inequality; by advancing their own interests in litigation, the haves advance their advantages over the have-nots. As an obvious example, when upperdog litigants seek mandatory arbitration or try to limit the availability of class actions, they are challenging the means by which underdogs might mitigate their disadvantaged position in politics, law, and economics and on social issues.

But do more powerful litigants in fact tend to seek less equality through lawsuits? Not always. There is actually a good amount of variability in the extent to which different types of parties seek equality. Figure 3.7 reports the preferences of the litigants for equality, based on an analysis that "stacks" the petitioners and respondents in this litigation (because the formal status of the litigant in the lawsuit is largely irrelevant).

As expected, individuals tend strongly to be involved in litigation in which their preference is for greater equality.[37] The surprise in these data is that relatively more powerful litigants, such as businesses and governments, tend to favor equality in a considerable number of cases. For instance, state governments seek equality in about one-third of their cases and inequality in two-thirds. Even large businesses favor a pro-equality outcome in about one-fifth of their cases. These data make it abundantly clear that we cannot simply equate higher litigant status or power with a uniform preference for inequality.

Figure 3.7 does not, however, consider the *relative* power of the litigants in the litigation. That is, the figure reports outcome preferences according to our measure of absolute litigant power, not relative power within the lawsuit. Table 3.4 makes that adjustment. Note, however, that table 3.4 also

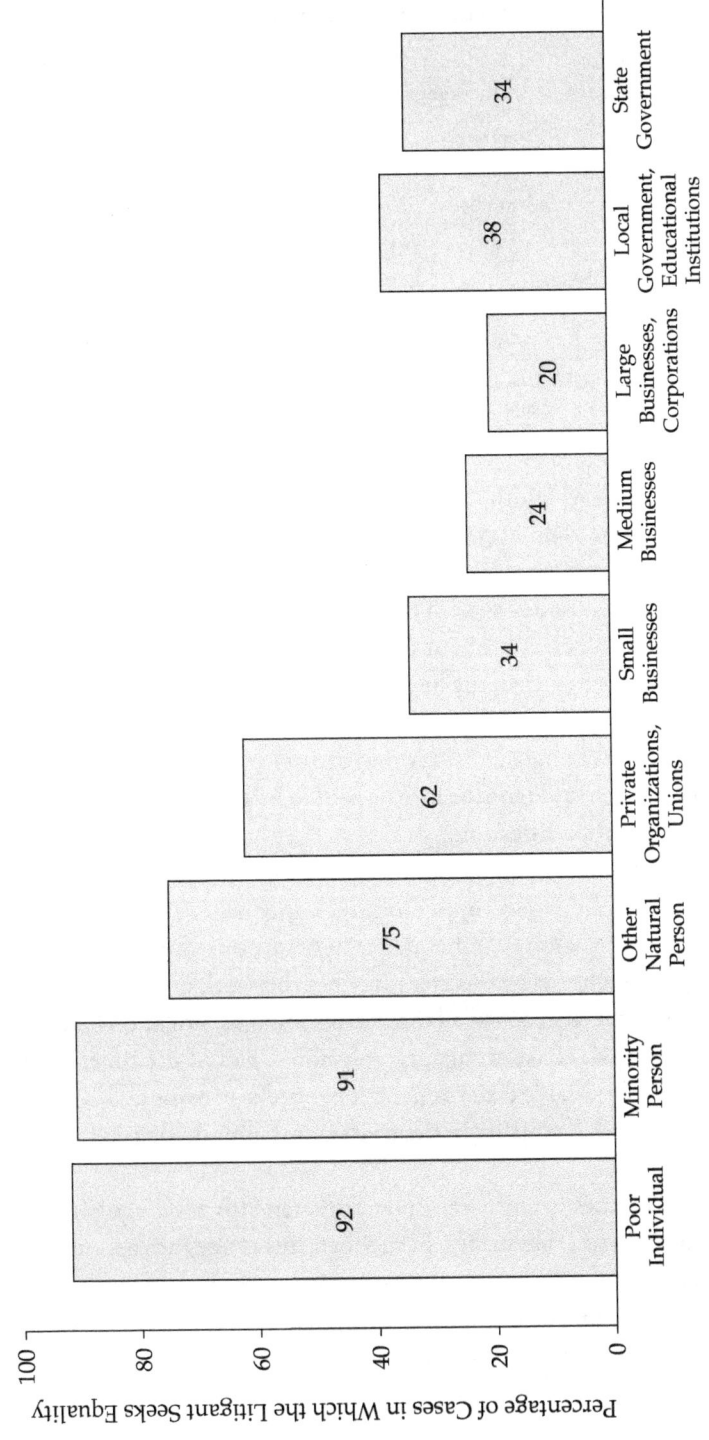

Figure 3.7 Seeking Equality in Litigation in State High Courts, by Type of Litigant

Source: Gibson and Nelson, State High Court Inequality Database, 1990–2015.
Notes: Total $N = 11{,}669$. This figure combines petitioners and litigants (in a "stacked" data set). Difference of percentages across litigant type: $F = 390.9$; $p < .001$; eta $= .46$; Pearson's $r = -.38$. Cases are weighted by weights associated with the three issue domains.

Table 3.4 Litigant Status and Goals in Litigation before State High Courts

Issue Area	Underdogs		Upperdogs		Equal Litigant Power	
	Percent Seeking Equality	N	Percent Seeking Inequality	N	Percent Seeking Equality	N
Minority rights	68.5	1,272	62.2	333	55.3	273
Rights of workers and employees	87.3	1,135	84.1	698	58.5	94
Access to justice institutions	72.0	719	78.6	873	49.2	358
All cases	76.1	3,127	77.7	1,904	52.6	726

Source: Gibson and Nelson, State High Court Inequality Database, 1990–2015.

Notes: This table is based on weighted numbers of cases.

reports the cases in which the status of the two litigants is equal—that is, cases in which there is no upperdog.

Table 3.4 provides a more comprehensive view of the connection between litigant status and the policy goals of the litigants. As presented in the bottom row of the table ("All cases"), about three-fourths of the underdogs seek an outcome favoring equality in the litigation, while a comparable percentage (78 percent) of the upperdogs seek inequality. Overall, nonprototypical policy outcomes are sought in about one-quarter of the cases. The data in table 3.4 support the same conclusion: upperdog litigants do not necessarily seek inequality in their litigation.

Table 3.4 also reveals some variation across issue domains. For instance, in minority rights litigation, upperdogs seek inequality in slightly fewer than two-thirds of the cases and equality in about one-third of the cases. Underdogs are roughly as inconsistent in what they seek in their litigation. It is also noteworthy that, across all three issue domains, litigation involving litigants of equal power seeks equality only about half of the time. Again, the conclusion of this table is the same: it is a mistake to assume that upperdogs necessarily seek inequality in the courts, or that underdogs necessarily seek equality.

In most issue areas, however, underdogs tend to seek equality and upperdogs tend to seek inequality. Even when this is not the case, the data make some sense. Consider gay rights litigation. At first glance, it may seem odd that a sizable percentage of gay rights cases, 17 percent (data not shown), feature underdogs who seek to advance *inequality*. In prototypical gay rights cases, like the Iowa Supreme Court's *Varnum v. Brien* decision, a gay or lesbian individual (the underdog) seeks greater equality through lawsuits against higher-status parties (often a government entity because the litigation addresses public policy).[38] But this is not true of all gay rights cases. In other such cases, the underdog is a conservative litigant suing an upperdog (often a government) to stymie the progress of gay rights. Consider *Alons et al. v. Iowa District Court*, in which a conservative Iowa pastor sought standing to sue the Iowa District Court to halt that court from allowing a gay couple to divorce.[39] Or *Mabon v. Keisling et al.*, in which the conservative proponent of a ballot proposition that would have stopped Oregon from recognizing LGBT people as a protected class sued the state attorney general regarding the ballot language for that proposition.[40] These and many other cases vividly demonstrate the need to move beyond litigant resources to determine what it is underdog and upperdog litigants are trying to achieve in their court cases.

That the analysis of the absolute and relative status of the litigants produces the same conclusion is important. The relative measure, which, of course, compares the status of the litigants in the case, could be misleading if a relatively high-status party is involved in litigation with a party of lesser but still high status, as in litigation involving a large business entity and a smaller business entity. Our findings indicate that powerful litigants sometimes seek equality through litigation and that the more powerful litigants in a lawsuit also sometimes seek equality in a lawsuit. Both the absolute power and the relative power of the litigants are less than perfect guides to whether they are in favor of political, legal, economic, and social inequality or oppose it.

The literature addressing the question of whether the haves come out ahead makes two implicit assumptions: that haves litigate to advance their interests, and that their interests are generally conservative and, in the context of equality-relevant cases, favor inequality. These assumptions, however, seem to be incorrect. Yes, upperdogs usually favor inequality and underdogs usually favor equality, but litigant interests do not align with litigant status in a substantial number of instances. These nonprototypical cases represent measurement error to the extent that the analysis assumes that upperdog litigants favor conservative and pro-inequality outcomes. From the liberal point of view, it may actually be a good thing in some cases that the haves come out ahead.

In the analysis that follows, we refocus our attention on prototypical cases in which upperdogs seek inequality and ask: Do the haves come out ahead in litigation in which they seek to bolster or maintain political, legal, economic, and social inequality? Consequently, we discard those nonprototypical cases in which upperdogs seek equality and in which underdogs seek inequality (as well as those cases in which the parties are of equal power). This allows us to consider a measure of court outcomes that is not confounded by heterogeneity in the objectives of the litigants in the cases. This analytical strategy does, however, significantly reduce the size of our database.

When the upperdog litigants seek to enhance or maintain political, legal, economic, and social inequality, they win 55 percent of the time ($N = 3,860$).[41] There is not a great deal of variability in win rates across issue domains. In minority rights cases, the upperdog seeking inequality wins 51 percent of the time, in contrast to access-to-justice cases, 58 percent of which are won by an upperdog seeking inequality.

We find only minor differences in win rates when we purify the data by the preferences of the litigants. Nevertheless, the variance in this new indicator is more homogeneous, which is to say, there is less error variance.

It does seem clear, however, that, by our definitions, we cannot assume that a finding that the haves come out ahead necessarily means that greater inequality is produced. A more general conclusion for research on litigant status is that it is useful, *if not imperative*, that both litigant status and substantive policy outcomes be evaluated when assessing whether state court rulings contribute to inequality in the United States and abroad. The assumption that more powerful litigants always seek to upend the equal distribution of resources is simply not borne out by these data.

Comparing Corrected and Uncorrected Upperdog Win Rates

Our innovation of ensuring that we analyze cases in which the upperdog is actually seeking inequality produces results for a subset of the total cases: those in which the upperdog is litigating in favor of inequality. Within those cases, the outcomes are, of course, identical for both approaches to calculating upperdog win rates.

When upperdogs are seeking inequality, they win 55 percent of their cases. In the nonprototypical cases (those in which the upperdog favors equality), the upperdog wins 59 percent of the time. Consequently, in this particular data set, our adjustment for the typicality of cases does not greatly affect our conclusions at the aggregate level. The haves come out ahead in about 55 to 59 percent of the cases they litigate. We consider the 55 percent figure to be the most substantively interesting because it is relevant to the way in which courts are used to create and bolster political, legal, economic, and social inequality in the United States.

State-Level Analysis

There are at least two major potential sources of the variability in upperdog litigation success: geography and time. We turn now to the consideration of these independent variables.

The win rate of upperdogs seeking inequality does not vary significantly over time, based on our analysis of yearly and decade-long trends. Furthermore, whatever slight trends may exist in the data are not linear over time. Thus, for the analysis that follows we can safely ignore the year of the decision and focus on the entire database.[42] This is not particularly surprising inasmuch as the judges who compose any given state high court change very slowly over time.

As we have previously noted, Brace and Hall have discovered considerable interstate variability in the degree to which the haves come out ahead. The state high courts in our data differ substantially in the degree to which their rulings in these equality cases favor the upperdogs in the litigation. Focusing on cases in which the upperdog sought an outcome favoring inequality, at one extreme, we find that about 74 percent of the cases decided by the Texas high courts favored the haves; at the other extreme, only 23 percent of the cases decided by the Arizona Supreme Court favored the haves. Figure 3.8 reports the percentages for each state. Significant but not extreme interstate variability exists: an F-test for differences across the states is significant at $p < .001$. However, eta is only .21, indicating that the identity of the state does only a little to predict whether the haves come out ahead.

Finally, figure 3.9 reports a slightly different take on whether the haves come out ahead when they seek inequality versus when they seek equality. This figure reports the difference between the percentage of cases in which the upperdog sought inequality and won and the percentage of cases in which the upperdog sought equality and won. This provides a more stringent measure of the degree to which a state supreme court favors the haves because it indicates the advantage to the upperdog when it seeks inequality.

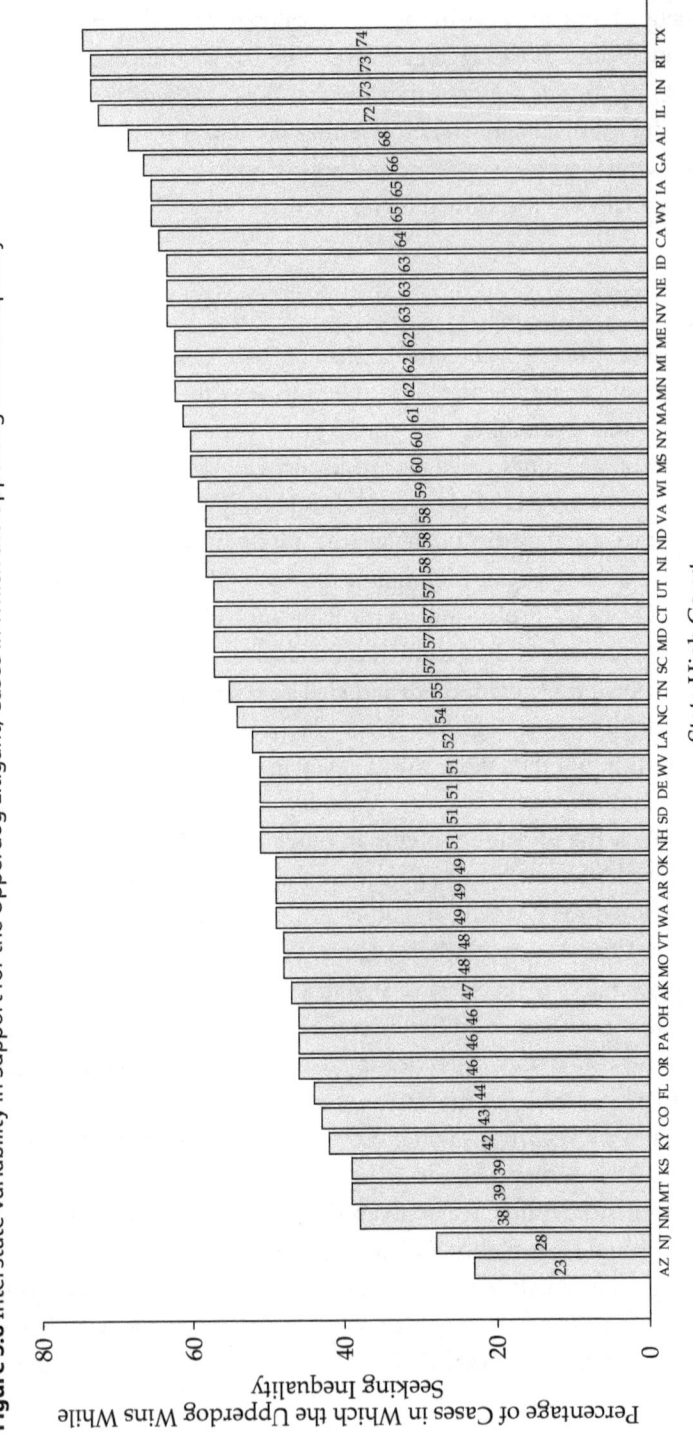

Figure 3.8 Interstate Variability in Support for the Upperdog Litigant, Cases in Which the Upperdog Seeks Inequality

Source: Gibson and Nelson, State High Court Inequality Database, 1990–2015.
Notes: The bars plot the percentage of cases in which the upperdog party won while seeking to advance inequality. The percentages within each bar provide the state-level percentage. Cases are weighted by weights associated with the three issue domains.

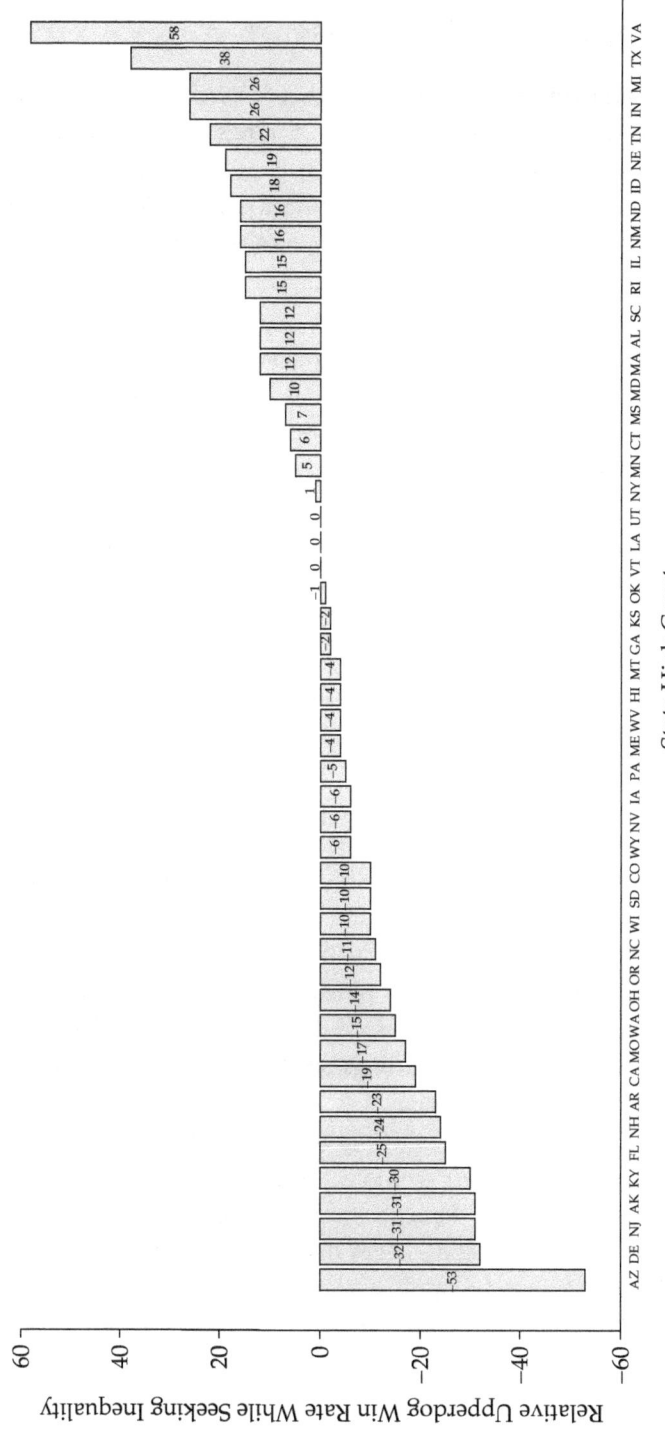

Figure 3.9 Interstate Variability in Differential Win Rates by Whether or Not the Upperdog Litigant Seeks Inequality

Source: Gibson and Nelson, State High Court Inequality Database, 1990–2015.
Notes: The bars plot the difference in the percentage of cases in which the have party won while seeking to advance inequality from the percentage of cases in which the have party won while seeking to advance equality. Positive values on the y-axis indicate that haves won more often while seeking to advance inequality than when they sought equality. The percentages in the middle of each bar provide the state-level percentage.

Discussion and Concluding Comments

Several important findings emerge from this research, the most general of which arose from the issue of whether upperdogs have been able to use the state judiciaries to advance their interests in political, legal, economic, and social inequality. Like earlier studies before ours, we find that upperdogs do indeed come out ahead in the state high courts. They do so both when they are seeking equality and when they are seeking inequality, but according to our analysis, a majority of the cases in the state high courts are won by upperdogs seeking greater inequality.

At the same time, our analysis has given us little confidence in research on litigant resources. The resources of litigants are measured in the crudest of ways (East St. Louis, Illinois, and Chicago are both scored as city governments), and the type of litigants involved in cases are not really a reliable guide to the amount of resources brought to bear in the litigation. There was obviously more, for instance, to Linda Brown than the individual Linda Brown (of *Brown v. Board of Education*). With litigant resources measured so poorly, it is surprising that any significant findings emerge.

But they do. Our findings in political, legal, economic, and social inequality litigation are much like those of earlier studies. The haves do come out ahead, but only by a relatively small margin. This is one simple fact of inequality in America.

The state high courts certainly vary, however, and the variation is startling. As we have reported, in Texas, Rhode Island, Indiana, and Illinois, upperdogs seeking inequality won about three-fourths of their cases, but in the Arizona and New Jersey high courts the comparable figure was closer to one-quarter. Some of these results satisfy our intuitions and prejudices (for example, about Texas and New Jersey), but others do not (Rhode Island and Arizona). These descriptive findings beg for a theoretical explanation that is tested against empirical data.

We say that courts vary, but courts do not make decisions—judges do. The "active ingredient" in these court decisions is the judge sitting on the high bench, casting votes in these decisions. It is to the characteristics of the judges who rendered these decisions that we turn in chapter 4.

CHAPTER 4

The Backgrounds and Ideologies of State Supreme Court Justices

THROUGHOUT THE UNITED STATES, state supreme courts are important policymakers that affect the distribution of rights and resources among their constituents. But courts do not cast votes in lawsuits; judges do. In this chapter, we turn our attention away from the litigants who bring cases before state supreme courts and focus instead on the judges who are responsible for making these public policies. The literature on judicial behavior is vast, teaching us that judicial decisions are a function of case attributes, the characteristics of the judges who decide the cases, the bargaining among those judges, the institutional structure of the judiciary (such as the rules by which judges are selected and retained), and state-level attributes such as public opinion and temporal differences.[1] But at the heart of all these factors are the people who actually make the decisions—the individual judges on each court.

In the remaining chapters of this book, we develop and test a model of judicial decision-making on state supreme court cases implicating political, legal, economic, and social inequality. Our comprehensive model acknowledges that individual judges decide cases with litigants in particular institutional circumstances. Broadly, we expect that these institutional features have particularly far-reaching consequences for state supreme court legal policies by affecting what sorts of people become judges on these courts and, subsequently, the decisions that they make once they reach the state

Figure 4.1 A Simple Model Connecting Backgrounds with Attitudes and Behavior

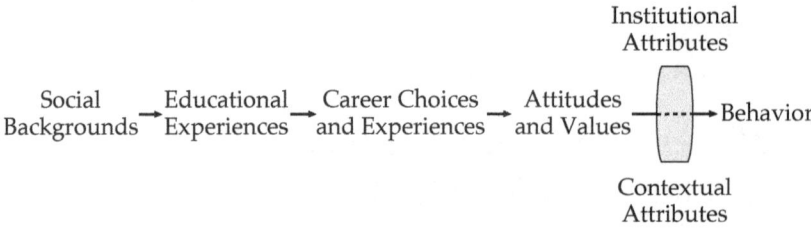

Source: Authors' compilation.

---

high court. Judges are at the center of this process, just as they are at the center of this chapter.

Our focus here is on the backgrounds and values of state supreme court judges. We revisit the canonical "attitudinal model" of judicial decision-making, which connects judges' background attributes with their attitudes and values and their votes in cases.[2] Our interest in judicial backgrounds is driven by two different mechanisms: (1) methods of judicial selection, which might privilege or advantage judicial candidates with particular types of backgrounds; and (2) judges' backgrounds, which might affect the attitudes that they hold and seek to embed in public policies as they decide cases. The simple (and simplified) model that guides our research is presented in figure 4.1.

Before discussing the analysis in this chapter, we should clarify one last important point. As the previous chapters have documented, the legal policies we investigate pertain to political, legal, economic, and social inequality. Consequently, our case database codes each of nearly six thousand decisions as either pro- or anti-equality. But ideology is clearly overlaid on our concern for political, legal, economic, and social inequality: liberals tend to favor more equality and conservatives tend to favor less equality. Or, to put this more squarely in focus using the language introduced in chapter 3, liberals tend to favor the interests of underdogs whereas conservatives favor the interests of upperdogs.[3] In this sense, our inquiry is no different from the hundreds of earlier projects seeking to explain why some court outcomes are liberal and some are conservative. So, when casting hypotheses, we treat "pro-equality/pro-underdog" as synonymous with "liberalism" and "anti-equality/pro-upperdog" as synonymous with "conservatism."[4]

We focus in particular on two characteristics of judges' backgrounds that are likely to influence their attitudes: their social class origins and their professional experiences. With regard to class origins, we hypothesize that judges from relatively less privileged backgrounds are more likely to espouse more liberal values. And with regard to professional experiences, we generally hypothesize that those whose careers have been defined by public service are more likely to be pro-equality than those who spent their careers prior to joining the bench in private practice.

Our analytical strategy in this chapter is twofold. First, we introduce a new data set of state supreme court justices who sat on the state high courts from 1990 to 2015, focusing in particular on their social class origins and their professional histories. Second, we test the linkages among social class origins, on-the-job experiences, and judicial attitudes (using two measures of judicial attitude).

Out of this analysis comes evidence that certain backgrounds and career attributes push judges toward more liberal, pro-equality values. In subsequent chapters, we expand on this conclusion as we consider whether these values influence judges' decisions in cases related to political, legal, economic, and social inequality.

Understanding Judicial Choice in the States

A dominant model of judicial behavior in political science is the attitudinal model, which posits a primary (if not dominant) role for judicial attitudes and values in the calculus of judicial choice.[5] While this model has achieved widespread support at the U.S. Supreme Court level, its application to lower courts has been somewhat less successful.[6] One reason for this disparity is that the judges on the U.S. Supreme Court and the judges on state supreme courts operate in very different institutional contexts. Compared to most lower court judges (including state supreme court justices), U.S. Supreme Court justices are given very high levels of discretion, coupled with almost vanishingly low requirements of accountability. They are endowed with a uniquely broad ability to choose the cases they wish to decide (or not to decide).[7] Justices also serve life terms, are subject to no practical means of being removed from office, and decide themselves whether to be "constrained" by legal doctrines such as precedent and stare decisis.[8] Moreover, they face no fear of reversal from a higher court (and quite limited fear of statutory and/or constitutional overrides of their decisions).[9] Finally, few justices harbor ambitions for "higher" offices.[10] If the attitudinal model were ever to apply to any court in the world, it would apply to the justices of the U.S. Supreme Court.

While state supreme court judges are certainly subject to more constraints than U.S. Supreme Court justices, they are still endowed with considerable discretion and burdened by only limited mechanisms of accountability. As an easy example, these courts have access to the common law, which means in a nutshell that they are allowed to decide cases on the basis of what is just, not just what is legal (for example, "common law marriages"). While not all these courts control their own dockets, most have at least some form of docket control.[11] Virtually all state supreme court judges are subject to some mechanisms of accountability, but often these mechanisms are weak at best (for example, retention elections), and long periods of time intercede between formal accountability calls. (For example, the lengthiest state supreme court terms are fourteen years, with a median of six years.)[12] The rulings of state supreme courts are not reviewable by a higher court when they are based on state law and state constitutions (unless a conflict with federal law and constitutions is alleged).[13] Even in cases that are subject to review, the number of cases per year in which the U.S. Supreme Court decides to formally review a state supreme court decision does not even approach one case per state.[14] Considering that a minority of state supreme court decisions involve dissenting opinions, we acknowledge that norms of consensus may constrain judges' ability to express their values through dissents.[15] At the same time, however, the actions of the U.S. Supreme Court are often under widespread and intense media scrutiny, while many state supreme courts labor in relative obscurity.[16] Perhaps state supreme court judges have less decisional freedom and discretion than U.S. Supreme Court justices, but there can be little doubt that liberal judges have ample opportunity to vote liberally in cases before these courts, just as conservatives have ample opportunity to vote conservatively.

We certainly concede that the attitudinal model is more difficult to investigate at the state high court level. To take an easy example, the views of newspaper editors and their boards provide one source of information about the ideological proclivities of U.S. Supreme Court justices.[17] Such information is not uniformly available for the judges of the fifty state supreme courts. Whereas scholars of the U.S. federal judiciary can rely upon measures of judicial preferences that span decades, valid and reliable measures of judicial attitudes are much harder to come by at the state level.[18]

Some approaches, like Paul Brace, Laura Langer, and Melinda Gann Hall's party-adjusted surrogate judge ideology measure (PAJID), rely on other measures of state ideology (here, the ideology of a state's citizens and elites) that are comparable over space and time, adjusting those measures based on a state's methods of judicial selection and retention to create judge-level ideology scores.[19] As the name of the concept acknowledges, this is a surrogate measure of judges' attitudes and values (at best).

Other, newer approaches, such as the scores developed by Adam Bonica and Michael Woodruff and by Jason Windett, Jeffrey Harden, and Matthew Hall, rely heavily on public reporting about political donations.[20] Such methods, while innovative, have their limits. For example, not all judges are equally likely to donate to political candidates, and there is also the risk that a willingness to donate to a candidate in the first place may correlate with a judge's ideology. Moreover, the fact that judges do not all make political donations requires that some other metric be used to estimate an ideology score for nondonating judges. In these cases, many scholars resort to the old standby: the indirect measure of assessing the partisanship of the judges (or those who appointed them to office).[21] That these newer measures have only been available for less than two decades also somewhat limits their utility.

When it comes to measuring the attitudes and values of state supreme court judges, all roads lead, ultimately, to party attachment as a key indicator. Even the most innovative measures of state judicial ideology rely heavily on nothing more than partisanship to indicate judges' attitudes.[22] Similarly, many well-regarded studies of state supreme court decision-making published in the last decade or so employ partisanship as their measure of judicial ideology, including studies published in the discipline's best journals.[23] Further evidence that the partisanship of judges is a reasonable measure of the attitudes of judges on modern state supreme courts is found in the fact that many state supreme court judges run for office directly on the basis of their partisanship; moreover, another huge proportion of judges are appointed to the bench by partisan legislators or governors—who likely filter candidates on the basis of party and ideology to ensure that their chosen judges will be reliable agents on the bench.[24] And as partisan polarization has grown in the United States, including in the American states, the utility of partisanship as a measure of ideologies has grown.[25] Consequently, as we explain in further detail later in this chapter, we rely on partisanship as one of our main indicators of judges' attitudes, though not the only one.

Where Do Attitudes Come From?

The empirical limitations of the attitudinal model join up with a further theoretical lacuna: Where do attitudes come from? Most existing tests of the relationship between judicial values and judicial decision-making take attitudes as exogenous, paying little attention to the rich literature on political socialization that has informed decades of research on the origins of partisanship and ideology among the American people and political elites.[26]

To be sure, scholars have long sought to determine how judges' backgrounds affect their decisions. From studies probing the effects of party affiliation or ideology, demographic characteristics, and background characteristics, such as judges' prior professional experiences, their religious backgrounds, and the context in which they live and work, we have a rich and textured understanding of the ways in which the characteristics of the judges who hear and decide cases affect the likelihood that they will rule for or against a particular policy position.[27] Just as the rich literature on political behavior has taught us that the processes of socialization powerfully shape the predilections of the mass public, we expect similar processes to shape the preferences of judges.[28]

Virtually all research on backgrounds and attitudes accepts the model we depict in figure 4.1, even if only implicitly. Obviously, if backgrounds and experiences are employed as an operationalization of attitudes, the connection between the concepts cannot be investigated empirically. Relatedly, if direct measures of attitudes are available and the only effect of backgrounds and experiences is exclusively through attitudes, then there is little reason to investigate the linkage between backgrounds and attitudes.

In our research, we take a hybrid approach. Initially assuming that partisanship measures ideology, we attempt to validate that assumption empirically, and then we investigate the linkages between backgrounds and career experiences and judges' ideologies. Because we do not assume that backgrounds and experiences affect behavior only through their connection with attitudes (for example, background may have ingratiated a nominee with the dominant elites in a state, irrespective of ideology, or the nominee may be put on the bench for descriptive representation purposes), our analysis includes both attitudes and backgrounds and experiences as predictors of judges' behaviors in cases related to political, legal, economic, and social inequality.

Understanding how judges' backgrounds shape their preferences is particularly important at the state level, where, in contrast to judges serving in the federal judiciary, judges' backgrounds vary widely. At the federal level—and especially at the U.S. Supreme Court—the range of judicial backgrounds has contracted in recent years. Modern-day justices tend to have attended elite law schools and to be drawn almost exclusively from the ranks of lower court judges. They are also younger than ever before.[29] It is perhaps not an accident that the first U.S. Supreme Court entirely comprising justices who all attended law school at either Harvard or Yale is also one of the most pro-business and conservative courts in American history.[30]

In short, we argue that judges' backgrounds are useful because they provide us with a window into their social and political origins and the formative experiences in their lives, both of which affect the ideologies they bring to the bench. Our analysis focuses on two types of backgrounds: social class origins and on-the-job experiences. We turn now to an explanation of these two types of attributes.

Social Class and Judicial Attitudes and Values

First, we hypothesize that judges' social class origins are likely to shape their ideologies and therefore their on-the-bench behaviors. Briefly, social class is a concept that refers to the position or status of a person in a society. As Nicholas Carnes, in his pathbreaking book on social class in American legislatures, writes:

> Societies tend to be organized or stratified along widely accepted economic and status dimensions. Some people are well off and well regarded. Others are not. And most observers agree about which people are which. Scholars refer to groups of people who occupy comparable positions on these dimensions as *social classes*. . . .

In the United States, a person's class is one of the best predictors of a variety of behaviors ranging from matters of taste such as entertainment, art, and consumption, to decisions about where to live, whom to invite into our social circles, how to speak, and how to raise our children. Class predicts significant differences in health outcomes and incarceration rates. It creates material interests that pit people from different classes against one another in a variety of settings, and it affects how involved people are in civic life, how they think about a wide range of political issues, and how they vote on election day.[31]

Indeed, the distinction between the haves and have-nots that has animated this book relates squarely to the concept of social class: some litigants tend to have the common markers—especially the resources—of privileged social classes, while other litigants do not.

That political elites vary in their social class origins is well documented. As Donald Matthews noted in 1954, "almost everywhere legislators are better educated, possess higher-status occupations, and have more privileged backgrounds than the people they 'represent.'"[32] Carnes, for example, reports that while 54 percent of American citizens are employed in a working-class job, only 2 percent of members of Congress—and no postwar president or U.S. Supreme Court justice—had a working-class job immediately before assuming office.[33] Similarly, while 73 percent of Americans lack a college degree, only 25 percent of state legislators, 8 percent of postwar presidents, and 1 percent of members of Congress lack that credential; every postwar U.S. Supreme Court justice has had a college degree. That the typical American politician comes from a social environment different from that of the average American is obvious and beyond dispute.

Moreover, existing research suggests that social class origins shape the preferences of both the mass public and political elites. For example, Gilens has persuasively documented that class origins determine the attitudes and values of everyday Americans.[34] And at the elite level, Carnes has demonstrated that legislators from the working class are significantly more liberal than other types of legislators on issues related to economics.[35]

At least in terms of legislative behavior, researchers have documented that social class background affects the behavior of political elites. Indeed, as Carnes states, the differences in elite political behavior are prominent on issues—especially economic ones—that split the haves and the have-nots:

> The shortage of working-class people—who tend to be more liberal on economic issues—appears to bias policy on issues like the minimum wage, taxes, and welfare spending towards the more conservative positions typically favored by affluent Americans. . . . Social safety net programs are stingier, business regulations are flimsier, tax politics are more regressive, and protections for workers are weaker than they would be if our political decision-makers came from the same mix of classes as the people they represent.[36]

This research confirms that legislators with working-class origins tend to be more liberal than their counterparts from society's upper classes on economic issues such as those we investigate in the state high courts.

These findings inform our expectations about the effect of social class on judicial decisions related to political, legal, economic, and social inequality. Our overriding expectation is one first suggested by Jilda Aliotta: "Justices of higher socioeconomic status might be expected to be less sympathetic to claims for equality of treatment than justices of lower socioeconomic status."[37] This has obvious relevance for the legal and political issues we investigate in this book.

This relationship might hold for two reasons.[38] First, individuals' social class origins affect their socialization, which, in turn, affects their values.[39] Individuals from the less privileged classes have, on average, very different everyday experiences from those of the more privileged classes. These life experiences shape individuals' values and choices as they move through the world. More specifically, existing research demonstrates that politicians' previous life experiences can influence their values, experiences, perceptions of self-interest, and general ideological orientations.[40]

Second, rational self-interest is another mechanism linking social class origins and elite behavior. Judges who come from less privileged class backgrounds stand to benefit the most in the short term from economically and socially liberal policies, which may explain why individuals from these class origins are more likely to favor liberal politics in general.[41] The same could be said about the relationship between privileged backgrounds and conservative policymaking.

Thus, regardless of the mechanism—socialization or rational self-interest—we expect that judges with less privileged class origins will tend to have more liberal ideologies on average.

On-the-Job Experiences and Judicial Ideologies

The second characteristic of interest is the prior professional experience or career path of judges. The legal profession is heterogeneous, and individuals often have a variety of different professionalizing experiences before they reach the bench. These experiences are important because they can "resocialize" a lawyer, potentially amplifying or overriding the socialization attributable to social class origins. On-the-job experiences teach people lessons about the way the world works that may either change or reinforce their values. These career experiences also shape judges' personal and social networks by determining the types of people they come into contact with on a daily basis, and those social contacts may shape a prospective judge's ideology as well.

Indeed, there may be a relationship between ideology and on-the-job experiences, for at least three reasons. First, certain types of people may self-select into particular positions.[42] As one example, a liberal-leaning law student may graduate from law school and then work as a public defender as a way to champion the cause of social justice. Similarly, conservative law school graduates might seek employment only at white-collar law firms because the caseload at that type of firm could advance the sort of policies they favor.

Second, the experience of having a particular type of job may affect a legal professional's values. For example, attorneys who work closely with society's underdogs on a daily basis, as many public defenders do, may learn about the intersections of race, class, and justice in the United States and as a consequence adopt (or commit more resolutely to) more liberal preferences. Conversely, defending the actions of corporate white-collar executives might increase a lawyer's sympathy for the worldviews (and resources) of those clients, thereby leading the lawyer to adopt a more conservative ideology.[43] People often become what they do.

Finally, working in certain types of jobs may shape judges' social networks in ways that influence their attitudes and define their opportunities. Prior to ascending to the Supreme Court, many U.S. Supreme Court justices have been active on the Washington cocktail party circuit, just as many white-collar firm partners attend the same charity balls and holiday parties. These social connections are important not only because they affect an individual's ability to attain judicial office but also because they define the social milieu in which prospective judges find themselves. These social networks may, in turn, affect the arguments and ideas—especially ideas about justice—that judges find compelling. Prospective judges whose social circles comprise people from more privileged classes are likely to find a particular type of political view socially reinforced, while nonconforming views are often snuffed out.[44]

Regardless of the mechanism, existing research demonstrates that there are differences in ideology across segments of the legal profession. Using data on the donation patterns of attorneys, Bonica and Sen find that law professors, public defenders, and government lawyers tend to be more liberal, while partners and attorneys at prestigious law firms tend to be more conservative.[45]

These patterns fit well with the folk wisdom about the ideologies associated with different segments of the legal profession. Those individuals who work in private practice—especially at white-collar firms—tend to live and work in professional networks dominated by friends and colleagues from more privileged social classes. On the other hand, individuals who have spent the majority of their career in public service, working as public defenders or even as prosecutors, are likely to have very different social networks and to take home far less bountiful paychecks than their peers who pursued careers in white-collar law firms. Lawyers with a background in public service are also disproportionately likely to have been exposed to caseloads involving society's underdogs, and this experience may have engendered a sense of justice associated more with liberalism than with conservatism.

We certainly realize the complexity of the connections between ideology and social background. Experience as a prosecutor may harden a lawyer's views toward underdogs, and graduating from law school at Harvard or Yale certainly does not guarantee that a lawyer has adopted liberal values. Consequently, while the analysis below is guided by rough hypotheses, much of our investigation of the interconnections of backgrounds, experiences, and values is exploratory in nature.

A New Data Set on the Attributes of State Supreme Court Justices

Determining the relationships among the social class backgrounds of state supreme court justices, their career trajectories, and their values requires fine-grained information on those justices' lives. While scholars, including

Laura Langer, Kathleen Bratton and Rorie Spill, and Greg Goelzhauser, have created databases with some information on the demographic characteristics of state supreme court judges, no existing database has the rich information on educational and career experiences required to test our theory.[46]

To test our theory, we created a new database, the State High Court Justices Database, cataloging important characteristics of state supreme court justices who had served on the bench since 1990. We hired law student and undergraduate coders to compile information on judges' demographic characteristics, educational experiences, pre- and post-court professional experiences, party affiliations, and the methods by which they attained and left office. Appendix 4.A reports the details of this process.

We define the universe of judges for this project as those who sat on a state high court from 1990 through 2015.[47] This yields a total of 981 judges.[48] Of these, six judges became formal members of the state supreme court after 2015, but they voted in cases decided in the 1990 to 2015 period as an irregular judge. We have decided to keep those judges in the database for the analyses in this chapter. Counting those six judges as serving more than one noncontiguous term, there are eleven judges who sat on a court, left it, and then returned to the court later (with Roy Moore of Alabama being the most prominent example). Since the unit of analysis for this chapter is the judge, we count these judges only once. With these various minor nuances, our analyses in this chapter are based on 981 judges.[49]

Nearly one-fourth of these judges (23 percent) are women, and 88 percent of the judges are White. Blacks are the minority group with the highest level of descriptive representation: 7 percent of the judges are African American, followed by 3 percent who are of Hispanic origin. On average, these lawyers were fifty-three years old when they first joined their state supreme court. Their median year of birth is 1943. Almost 56 percent of the judges are Democrats (discussed further later).

Operationalizing Judicial Backgrounds

Before we can summarize our new data on these judges, we must first explain and defend our measures of our two key independent variables: judges' social class origins and their prior professional experiences. We discuss each in turn, beginning with a review of previous attempts to measure judges' social class origins.

Previous Attempts to Measure Judicial Social Class Origins

The social class origins of judges present a thorny measurement issue. To estimate the effect of social class background on judicial behavior, we must develop a reliable and valid classification scheme to categorize judges by their social class origins. Although attention to the relationship between social class and judicial behavior is rare in contemporary judicial politics research, earlier generations of scholars—especially those writing in the 1950s and 1960s—discussed this topic in detail, conceptualizing and measuring the social class of American judges in a variety of ways that are useful to review as we seek to devise a measurement scheme applicable to contemporary state supreme court judges.[50] Here, we consider the major approaches and discuss the strengths and weaknesses of each.[51]

It might initially seem that the best way to measure judicial social class is to ask judges directly. Whereas John Wold and James Gibson (among others) were able to interview judges to acquire firsthand reports of their backgrounds, this approach is obviously not practical for us.[52] For example, many judges who served between 1990 and 2015 are no longer living. And among those who are, the relatively low response rates expected from a survey of political elites would require us to eliminate many (and likely most) of the judges from our empirical analyses. Finally, to compound the issue, survey respondents—especially public servants—are generally reluctant to label themselves "upper class," which could lead to issues of measurement validity.[53]

Second, some studies that consider the relationship between social class and judicial behavior relied on information about judges' backgrounds using their father's occupational status. This is the measure of social class used by John Schmidhauser in his pioneering studies on the social class backgrounds of U.S. Supreme Court justices.[54] More recently, Thomas Marshall created an indicator of judicial social class for U.S. Supreme Court justices.[55] As he describes the measure:

> The justices' parents were grouped into three groupings: high status (professional, large property owners, high managerial); middle status (middle management, civil servants, shopkeepers, clerical, or stable blue collar); and lower status (described in accounts as poor, needy, or impoverished). The high status justices included Reed, Clark, Harlan, Stewart, Stevens, O'Connor, Scalia, Kennedy, Burton, and Powell; the middle status justices included

Black, Jackson, Minton, Brennan, White, Marshall, Burger, Blackmun, and Rehnquist; the low status justices included Frankfurter, Douglas, Warren, Whittaker, Goldberg, and Fortas.

This measure, too, suffers from both practical and empirical problems. In terms of practicality, students of the U.S. Supreme Court can rely on the detailed information about the justices' childhoods from the rich U.S. Supreme Court Justices Database compiled by Lee Epstein and her colleagues, as well as from other sources.[56] But no similar fount of data exists for state supreme court judges, and collecting such detailed information—especially moving backwards in time—is simply impossible. Moreover, social mobility in the United States, especially in the post–World War II era, makes any empirical evidence linking parents' occupational status to their child's political views as an adult surprisingly weak.[57]

Third, following the work of Carnes and others, we might look at a person's prior professional experiences to derive a measure of social class. After all, Matthews argues, "the most important single criterion for class ranking in the United States is occupation. While an individual's occupation is by no means a certain index to his social standing, it is the closest approach to an infallible guide."[58] Here the categorization scheme that is useful for classifying legislators fails in the judicial context for one simple and obvious reason: nearly all judges were lawyers immediately before they ascended to the bench![59] A measure with no variation is unrealistic and lacks utility and therefore must be rejected.

Finally, while scholars often do not explain it as such, perhaps the most common indicator of social class background for judges is their educational experience. This measure is generally easy to code because information on judges' educational histories is widely available in their publicly available biographies. Moreover, nearly all (but not all) contemporary state and federal judges have both a bachelor's degree and a law degree, which provides common metrics by which to assess the educational backgrounds of judges.

At least historically, there has been wide variability in judges' educational backgrounds.[60] Until Amy Coney Barrett joined the Court, the Trump-era U.S. Supreme Court was made up entirely of former Harvard and Yale law school students, but such a narrow range of prior educational experiences has been historically rare.[61] Moreover, the educational backgrounds of lower federal court and state court judges are much more varied, in part because of the geographic dispersion of the judiciary and also because of the diverse professional networks that are useful in attaining these judgeships.[62]

A New Measure of Judges' Social Class Origins

Consequently, we are left with only a single workable indicator of judges' social class origins: their educational backgrounds. However, while we recognize that a focus on educational backgrounds is not ideal, a potential saving grace of our approach is that we broaden the concept of educational experience beyond legal education, examining *both* undergraduate and legal education.[63]

Examining both types of educational institutions recognizes the fact that people often choose their undergraduate and law schools for different reasons. On the one hand, holding a diploma from a prestigious educational institution can provide a useful boost for some judicial candidates by burnishing their résumé and providing them with access to influential political networks. On the other hand, graduating from an in-state educational institution may provide "native son" credentials that, in turn, provide state court judges in particular with access to different, but equally important, political networks. Because judges received their undergraduate degree before attending law school (that is, at a time more distant from the point at which they became a state high court judge), we think it likely that their choice of an undergraduate institution was not a long-term strategic political calculation but rather a reflection of socioeconomic realities such as financial and geographic accessibility. To take just one example, many undergraduate students change their major and career plan during their time in college. It is less likely that those who altered their career plans in college selected their undergraduate institution in an attempt to build their credentials for a later run at a high court judgeship.

Previous research supports the assertion that undergraduate and legal educational experiences are differentially linked to social class. James Brudney, Sara Schiavoni, and Deborah Merritt explain that, while there is some relationship between class and the quality of one's law school, "law school status is less emphatically related to socioeconomic class than is college status."[64] Or, as Aliotta explains: "Justices with prestigious prelaw educations probably came from families of more comfortable circumstances than justices who received a less prestigious education. Furthermore, attendance at a prestigious law school has been shown to ease entry into the higher status, more lucrative strata of the legal profession."[65] Thus, there is good reason to examine both undergraduate and legal education, and individuals' undergraduate education is likely to be more closely associated with their social class origins than the prestige of their law school.

As they pursue an undergraduate degree, individuals' preferences are shaped by their experiences inside and outside the classroom. Inside the classroom, the undergraduate experience exposes students to new ideas and concepts that may change how they view the world, their preferences for how rights and resources should be distributed, and their perceptions of "right" and "wrong" or "fair" and "unfair." Outside the classroom, many young adults' undergraduate education is their first extended experience away from parental supervision, and the social ties that they form during their undergraduate years set the trajectory for their social networks as they leave college and enter the professional world. In this way, we expect that the socializing experiences associated with undergraduate education are powerful and can help shape the way judges behave on the bench.[66]

Of course, not all undergraduate institutions are the same, and the undergraduate institution from which an individual graduates is, on average, related to his or her social class background.[67] Individuals from more privileged class backgrounds are more likely to graduate from prestigious undergraduate institutions for a variety of reasons: they have the means to afford the expensive tuition charged by these institutions; they benefit from alumni preference in the admissions cycle; they are immersed in personal and parental social networks that value the status conferred by prestigious undergraduate diplomas; and they have access to counseling and other resources that reinforce the lesson that "good" students attend these sorts of institutions. On the other hand, individuals not from the more privileged classes are less likely to attend these sorts of institutions, perhaps because of financial and geographic constraints or because they were not encouraged to apply to these institutions in the first place.[68]

Despite the efforts of colleges to diversify their admissions criteria, these deeply embedded structures create student bodies on college campuses that reinforce the social class backgrounds of their students. In other words, social class background helps to shape the sort of students who make up an undergraduate institution's student body. This homogeneity amplifies the socializing power of the undergraduate experience. Moreover, that the class-based nature of undergraduate admissions is structural ensures that even those individuals who are not from their institution's modal social class background are exposed to a peer network inside and outside the classroom that comes from that social class background. This homogeneity, in turn, unifies and intensifies the type of socialization experiences each type of undergraduate institution produces.

The judges who served on the state high courts from 1990 to 2015 attended around four hundred distinct undergraduate institutions. Overall, about 53 percent of the judges attended a public institution, 30 percent attended a private secular school, and 17 percent attended a religiously affiliated undergraduate institution. Most judges (60 percent) attended a school located in the state in which they ultimately served on the state high court.[69] This figure, however, masks enormous variability across the states: in Alaska, none of the fourteen judges serving on the supreme court went to an Alaskan undergraduate school; in Ohio and Louisiana, seventeen of the twenty judges in each state (85 percent) who served on the state supreme court went to an in-state undergraduate school (see figure 4.2). We shall return to this variability in later analyses.

It turns out that a wealth of information about colleges and universities is available from the federal government's Integrated Postsecondary Education Data System, created by the National Center for Education Statistics.[70] We use the NCES's database of institutional characteristics from 1980 for information on each judge's undergraduate institution; this is the earliest year of data available through the U.S. Department of Education. In using the database from 1980, we recognize that most of these judges attended these institutions well before 1980. Indeed, if we assume that everyone went to undergraduate school when they were eighteen years old, these judges first matriculated between 1930 and 1994, with a median year of matriculation of 1961. We take some comfort in the fact that the era of rapid change in the nature of institutions of higher education most likely occurred after 1980.[71] In any event, these are, to our knowledge, the earliest data about school characteristics available from the Department of Education.

The NCES database reports the tuition charged at these institutions in 1980. For private schools, the average tuition was $5,086 (median = $5,515). Religious private schools (as defined by NCES) were considerably less expensive (mean = $3,577; median = $3,575). And in-state tuition at public

Figure 4.2 State High Court Justices' Undergraduate Institutions, In-State versus Out-of-State, by State

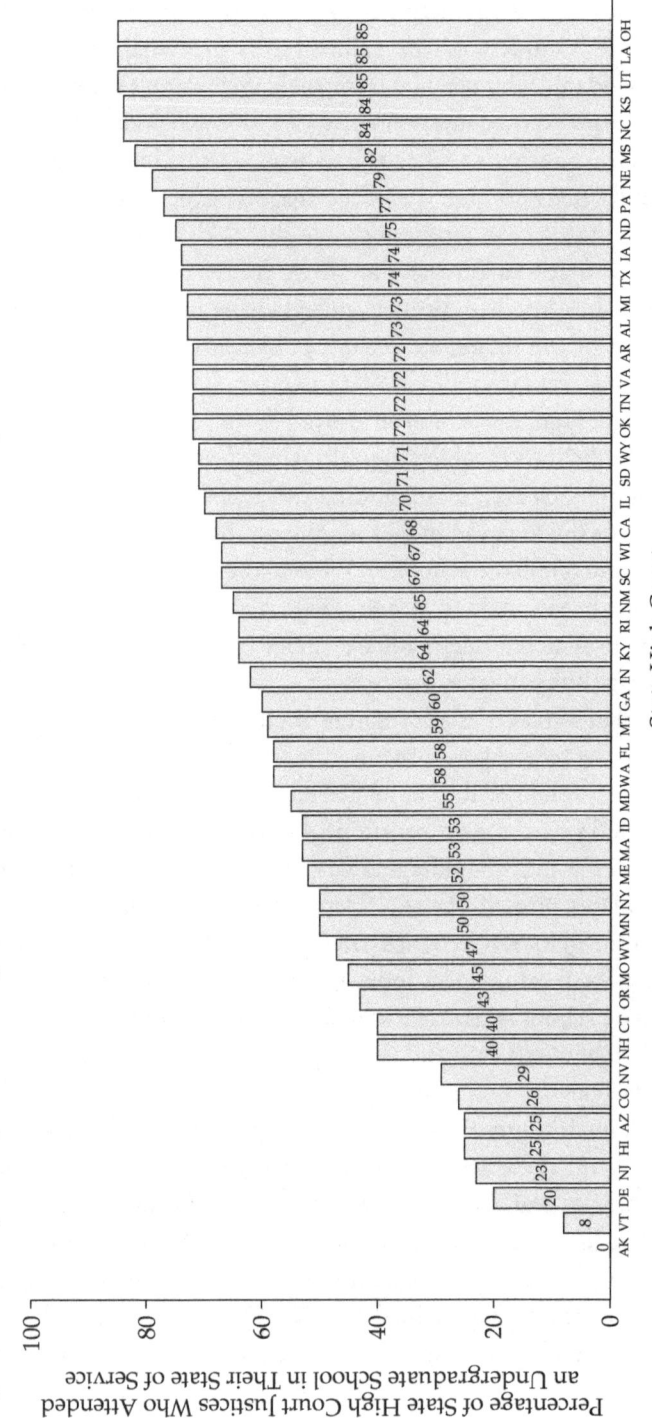

Source: Gibson and Nelson, State High Court Justices Database, 1990–2015.
Notes: $N = 981$. The undergraduate institutions attended by the state supreme court justices were coded as being either in the same state as the court or not in the same state as the court. The figure shows, for example, that none of the justices in Alaska received their undergraduate degree from an Alaskan university. Difference of proportions: $p < .001$, eta = .40.

schools was a real bargain at an average of $823 (median = $766).[72] We are fully cognizant of all the vagaries associated with calculating the true and actual cost of a college education. Nonetheless, we believe that three conclusions from this analysis are warranted: public schools cost a great deal less than private schools; religious private schools cost less than secular private schools; and the cost differentials in tuition were sufficiently great that, even with considerable measurement error, these tuition figures can stand for a reasonable approximation of social class origins.[73] We also observe that these figures are perhaps a better measure of the social classes from which the schools drew than a simple distinction between private, public, and religious institutions. For instance, the range of tuitions for religious private schools was $970 to $4,970, and similar variability characterizes the public and private institutions.

We have developed two additional measures: for public undergraduate institutions, whether the school is a "flagship" school for the state; and for all schools, the quality of the institution. To be considered a flagship university, the school must be a public school that offers a PhD and is classified as a "university" (a classification that, in the past, meant something).[74] Several states (for example, Connecticut) have only one flagship school in the judge database, while a few states (Massachusetts, Rhode Island) have no flagship public schools by this measure.

The NCES school quality variable has three categories: admission contingent upon "ability to profit from attendance"; high school graduation or equivalent; or high school graduation plus superior academic aptitude. Given that only 2 percent of the judges attended the lowest-quality school, this variable is essentially a dichotomy, with 44 percent of the schools requiring superior academic aptitude.

These five variables measure different aspects of the undergraduate institutions, and therefore we do not expect them to scale on a single underlying dimension of "quality." Some of the variables, however, are very strongly intercorrelated. For instance, the type of school is correlated with the price of tuition at $r = .91$.

Having discussed our data on undergraduate schooling, we now move to the judges' legal education. We note at the outset that law school is also a powerful socializing experience. As James Gibson explains, "one of the major agents of early adulthood socialization is the law school."[75] Individuals who graduate from a high-status law school have easier access to white-collar law firms, résumé-burnishing judicial clerkships, and other markers of privileged status that are more difficult to attain for students who hold a diploma from a lower-status law school. Moreover, graduates of higher-status law schools are exposed to law school classmates and professors, many of whom have easy access to life's advantages. Together, we expect that these experiences create a unique type of early adulthood socialization experience.

But it is perhaps not quite so simple. As Gregory Sisk, Michael Heise, and Andrew Morriss write: "Justice Frankfurter once opined that 'the law is what the lawyers are. And the law and lawyers are what the law schools make them.' Law school faculties in general, and those at the leading law schools in particular, are ideologically unrepresentative of the general population and tend to be identified with liberal causes and attitudes."[76] Thus, as we have already acknowledged, many of the highest-status schools in the country are strongly associated with liberal, not conservative, values.

This contention is supported by recent empirical research. Bonica and his colleagues note that only 15 percent of law professors in 2012 (unlike 35 percent of lawyers overall) were politically conservative and that more prestigious law schools tended to be more liberal.[77] Likewise, Bonica and Sen find that judges who attended more prestigious law schools tend to be more liberal than lawyers who graduated from lower-ranked law schools.[78] Thus, and as we discuss in further detail later, one must be cautious before assuming that exposure to a prestigious educational institution is necessarily associated with anti-equality values.[79]

The result, as Gibson explains, is a complete reversal of this conventional wisdom: "Indeed, to the extent that generalization is possible, it seems that the traditional assumption about social class and liberalism is undermined—judges trained in high-status law schools tend to be somewhat more liberal than judges trained in low-status schools."[80] For this reason, *we expect that more prestigious law school experiences are associated with greater liberalism*, even though elite legal education is an experience traditionally associated with society's upperdogs.

Additionally, we draw a distinction between in-state and out-of-state educational institutions. We expect that judges who graduated from out-of-state law schools were more likely to be exposed to ideas about the law and legal systems that differed from the modal ways of thinking in their home states.[81] These new ideas, by extension, may have expanded a judge's intellectual horizons and views about the "right" way to decide cases. We expect a similar mechanism to hold for judges with a diploma from an in-state educational institution. On the whole, these judges were less likely to be exposed to a diversity of thought, and we therefore expect these judges to be more conservative. This framework, in turn, motivates our prediction that *judges who received their undergraduate or law degrees from in-state educational institutions will tend to be more conservative, on average, than judges who graduated from out-of-state institutions.*

The federal government school database also includes a measure of the amount of the tuition for graduate schools. Under the fairly safe assumption that law school tuition differs little from graduate school tuition (at least during the relevant time frame), we can also measure the approximate cost of the law schools attended by these judges. By tying the law schools to their primary educational institution, we were able to calculate the tuition costs at various types of schools. For public law schools, the average tuition in the federal database is $958 (median = $900), $3,465 for religious schools (median = $3,592), and $4,678 for private schools (median = $4,735). Again, the most important point we want to make from this analysis is that there are vast differences in the costs of legal training across types of law schools.

Measuring law school quality decades ago is a demanding task. Under the assumption that the highest-quality schools have changed little, even if lesser law schools may have changed in significant ways, we employ a simple dichotomy to measure law school quality: whether or not the school is in the "T14" category of law schools.[82] About one in five (22 percent) of these judges graduated from one of these elite law schools.

About 61 percent of these judges attended a law school located in the state in which they eventually served as a judge. Putting together undergraduate and law school training, 47 percent of these judges studied at both an in-state undergraduate institution and an in-state law school, compared to 26 percent who received both their undergraduate and legal degrees outside the state in which they served as a judge.

The states vary enormously in the percentage of judges who acquired both their undergraduate and legal training from in-state institutions (see figure 4.3). In Louisiana and Kansas, nearly all judges were trained within the state, whereas in five states (Alaska, Delaware, New Hampshire, Nevada, and Rhode Island) none of the state high court judges received their undergraduate and legal degrees from in-state institutions. Obviously,

Figure 4.3 Percentage of State High Court Justices Who Attended Both an Undergraduate School and a Law School in the State Where They Served as a Judge

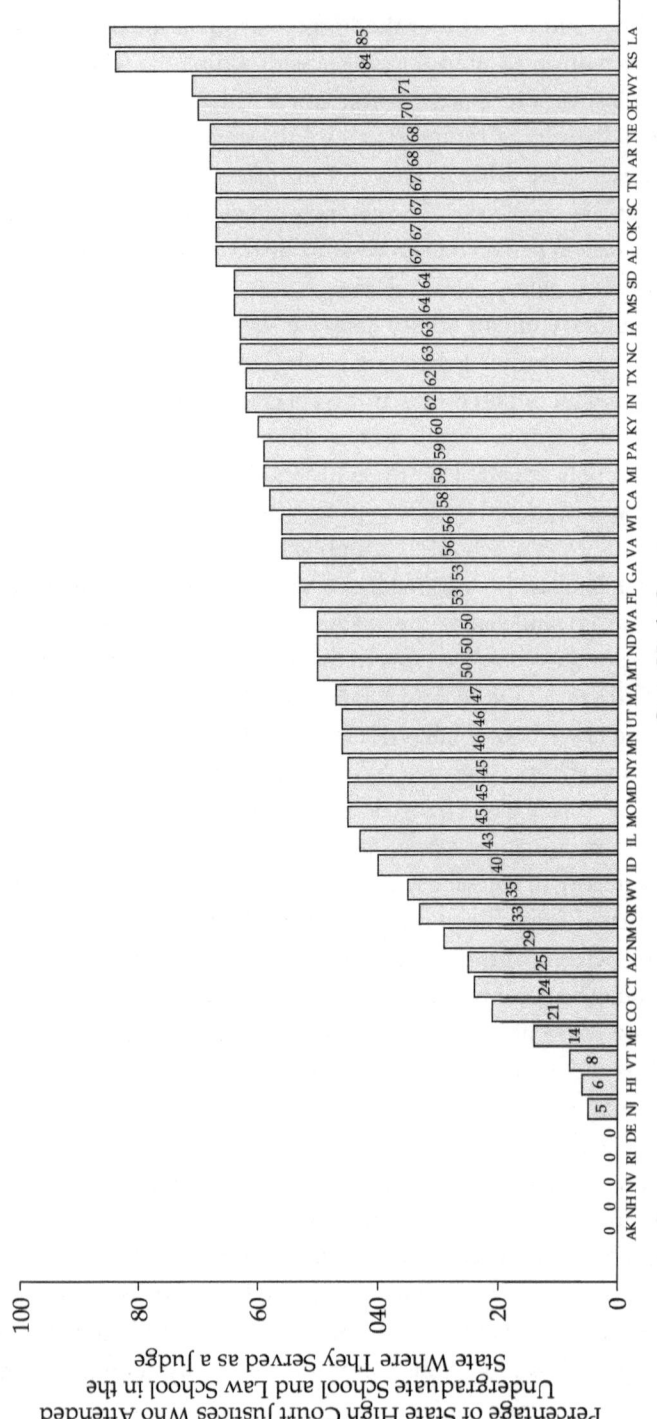

Source: Gibson and Nelson, State High Court Justices Database, 1990–2015.
Notes: $N = 981$. The figure shows, for example, that none of the justices in Alaska received both their undergraduate and law degrees from an Alaskan university. Difference of proportions: $p < .001$, eta $= .45$.

these judges' ties to local educational institutions differ just about as much as they possibly could across the fifty states.

What conclusions can we draw from these educational data about the social class origins of the judges? We have created a variable that is the sum of the cost of the undergraduate and law school training for each judge, assuming that each judge attended four years of undergraduate school and obtained three years of legal education. Importantly, this figure does not reflect the full costs of education, as it is based only on the nominal tuition costs, not on the actual amount paid by any given individual.[83] Nevertheless, recognizing that we have no other indicator of social class background, this variable must suffice as a somewhat coarse measure of the background of each judge.

The combined average educational cost for both undergraduate and legal education for these justices is $18,037. There is significant variability in the costs, however, with the variable ranging from just over $2,000 to more than $44,000. Interestingly, by our measure, Justice Roy Moore, who attended the U.S. Military Academy as an undergraduate and the University of Alabama Law School, had one of the least costly educations.[84] The highest education costs are associated with the handful of justices who attended both Harvard and Yale, in any combination (for example, Edward M. Mansfield of Iowa).

Measuring On-the-Job Experiences

We are particularly concerned with six common legal experiences: prior service as a judge, as a prosecutor, as a public defender, as a law professor, as a law clerk, and as an attorney in private practice. We expect each of these professionalizing experiences to shape judges' ideologies.

We collected data on the judges' career experiences from various bibliographical sources. We scored a judge as having a particular experience only if we found an affirmative statement that the judge in fact served in that role. Therefore, the category "no such experience" should actually be understood as meaning "no evidence of such experience." The category "has the experience" contains considerably less measurement error (but not zero error, owing to mistakes in reporting or mistakes in understanding exactly how a given position ought to be coded) than the category "no evidence of such experience." Figure 4.4 reports the frequency distributions on these career experience variables.

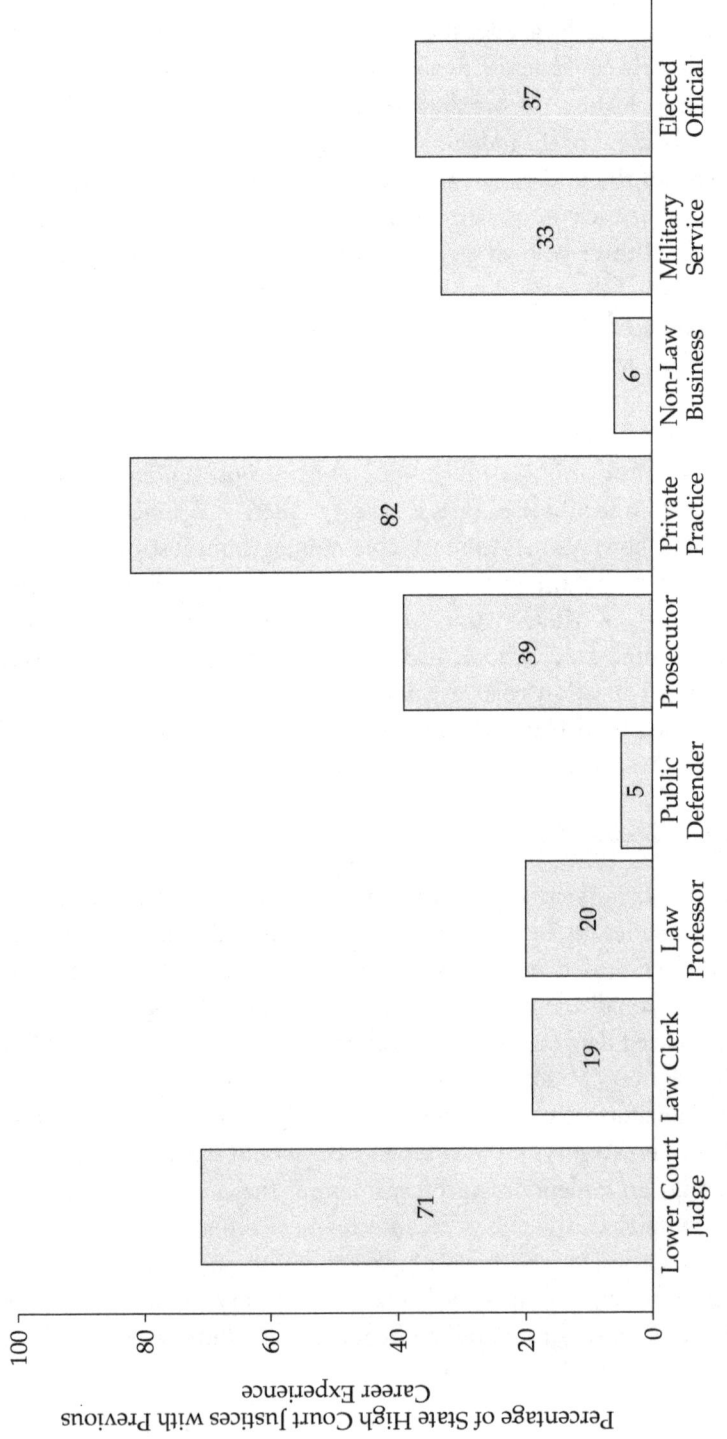

Figure 4.4 The Previous Career Experiences of State High Court Justices

Source: Gibson and Nelson, State High Court Justices Database, 1990–2015.
Notes: N = 981 state high court justices. We hypothesize that law professors, public defenders, and elected officials tend to be liberal while justices with experience as lower court judges, law clerks, prosecutors, in private practice, in business, and/or in the military tend to be conservative.

First, we expect that *prior service in the judicial branch—as a lower court judge or as a clerk—is associated with an increase in the probability that a judge will hold liberal attitudes.*[85] Both of these experiences expose future state high court judges to a breadth of legal issues and litigants. These experiences, by extension, should expand judges' worldviews and make them more sympathetic to claims that seek to advance inequality.[86] About 71 percent of these justices served as lower court judges, although only 19 percent worked as law clerks. Of those who served as law clerks, a majority went on to become a lower court judge (62 percent). And of the entire set of justices, 78 percent were either a lower court judge or a clerk to a judge before becoming a state supreme court judge.

As mentioned previously, law professors are predominantly liberal.[87] We expect that they would take these preexisting views with them to the bench. As a result, *we hypothesize that work as a law professor is associated with an increase in the probability that a judge will hold liberal attitudes.* Only about 21 percent of the justices had been a law professor at some point prior to joining the state's highest court.

Second, *we expect that judges who previously worked in public service, as a prosecutor or as a public defender, will be more likely to hold liberal attitudes* than those who spent most of their previous career in private practice. Public interest lawyers are exposed to a caseload that is disproportionately stocked with litigants who come from society's have-nots. We hypothesize that repeated and prolonged exposure to these types of litigants has a liberalizing effect on a prospective judge's ideology and is likely to be associated with greater support for claims that seek to advance equality. Not many of these judges had prior experience as a public defender (5 percent), but a sizable proportion had served as a prosecutor (39 percent).

Finally, *we expect that judges who previously worked in private practice to be less likely, on average, to hold liberal attitudes.* We fully acknowledge that "private practice" is a heterogeneous classification that includes white-collar law firms, plaintiffs' attorneys, and solo practitioners. However, private practice is distinct from other types of professional legal experience because attorneys in private practice have some profit motive to their work. These motives can differ widely: for example, compare the first-year associates at a big firm who need to bill hundreds of hours every month with a solo practitioner who simply needs enough revenue to keep the office lights on. We believe that these profit-based pressures engender a worldview that emphasizes the need to amass and protect resources. This worldview, we hypothesize, is associated with anti-equality attitudes and behaviors on the bench. A very large percentage of these judges (82 percent) worked in private practice at some point prior to becoming a state supreme court judge.

Similarly, just as we expect public interest attorneys to expand their worldview through working on cases involving society's have-nots, we expect the worldviews of private practice attorneys to be influenced by their frequent work representing the claims of society's upperdogs in the legal system. Given that, in many cases, society's haves seek to advance inequality, repeated exposure as an attorney in private practice to these types of claims may be associated with a decrease in the probability that a judge will vote for the pro-equality position in a given case.

We also examine work in three other sectors that we expect to have particularly powerful professionalizing influences: service in the military, employment in business, and service as an elected public official.

We expect that professional experiences in business and the military are associated with a decrease in the likelihood that a judge will hold liberal attitudes. Both of these sectors of the workforce are renowned for their emphasis on authority, hierarchy, and maintenance of the status quo, which are not exactly liberal values. We therefore expect judges who worked in these two sectors to have been exposed to these values and to be likely to have incorporated them into their worldview, thereby affecting their behavior on the bench. Not many of these judges worked in a business that was not engaged in legal practice (6 percent), but a sizable percentage served in the military (33 percent).

On the other hand, *we expect individuals who have previously served as an elected official to be more likely to hold liberal attitudes.* Through the electoral process, casework, and learning about their constituents' trials and tribulations, service as an elected official expands people's worldview. We expect that state high court judges with a background in elected office will be more likely to view the law as a tool to help those in need, and thus more likely to support a pro-equality position when they are on the bench. More than one-third of these judges served as an elected official (37 percent) before joining the state supreme court.

In short, we are interested in a range of professionalizing experiences that a judge had before reaching the state supreme court. We expect that different types of legal practice expand a judge's horizons and expose him or her to a panoply of views. These diverse experiences, we hypothesize, affect a judge's decisions on equality-relevant cases. Therefore, judges' social backgrounds and career experiences are expected to affect their on-the-bench behavior.

Operationalizing Judicial Ideologies

An overarching hypothesis of this research (as shown in figure 4.1) is that judges' decisional behavior is affected by their values and ideologies. This hypothesis has been supported over and over again in hundreds of studies of judicial behavior.[88]

In light of the difficulty of measuring values and ideologies, scholars have overwhelmingly gravitated to a very simple indicator: judges who are Democrats are assumed to be more liberal than judges who are Republicans. While a seemingly crude measure, earlier research has shown that this simple distinction predicts decisional behavior across a wide range of policy domains.[89]

We were able to score each judge in our database as either a Democrat or a Republican.[90] Democrats dominated; about 56 percent of the judges were Democrats and the remaining 44 percent were Republicans.[91] The conventional wisdom is that Democrats tend to be at least somewhat liberal and that Republicans tend to be at least somewhat conservative. That assumption, however, is subject to some necessary empirical verification.

To validate this assumption, we refer to the work of Bonica and Woodruff, who have developed a measure of state supreme court judges' ideologies that is useful for us.[92] The measure is derived from a mixture of campaign contribution data and the party of the appointing authority (typically the governor). There is significant overlap between the judges in our data set and the judges examined by Bonica and Woodruff. Of the roughly 1,000 judges in our data, 823 had received a Bonica-Woodruff ideology score. The measure does not vary across time, so judges in our database who were serving in 2015 received the same score that the researchers assigned to these judges in 2010. According to this measure, Justice Alan M. Wilner (Maryland, Democrat) is the most liberal state high court judge in America,[93] and the most conservative judge is Justice Dale V. Sandstrom (North Dakota, Republican).[94] The most liberal Republican in our database is Justice Frederic Allen (Vermont),[95] and the most conservative Democrat is Justice Larry L. Lehman (Wyoming).[96]

Figure 4.5 The Distribution of State High Court Justices' Ideologies, by Party Affiliation

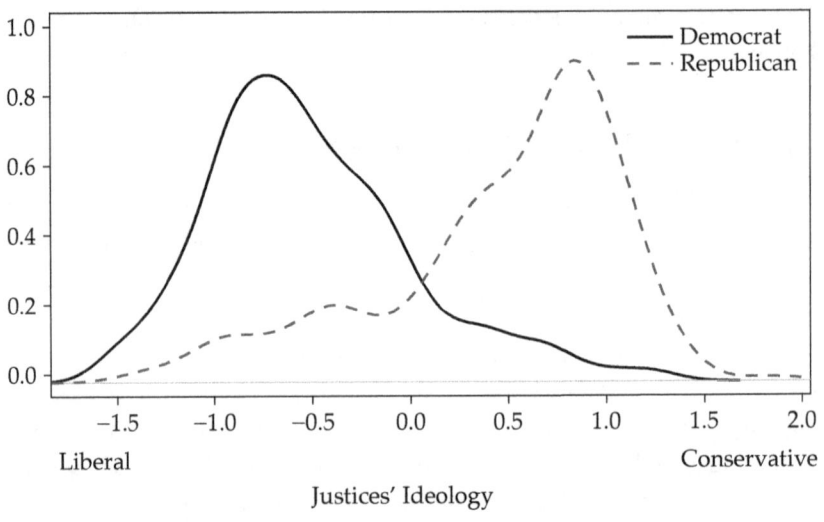

Source: Gibson and Nelson, State High Court Justices Database, 1990–2015; Bonica and Woodruff 2015.
Notes: N = 981. This figure shows the distribution of ideology scores for state supreme court justices who are Democrats and those who are Republicans.

Based on this measure of ideology, Democratic and Republican judges differ greatly (see figure 4.5). The measure varies from –1.60 (liberal) to 1.90 (conservative).[97] The correlation of the Democratic judge indicator and this ideology measure is –.63, meaning that, on average, Democratic judges are very much more liberal than Republican judges.[98] The mean for Democratic judges is –.50 (standard deviation = .56; median = –.59), while the mean for Republican judges is .47 (standard deviation = .64; median = .68). Thus, the mean for the Republicans is nearly two standard deviations distant from the mean for the Democrats. Overall, this analysis suggests that simple party affiliation is in fact a strong indicator of judges' ideological position.[99] Throughout the analysis that follows, we employ both measures of judges' ideologies: their partisan attachments and their ideology scores.

Connecting Backgrounds with Ideologies

To what degree are judges' ideologies related to their backgrounds and educational experiences? In table 4.1, we report the results from regressing

Table 4.1 Predictors of a State High Court Justice's Ideology and Political Party

	OLS Regression			Logistic Regression		
Predictor Type	Justice's Ideology			Justice's Political Party		
Predictor	*b*	s.e.	*r*	*b*	s.e.	*r*
Demographic attributes						
Gender	.03*	.02	.04	.37*	.18	.02
Whether Asian	−.17**	.06	−.11	−1.23	.68	−.06
Whether Black	−.11***	.03	−.11	−1.71***	.35	−.17
Whether Hispanic	−.12**	.04	−.08	−.75	.45	−.03
Year born	.22***	.04	.12	3.45***	.48	.19
Military experience	.04*	.02	.01	.39*	.18	−.04
Social class origins						
Cost of education	−.04	.04	−.14	.48	.41	.01
Undergraduate education						
Quality	−.03	.03	−.05	.12	.27	.01
Whether in-state	.01	.02	.12	.05	.17	.03
Whether religious institution	−.00	.02	−.11	−.34	.23	−.03
Law school education						
Quality	.01	.02	−.08	.21	.21	.02
Whether in-state	.04**	.02	.16	.36*	.18	.04
Career experiences						
Age on joining supreme court	−.07	.05	−.09	.31	.56	−.06
Whether public defender	−.05	.03	−.09	−.42	.33	−.06
Whether prosecutor	.02	.01	.02	.11	.15	.00
Private practice experience	.05**	.02	.11	.46*	.20	.10
State-level attributes						
Whether former Confederate state	.07***	.02	.18	−.35*	.17	−.05
Control						
Whether ideology is imputed	−.03	.02	−.03	−.38*	.20	−.02
Equation						
Intercept	.29***	.05	—	−2.88***	.52	—
Standard deviation—dependent variable	.21					
Standard error of estimate	.20					
R^2	.13***			.15***		
N	981			981		

Source: Authors' compilation.

Notes: All variables are scored to range from 0 to 1. For the logit analysis of the judge's political party, we report the Nagelkerke R^2. Significance of unstandardized regression coefficients (*b*): ***$p \leq .001$; **$p \leq .01$; *$p \leq .05$; s.e. = standard error of unstandardized logit regression coefficient; *r* = bivariate correlation with justice's ideology or political party.

our two measures of ideology on a variety of attributes of the judges. For the judge's ideology, a continuous variable, we use OLS regression; for political party affiliation, a dichotomous variable, we use logistic regression. It is perhaps worth reiterating that the correlation of the two dependent variables is .64, and that it is not larger owing especially to the fact that Democratic judges are internally heterogeneous in their ideologies (in part because of relatively conservative southern Democrats). We consider first the predictors of the judge's ideology.

The single strongest predictor of judicial ideology reported in table 4.1 is the year in which the judge was born. The results indicate that judges born more recently—younger judges—are more likely to be *conservative*. To understand this relationship, we examine the bivariate relationship between this variable and ideology, which is depicted in figure 4.6.

This figure shows clearly the tendency for younger judges—who joined their state high court more recently—to be more conservative. The change seems to be centered on judges born around 1950, which roughly equates to those who became state supreme court justices about fifty years later. This corresponds with the period in which Republicans were becoming more successful in capturing the supreme courts of the American states, a trend we explore in greater detail in chapter 5.

The data also reveal that minority state supreme court justices tend to be less conservative (more liberal), particularly Black judges (7 percent of the judge population). Note that the regression coefficients reported in table 4.1 depict the difference between each of the three categories of race in comparison to White judges. Asian, Black, and Hispanic judges are all significantly less conservative than their White peers. At the same time, we note that female judges, on average, are neither more liberal nor more conservative than male judges.

Two of the background variables—obtaining an in-state legal education and working in private practice—have significant effects on judicial ideologies. Those who attended an in-state law school and those who were in private practice prior to coming to the supreme court are both significantly more conservative. Even our crude measure of private practice (which is unable to distinguish among types of private practice) is connected to ideological conservatism (as compared to those judges with no notable experience in private practice). We have more to say about in-state legal training later, but here we have one initial takeaway from our results: as we predicted, homegrown judges are more conservative than judges who

Figure 4.6 The Relationship between Justices' Year of Birth and Conservative Ideology

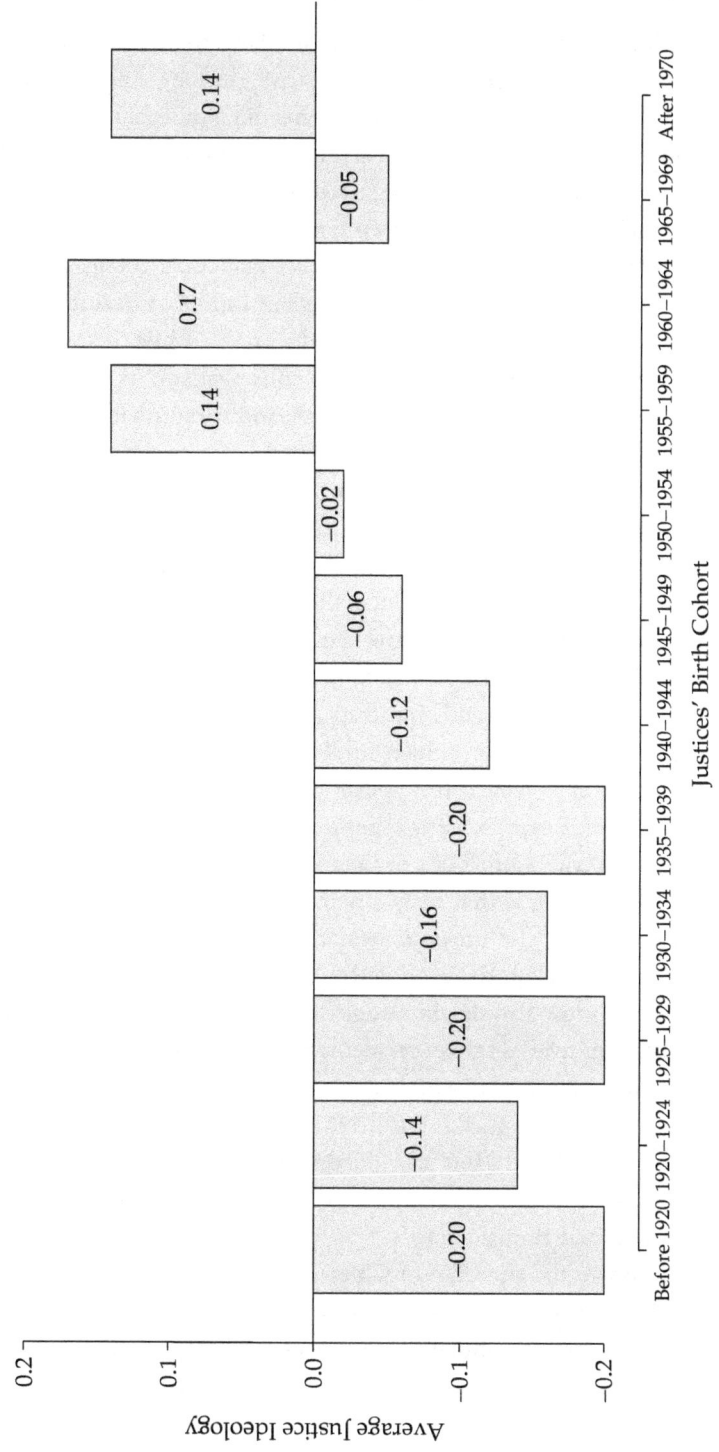

Source: Gibson and Nelson, State High Court Justices Database, 1990–2015; Bonica and Woodruff 2015.
Notes: This figure depicts the average ideology score (higher scores indicate greater conservatism) according to the year in which a justice was born.

received their legal training in another state. Similarly, there is a positive association between military service and conservative ideology. Another notable finding is that judges serving in the states of the old Confederacy are significantly more conservative than judges serving elsewhere in the nation. The history of conservatism in the South and the recent ascendance of Republicans in its state politics are likely to account for this relationship.[100]

Several of the variables that do not predict justices' ideologies are also noteworthy. Most important in this group is our primary measure of social class background: the cost of the justice's education. While this variable is one of the strongest bivariate predictors of conservatism, its independent and direct effect in the multivariate equation is indistinguishable from zero. This result is likely due to the strong relationship between the cost of education and the other variables in the equation, especially whether the justice's undergraduate school was a religious institution.[101] In many respects, this is not surprising given that the influence of social class background is likely to be filtered through career experiences during adulthood.[102] We also note that the cost of the judge's education is measured about three decades prior to the measurement of the judge's ideology. And as we report later, the effect of this variable varies between Democrats and Republicans.

Table 4.1 also reveals that neither service as a public defender nor service as a prosecutor is related to judicial ideology. There is some bivariate relationship between experience as a public defender and judicial ideology; however, that effect is washed out in the multivariate equation. One explanation for this finding is that only 5 percent of these judges ever served as a public defender. The previous explanation does not hold, however, for the effect of prosecutorial experience. Prior experience as a prosecutor is far more common among the judges (39 percent) and has neither a bivariate nor a multivariate effect on ideology, perhaps because we have cast our net broadly in measuring whether the judge ever served as a prosecutor (including, for instance, assistant attorneys general, even those who never came near a criminal case). But it could also be that the job has changed in recent years and now attracts less conservative lawyers such as, for example, Amy Klobuchar and Kamala Harris.[103]

We turn now to the equation in table 4.1 that predicts the judge's party affiliation. Most of the conclusions we have drawn about the effects on conservative ideology are similar for the effects on being a Republican. For example, experience in private practice is associated with both conservativism and Republican affiliation. Similarly, younger judges are considerably more likely to be Republicans.

A few differences stand out when comparing the two equations reported in table 4.1. For instance, some of the racial and ethnic background variables perform differently, although some of these categories (for example, Asian origin) include only small numbers of judges.

The most important difference between the equations concerns whether the judge serves in one of the former Confederate states. While these judges tend to be more conservative, they also tend to be significantly more Democratic (less Republican). This obviously reflects the fact that our data summarize the period from 1990 to 2015, a period when many Democrats served on southern supreme courts. From a slightly different vantage point, this finding also suggests that the Bonica-Woodruff scores are more valid as measures of judicial ideology than simple political party affiliation.

But party affiliation is still important for these relationships. Table 4.2 reports the results of regressing the ideology measure on the various predictors *within* Democrats and *within* Republicans. The table reveals some important differences across the two parties.

We first note that there is considerable systematic internal variability among Democrats and among Republicans. While 20 percent of the variation in ideology among Democrats is explained, only 13 percent of the variation in ideology for Republican justices can be explained. For Democrats, the variable indicating whether the justice's state is part of the former Confederacy is by far the strongest predictor of ideology. For Republicans, however, there is no difference between judges serving in Confederate and those serving in non-Confederate states. Rather, the strongest predictor of ideology among Republicans is social class (cost of education): as the cost increases, conservatism *decreases*. In contrast, the effect of educational cost on ideology among Democrats is indistinguishable from zero, although Democrats who attended a higher-quality undergraduate school tend to be slightly less conservative. We note as well that, while youth is associated with conservatism among Republican judges, this is not the case among Democratic judges.

The picture that emerges from these analyses has several noteworthy parts. First, even a fairly crude model linking backgrounds to ideologies reveals some important connections. Perhaps contrary to conventional wisdom, Republican judges who are younger and who hail from a relatively

Table 4.2 Predictors of a State High Court Justice's Ideology, by Political Party

Predictor Type / Predictor	Democrats Justice's Ideology			Republicans Justice's Ideology		
	b	s.e.	r	b	s.e.	r
Demographic attributes						
Gender	.01	.02	.09	.01	.02	–.02
Whether Asian	–.06	.04	–.10	–.23*	.10	–.12
Whether Black	–.00	.02	.02	–.05	.05	–.02
Whether Hispanic	–.06	.04	–.11	–.09	.06	–.03
Year born	–.06	.04	–.17	.17**	.06	.19
Military experience	.01	.02	.12	.03	.02	–.04
Social class origins						
Cost of education	.02	.04	–.19	–.14**	.05	–.19
Undergraduate education						
Quality	–.06*	.03	–.11	–.00	.03	–.04
Whether in-state	.00	.01	.14	.01	.02	.11
Whether religious institution	–.01	.02	–.14	.05	.03	–.08
Law school education						
Quality	–.03	.02	–.19	.04	.03	–.07
Whether in-state	.02	.02	.20	.04	.02	.15
Career experiences						
Age on joining supreme court	–.03	.05	.03	–.12	.07	–.17
Whether public defender	–.03	.03	–.09	–.03	.04	–.04
Whether prosecutor	.00	.01	.02	.01	.02	.03
Private practice experience	.00	.02	.03	.04	.03	.07
State-level attributes						
Whether former Confederate state	.11***	.01	.38	.04	.02	.17
Control						
Whether ideology is imputed	.00	.02	–.03	–.04	.02	–.01
Equation						
Intercept	.34***	.04		.50***	.07	
Standard deviation—dependent variable	.15			.18		
Standard error of estimate	.14			.17		
R^2	.20***			.13***		
N	544			437		

Source: Authors' compilation.

Notes: All variables are scored to range from 0 to 1. Significance of unstandardized regression coefficients (*b*): ***$p \leq .001$; **$p \leq .01$; *$p \leq .05$; s.e. = standard error of unstandardized regression coefficient; *r* = bivariate correlation with justice's ideology.

less privileged social class tend to be more conservative. Neither age nor social class origin is associated with ideology among Democratic judges. For Democrats, judges serving in the South are significantly more conservative than judges elsewhere, as are those who attended undergraduate institutions of more plebian reputation, although to a lesser degree. For both Democratic and Republican judges, career experiences seem to have limited consequences for ideology: neither experience as a prosecutor nor experience as a public defender has a significant impact on conservative or liberal ideology.

Summary and Concluding Thoughts

The analyses in this chapter are varied and far-reaching. Therefore, it is useful to try to pull together and summarize our most important conclusions.

- Following extant research, we have developed two measures of the ideological proclivities of all state supreme court justices who served from 1990 to 2015: the party affiliations of the justices and their scores on the Bonica-Woodruff conservatism index.[104] We discovered, as expected, that these two measures are strongly correlated. But owing to the conservatism of southern Democratic justices, the Bonica-Woodruff conservatism measure seems to be the best indicator of justices' ideologies.
- We hypothesized that justices' attitudes and values (ideologies) are related to their demographic attributes, their social class backgrounds, and their career experiences. Some of the conventional hypotheses have been supported. For example, those whose pre-court careers were spent in private practice are more likely to be Republicans and are more conservative. Similarly, minority justices tend to be more liberal than their White peers.
- Other findings ran counter to our expectations. For instance, younger judges, especially younger Republican justices, tend to be more conservative than older justices. For Republicans, those from more privileged social classes (as indicated by costly undergraduate and law school education) tend to be *less* conservative than their colleagues who attended more plebian schools. In contrast to the common assumption that those with prior experience as a prosecutor tend to be more conservative,

we find no association between prosecutorial experience and party affiliation or ideology.
- One of our more intriguing findings is that homegrown justices tend to be more conservative than those educated outside their state of service. Backgrounds are indeed connected to justices' attitudes and values, but not necessarily in simple and direct ways.
- A venerable political science adage has it that "it's always different in the South!" That is certainly true with these judges and court data. The former Confederate states stand out as distinctive in many respects. The justices from these states are certainly more conservative than justices serving elsewhere, but because of the region's political history, they are also more likely to be Democrats. There is probably no relationship we have discovered in this chapter that is not connected in some way or another to this fundamental regional divide.
- The growing conservatism of these state supreme court justices strongly suggests that support for political, legal, economic, and social inequality in judicial decisions will have increased over time. Assessing the connection between ideologies and judicial behavior—as well as a variety of other theoretically derived variables—is the most important objective of the remainder of this book.

What, in the end, do we conclude about the social class origins of these justices? Our analyses suggest the possibility of a curvilinear relationship with attitudes and values. It may well be true that those from less privileged backgrounds tend to be more liberal and are therefore more likely to favor greater equality than those from more privileged backgrounds. But as privilege grows—to the point, for example, of being able to afford to attend Harvard or Yale—conservatism seems to decline. This may well have something to do with the liberalizing influences in elite legal education, but we do not want to speculate too far beyond our data. Nevertheless, the analysis in this chapter provides at least some evidence that class still matters, even for state supreme court justices.

Appendix 4.A: Coding Judge Attributes

After undergoing training, the coders followed the precedent of the coders who read and coded the case data by entering the information they collected into an online Qualtrics form we created. The Qualtrics form had many advantages for reliability over a simple spreadsheet-based approach. For example, the form limited the possible response options for each piece of data, thus ensuring that coders did not enter an incorrect state abbreviation, because they were required to select a state name from a dropdown list. The form also made only applicable questions available to be answered. For example, party control of the appointing legislature was an available coding option only for judges identified by coders as having been appointed by a legislature; coders were asked to code information about a judge's postcourt history only if they had indicated that the judge was no longer on the bench.

After the initial coding for each judge was completed, we took several steps to examine the reliability and validity of the data. First, we asked coders to record the source of every piece of information they coded and to indicate their level of confidence in each section of data they completed (for example, educational background, or prior professional experiences). This enabled us to prioritize judges who needed a second look by another coder. Second, we compared variables that were common across our data set and the data sets created by Goelzhauser to examine reliability empirically.[105] Among the judges coded by both our coders and Goelzhauser, the coding was the same for the vast majority of them. For example, we differed on the gender of 1.2 percent of the judges, the race of .8 percent of the judges, the party of the appointing governor (conditional on the judge being appointed by a governor) on .2 percent, judges' prior clerkship experience on 6 percent, and judges' prior judicial experience on 6 percent.[106] Inconsistent codings required us to go back to the various data sources to reconcile the competing scores.

CHAPTER 5

The Institutions

WE HAVE JUST seen that judges with heterogeneous backgrounds serve on the state supreme courts, and we have shown that these background characteristics are important because they can predict the attitudes that judges bring to the bench. Of course, before someone can vote as a judge on a state supreme court, he or she must actually become a judge on that state supreme court. Many people are attorneys, but only a tiny fraction become state supreme court justices. Moreover, the processes through which state supreme court justices are selected may privilege certain types of people over others. And since these background characteristics are associated with judges' attitudes, being familiar with methods of judicial selection could be critical to understanding the role of state supreme courts in exacerbating or mitigating inequality in the U.S. states.

By far the most important—and unique—institutions that might affect the behavior of state supreme court justices and the composition of these high courts are the rules that govern how judges first acquire their seat on the bench and determine whether they can keep their position. Methods of judicial *selection* refer to the institutions that govern how judges join their state supreme court. Methods of judicial *retention* are the rules that determine whether judges stay in office when their term expires.

The remainder of this book explores how these institutions affect judicial policymaking across the United States. We theorize and test the effects of both methods of judicial selection and methods of judicial retention on the propensity of state supreme courts to advance equality through their rulings.[1] Our overarching claim is that judicial elections make it possible to disrupt the ability of dominant political elites in a state to control a state supreme court and its policymaking by limiting the influence of these elites over deciding who serves in these courts. But in practice that possibility is rarely realized: the composition of state courts usually mirrors the state's dominant political coalition in power.

We begin our argument with a brief digression to summarize the rich historical and social-scientific literature on the adoption of judicial elections, which were not adopted in a vacuum but instead were responses to major political moments in American history. States implemented judicial elections as a strategy in drawn-out political battles often aimed explicitly at controlling the sorts of people who would become judges and the types of decisions they would make once in office.[2] As we will see, the adoption (and rejection) of various methods of judicial selection and retention is tightly connected to the rise and fall of populist movements in the United States.

We next move from history to the present to categorize the various methods employed by states to select and retain their judges. We make the important distinction between the "formal" institutions that states purportedly use for these purposes and the "informal" ways in which these institutions operate in practice. These distinctions are important, we argue, because a failure to account for these de facto practices could bias scholars' understandings about the impacts of these institutions on judicial behavior. In one of our major conclusions, we find that, even where judges are nominally elected to the state supreme court, many do *not* acquire their seat on the court by election. Instead, these "elected" judges are actually appointed to their position. As a consequence, political elites maintain a good deal of influence over the staffing of most elected state supreme courts even when the public is formally involved in the selection of its judges. This has important consequences for the elite capture of state supreme courts.

Third, having described how state supreme court judges in the United States reach their position, we turn to an in-depth analysis of the consequences of judicial selection institutions in order to test a powerful alternative to our theory. It may be the case that systems of judicial selection—regardless of who is in power in a state at a particular point in time—put different types of people on the bench. Because judges' background characteristics can relate to their attitudes (as we saw in chapter 4), selection systems that privilege particular types of background characteristics might have *direct* consequences for whether a court tends to be pro- or anti-equality. Moreover, if it is the case that, regardless of background characteristics, selection systems privilege liberal or conservative justices on average, the mere presence or absence of particular institutions might explain why some courts tend to favor equality more than others. This explanation stands in direct contradiction to our theory that state supreme courts are captured by the dominant political coalition in a state.

Most generally, we find few differences in the background characteristics of judges who were initially elected to their position compared to those who were initially appointed to the bench. And with rare exception, the differences that we do find—particularly judges' educational background, social class background, and racial-ethnic background—are substantively rather small. Indeed, elected and appointed courts look fairly similar to one another. Perhaps most importantly, we find that a near-majority of judges who work on elected courts were initially appointed to their state supreme court position. Thus was the way paved for elite control over state supreme courts, just as our theory predicts.

A Short History of Judicial Selection in the United States

While most judges throughout the world reach the bench through some sort of appointment procedure and serve for a fixed term of office, many judges in the U.S. states face a unique constraint: they need to satisfy voters in an election in order to earn their position on the bench. Once they are in office, *most* judges in the U.S. states must continue to win elections in order to remain on the bench.[3]

That so many U.S. state judges must face the electorate is unique. The only other country that uses judicial elections to select judges for courts with important policymaking powers is Bolivia, and that country only began the practice in 2011.[4] In the United States, states have used judicial elections to select their judges for over a century.[5] The history of judicial selection in the United States is tied inextricably to populist political movements. While concerns about partisanship and professionalism have loomed large in these discussions, the debate about the "best" method of judicial selection is fundamentally about the proper influence of political elites over the judicial branch.

At the time of America's founding, judges were selected through elite appointment processes; some states granted the governor the authority to make these appointments, while others empowered the state legislature to fill the state's highest court. Beginning in the early 1800s, states began selecting their judges through popular elections. Interestingly, elections were initially adopted as a way of empowering *independent* state judiciaries to use their power of judicial review to curb legislative overspending and financial excesses.[6] By removing the tight linkage between state legislatures and state supreme courts, reformers hoped (correctly) that they could induce state supreme courts to be responsive to the people rather than the legislature and to use judicial review to curb legislative excesses.[7] In this way, judicial elections were designed to foster greater judicial independence from the political elites who had previously selected state judges, or at least to redirect some degree of judicial dependence from those elites to the mass public.

The next major wave of judicial selection reforms emerged from the same concern over elite dominance of state supreme courts. But this time the elites with "too much" power were party elites, whose control of state and local party machines enabled them to tightly control access to the party's nomination, thereby limiting the ability of the average voter to have much meaningful effect on the composition of the bench. Thus, as time passed and state and local party machines consolidated their power, reformers sought again to increase judicial independence by altering methods of judicial selection. Worried that partisan elections had produced an unfavorable tie between state courts and partisan politics, reformers successfully encouraged many states to remove party labels from the ballot in the hope that these new elections would transfer the power to select judges from the leaders of party machines to the voters. As a result of these efforts, nonpartisan elections became an increasingly popular mechanism to staff the judicial branch during the mid-1900s.[8]

The final shift in state supreme court selection methods came as part of the "good governance" movement that swept the nation during the second half of the twentieth century. These reformers were skeptical of the ability of the average American voter to make an informed decision on a judge at the ballot box. Indeed, as we explain in more detail later, this movement was premised on the fact that elite influence over formally elected courts was so strong *that it could not be broken*.⁹ Consequently, these reformers encouraged states to abandon the existing opaque methods of elite dominance and make the elite appointment of judges transparent to the public. The eventual proposal culminated in the adoption by many states of a commission-based system of judicial selection, alternatively called the "Kales plan" (after Albert Kales, the leader of the American Judicature Society, who created the plan), the "Missouri plan" (after the first state to adopt the system), or "merit selection" (referring to reformers' hopes that merit rather than politics would be the foremost priority among commission members who vetted judges under the plan).[10]

This *very* brief review of the historical evidence on the evolution of judicial selection in the United States leads us to one major conclusion: a major concern in each wave of judicial selection reform focused on the appropriate balance of power between the people and political elites. What was largely assumed in the debates surrounding the adoption of these institutions was that popular elections would make judges more responsive to the people and less responsive to elites. Our investigation aims to uncover whether that assumption is borne out in the contemporary United States.

Contemporary Judicial Selection Systems

Today states use myriad systems to select their high court justices. Table 5.1 provides a summary of the formal selection and retention systems employed by each of the fifty states in 2015.[11] The rows of the table show each state's method for selecting state supreme court justices in 2015, and the columns show the method of retention it uses for its state supreme court. Texas and Oklahoma have two state supreme courts, but the methods of selection and retention for the two supreme courts in both states are the same.

We begin by discussing the four major categories of state judicial selection in use in the contemporary United States. First, in *partisan elections*, multiple candidates can appear on the ballot, typically after being nominated in a partisan primary election; in a partisan election, voters have the aid of a party label next to each candidate's name on the ballot. As can be seen in the left-hand panel of figure 5.1, these elections look no different from typical legislative or executive electoral contests. Indeed, in most of

Table 5.1 Methods of Judicial Selection and Retention for State High Courts, 2015

	Method of Judicial Retention					
Method of Judicial Selection	Partisan Election	Nonpartisan Election	Retention Election	Gubernatorial Reappointment	Legislative Reappointment	Commission Reappointment	No Retention
Partisan election	AL, LA, MI, OH, TX, WV		IL, NM, PA				
Nonpartisan election		AR, GA, ID, KY, MN, MS, MT, NV, NC, ND, OR, WA, WI					
Gubernatorial appointment			AK, AZ, CA, CO, FL, IN, IA, KS, MD, MO, NE, OK, SD, TN, UT, WY	CT, DE, ME, NJ, NY	VT	HI	MA, NH, RI
Legislative appointment					SC, VA		

Source: Authors' compilation.

Figure 5.1 Judicial Election Ballot Types

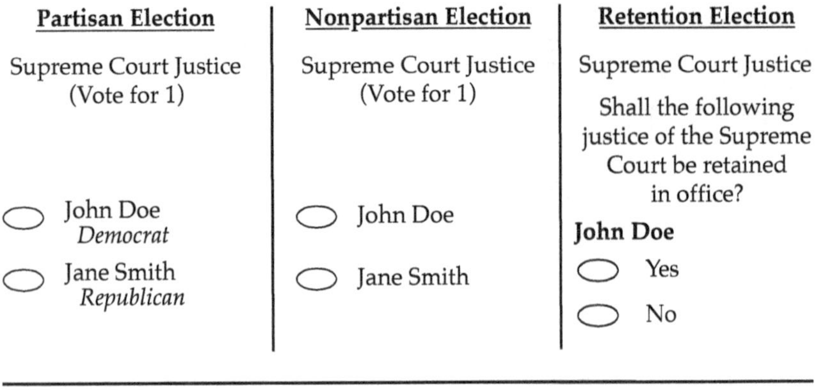

Partisan Election	Nonpartisan Election	Retention Election
Supreme Court Justice (Vote for 1)	Supreme Court Justice (Vote for 1)	Supreme Court Justice
		Shall the following justice of the Supreme Court be retained in office?
◯ John Doe 　　Democrat	◯ John Doe	**John Doe**
◯ Jane Smith 　　Republican	◯ Jane Smith	◯ Yes ◯ No

Source: Authors' compilation.

these states, voters who vote for parties rather than candidates (via the "party lever") are able to vote for the party's judicial candidates as well. Second, in a *nonpartisan election* (shown in the middle panel of figure 5.1) multiple candidates compete for a seat simultaneously, and there is no indication of a party affiliation on the ballot. Third, the majority of states use some sort of *gubernatorial appointment* to select the judges of their state supreme courts. The rules governing these appointments differ from state to state; while some states grant governors unilateral authority to place judges on the state high court, other states use a gubernatorial appointment coupled with legislative confirmation, and still other states use a commission to vet candidates. In the last set of states, the commission passes a list of names to the appointing authority (typically the governor), who appoints a judge from the list.[12] Finally, South Carolina and Virginia use a legislative appointment system to select their state supreme court judges; in these systems, state legislators select judges for the high court by a majority vote.[13]

Two states pose a special measurement challenge. While the judges of the Ohio and Michigan high courts run in formally nonpartisan general elections, they must first pass a formally partisan nomination process in order to appear on the ballot.[14] Ohio Supreme Court justices run in partisan primary elections to qualify for the nonpartisan general election ballot, while Michigan Supreme Court justices are typically nominated by party conventions before they appear on the general election ballot.

These two states are unique in that no other states with nonpartisan judicial elections employ overtly partisan processes to place judges on the general election ballot.[15]

Scholars have dealt with these two states in a variety of ways, from classifying them as nonpartisan elections or as partisan elections to treating them as a unique "hybrid" type of election.[16] Because in Michigan and Ohio political parties play such an important, formal role in the selection of judges—who typically must receive the formal backing of the party before they can face voters on the day of the general election—we believe that it is more useful to label the judges in these states as partisan election judges. In this way, we follow Michael Nelson, Rachel Caufield, and Andrew Martin in classifying Ohio and Michigan as partisan rather than nonpartisan election states.[17]

Contemporary Judicial Retention Systems

The rules used by states to decide whether or not justices should keep their position are more numerous and varied than those used to select judges. As table 5.1 shows, most states that choose their state supreme court judges through partisan or nonpartisan elections use the same processes to retain them. However, the most common method of judicial reselection is a *retention election* based on the Missouri plan. These elections are single-candidate affairs: no alternative candidate is shown on the ballot, though foes are not prohibited from challenging whether the judge should be given a new term. Voters are presented with a binary choice: Should Justice X be kept on the bench or not? If a state supreme court justice receives less than a set percentage of the vote (normally 50 percent), he or she is removed from the bench, and a new justice is selected for the court, typically via gubernatorial appointment.[18]

A handful of states retain judges through elite reappointment, although there are many variants to this approach. For example, Hawaii's judicial retention system relies on the vote of a judicial selection commission to determine whether judges remain in office.

Finally, Massachusetts, New Hampshire, and Rhode Island do not employ a retention method. In Massachusetts and New Hampshire, judges serve until they are seventy years old, while judges in Rhode Island, like federal judges, serve for life. New Jersey uses reappointment at the end of the initial term, after which the justice serves until reaching mandatory retirement age.

Points to Keep in Mind

Before moving forward, we briefly pause to make three points about judicial selection and retention that are important for our analyses in the remainder of this book. First, note that in many states the methods of judicial selection and retention are not the same. These distinctions are important and are too often conflated in previous research.[19] The Missouri plan, most notably, pairs initial appointment with periodic retention elections, while other states, such as Pennsylvania, New Mexico, and Illinois, use very different types of judicial elections for the purposes of selection and retention. Thus, to treat selection and retention as the same is to systematically misclassify the institutions used by the states.

Second, as noted in our brief review of the history of judicial selection and retention, most of the states have changed their methods of judicial selection and retention over time. Of particular concern to us are changes in judicial retention systems during the 1990–2015 time period covered by our case-level data. During this period, three states switched from partisan elections to nonpartisan elections: Arkansas (2000), Mississippi (1994), and North Carolina (2004). One other state switched during this period: Tennessee transitioned from partisan elections to retention elections in 1994. Still, aside from this small handful of changes—which we account for in our analyses—the quarter-century covered by our analysis is a time of relative stasis in states' methods of judicial retention. This is not to say that there was no support for changes during this time; in fact, there were several failed attempts to manipulate retention systems.[20] It is just that, in the evolution of these systems in the United States, the period covered by our data widely favored the status quo.

The final important substantive point to remember about methods of judicial selection and retention is that they are not randomly assigned to states. To the contrary, the methods of judicial selection and retention have typically engendered intense political struggles within states over time and represent the culmination of political battles and compromises among lawyers and nonlawyers, Republicans and Democrats, and judges and laypeople in states at particular moments in time.[21] Moreover, there has historically been significant geographic correlation with the adoption of these systems. While partisan elections have traditionally been more common in the southern United States than in other regions, a wave of midwestern states adopted commission-based systems of judicial selection coupled with retention elections. Methodologically, this requires us to account for various ways in which states might vary over time, further informing the specification of our empirical model reported in chapters 7 and 8.

The Importance of Informal Selection Institutions

When reviewing the methods of judicial selection and retention used by states, we have discussed the formal methods of judicial selection and retention—that is, the procedures used to select judges for full terms of service. Importantly, these formal methods of judicial selection do not fully capture the actual pattern of accession to state high courts. Many judges do not serve their full term of office because they die, retire, or resign in the middle of their term. Holding a special election to fill a judicial vacancy is expensive and risky, so many states that formally use elections to fill their state courts do not consult the voters when justices leave office before their term expires.[22] Instead, these states rely on some method of appointment—usually by the governor—to fill the vacancy. In some states the interim appointee will serve out the term, while in other states the interim appointee must seek the assent of voters in the next election.[23]

That many judges leave in the middle of their term and judicial vacancies are filled by appointment—even in elective states—has important practical consequences for the composition of the bench. Indeed, as Lisa Holmes and Jolly Emrey have found, most state supreme court judges in states that formally used elections to staff their state supreme court between 1962 and 2004 *were actually chosen through an appointment process.*[24] Importantly, these findings are not time-bound. James Herndon found that between 1948 and 1957 only 56 percent of state supreme court judges in states with judicial elections were initially elected. Similarly, Kate Berry and Cathleen Lisk, writing for the Brennan Center for Justice, found that 45 percent of judges sitting on elective state supreme courts in 2016 were initially appointed, *including the entire Georgia, Minnesota, and North Dakota state supreme courts.*[25]

Judicial retention systems are also not as simple as they appear. Formal methods of judicial retention are deceiving because states vary widely in the likelihood that judges will lose their job. Some of this variation is tied to the specific formal method of retention. For example, judges who face Missouri-plan retention elections are much less likely to lose their seat than those who face partisan or nonpartisan elections.[26] Other variation is tied to the state's level of electoral competitiveness. In states that are dominated by a single party, for example, a judge from that party is relatively "safe" in the general election so long as he or she was successfully nominated in the primary election. In other states, judges have little practical worry of losing an election because challengers rarely appear on the ballot.[27] Even in reappointment systems, the odds of reappointment are high. In New Jersey, for example, from 1947 to 2010, when Chris Christie refused to reappoint Justice John Wallace to the state's high court, no supreme court justice had ever not been reappointed by a New Jersey governor.[28]

Judicial Selection and Elite Control of State Courts

So far in this chapter we have established that states use diverse methods of judicial selection and retention to staff their state supreme courts, that these selection methods were adopted in response to controversies regarding the proper influence of political elites over state supreme courts, and that many (if not most) judges who sit on formally elected courts were initially appointed to their position. Our original interest in these institutions, however, was in understanding how they affect the ability of state supreme court justices to translate their ideological preferences into public policy (see figure 4.1).

Our overriding contention is that state judicial selection systems operate in a way that gives elites a de facto ability to shape the composition of the bench. In a pure appointive system, political elites have the opportunity to screen potential judges and select the judicial candidate who they believe will be their best agent on the court. The appointing authority (usually the governor) then places that person on the court. In this way, judicial appointments function as a strong source of ex ante control by elites over judicial policymaking.[29]

In an idealized electoral environment, political elites' ability to place their chosen candidate on the bench is substantially constrained because *voters*, rather than *elites*, make the final choice about who will serve on the bench. Although elites may still have a preferred candidate, and elite influence may still play an important role in shaping the electoral process (when, for example, "the party decides"), at the end of the day a candidate who appeals to voters can steamroll the elite's wishes.[30] (See, for example, the election of Donald Trump to the U.S. presidency in 2016; see also the election and reelection of Roy Moore to the Alabama Supreme Court.)

In judicial elections, elite influence is likely to be particularly strong when electoral contests are not salient to voters and parties are centralized and strong. Indeed, these conditions characterized political parties in the United States in many localities at the turn of the last century, and party elites deftly controlled the outcomes of judicial elections. Consider the account of these elections from the reformer Albert Kales:

> In a great metropolitan district like Chicago, for instance, where we have a typical long ballot and the party machines are well organized and powerful, our judges, while they go through the form of election, are not selected by the people at all. They are appointed. The appointing power is lodged with the leaders of the party machines. These men appoint the nominees. . . .
>
> Even outside of such metropolitan districts as Chicago, if party organizations are strong and well led, and the form or elections aid these party organizations, the same process of appointment will be found to prevail, although owing to the smaller sized electorate the confirming of the appointees by the people may be somewhat more intelligent.[31]

Where party leaders have tight control over ballot access and voters are not offered incentives to participate in these elections (see Kales's "a typical long ballot"), elites control who appears on the ballot, and only relatively sophisticated voters are casting their ballot in the election (since more educated voters are less likely to "roll off"—vote in higher-level contests but not in lower-level races—in judicial elections).[32]

At least two factors in contemporary American politics make the sort of elite dominance over elective systems that worried Kales unlikely to unfold broadly today. First, partisan elections have largely been replaced with nonpartisan elections. In nonpartisan election systems, elite control over the candidate selection process is lessened because parties do not have a set ballot line to fill in each election with a candidate of their choice. Moreover, since the early 1900s, parties in the United States have become weaker and more decentralized; party elites today are simply less powerful than those who ran the party machines of olden days.[33] Finally, nonpartisan elections open the door to issues (and, by extension, interest groups) that have a more powerful influence on voters' choice.[34]

Second, the adoption of television advertising, among other changes, has raised the salience of judicial elections. Far from the "sleepy" contests of old, today's judicial elections are often just as competitive as other types of elections in the United States.[35] As voter interest in these elections grows, elite influence over their outcome weakens. Elections that are more salient and interesting to voters have higher levels of voter participation.[36] And as more voters participate in elections, the threat of an unconventional and perhaps even extreme candidate looms larger.[37] When voter turnout is low, typical voters are well educated and sophisticated. But as voter turnout increases, traditional nonvoters—people who are less politically sophisticated and less educated—turn out to vote, shifting the location of the median voter away from the elites' preferences and increasing the risk that the voters will choose a candidate who is a poor agent for elite policy preferences.

Thus, judicial elections in the contemporary United States introduce uncertainty over candidate selection, lessening elites' ability to influence the outcomes of the judicial selection process, and, by extension, the composition of the state supreme court. For elites, elections are to be feared.

This is not to say that elites are unable to influence the composition of the bench in states that use judicial elections. Recall that nearly all states that formally use elections allow for interim appointments when judges leave the bench before completing their term. These interim appointments give elites substantial influence over the composition of the high court in these states. Indeed, many (if not most) judges who sit on these state supreme courts are initially appointed to their position. Kales describes the power of interim appointments colorfully:

> Most people in this country, who think about the subject at all, suppose that there are only two methods of selecting judges—by appointment and by election. This is a fundamental error that we must avoid *in limini*. There is, speaking generally, only one method of selecting judges and that is by appointment. There are, of course, different kinds of appointment . . . but except, perhaps, in the most primitive frontier communities, there is no such thing as the selection of judges by the people. . . . It is one of our most absurd bits of political hypocrisy that we actually talk and act as if our judges were elected by the people whenever the method of selection is in form by popular election.[38]

Once these interim appointments are on the bench, they must run for reelection, though some will be retained in office without ever facing a challenger at the polls.[39] All will face voters with the benefit of incumbency on their side.[40] This incumbency advantage can help protect these appointees from attacks and bolster their chances of retaining their seat on the bench.[41]

We expect that the widespread use of interim appointments improves elites' capacity to influence the composition of the bench. We acknowledge that strategic elites are forward-looking and therefore likely to appoint the sort of candidate who is able to win a future election. The pool of eligible potential judges is vast, providing elites with ample opportunity to select an interim appointee who is both sympathetic to their policy preferences and capable of securing an eventual electoral victory.

Judicial Selection and the Composition of the Bench

Do the characteristics of judges who were initially appointed to their position differ from the characteristics of those judges who gained their seat through election? In trying to answer this question, we focus on the backgrounds, experiences, and ideologies of the judges selected through different systems. In examining the relationship between judges' background characteristics and methods of judicial selection, we contribute to a voluminous literature that has sought to determine whether judicial elections advance or impede the diversity and quality of the bench.[42]

Our purpose in this analysis is to adjudicate a powerful rival explanation to our theory. Recall Jed Shugerman's argument that the adoption of judicial elections has important consequences for economic policy because the judges who are placed on the bench through early judicial elections are strikingly less willing to go along with budgets passed by state legislatures.[43] In other words, judicial elections seemingly select judges whose preferences are very different from the preferences of their appointed predecessors.

This hints at an important alternative explanation for why some courts are more pro-equality than others. While we argue that elites have co-opted both elective and appointive methods of selection, resulting in a bench that reflects the dominant political coalition in power in a state at a particular point in time, it may be the case that judicial selection institutions have effects *regardless of who is in power*. In other words, judicial elections might put different types of people on the bench than judicial appointments. To the extent that these systems select individuals with particular characteristics or attitudes, they might have direct effects on the propensity of a court to rule in favor of equality regardless of which party is in power in the state. This is not a fringe theory. Indeed, one of the major arguments made by proponents of merit selection systems is that voters do not select the most qualified judges for the bench; proponents of judicial merit selection argue that initial appointments do a better job of placing qualified judges on the bench.[44] In other words, that a bench filled through elections differs substantially from a bench filled through appointments is a claim that sits at the crux of the debate over the "best" way to select judges; our theory, by contrast, suggests that we should observe few differences across methods of selection.[45] We therefore test this proposition: Do elected and appointed courts look different from one another?

Formal and Informal Selection Systems

We begin our analysis of the effect of judicial selection methods on the composition of the bench with the aid of three new variables. The first variable measures the formal judicial selection method on the books in the year in which the judge was initially selected to the state high court. This variable was derived from Andrew Hanssen and the Judicial Selection in the States website, which is maintained by the National Center for State Courts.[46] States that formally use legislative or gubernatorial appointment to select judges were coded as appointive states, and states that use partisan or nonpartisan elections were coded as elective states. About half (48 percent) of our judges took office in a state that formally uses judicial appointment to select its judges.[47]

To measure the judges' *actual* methods of selection, we (and our research assistants) scoured news reports and official biographies to determine the method by which the judges acquired their seats on the court. Of the state supreme justices in our database, 52 percent joined the state supreme court under a formal selection system involving either a partisan or a nonpartisan election, while the remainder (48 percent) joined the court via some sort of appointed system. However, 73 percent of the justices in our database were in fact initially appointed to their positions! Obviously, all of those selected under a formal appointment system are appointed to their positions.

Of those in formally elected systems, however, only 52 percent first joined the state supreme court via an election, compared to the 48 percent who were initially appointed. This number, if anything, is slightly lower than that found in past studies, which rely on earlier time periods and have reported that a slight *majority* of judges who reach the bench in elected states were initially appointed.[48] These data drive home the conclusion that most justices on the state supreme courts (nearly three-fourths) initially became a justice via some sort of appointment process not directly involving the mass public in the state.

Figure 5.2 reports the percentages of state supreme court justices who initially joined the state supreme court via an interim appointment. Note that this figure examines the selection method in use *at the time the justice was appointed*, even if that system was no longer in use during the 1990–2015 period. The Louisiana Supreme Court fills its vacancies by special election, rather than gubernatorial appointment. The striking figure in this diagram belongs to Minnesota, which uses nonpartisan elections to select its replacement justices. Notably, of the twenty-six justices serving on the Minnesota Supreme Court from 1990 to 2015, all but one joined the court via an interim appointment. Other states have very high percentages as well. It hardly seems possible that in Minnesota twenty-five justices left the bench before the completion of their term owing to chance factors such as untimely death. Instead, these departures seem to be strategically timed. These trends must be political in nature; as such, it is necessary to focus on *who* selects a judge's eventual replacement, just as our theory suggests.

Finally, as we examined the effects of formal and informal methods of judicial selection on the characteristics of judges, we created a trichotomy that summarizes the previous two variables, differentiating judges who were appointed in systems that formally use elections, judges who were initially elected in formal election systems, and judges who were appointed in states that use appointments to formally staff the bench. To illustrate the differences across formal and informal methods of selection, table 5.2 displays, for each judicial characteristic we examined using this trichotomy, the percentage of judges with a particular background characteristic (for dichotomous characteristics) or the average value of the characteristic for the judges in that category (for continuous-level characteristics). We tested for selection system differences across four categories of judges' attributes.

Figure 5.2 Percentage of Appointed Interim State High Court Justices in States with Formal Judicial Elections

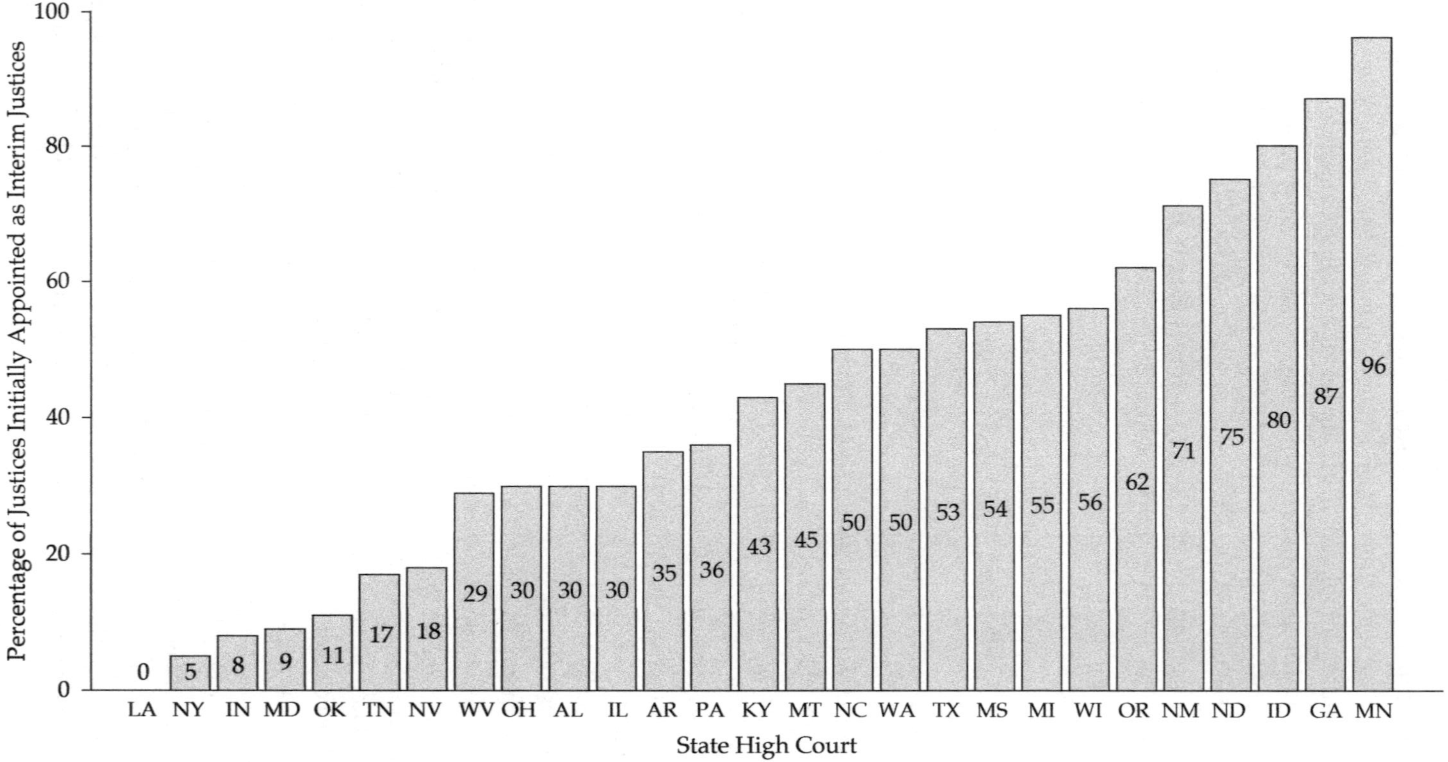

State	%
LA	0
NY	5
IN	8
MD	9
OK	11
TN	17
NV	18
WV	29
OH	30
AL	30
IL	30
AR	35
PA	36
KY	43
MT	45
NC	50
WA	50
TX	53
MS	54
MI	55
WI	56
OR	62
NM	71
ND	75
ID	80
GA	87
MN	96

Source: Gibson and Nelson, State High Court Justices Database, 1990–2015.

Table 5.2 Background Characteristics and Attitudes of State High Court Justices, by Initial Selection

	Appointed in Elected System	Elected in Elected System	Appointed in Appointed System	p-value
Demographic attributes				
Female justice	25%	22%	22%	.562
Minority justice	19%	3%	13%	<.001
Age at appointment	52 years	53 years	53 years	.345
Prior military experience	30%	38%	31%	.071
Social class backgrounds				
Cost of education	$15,447	$13,863	$20,245	<.001
High-quality undergraduate school	39%	37%	51%	.001
In-state undergraduate school	63%	70%	52%	<.001
High-quality law school	15%	11%	32%	<.001
In-state law school	68%	70%	53%	<.001
Prior professional experiences				
Prior judicial service	63%	73%	74%	.007
Prior prosecutorial experience	40%	39%	39%	.964
Prior public defender experience	6%	3%	6%	.225
Prior law professor experience	20%	19%	22%	.535
Prior private practice experience	83%	80%	83%	.408
Prior law clerk experience	20%	15%	22%	.073
Prior business experience	7%	6%	6%	.619
Prior elected office experience	43%	58%	23%	<.001
Ideologies and partisan attachments				
Justice's conservative ideology	.45	.45	.42	.049
Republican justice	46%	41%	45%	.460

Source: Authors' compilation.
Notes: This table displays the distribution of judicial characteristics by method of initial selection. For dichotomous variables, the cell entries indicate the percentage of justices who have a particular background characteristic (for example, 25 percent of justices appointed in elected systems are women). For continuous variables, the cell entry is the average value of the variable for justices in that category (for example, the average age of justices appointed in formal appointment systems is fifty-three). The p-values test for differences across the rows, using Chi^2 tests for the categorical variables and F-tests for the continuous variables.

Initial Selection and Demographic Attributes

These data enable us to probe the relationship between the characteristics of a judge and the methods by which they reach the bench.[49] We begin by analyzing the relationship between the demographic characteristics of these state supreme court justices and the method by which they attained their seat on the bench.

Figure 5.3 Percentage of Female State High Court Justices Serving under Different Selection Systems

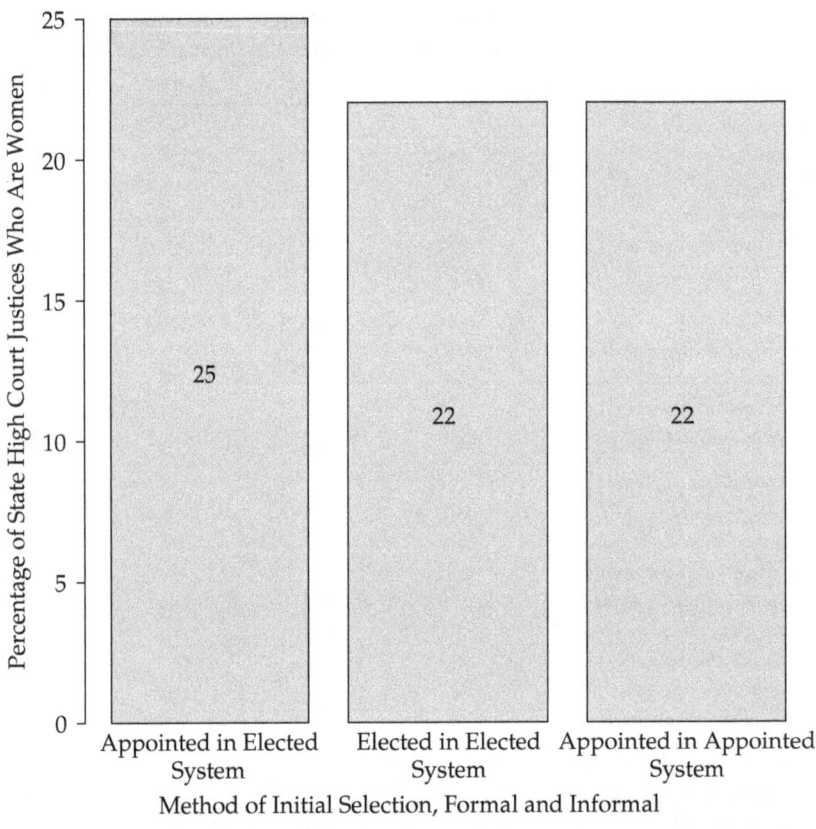

Source: Gibson and Nelson, State High Court Justices Database, 1990–2015.
Notes: N = 981. Difference in proportions across selection systems: $p > .05$; eta = .03.

Somewhat contrary to the findings of earlier studies, we find no evidence that different selection systems, either formal or informal, produce different numbers of female justices.[50] Figure 5.3 reports the percentage of female justices across the three types of formal and informal selection systems. In each, the percentage of justices who are female is between 20 and 25 percent, and the difference across systems is not statistically significant ($p > .05$). We suspect that this discrepancy arises, in part, because Bratton and Spill find that governors are particularly likely to use appointments to place women on the bench when only men are serving on their state high court, a circumstance

Figure 5.4 Percentage of Minority State High Court Justices Serving under Different Selection Systems

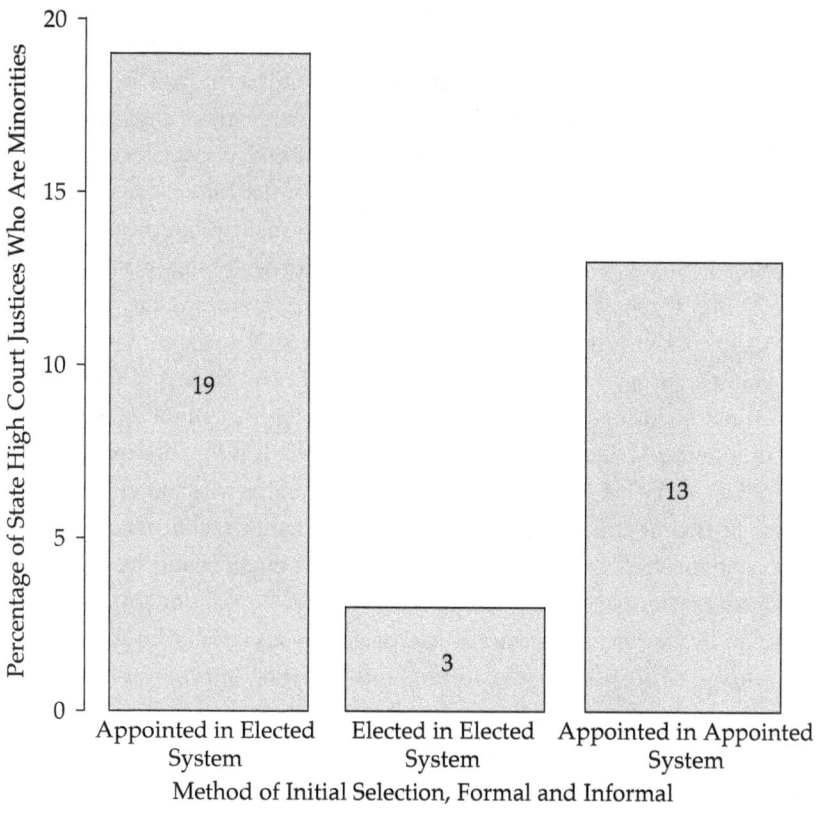

Source: Gibson and Nelson, State High Court Justices Database, 1990–2015.
Notes: N = 981.

that is less common in the (more recent) years covered by our data.[51] We do note, however, that in systems that formally use nonpartisan elections, 30 percent of the justices are women, whereas in states that use partisan elections, only 15 percent of the justices are women. This may reflect the fact, however, that many partisan elections are held in southern states.

We observe a statistically significant ($p < .001$) relationship between judicial selection methods and the racial and ethnic diversity of the bench. Figure 5.4 illustrates this relationship. While the numbers of minority justices are often small (for example, only eight minority justices have been elected in elected systems), it does appear that appointment, in either appointed or elected systems (the difference between these two is not statistically significant), is the most effective means of getting minorities on the state high courts. These findings are in line with a variety of studies that herald the benefits of judicial appointments for enhancing judicial diversity.[52] Importantly, these findings disappear when we analyze a state's formal method of judicial selection. Focusing on the 116 non-White judges in our data, 62 (13 percent) reached the bench in states that formally use judicial appointment, and 54 (11 percent) served in states that formally use judicial elections to staff the bench, a relationship that is not statistically significant.

Moving to the age of the judge at the time of appointment, one might expect governors, given the chance to shape the bench, to appoint judges who are younger, on average, than those who are initially elected. This expectation is not at all supported by the data. The average age of judges elected in election systems is identical to the average age of judges initially appointed to the bench: fifty-three years. We observe no differences whatsoever in the ages of the justices at appointment across any of the various selection systems. In both systems, fairly young people become state supreme court justices.

Finally, we observe no statistically significant relationship between prior military experience and initial selection method. About the same percentage of justices in the formal and informal appointment systems served in the military, but those who were initially elected to the bench were somewhat more likely to have served. This, no doubt, reflects the assumed value of military services in the eyes of the electorate. However, the difference across the three conditions is not statistically significant ($p = .07$).

Initial Selection and Social Class Background

We turn next to the relationship between social class background and methods of judicial selection. Generally speaking, we hypothesize that justices who are appointed to a seat on the state supreme court will hail from more privileged social class backgrounds.

We begin our analysis by examining the relationship between judicial selection methods and our measure of the justices' social class background, using the indicator explained in chapter 4: the total value of a judge's education. We find a large difference among selection systems in this regard. Across the three types of formal and informal selection systems, pure appointment systems are significantly more likely to tap lawyers from a more privileged social class for the bench. Those who initially reach the high court via election are significantly more likely to be from less privileged classes. (Those who are appointed in elected systems have education costs indicating a social class background in between.)[53] The same pattern holds if we limit the data to include only judges in states that use judicial elections as a formal selection method; however, the difference in class backgrounds weakens to the point that it is no longer statistically significant ($p = .09$).

There are also some similar significant differences relating to the quality and location of a judge's undergraduate institution. Of judges who were initially appointed to the bench, 51 percent attended an undergraduate school that required high school graduation plus superior academic achievement, while only 37 percent of elected judges graduated from an undergraduate institution of that caliber. This difference is statistically significant ($p < .001$). Within states that elect their judges, there is no significant difference in the quality of judges' undergraduate schools between those initially appointed and those initially elected to the bench.

We observe a substantial relationship between the location of a judge's undergraduate education and the method of judicial selection. Of those justices in formally elected systems, 67 percent received their undergraduate degree in the same state where they eventually served on the state supreme court. In contrast, of those in formally appointed systems, only 52 percent attended an in-state undergraduate school ($p < .001$). Within states with formal elections, the difference in percentages between those initially elected and those initially appointed are indistinguishable from zero. Elections thus seem to favor "native sons."

Almost exactly the same relationships hold for judges who attended law school in the same state in which they served: 32 percent of judges who were appointed in appointed systems went to an in-state law school. That figure is 15 percent for justices originally appointed in formally elected systems and only 11 percent for justices who were initially elected to the bench.

In addition, the identical pattern describes the effect of law school quality: justices in states with appointed systems are much more likely to have attended a high-quality law school (32 percent) than elected justices (13 percent). Within formally elected systems, however, there is no difference between judges based on whether they were initially elected or appointed to the state supreme court.

Initial Selection and Prior Professional Experiences

We move now to the relationship between methods of judicial selection and judges' prior career experiences. Here the results are mixed. There is some relationship between method of ascension and prior judicial service, with appointed judges more likely to have had prior judicial experience (74 percent versus 68 percent, $p = .04$). A substantial difference exists among justices from systems that formally use judicial elections: those initially appointed to the bench are less likely to have served as a lower court judge (63 percent versus 73 percent, $p = .017$). On the other hand, we find no evidence of career differences between methods of judicial selection and experience in business or prior work as a prosecutor, public defender, law professor, attorney in private practice, or law clerk.

Additionally, experience with the electoral process does not help judges reach the bench through appointment. Only 23 percent of those in formally appointed systems had previous experience in elected office, whereas 51 percent of those in formally elected systems had such experience. Moreover, within formally elected systems, those justices initially appointed to the bench had significantly less experience as public elected officials than justices who got to the state supreme court in the first place via an election (43 percent versus 58 percent).

Initial Selection and Justices' Ideologies and Partisan Attachments

In this final section, we consider whether different selection systems tend to select justices with particular ideologies and partisan attachments. Theories of majority empowerment would suggest that the more the public is involved in the selection process, the more liberal and more Democratic the justices will be.[54]

Using the three-category variable, we find a (barely) statistically significant difference in justices' ideologies across the formal and informal selection processes ($p = .049$). The data reveal that formally elected justices tend to be more *conservative* than appointed justices. The difference in formal selection system may be driven by the fact that many southern states are both conservative and use elections. The difference is statistically significant for all states ($p = .02$), but that difference disappears when we remove the southern states from the analysis ($p = .90$). However, it matters not at all whether a justice in an elected system comes to the bench initially via election or appointment. There is no difference in ideology based on actual method of judicial selection for all states ($p = .31$) and for all nonsouthern states ($p = .53$). As a consequence, when we compare the justices in formally appointed systems with those in formally elected systems, the difference in their ideologies is stronger ($p = .014$), although the correlation is still far from strong ($r = .08$). This relationship is no doubt affected by the fact that the northeastern states, where the justices tend to be more liberal, typically appoint their justices. Still, we do not make much of this finding: the difference between the formally appointed and formally elected justices is a mere .04, a difference of only 18 percent of the standard deviation of that variable. Thus, while there is some statistically significant evidence relating selection method to ideology, the substantive size of the effect is not impressive.

The relationship with the justices' party affiliation is weaker still and does not approach statistical significance. The percentages of Republicans across the three types of selection systems are 46 percent for appointed judges in elected systems, 41 percent for elected judges in elected systems, and 45 percent for appointed judges in appointed systems.

The most important conclusion from this portion of our analysis—a conclusion that is quite relevant to our hypotheses about the role of public opinion in shaping court decisions regarding political, legal, economic, and social inequality—is that more popular involvement in the selection of supreme court justices has little substantive relationship with the typical attitudes of a state high court's justices. While there is some evidence that elections are associated with more conservative justices, the size of that effect is minute. This result strongly contradicts the prediction of majority empowerment theories: not only is the effect size small, but more popular control is associated with *conservative* attitudes rather than, as expected, liberal attitudes.

Conclusions

Perhaps our most unexpected conclusion from this analysis is that informal methods of selecting justices to the state supreme courts—in particular, filling vacancies in elected systems by appointing justices—rarely seems to make much of a difference in the type of justice named to the court. The most significant of the handful of differences we find are with social class background and whether the justice is a minority. But generally, appointed justices differ little from those who come to the bench initially via elections in systems that are nominally elected. This may very well be related to the incentive that the appointing official (typically the governor) may have to name an interim justice who can later win an election.

We do find some sporadic differences between formally elected and appointed systems. Justices who come to the bench via appointment in appointive systems tend to be drawn from more privileged social classes, are trained at higher-quality law schools, and are less likely to have attended in-state undergraduate and law schools. Elected systems seem to place a premium on "homegrown" justices. But overall, perhaps the most striking finding of this chapter is that, contrary to the fears of many judicial reformers, there are no particularly large differences between courts that are formally (or informally) appointed and those whose justices are initially elected.

This finding has important consequences for the theory that we advance throughout this book. Recall that our overriding argument is that state supreme courts are inextricably part of the dominant political coalition in a state at a given point in time. A major goal of the empirical analysis in this chapter was to test a rival explanation: that methods of judicial selection, regardless of the identity of the dominant political regime, have direct effects on the policymaking of state supreme courts by altering the composition of the bench. While we did observe some slight differences across methods of selection, we found many nonrelationships as well. The differences between elected and appointed judges on many background characteristics—particularly those related to prior professional experiences—are indistinguishable from zero. Aside from class, education, and race, elected and appointed judges have broadly similar backgrounds. This too is an important finding. Indeed, the major conclusion of this chapter is that *there appear to be few direct effects of judicial selection method on the composition of the bench*.

This is not to say that the empirical evidence in this chapter does not help us advance our own theory. Indeed, our analysis, consistent with other studies of methods of judicial selection, has emphasized an important way in which political elites are able to co-opt methods of judicial selection to fill the bench with judges they endorse.[55] That so many judges—even in nominally elected systems—are actually appointed means that the opportunity for political elites in a state to shape the composition of the bench is broader than it may initially seem. But is it the case that the composition of the bench does indeed reflect the dominant political coalition in a state at any given time? Answering that question is the focus of the next chapter.

CHAPTER 6

The Capture of State Supreme Courts by State Political Regimes

AT THIS POINT, we have described the cases we study, the judges who decided those cases, and the institutional constraints under which those judges decided those cases. The stage is now set for us to begin to test our theory about the role of state supreme courts with regard to policies relevant to political, legal, economic, and social inequality.

As we noted in chapter 1, our theory suggests that elites seek to adopt and implement their chosen policies.[1] Courts can frustrate this process by ruling policies unconstitutional or interfering with the implementation of the ruling regime's agenda. By contrast, and far from the traditional view of courts as the last bulwark of the underdogs, we hypothesize that courts tend to be part of the dominant political coalition in a state at a given point in time. Because judges have discretion in many cases and tend to vote in ways that match their ideology when they have discretion, elites seek to control the membership of courts, as they do with legislatures and executives. A court whose members have policy preferences that align with the legislature and the governor in a state is likely to produce policies that are acceptable to those legislators and the governor. As a result, our theory suggests that *we should observe a high level of congruence between control of the legislative and executive branches of government and the composition of the bench*. Testing for this connection is the major focus of this chapter.

We begin with a brief theoretical discussion, explaining why we should expect the composition of state supreme courts to mirror that of the traditionally elected branches of state government. We discuss how judicial elections might disrupt the ability of elites to steer the ideological direction of their state high court and how, in practice, the promise of judicial elections to disconnect control of the state supreme court from control of the legislature and the governor's office is unlikely to be met. We embed our expectations about the composition of state supreme courts in a theory introduced long ago by Robert Dahl, who posited that courts are not really independent institutions but rather part of a "governing coalition"—part of the "political regime"—in a state.

A second purpose of this chapter is to introduce our measures of the ideological composition of state governments and state supreme courts, testing formally the degree to which state supreme courts have ideological orientations that mirror those of the legislature and governor. To preview one of our most important conclusions, we find a remarkably high level of congruence between control of the legislative and executive branches of government and the partisanship and ideology of the state supreme court.

Third, we introduce public opinion into the equation. After all, public preferences, which also determine to a considerable degree who is elected as a legislator or governor, may play an important role in shaping the ideological direction of state supreme courts. To this end, we introduce our measures of public opinion and explore the relationship between public opinion and the composition of state supreme courts. We uncover a relationship between public preferences and the ideological composition of the court, although that relationship is slightly weaker than that between elite dominance and the court's preferences.

We conclude the chapter with a formal test of our theory: To what extent does the composition of the state supreme court mirror that of the other branches of government (or public opinion), all else equal? We find that both public opinion and elite dominance of other political institutions have independent statistical and substantive effects on the average ideology and partisanship of a state supreme court in any given year. Moreover, we find that the extent to which elites can control the ideological direction of a state supreme court depends substantially on the methods by which judges are retained. Counterintuitively, however, it is through *elections* that elites' preferences are best represented on a state supreme court. This is true because of what we term "judicial hangover": judges from an earlier coalition continuing to serve when a new regime takes office. Because judges who face reappointment or retention elections tend to have longer tenures than judges who face partisan or nonpartisan elections, courts in states that use the former two retention methods are more likely to be out of step with the preferences of the current legislature and executive than courts that face the two types of elections that have higher rates of defeat. Thus, we once more conclude that the methods by which state supreme court justices are selected and retained have important consequences for political, legal, economic, and social inequality in the U.S. states.

Courts and the Dominant Political Coalition

A traditional view of courts suggests that these institutions stand apart from the legislative and executive branches of government, protecting the rights of less privileged citizens from overreach by society's upperdogs. By this view, courts are strong proponents of equality against upperdogs, who would otherwise seek to encroach on the rights of the less fortunate.

Courts in the United States, by this logic, are able to fulfill this role because of the de facto and de jure independence that they enjoy. Judges are traditionally not impeached when they make rulings that defy the public, they have terms of service that are lengthier than those of governors and legislators, and they often are constitutionally protected against reduced compensation or other types of reprisal. In other words, judges have substantial independence that may enable them to protect the rights of underdogs and, by extension, promote equality from the bench.

But judicial independence does not *necessarily* lead to a greater respect for the rights of underdogs. Rather, it provides judges with the opportunity to enact their policy preferences into law without fear of non-implementation or loss of their job. Indeed, these substantial grants of judicial independence, in practice, might simply make it easier for judges to be effective policymakers—to do, as they see it, "the right thing."[2]

As a result, courts present a potentially dangerous threat to the governing coalition that runs the legislative and executive branches of government. A court with preferences that are not aligned with elites' policy goals could present a substantial hurdle to the enactment of the dominant political coalition's policy goals. Thus, courts with divergent policy preferences may present an existential threat to the ability of traditionally elected branches of government to make the policies their constituents sent them to the capital to enact. In the eyes of these elites, it is important to do what they can to ensure that the state's judiciary does not go astray.

Luckily for these elites, decades of political science research suggest that, contrary to the rosy view of the majestic judiciary, courts tend to be quite "well behaved," rarely presenting much of a real threat to the ability of the legislative and executive branches to enact their policies.[3] Indeed, in the words of Dahl: "The fact is, then, that the policy views dominant on the [U.S. Supreme Court] are never for long out of line with the policy views dominant among the lawmaking majorities of the United States. Consequently it would be most unrealistic to suppose that the Court would, for more than a few years at most, stand against any major alternatives sought by a lawmaking majority."[4] Dahl goes on to explain that "the main task of the Court is to confer legitimacy on the fundamental policies of the successful coalition."[5] Thus, rather than presenting an obstacle to the policies of the dominant political coalition, courts actually serve to *protect and advance the coalition's interests.*

Dahl suggests that judicial selection is the key mechanism that keeps courts and elites on the same page. If policymakers are dissatisfied with a court's policies, they may find their efforts to adjust them frustrated, because judges can serve for decades. Indeed, it is often noted that presidents have a powerful "judicial legacy" through their nominations to the federal judiciary.[6] Presidents' nominations of federal judges, who often serve for a decade or more after they themselves leave office, can be a powerful tool for entrenching their policy views in federal law.[7]

This combination of a partisan selection process (which has increasingly paid close attention to ideology) and life tenure makes it possible for an incoming president to be stymied by a federal judiciary that is composed of a large number of out-partisans.[8] We term this disconnect between a new regime and the judges of an old regime "judicial hangover." Donald Trump, for example, felt this hangover effect with full force when several Barack Obama appointees overturned various immigration policy proposals that he tried to enact in his first years in office.[9]

Yet, while new presidents may experience some judicial hangover in their initial years in office (Franklin D. Roosevelt is another example), their opportunity to make new appointments to the federal judiciary allows them to bring the judiciary in line with their policy views, reducing the hangover they experience. And because presidents are themselves democratically elected, regular presidential appointments to the federal judiciary help to ensure that the courts are never too far out of line with mainline public sentiment (or at least have done so in the past). By Dahl's argument, courts are agents of the current, dominant political alliance because that current political regime has some ability to place its chosen judges on them.

But Dahl was writing about the U.S. Supreme Court! At first glance, it appears that state judiciaries should be harder for the governing coalition to control than the national judiciary because formal elite control over the composition of the bench is weaker in the states than at the federal level. The terms of service typically set for judges on state supreme courts require them to please a retention authority (most often the public) in order to keep their job. And many state supreme court judges sit on courts whose seats are filled through elections rather than by political elites. All of these conditions should combine to keep state supreme courts in line with public sentiment.

Nevertheless, some pieces of evidence we have gathered so far in this book give us good reason to doubt the effectiveness of judicial elections at frustrating the ability of political elites to limit the amount of policy disagreement between the judicial branch and the governing coalition.

For one, consider what we learned in chapter 5 about initial selection. Besides the large number of judges who are formally appointed to their position, *almost half of "elected" state supreme court justices are also initially appointed to their offices.* That a vast majority of state supreme court justices are placed on the bench by elites rather than by the mass public is strong suggestive evidence that state supreme courts may be largely congruent and compatible with the other branches of state government.

Or consider judicial elections. While state supreme court justices regularly face the electorate, the incumbency advantage is strong in judicial elections, and judges who face reappointment (rather than reelection) are nearly always reappointed. As a result, many state supreme court justices serve for long periods of time. This fact amplifies the importance of initial selection, which, again, is typically the prerogative of political elites.

Moreover, as we have argued throughout this book, state supreme court justices do not function in a vacuum. To name just a few factors, the executive and legislative branches of government are involved in selecting the justices of these courts, the political parties nominate candidates for the high bench and help them get elected, state governments do all they can to ensure that state high courts do not upset their policy agendas with their rulings, and some state supreme court justices (albeit not a lot of them) move on to higher partisan and nonpartisan offices when they leave the bench.

This discussion leads to a series of conclusions. First, because these courts have an important policymaking role in state government and enjoy a good deal of practical freedom to rule as they desire, a state's political elites will do what they can to limit the amount of policy divergence between themselves and the judiciary.

Second, because elites play such a strong role in the initial selection, and involuntary removal from office is relatively rare for state supreme court justices, the composition of state supreme courts should mirror the composition of the dominant political coalition in power in a state at a particular period of time.

Third, because involuntary removals are relatively rare, many state supreme court justices serve for a long time. Because elites can influence the composition of the court only when there is a vacancy, their ability to shape the ideology of a court is far from absolute. Instead, these long terms of service may create a hangover effect as court policymaking is increasingly out of step with the preferences of democratically elected governors and legislative majorities, which have had no opportunity to manipulate the ideology of a court through replacement. Absent the opportunity to move a state supreme court's center of gravity, these actors face an uphill battle against a court whose policy views are not aligned with their own.

The Ideological and Partisan Composition of State Supreme Courts

We begin our analysis of the theory of court capture—using the "court-year" as our unit of analysis—by examining the partisan and ideological composition of state supreme courts between 1990 and 2015.[10] To do so, we must know which judges "constituted" the court within any given year. For most court-years, this is unambiguous because no judges left the court and no judges joined the court. But many years did see some turnover.[11]

Because turnover is not rare, we think it is unwise to characterize a court-year by all judges who served in that year—especially since it appears that January 1 of many years is a popular date on which to leave a court. Therefore, we define a court-year by the judges who spent the greatest number of days that year on the bench. We will use "sitting judges" as the term of art for the group of judges that defines the court-year.[12]

Armed with the identities of the judges who constituted each court in each year, we can now examine the partisan and ideological composition of the court over time. We begin by examining the overall temporal trend in the partisanship of state supreme courts, measured as the percentage of sitting judges who were Republicans. Figure 6.1 reports the fifty state averages of the percentage of Republican judges for each of the twenty-six years in our database. Because these averages across the fifty states summarize extreme variability within each year, they are much more stable than the individual state figures.

Nevertheless, figure 6.1 reveals a clear trend: the slow but steady increase of Republican dominance on the state supreme courts, from about one-third Republican in the early part of the time series to about one-half Republican in the later parts of the time series. This Democratic decline (Republican ascendancy) does not necessarily characterize each of the individual states, but the state high courts as a whole became much more evenly divided between Democratic and Republican judges over this twenty-six-year period.

We can also examine change in the ideological character of the fifty state supreme courts over time. Figure 6.2 reports the average conservatism scores for each of the twenty-six years. It is worth recalling that the individual-justice ideology scores vary from about −1.60 to +1.90.

As with partisanship, the state supreme courts as a whole have become considerably more conservative over time. In the early part of the time series, the courts tilt toward being liberal. At the end of the time series this tilt has righted itself. The ideology scores are relative, not absolute scores, so zero has no inherent or substantive meaning, but in light of our finding of a roughly fifty-fifty split on partisanship, we might reasonably conclude that the state supreme courts, as a whole, have become at least somewhat more ideologically balanced in more recent times.

Our analysis of change within individual states reveals a great deal of variability across the states. States such as Maryland, New Mexico, and

Figure 6.1 Average Partisan Makeup of State High Courts, 1990–2015

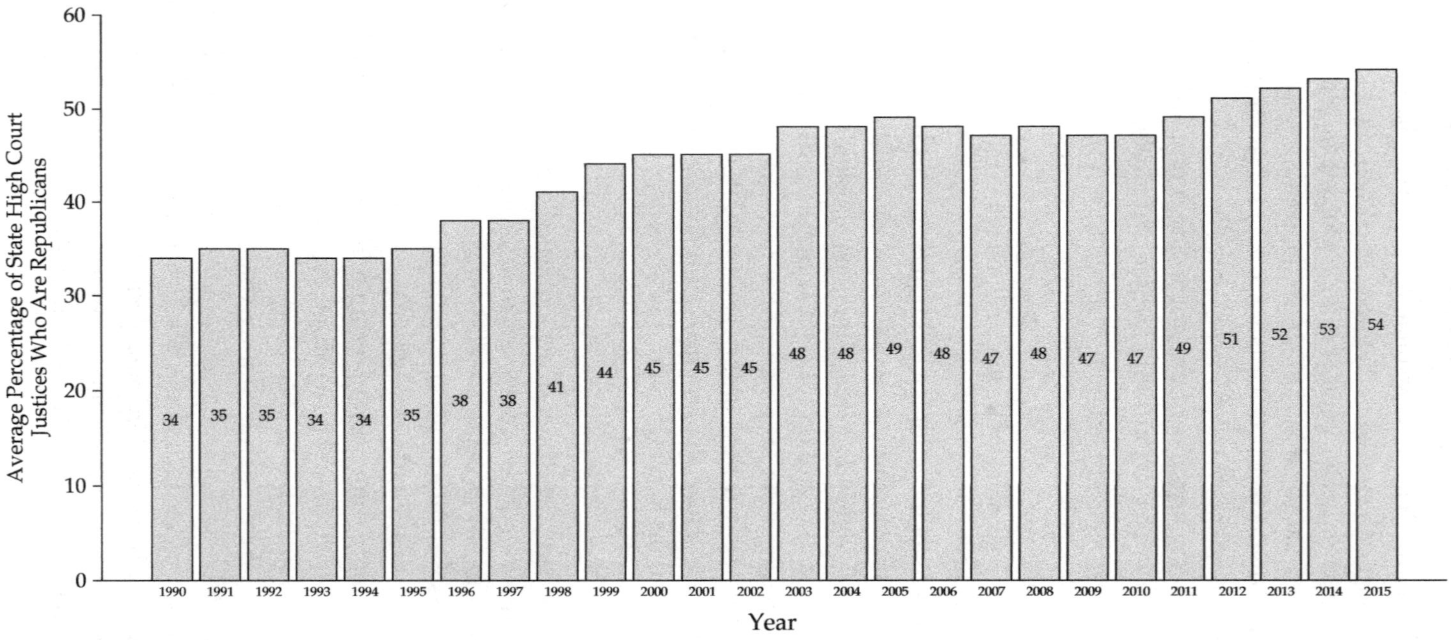

Year	Average Percentage of State High Court Justices Who Are Republicans
1990	34
1991	35
1992	35
1993	34
1994	34
1995	35
1996	38
1997	38
1998	41
1999	44
2000	45
2001	45
2002	45
2003	48
2004	48
2005	49
2006	48
2007	47
2008	48
2009	47
2010	47
2011	49
2012	51
2013	52
2014	53
2015	54

Source: Gibson and Nelson, State High Court Justices Database, 1990–2015.
Notes: Differences in percentages across year: $p < .001$; eta = .22; r = .21.

Figure 6.2 Average Ideological Conservatism Score of State High Courts, 1990–2015

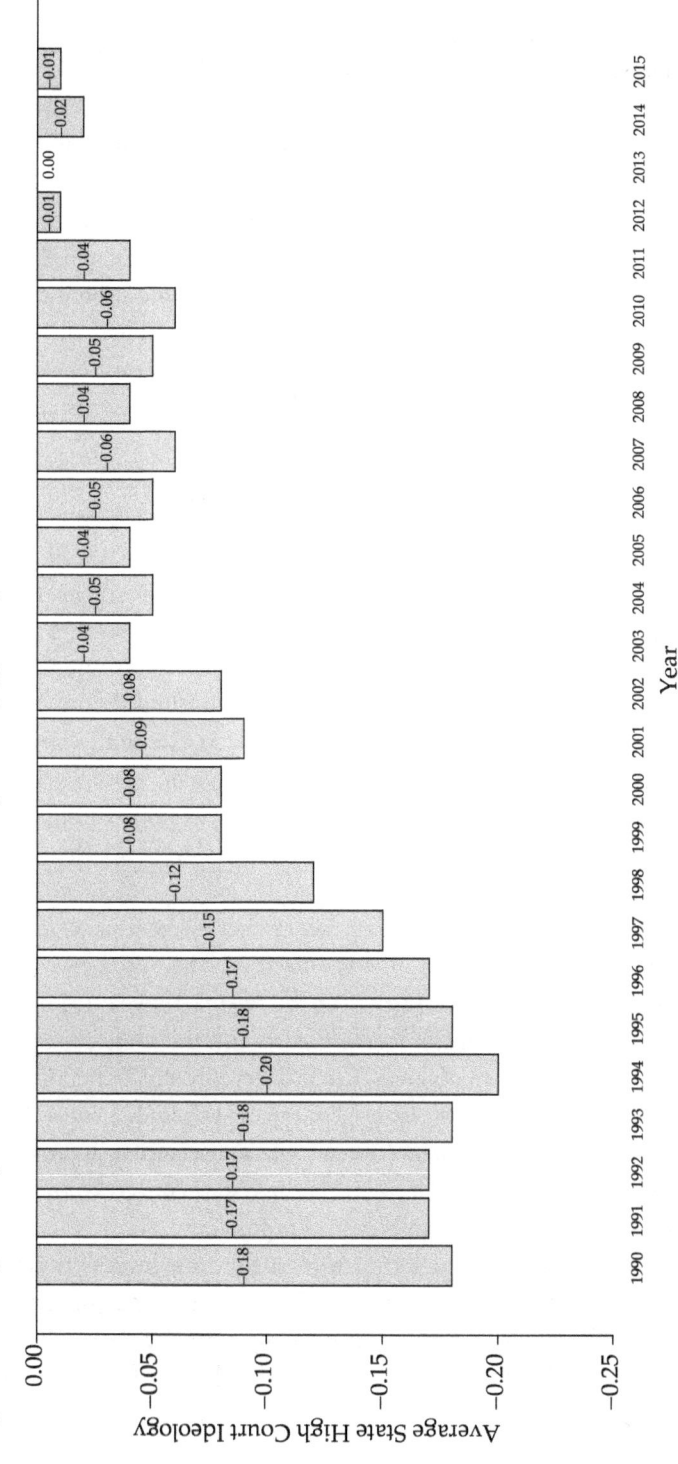

Source: Gibson and Nelson, State High Court Justices Database, 1990–2015; Bonica and Woodruff 2015.
Notes: Differences in average ideology across year: $p < .05$; eta = .13; r = .12. Lower average scores indicate greater judicial liberalism.

South Dakota reveal practically no change at all over time. On the other hand, Alabama changed from a supreme court made up of nearly 100 percent Democratic judges to a court that had no Democrats in 2015! It is almost impossible to imagine how there could be greater variability across the American states.

The last two figures, of course, summarize a great deal of interstate variability. We therefore shift our perspective from the temporal to the geographic to provide a much clearer perspective on how state supreme courts differ. For each court, we calculate the percentage of judges serving on each state supreme court between 1990 and 2015 who were Republicans. Figure 6.3 reports these percentages for each state over the entire twenty-six-year period.[13]

Care must be taken with this figure because it summarizes for each state a lengthy period of time (twenty-six years) during which considerable change was taking place in some states (particularly southern states). But not in Maryland and South Dakota! In Maryland, nearly every state supreme court judge who sat on the court from 1990 to 2015 was a Democrat; at the same time in South Dakota, almost every state supreme court judge was a Republican. Figure 6.3 shows extreme variability across the states, from some states that can be characterized as essentially one-party courts to other states where courts are closely divided between Democratic and Republican judges. Three states—New Jersey, Rhode Island, and Wyoming—had an equal number of Democratic and Republican judges serving during this period.

Figure 6.4 shows the same fifty states, but ranked by the average ideology scores for the justices serving from 1990 to 2015. The figure reveals that the most liberal court in the country over the twenty-six-year time period of this study was the Vermont Supreme Court, and the most conservative court was the Texas Supreme Court. The most evenly divided courts were the Pennsylvania and Georgia Supreme Courts (although they were not necessarily evenly divided between liberals and conservatives in any given year). Again, the conclusion we draw is that these state courts exhibit a huge amount of variability in their ideological composition.

We earlier reported that the correlation at the state level between the percentage of judges who are Republicans and the average conservatism score is .50. In figure 6.5, a scatterplot showing the relationship between the two indicators, higher values of the *x*-axis indicate more Republican

Figure 6.3 Variability in the Partisan Composition of State High Courts, 1990–2015

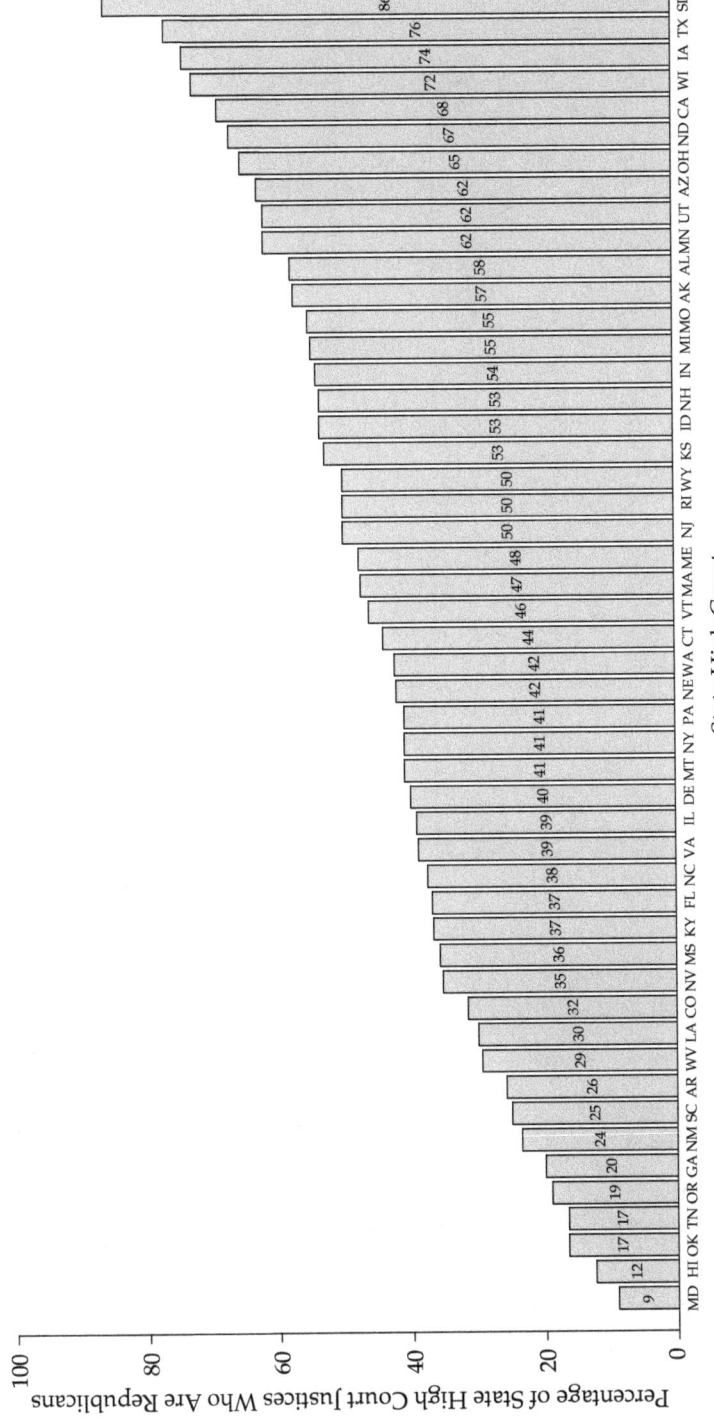

Source: Gibson and Nelson, State High Court Justices Database, 1990–2015.
Notes: Difference of percentages across states: $p < .001$; eta = .35.

Figure 6.4 Variability in the Ideological Composition of State High Courts, 1990–2015

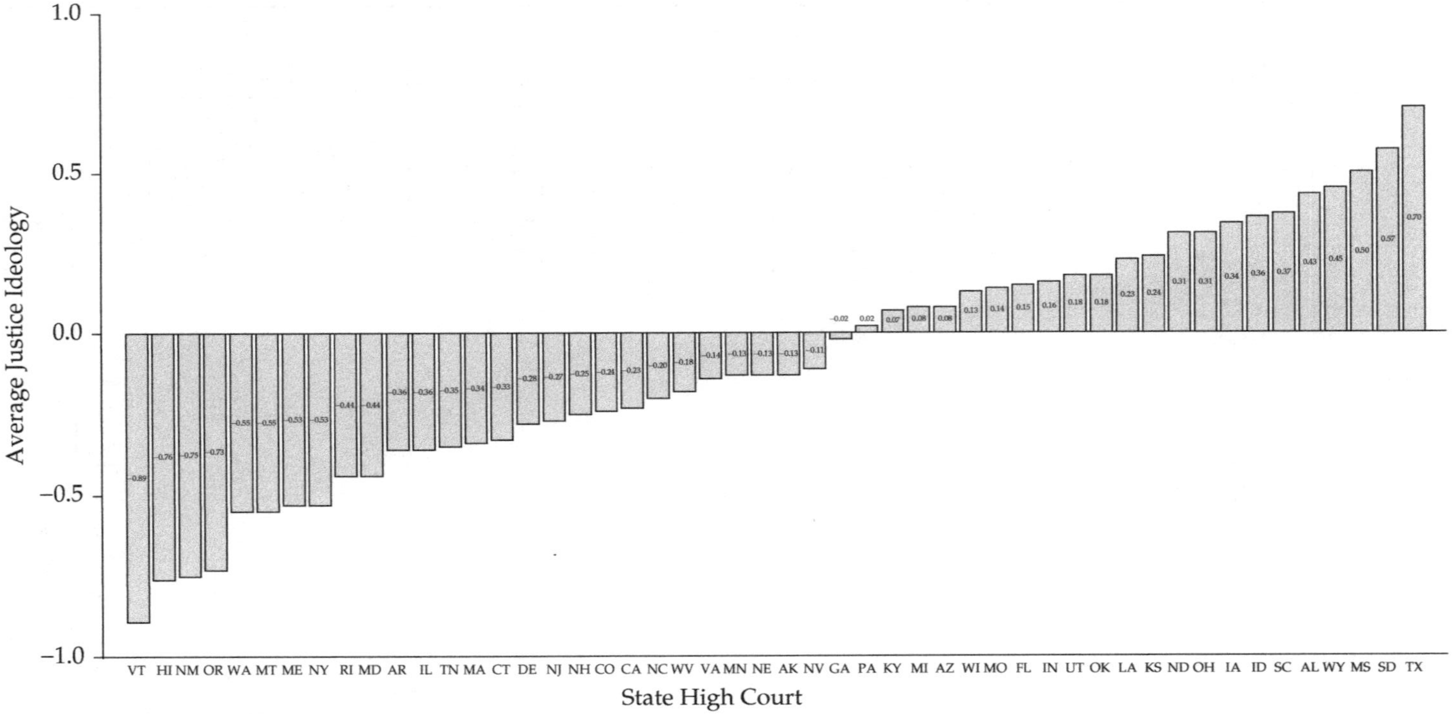

Source: Gibson and Nelson, State High Court Justices Database, 1990–2015; Bonica and Woodruff 2015.
Notes: Higher scores on the ideology index indicate greater conservatism. Ideological conservatism is measured via the Bonica and Woodruff index. This figure is based on averaging conservatism within each state across twenty-six years. $N = 1,300$. Difference of means tests: $p < .001$; eta $= .86$.

Figure 6.5 The Relationship between Partisanship and Ideology on State High Courts, 1990–2015

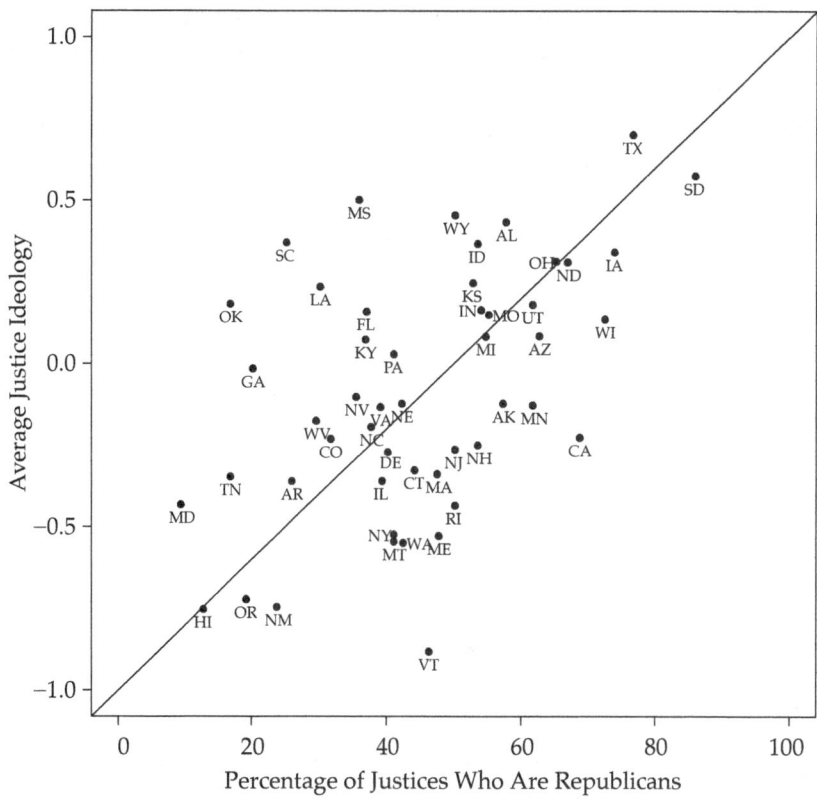

Source: Gibson and Nelson, State High Court Justices Database, 1990–2015; Bonica and Woodruff 2015.
Notes: $N \approx 50$ states. Higher scores on the ideology index indicate greater conservatism. Ideological conservatism is measured via the Bonica and Woodruff index. Pearson correlation = .50.

courts and higher values of the *y*-axis indicate more conservative courts. That the correlation is positive suggests that courts with a higher percentage of Republican justices tend to be more conservative.

While the relationship is fairly strong, we can readily see why it is not stronger. The Vermont Supreme Court, for instance, has been relatively balanced between Democrats and Republicans, but given how liberal the court is, the Republicans themselves must be (and are) fairly liberal. Conversely, the Maryland and Oklahoma Supreme Courts have been mostly

Democratic, but on average the Democratic justices are not as liberal as the justices in other heavily Democratic courts. The Texas and South Dakota Supreme Courts stand out for being heavily dominated by Republican justices who are quite conservative. Generally speaking, courts above the regression line are more conservative than they "ought to be" in light of their partisan composition, and courts below the line are more liberal than indicated by their partisan makeup. Party and ideology are correlated, but far from perfectly.

The Ideological Polarization of State High Courts

We are also interested in the degree to which each of these courts is characterized by ideological polarization. Our measure of polarization indicates the number of Republican judges with an ideology score that is more liberal than the most conservative Democratic judge and the number of Democratic judges with an ideology score that is more conservative than the least conservative Republican.

By this measure, the Alabama Supreme Court scores at the highest level of polarization over the period from 1990 to 2015. The most conservative Democratic judge has an ideological score of .42 (high scores equal more conservatism), and the least conservative Republican judge has a score of .62. Therefore, all fourteen Democrats serving on the Alabama Supreme Court during this period are more liberal than the most liberal Republican, and all nineteen Republican judges are more conservative than the most conservative Democrat. Party almost perfectly aligns with ideology on the Alabama Supreme Court.[14] This pattern of all Democrats being more liberal than the most liberal Republican characterizes fourteen state high courts. In fourteen courts, all Republicans are more conservative than the most conservative Democrat. These are in fact (but not by design) the same fourteen states. For an overall measure of ideological polarization for the state high courts, we take the average of the two polarization scores (for Democrats and for Republicans). Over this time period, the Tennessee Supreme Court was the least polarized of all the state high courts; examples of courts with maximal polarization are Alabama, Indiana, New Hampshire, New Mexico, and West Virginia. Of the fifty state high courts, 54 percent have scores of less than .5 on this measure of polarization, and 46 percent have scores greater than .5.

State-Level Political Regimes: Supreme Courts and the Governing Coalitions

The analyses in the previous section have established a breathtaking amount of variability in the ideological and partisan composition of the nation's state high courts. But our goal in this chapter requires us to go a step further. We must examine whether this variability is tied to another source of change in state politics: partisan control of the state legislative and executive branches. We therefore need to measure the degree of political party dominance over the executive and legislative branches of the state governments so that we can determine whether those branches are successful at serving with like-minded courts and justices.

State-Level Partisan Dominance

State legislative and executive branches, just like state high courts, vary greatly in the degree to which the Republican and Democratic Parties control the legislative and executive branches of government.[15] Beginning with Austin Ranney, scholars of state politics and policy have relied upon the so-called Ranney index to measure Democratic Party strength in the two-party political system within each state at particular points in time. The index averages four indicators: the proportion of seats won by the Democratic Party in the *lower* house of the legislature; the proportion of seats won by the Democratic Party in the *upper* house of the legislature; the percentage of the vote received by the Democratic candidate for governor; and the presence of unified Democratic government in a state over a particular time period (often four years), based on a moving average.[16] This index therefore measures the strength of the Democratic Party in state governments at any given point in time.

We calculated the Ranney index with two minor adjustments. First, following Carl Klarner's recommendations, we adjusted the fourth item in the index to be scored 0 for unified Republican control of state government, 1 for unified Democratic control of state government, and .5 for split control of state government.[17] The traditional calculation of the measure lumps split control of state government and unified Republican control together as a single category, conflating two very different things. Second, using newspaper sources and official records of the Nebraska legislature, we were

Figure 6.6 Change in Democratic Party Dominance in the Fifty States, 1990–2015

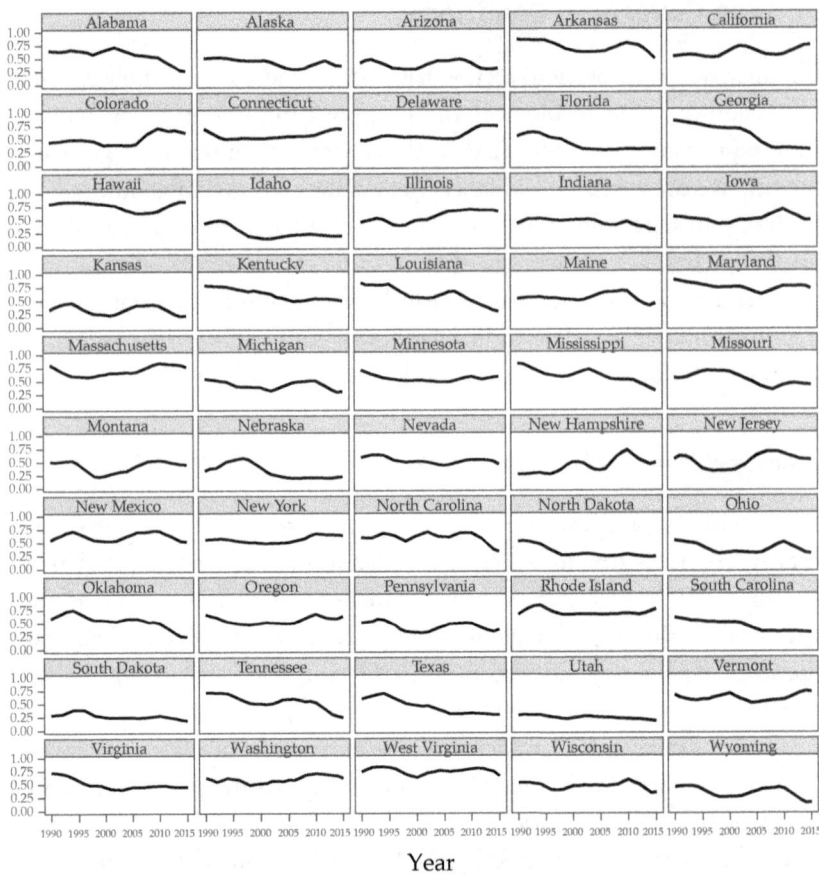

Source: Authors' update of Jordan and Grossman 2020 and Klarner 2013.
Notes: This figure reports the average index of Democratic Party dominance in the state (aka, the Ranney index) across the twenty-six years in our database.

able to compute the partisanship of that state's ostensibly nonpartisan legislature. Because the Nebraska legislature is also unicameral, the values for that state are a moving average of only three indicators (because there is no upper house of the legislature to include in the calculation).

Figure 6.6 shows trends in the Democratic Party dominance measure within each of the fifty states over time. Perhaps the most notable trend in the plots is the stark erosion of Democratic control in southern states. As the graphs for most of the southern states show clearly, the Republican

Party has gained a great deal of ground as the South moved toward strong one-party (Republican) control in recent years. Other states show the opposite trend. California, Colorado, Delaware, and Illinois are all states where Democratic control of state government was stronger in 2015 than in 1990. Still other states have remained relatively stable, although with very different intercepts. Utah was consistently a Republican-dominated state throughout this time period, while partisan control of Minnesota was relatively equally divided between the two parties during this quarter-century.

In sum, the most important conclusion we draw from this discussion is that partisan control of the fifty state governments between 1990 and 2015 was richly varied. While Republicans, on the whole, increased their dominance of state governments during this time period, those gains were neither universal nor synchronous across states. Instead, there are many unique trends in partisan control of state governments across the period.

State Supreme Courts and Partisan "Trifectas"

Having established that partisan control of state supreme courts and the legislative and executive branches of state government was marked by a great deal of variability from 1990 to 2015, we can now begin to shed some empirical light on our theory: Are the state supreme courts majoritarian or minoritarian institutions? Recall that the traditional view in the United States is that courts are minoritarian institutions in the sense of having relatively weak accountability ties to the majority. In our discussion to this point, we have cast suspicion on that view, in part because so many justices are actually appointed to their position by the political branches in the state, and in part because formal accountability in many states is owed to the majority of the voters in the state. Like Robert Dahl before us, we are concerned with the question of whether the state supreme courts stand apart from state governments, perhaps acting as a countermajoritarian balance, or whether, like the federal courts, the judiciary is part of the "governing coalition" in the state.[18]

To address this issue, we have computed three measures for each court-year for each state: whether the same political party controls the governorship and the state supreme court;[19] whether the state supreme court is part of a "branch trifecta," that is, uniform party control of the governorship, the legislature, and the state supreme court; and whether the supreme court

Figure 6.7 Governing Coalitions in the States: Party Control of the Branches of Government, 1990–2015

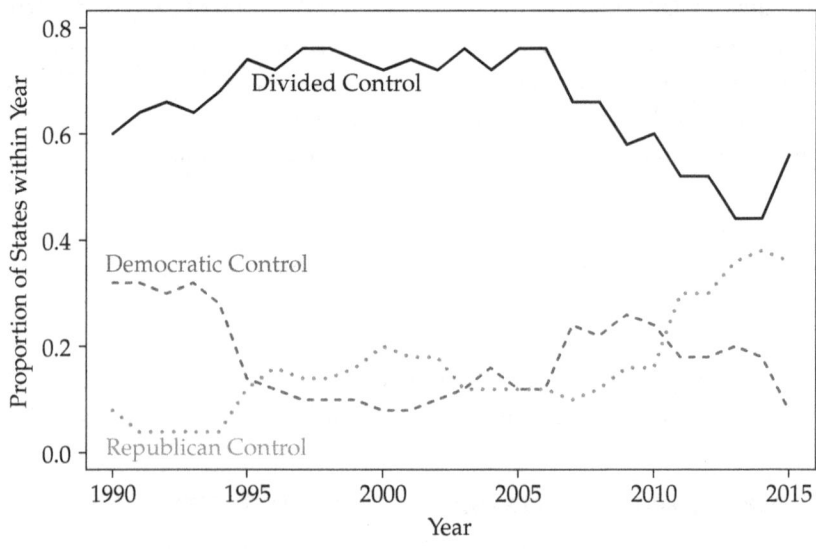

Source: Authors' compilation.
Notes: Within year, N ≈ 50. This figure reports the percentage within the year of states in which the three branches of government (the governor, the legislature, and the state supreme court) are controlled as follows:

> Democratic control: All three branches controlled by the Democrats
> Republican control: All three branches controlled by the Republicans
> Divided control: Split control across the three branches of government.

is the "odd branch out" in the sense that the governorship and the legislature are controlled by the same party, but it is not the party that controls the supreme court. We are able to score each year for each state during the twenty-six-year period.

Consider first the "branch trifecta." Figure 6.7 reports party control of the three branches of government within each year from 1990 to 2015. A party is said to control the branch if 50 percent of its members plus one person are members of the party. (A fifty-fifty split does not equal control of the branch.) This is, of course, a fairly stringent criterion.

In the early part of the time series, divided control of the three branches of state government was reasonably common. From about 1990 to 2005 or so, however, divided control increased significantly, largely as a result of nascent Republican ascendancy and Democratic decline. Then, beginning around 2006, that too changed, with divided control of the three branches of government plummeting to a low of 44 percent in 2013. It is interesting to note that in 1990 Republicans controlled all three branches in just 8 percent of the states (Kansas, Nebraska, New Hampshire, South Dakota), but their dominance climbed to a high of 38 percent by about 2013. Conversely, Democrats controlled all three branches of government in 32 percent of the states in 1990; by 2015, they had complete control in only 8 percent of the states (Delaware, Hawaii, Oregon, and Vermont). Perhaps one of the most interesting figures that can be derived from figure 6.7 is that, in 2015, 44 percent of the states (thirty-six percent Republican plus eight percent Democratic) had a state supreme court that was controlled by the same party as the governorship and the legislature. In 2012 and 2013, less than a majority of the states had divided party control across the three branches. Once more, the stories of this figure tell us about enormous variability across the states and remarkable change over time in Republican successes.

A different, less stringent way to look at these data has to do with whether the supreme court in a state is controlled by a party different from the governorship or a party different from the party that controls the governorship and the state legislature. Both of these measures address the issue of whether the state supreme court can stand as a countermajoritarian check on the state government. The relevant data are reported in figure 6.8.

The data reveal that it is relatively rare for a state supreme court to be controlled by a party different from the party controlling the governorship *and* the state legislature. Across the entire twenty-six-year period, the state supreme court stood alone, on average, in only 14 percent of the states. Relaxing the criterion just a bit so as to compare the supreme court and the governor, the figure of course rises (to 40 percent on average). It is uncommon to find that the governorship and the supreme court were held by different parties in a majority of the states. Usually, the state supreme courts were part of the state political regime.

These analyses point to a very important conclusion: in general, the supreme courts of the American states do not stand apart from the other political institutions in the state. Indeed, on average, the state supreme courts are creatures of the other branches of government. This, we believe, has very important implications for whether these institutions can act independently in cases involving political, legal, economic, and social

Figure 6.8 State High Court Alignment with Other State Political Institutions, 1990–2015

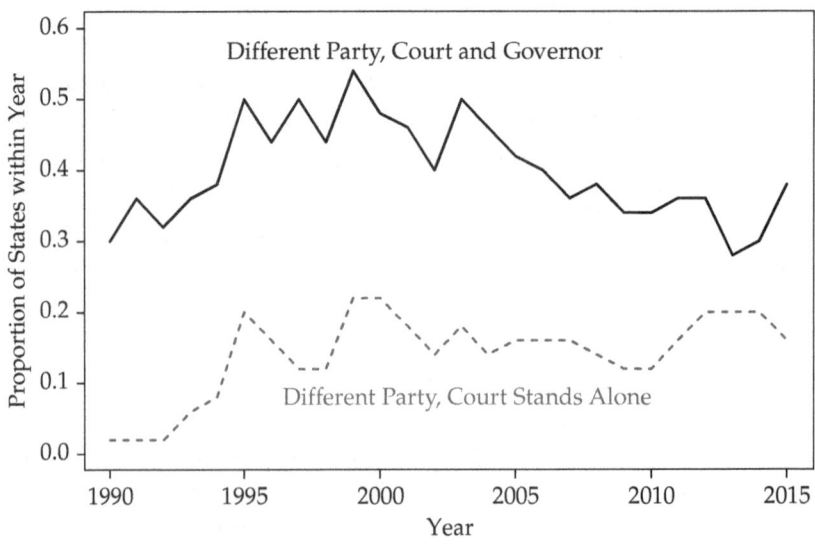

Source: Authors' compilation.
Notes: Within year, $N \approx 50$. This figure reports the proportion of state supreme courts within each of the years from 1990 to 2015 in which (a) the party dominating the state supreme court is different from the party of the state's governor ("Different Party, Court and Governor"), and (b) the party dominating the state supreme is different from the party controlling both the governorship and the state legislature ("Different Party, Court Stands Alone").

inequality. We do not contend that these courts are actively "controlled" by the state governments, but rather, that like-minded judges are put on the state high courts via mechanisms of selection and retention. We will have more to say about hangover judges later, but our most general conclusion is that these high courts are very much a part of the governing coalitions in their states.

The Role of Public Opinion

In addition to the relationship between the composition of the high court and the other branches of government, we suggested at the beginning of this chapter that public opinion may have an important role to play in shaping the composition of high courts. As Dahl suggests, the U.S.

Supreme Court's composition is likely to mirror public sentiment indirectly because political elites (themselves chosen by the people) have the opportunity to regularly place new justices on the bench.[20] And in some U.S. states where voters have the opportunity to select directly the judges they want to place on the bench, public sentiment can directly influence the composition of the bench. These direct and indirect relationships between public opinion and the composition of the court require us to present and defend measures of public sentiment to use in our empirical analyses.

We are fortunate that political scientists have earlier developed measures of relevant state-level public opinion.[21] Here we consider two aspects of public opinion: the public's social and economic liberalism and its attitudes toward equality.

Measuring State-Level Public Opinion

Measuring public opinion within the U.S. states is perhaps best accomplished using a bespoke survey, with a sample large enough to ensure sufficient respondents within each state. Two recent survey projects that use this method, the National Annenberg Election Survey and the Cooperative Congressional Election Study, each obtained responses from more than *fifty thousand* Americans.[22] Such surveys may produce high-quality data, but because they are hugely expensive and require collaboration across many investigators, they are rare. Nor have existing surveys of this design included measures of public opinion regarding political, legal, economic, and social inequality.

Another approach has been to aggregate existing survey data over an extended period of time to build a "mega-poll." This method is used by Robert Erikson, Gerald Wright, and John McIver in their groundbreaking work on macro-public opinion.[23] Similarly, James Gibson disaggregated the nationally-representative surveys to create state-level measures of mass and elite political intolerance.[24] Paul Brace and his colleagues followed suit in using aggregated General Social Survey data to measure nine opinion variables at the state level.[25] Yet even after aggregating twenty-four years of survey data, these researchers found that only forty-one states have samples of one hundred or more.[26] Of even greater concern is that only thirty-eight states featured two or more primary sampling units (PSUs) over this entire time period. Consequently, it is not surprising that, as Jeffrey

Lax and Justin Phillips as well as Julianna Pacheco have shown, estimates produced using this method of aggregation are unreliable in small and very small states.[27]

Faced with these limitations, scholars are increasingly turning to a method of model-based estimation known as multilevel regression with poststratification (MRP). Pioneered by Andrew Gelman and Thomas Little and by David Park, Andrew Gelman, and Joseph Bafumi, MRP utilizes a multilevel model to predict average opinion for thousands of demographic-geographic categories (such as Hispanic, college-educated women who are ages eighteen to twenty-nine and who live in Colorado).[28] These raw opinion estimates are then weighted by the population sizes of each demographic-geographic category and aggregated by state to create a post-stratified estimate of opinion.

MRP has captured the imagination of political scientists. It allows scholars to use existing survey data, even with typically sized samples of around 1,500 respondents, to reliably measure opinion within the states.[29] Some have urged caution, but the method has been validated using a variety of external data, including election results and very large aggregated polls.[30]

Fortunately for us, scholars have produced state-level measures of public opinion that are directly relevant to this project: indicators of social and economic liberalism, developed by Devin Caughey and Christopher Warshaw, and a measure of attitudes toward inequality, produced by William Franko and Christopher Witko.[31] Caughey and Warshaw have developed separate indicators of levels of economic and social public opinion liberalism for each state, over time.[32] Economic liberalism is defined in terms of attitudes toward such issues such as "taxes, social welfare, and labor regulations," whereas social liberalism concerns issues such as "alcohol, abortion, gay rights, women's rights, school prayer, and other cultural (but not racial) issues."[33] Over the course of the period from 1990 to 2015, the correlation of economic and social liberalism is only a minuscule −.02, indicating that these are entirely distinct aspects of public opinion in the American states. (Recall that higher values of each variable indicate more liberal public opinion.)

Like us, Franko and Witko are interested in how the mass publics in each of the states feel about equality, and they have developed a measure that we incorporate into our analysis.[34] They assembled public opinion data from a survey question asking respondents about whether "the rich are getting richer and the poor are getting poorer"—that is, whether the gap between the rich and the poor is growing.

We regard this measure as not ideal but still usable for our purposes. Strictly speaking, the question should be understood as an empirical perception; the rich *are* getting richer and the poor *are* getting poorer; the gap between the two *is* growing. It is not a normative measure of whether the rich *should* get richer and whether the poor *should* get poorer. Some may believe that it is desirable for the rich to get richer and the poor to get poorer. However, we suspect that the vast majority of Americans would attach the following qualification to their responses to the empirical observation: ". . . and it's a bad thing!" While we are careful in our analysis not to claim too unequivocally that this question measures preferences, we strongly suspect that, were a preference measure available, the answers to this empirical question would correlate highly with it. However, we acknowledge that we have no data to support or oppose this presumption.

Using MRP, Franko and Witko provide state-level estimates for forty-eight states (excluding Alaska and Hawaii) for the period 1987 to 2012.[35] Across 1,152 state and year data points, the smallest observed percentage believing that the rich are getting richer is 60 percent; the largest is 84 percent. Across the entire time series, Mississippi is the state in which most people are likely to believe the rich are getting richer (77 percent), and Utah is the state where the average is lowest (69 percent). Thus, in every state, a majority of residents seems to perceive greater inequality. Across time, for all states, there is a fairly strong and somewhat surprising tendency for the percentage of those believing that the gap between the rich and the poor is increasing to *decline*. Of course, this trend varies within individual states.

Using a process of statistical imputation, we were able to estimate public attitudes toward inequality over our entire time period for each state (for details, see appendix 6.A). At the aggregate level, for this period of years and across the fifty states, equality opinion is moderately correlated with economic liberalism ($r = .43$), but not at all with social liberalism.[36] Higher values of economic liberalism correspond to a higher percentage of the population believing that "the rich are getting richer and the poor are getting poorer." For the analysis that follows, we therefore have at our disposal three variables as our measures of public opinion in each state: general social liberalism, general economic liberalism, and beliefs about whether the gap between the rich and the poor is increasing.

Figure 6.9 Change in Public Opinion, 1990–2015

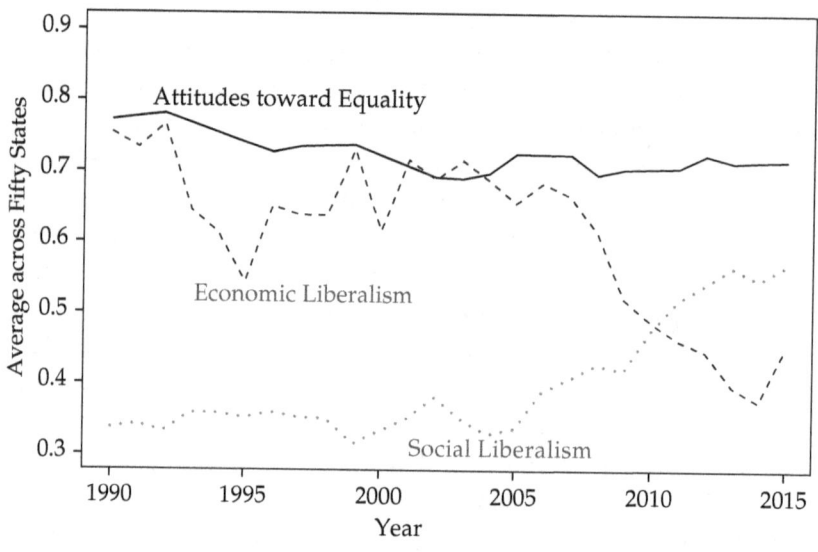

Source: Franko and Witko 2018; Caughey and Warshaw 2018.
Notes: The measure of attitudes toward equality is the proportion of respondents who see the gap between rich and poor as getting larger. The two measures of liberalism are the Caughey and Warshaw measures, scored to range from 0 to 1. The correlations of opinion and the year of the survey ($N = 26$) are: equality: $r = -.73$; social liberalism: $r = .38$; economic liberalism: $r = -.75$.

Figure 6.9 reports the trends in both the ideology and equality measures over time, using averages of the fifty states. One can see in this figure a slight change in attitudes toward equality in the time series, one that levels off from about 2000 onward. The two measures of public opinion liberalism change much more notably, with economic liberalism dropping rather dramatically from about 2005 onward and, contrariwise, social liberalism increasing during the same time period. These opposite trends on the two dimensions of public opinion liberalism go some distance toward explaining why the two measures are not intercorrelated.

The Interconnection of State Supreme Court Ideology and Partisanship with State Public Opinion and Partisan Control of State Government

Having discussed these three measures of public opinion, we now briefly consider the relationships between these variables and our measures of the ideological composition of the court. The correlation between the average ideology of the sitting justices on a state supreme court in a given year and the public's beliefs about equality is −.17; at −.22, the relationship between partisanship and those beliefs is similar. Recall that higher values of the inequality beliefs variable denote more widespread belief among the public that the gap between the rich and the poor is increasing. Higher values of the court composition variables indicate more conservative (or Republican) courts. Thus, the negative relationship suggests that, as the public's belief in a gap between the rich and the poor increases, their state high court tends to be more liberal (or more Democratic).

The relationship between economic liberalism and court composition is similar, with correlations of −.27 for court ideology and −.22 for court partisanship. Recall that higher values of economic liberalism indicate *more liberal* publics. Thus, the negative correlation is the expected one: as the public becomes less liberal, the court tends to be more conservative (and more Republican).

Finally, we observe fairly different relationships between the public's social liberalism and court composition. For the relationship between social liberalism and the ideology of the court, the correlation is the largest in magnitude we observe: −.41. More socially liberal publics tend to get less conservative (more liberal) courts. For partisanship, it is the *smallest*: .05. And note that this correlation is *positive*: more socially liberal publics tend to get more *Republican* courts. Of course, a correlation of .05 indicates that there is practically no relationship between the two concepts. We attribute this initially puzzling correlation to the large variation among the state political parties. Many "liberal" states like California, New Jersey, and Massachusetts had Republican governors during the 1990–2015 period *and* rely on gubernatorial appointments to staff their courts.

We take these correlations, on the whole, to provide some—albeit not particularly strong—evidence that the composition of the court in a particular state at a given point in time does tend to generally trend with public sentiment. However, with one possible exception—the relationship between social liberalism and court ideology—none of these correlations is as large as the relationship between our measure of Democratic dominance of state government (the Ranney index) and court composition: −.43 for partisanship and −.46 for ideology. Indeed, the relationship between court composition and control over the other branches of government is about twice the size of the relationship between the composition of the court and beliefs in inequality or the public's economic liberalism. We therefore draw the conclusion that the court's ideological composition is largely consistent with the public's attitudes, although the relationship is generally not as strong as the relationship between court composition and partisan control of the rest of state government. Indeed, elite control seems to effectively shape the composition of the court.

Of course, a better way to understand the relationship between the composition of the court, public opinion, and partisan dominance of the other branches of government is in a regression equation, which allows us to estimate the effects of each concept holding constant the effects of the other variables.

As we move forward with this analysis (and throughout the rest of the book), we focus on the ideology of the court rather than its partisanship, for two reasons. First, there is such widespread variation in the state political parties that the percentage of justices who are Republican is not particularly comparable across states: a Massachusetts Republican and an Alabama Republican tend to be quite different from one another. The ideology scores, which use donations to bridge across states, are more comparable across states. Second, the partisanship measure simply averages the number of people attached to a political party, which is to say, it averages the sum of a dichotomous variable. The ideology variable, by contrast, has much more variation and thus can describe differences *among* justices that the partisanship measure would treat as homogeneous. Because the ideology measure provides more valid and reliable cross-state comparisons and allows for more internal variation within courts, we use it as the superior measure of judicial attitudes for the remainder of this book.

To this end, table 6.1 reports the results of regressing the average court ideology for each year from 1990 to 2015 on the various contextual variables previously discussed. The predictors we include in the equation are: (1) public beliefs about whether the gap between the rich and the poor is growing; (2) economic opinion liberalism; (3) social opinion liberalism; (4) the degree of Democratic Party dominance in the state; and, as a control variable, (5) whether the state is part of the old Confederacy.[37] In the cases of the public opinion variables, the independent variables have been lagged by one year.

First, as is often the case with these data, a considerable amount of the cross-state and cross-time variance in state supreme court ideology can be

Table 6.1 Predictors of Average State High Court Ideology, 1990–2015

		Court's Ideology		
Predictor Type	Predictor	b	s.e.	r
Public opinion	Public beliefs about inequality	–.01	.04	–.17
	Economic liberalism	–.14***	.04	–.27
	Social liberalism	–.34***	.03	–.41
State-level attributes	Democratic dominance of state government	–.35***	.03	–.46
	Whether Confederate state	.08***	.01	.24
Equation	Intercept	.87***	.03	
	Standard deviation—dependent variable	.20		
	Standard error of estimate	.16		
	R^2	.36***		
	N	1,300		

Source: Authors' compilation.

Notes: All variables are scored to range from 0 to 1. See appendix table 6.B.1 for the distributions of the individual variables. Significance of unstandardized regression coefficients (b): ***$p \leq .001$; **$p \leq .01$; *$p \leq .05$; s.e. = standard error of unstandardized regression coefficient; r = bivariate correlation with court's ideology.

explained by this simple equation. On average, the best predictors of how conservative a supreme court is, at any given point in time, are Democratic Party dominance in the state government and social opinion liberalism: where the Democrats are in control and (not coincidentally) public opinion is more liberal on social issues, the state supreme court tends quite substantially to be markedly less conservative. Economic opinion liberalism is also negatively correlated with supreme court ideological conservatism, but the correlation is much weaker. Whether the public sees the gap between rich and poor growing is unrelated to whether the supreme court is conservative or liberal. Even in the multivariate equation, the legacy of being one of the Confederate states is independently related to supreme court conservatism. The most important general conclusion we draw from this analysis is that both partisan dominance of the legislative and executive branches of government and public opinion play an important role in shaping the ideological makeup of state high courts.

We simplify the findings from this section of our analysis with figure 6.10, which reports the bivariate correlations of the three main concepts: public opinion liberalism (two indicators), the degree of state government dominance by the Democratic Party, and the average ideological conservatism of the state supreme court. Above the lines connected to the public opinion variable, we report the results for public opinion liberalism on social issues;

Figure 6.10 The Relationship between Public Opinion Liberalism, Democratic Party Dominance, and State High Court Ideology

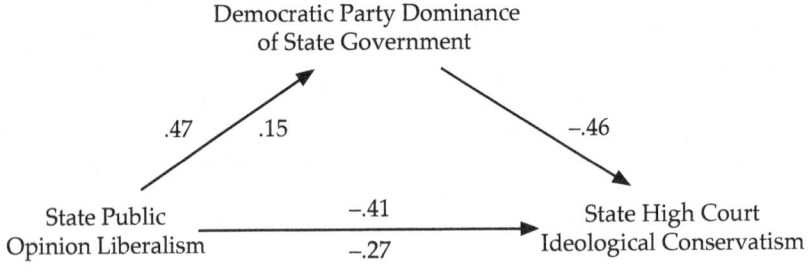

Source: Authors' compilation.
Notes: This figure reports bivariate correlation coefficients, based on 1,300 state-years (fifty states, twenty-six years). Two measures of state public opinion liberalism are used. The coefficients above the lines pertain to liberalism on social issues; the coefficient below the lines pertain to liberalism on economic issues.

the coefficients for liberalism on economic issues are shown below the lines. Since all these variables do indeed vary over time, the most telling unit of analysis is the state-year ($N = 1,300$). Recall that the public opinion and Democratic dominance measures are coded such that higher values correspond to more liberalism; the court ideology measure is coded such that higher values indicate more conservatism. Thus, we expect (and find) that the former two measures are negatively correlated with the latter measure.

This figure confirms one of the most important findings of our research. The ideological orientation of the state supreme courts is closely related to both public opinion in the state and party control of the state government. A simple story about the relationships in this figure goes as follows. Where the public is more liberal, it is more likely to elect Democrats to the state legislature and a Democratic governor. Where the Democrats exert more control over the state government, the state supreme court is more liberal (and, of course, more Democratic). We take this as evidence that the state supreme courts strongly reflect the political makeup of the states in which they function.

The Role of Judicial Elections

Methods of judicial selection and retention provide the last piece of our puzzle. On the one hand, these institutions threaten the ability of the governing coalition to dominate state supreme courts because, in most states, the public has a direct say in determining whether or not judges remain on the bench. On the other hand, elites appoint most state supreme court justices, and the relative rarity of incumbents being defeated in judicial elections provides justices with a good deal of job security. These factors, in turn, might solidify the ability of elites to control the composition (and by extension, the policymaking) of state high courts.

Some initial evidence on this front comes from the relationship between partisan dominance of state government and the composition of the state high courts. Recall that the overall correlation between these two concepts is quite strong: −.43 for court partisanship and −.46 for court ideology: greater Democratic dominance of the executive and legislative branches of government is associated with less conservative state supreme courts. However, these correlations mask substantial variation among retention methods. For partisanship, the correlations between the two concepts range from −.24 and −.34 for no-election and retention election states, respectively, to −.54 for nonpartisan election states to a strong −.74 for partisan election states. The relationship with court ideology is more muted: −.45 for no-election states, −.46 for retention election states, −.43 for nonpartisan election states, and a slightly stronger −.52 for partisan election states. While the magnitude of these relationships varies, the direction remains constant: courts tend to be most liberal when Democratic dominance of the other branches of government is at its highest.

We examine whether the relationship between elite control of state governments and court ideological composition varies by method of judicial retention in a multivariate setting in table 6.2. This table presents the results of a linear regression mirroring that shown in table 6.1, with the addition of indicator variables for the three judicial election systems (leaving no-election systems as the baseline category) and multiplicative interactions between those variables and the partisan dominance variable. We focus on judicial ideology as the dependent variable for this analysis because it is the harder test, as the correlations in the previous section suggest. We therefore test formally the hypothesis that the relationship between elite dominance and court ideological composition varies across selection methods.

We note at the outset that the addition of the retention method variables and their interactions does not disrupt or diminish the relationships between public opinion, Confederate status, and average court ideology that we observed in table 6.1. It is still the case that more economically liberal publics tend to have more liberal courts, as do more socially

Table 6.2 Predictors of Average State High Court Ideology, by Retention Method, 1990–2015

Predictor Type	Predictor	Court's Ideology b	s.e.
Public opinion	Public beliefs about inequality	–.02	.03
	Economic liberalism	–.14***	.04
	Social liberalism	–.33***	.04
State-level attributes	Democratic dominance of state government	–.22***	.05
	Partisan elections	.28***	.04
	Nonpartisan elections	.10*	.04
	Retention elections	.07	.04
	Democratic dominance of state government × partisan elections	–.30***	.08
	Democratic dominance of state government × nonpartisan elections	–.17**	.07
	Democratic dominance of state government × retention elections	–.09	.06
	Whether Confederate state	.06***	.01
Equation	Intercept	.79***	.05
	R^2	.40	
	N	1,300	

Source: Authors' compilation.

Notes: All variables are scored to range from 0 to 1. Significance of unstandardized regression coefficients (b): ***$p \leq .001$; **$p \leq .01$; *$p \leq .05$. See appendix table 6.B.1 for the distributions of the individual variables; s.e. = standard error of unstandardized regression coefficient.

liberal publics. Moreover, the sizes of these effects remain unchanged: the relationship between social liberalism and average court ideology is still twice as large as the relationship between economic liberalism and the outcome variable.

Additionally, table 6.2 suggests that the effects of Democratic dominance vary across retention regimes. The coefficient on Democratic dominance of state government is statistically significant, as are the coefficients on two of the interaction terms. Because it is a constituent term to an interaction, the coefficient on Democratic dominance represents the effect of that variable when all the election variables take values of zero: a no-election system. That the variable is negative and statistically significant illustrates that, in those states that do not use judicial elections, there is a relationship between Democratic dominance and the average court ideology in a state-

Figure 6.11 The Marginal Effect of Democratic Dominance, by Retention Method

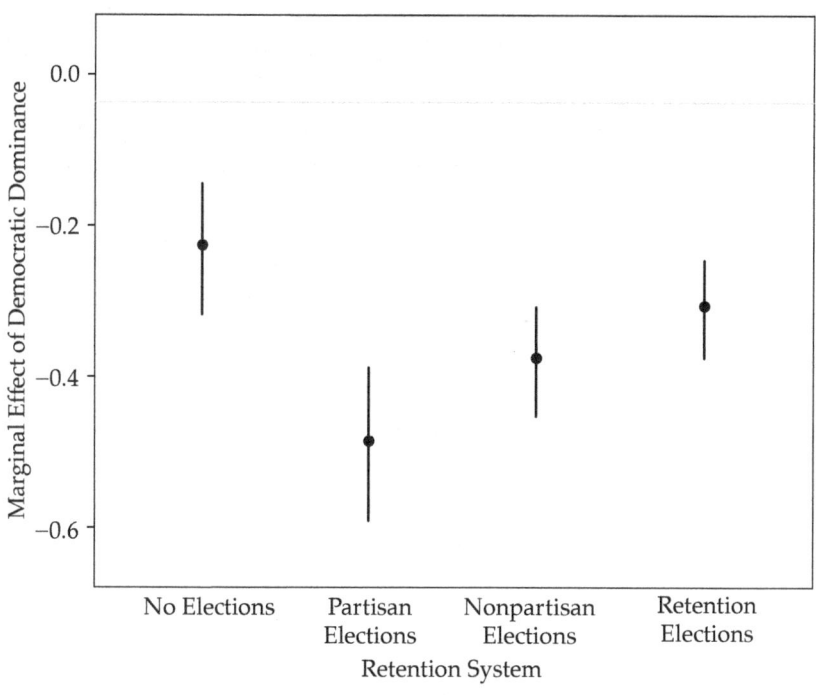

Source: Authors' compilation.
Notes: This figure shows the marginal effect of Democratic dominance of state government on the average ideology of the state supreme court in a given state-year, by retention system. The whiskers provide 95 percent confidence intervals around the estimates. These marginal effects are calculated holding all other independent variables at their mean (for continuous variables) or modal (for categorical variables) values. These estimates are derived from the model in table 6.2.

year: greater Democratic dominance is associated with more liberal state supreme courts.

To understand how this relationship varies across the four methods of judicial retention, we turn to figure 6.11, which plots the marginal effects of Democratic dominance of state government on the average ideology of the court in a particular state-year for each of the four retention systems. Essentially, these estimates are the coefficients on the Democratic dominance variable for each selection method; estimates that are larger in magnitude indicate larger relationships between the two concepts. A negative relationship is the expected one: greater Democratic dominance of the legislative and executive branches of state government should translate into *less* state supreme court conservatism.[38]

And this is exactly the relationship that we observe. For each judicial retention method, the estimate is statistically significant, illustrating a relationship between Democratic Party control of the legislative and executive branches and the ideology of the court. Somewhat surprisingly, however, the two weakest relationships come from the two systems in which nearly all judges are initially appointed to the bench—no-election systems and retention election systems. (Recall that some states that use Missouri plan–style retention elections, like Pennsylvania and Illinois, initially select their judges through partisan elections.) The largest relationship we observe is in partisan election states: there, the congruence between elite control of state government and the ideology of the court is twice as large as the relationship between those two concepts in states that do not use those elections (the baseline category).

This raises a puzzle: If elites dominate judicial selection, especially over initial appointments to state high courts, why is the congruence between control of state governments and state courts smallest in the states that allow elites total control over initial selection and largest in the states in which the mass public has nominal control of who becomes a judge?

Our answer to this question brings us back to the topic of judicial hangover mentioned earlier in the chapter. We say a court is "hungover" to the extent that its composition matches an earlier regime but not the current regime. So, for example, when Republican Sam Brownback took control of the Kansas governorship after a decade of Democratic governors, he faced a hungover judiciary; he would have opportunities to shape the Kansas Supreme Court's composition only when the existing justices on that court lost their retention elections (an event that never occurred) or decided to step down (a decision outside his control). In this way, long tenure lengths can frustrate the ability of elites to shape the composition of state supreme courts.

We see this phenomenon playing out in the state supreme courts. Over the twenty-six-year period under consideration in this book, quite different numbers of justices have served on these courts. The average number of judges is twenty (and the median is nineteen), with a range from twelve judges (in North Dakota and South Carolina) to thirty-four (in Texas—a count that includes only the Texas Supreme Court and excludes the Texas

Criminal Appeals Court). These relatively small numbers reflect the stability of these courts; once individuals join a state supreme court, they tend to stay a long while.

To examine the relationship between tenure length and selection method, we created a measure that is the number of days of service for the judges who were included in our analysis in chapter 4 *and* who had completed their service by December 31, 2015 (because the tenure of many of these judges had not yet concluded at the end of our time period). For judges who served multiple nonconsecutive terms on the bench, we summed together the lengths of their nonconsecutive terms. We divided the resulting number by 365 to create an outcome variable: years of service. This analysis therefore pertains to 784 judges.

We shift our interest slightly for this analysis from judicial *retention* to judicial *selection*. Because we care about the ability of elites to select new justices, we need to know how long judges will serve based on how they are *selected*, not how they are *retained*.

The average length of service in our data set was twelve years, with a substantial standard deviation of seven years. Two judges, Harry L. Carrico (Virginia Supreme Court) and Robert E. Lavender (Oklahoma Supreme Court), *each served over forty years on their court.* Judges who were selected via legislative appointment served sixteen years on average, while judges selected through other types of appointment served, on average, thirteen years. Judges formally selected through partisan and nonpartisan elections served eleven and twelve years on the state supreme court on average, respectively.[39]

Perhaps interestingly, there is little relationship between mandatory retirement rules and the average length of tenure on state supreme courts. Relying on data from the National Center for State Courts and from Elliott Ash and Bentley MacLeod, we coded state-years according to whether they (a) had no formal retirement provision, (b) required judges to retire at age seventy, (c) required judges to retire between ages seventy-one and seventy-four, or (d) required judges to retire at seventy-five.[40] While a one-way ANOVA analysis reveals a statistically significant difference between the four groups ($p = .03$), the relationship is not linear. The average length of service was 11.6 years for judges on courts with no retirement age, 12.6 years for judges forced to retire at seventy, 14.1 years for judges who had to retire in their early seventies, and 13.1 years for judges who had to retire at seventy-five. In no regression controlling for selection method—regardless of the baseline category used—are any of the coefficients for mandatory retirement statistically significant. Rather, there is no evidence that, accounting for method of formal selection, judges who faced more lenient mandatory retirement provisions tended to serve for longer periods of time on their state supreme court.

Thus, the major conclusion of this analysis is that judicial hangover is lessened somewhat in states that use popular elections and increased in states that use judicial appointment. Once judges go on the bench, they tend to serve, on average, a term that is equal to roughly three or more gubernatorial terms.

These results fit well with the accumulated wisdom about judicial elections. Judicial defeat rates are much higher in partisan and nonpartisan elections than in retention elections, and judges who face partisan elections tend to lose those elections at higher rates than judges who face nonpartisan elections.[41] This pattern helps to explain the differences in tenure length across methods of election just cited.

The conclusion here is a simple one: the partisanship of state courts tends to reflect the partisanship of the other branches of government when judges are retained through elections, especially those elections where the ballot looks like the ballot for the legislative and gubernatorial elections. As the distance grows between the public and the method of judicial retention, the congruence between the partisanship of the courts and the partisanship of the executive and legislative branches of state government becomes smaller. In other words, it appears that giving the public an active and meaningful role in the process of judicial retention is one way in which states can keep all of their institutions on the same partisan page. Judicial hangover, it seems, happens when elites have the opportunity to place their preferred judges on the bench and the public has no meaningful opportunity to remove those judges from office. Put simply, it appears that partisan elections are to political elites what ibuprofen is to many college students on a Sunday morning: the easiest way to cure a hangover.

Summary and Concluding Thoughts

From about 1990 onward, many—perhaps most—of the state supreme courts have been the object of an intense partisan and ideological struggle. As always, it is different in the South, and one way in which the South is different concerns the ascendancy of Republican justices and courts. Charles Geyh summarizes it well:

> In the South, a period of intense, two-party competition began with upstart Republicans initiating a pitched battle to end a century of Democratic Party control over state supreme courts—a battle that the Republicans won. Well-financed campaigns waged by the Chamber of Commerce and other business interests to repopulate state supreme courts with business-friendly judges—campaigns that bankrolled the new politics—have, for the most part, succeeded.[42]

No better example can be found than Alabama, a state that flipped over the twenty-six-year period from all conservative Democratic justices on its high court to a court filled with conservative Republican justices. Judicial politics is obviously not immune to the forces of ordinary politics. What Geyh does not say is that similar sorts of battles have taken place outside the South, although the Republicans have not been nearly as successful elsewhere as they have been in the South.

Our analysis focuses on the period from 1990 to 2015, a period, it turns out, of very considerable change in the composition of the state supreme courts. To characterize our most general finding, in the early days of this period Democrats and liberals seemed to have a considerable advantage in the state supreme courts. By the end of the period, partisan and ideological parity had been reached.

At the same time, a great deal of diversity characterizes the state supreme courts. Some courts, such as Hawaii, New Mexico, and Oregon, remain staunchly Democratic and liberal. Other courts, Arkansas, for example, are more ideologically diverse than might be expected on the basis of national politics. Still other courts are almost entirely controlled by Republican conservatives, as in South Dakota and Texas. And some courts are evenly divided between Republicans and Democrats—for example, Indiana, New Jersey, and Wyoming. Even with the Republican gains in the last couple of decades, it is difficult to imagine how the state supreme courts could be more ideologically diverse.

In general, we find that state supreme courts infrequently depart from the ideological preferences of the governing coalition in the state, as illustrated, for instance, by the fact that divided control of the three branches of the state governments is less common today than in the past. The ideological makeup of the state supreme courts is closely connected to the ideological preferences of both the courts' constituents—the people of the state—and the political regime in the state. That these relationships are not stronger is to some degree a function of judicial hangover: judges not leaving a state supreme court for a considerable period of time after they join it. Judicial inertia seems to be an important source of at least some degree of judicial independence, for better or for worse.

Importantly, however, the degree of congruence between the composition of the court and the partisan control of state government is not uniform. Rather, in states that do not elect judges or use Missouri plan–style retention elections, courts are somewhat less congruent with the traditionally elected branches of government than in states that use partisan or nonpartisan elections. This finding points to an important mechanism through which judicial elections might encourage judges to follow public opinion: elections can matter not just because they encourage judges to follow public opinion in their rulings, but also because competitive elections, in which incumbents are relatively more commonly defeated, can lead to increased turnover on a court. As a result, judges whose attitudes are more aligned with public opinion are elected, replacing judges who may be out of step with the public. Where elections are "sleepy" or judges otherwise have longer tenures, courts can become hungover and difficult for elites to control.

Thus, to return to the relationship between courts and equality, we cannot underscore enough that hungover courts are not uniformly "good" or "bad." Rather, hangovers signify nothing more than an entrenched judiciary. On the one hand, hungover judiciaries can slow down the policymaking process and frustrate the ability of a disliked majority coalition to make unfavorable policies with respect to inequality. On the other hand, for those who like the majority coalition in power, swift policy change is an asset and hungover judiciaries are bad. For this reason, there are no direct implications of our results in this chapter about the sort of methods of judicial retention or selection that are the best for those who seek to advance (in)equality in a state.

Rather, our central contention is that courts tend to reflect the views of the dominant coalition in a state. But that congruence is related to some degree to the methods by which judges are selected and retained. Long terms of service and reappointment systems—because they tend to go hand in hand—frustrate the ability of political regimes to tie the ideological composition of the court tightly to their own preferences. On the other hand, because so many "elected" judges are actually appointed to their seats, and because turnover is more frequent in partisan election states, highly visible partisan elections may also, counterintuitively (and also counter to Shugerman's theory), be the best way for elites to ensure that their preferences are reflected on a state high court. After all, the same public that put those elites into office would be the same public casting ballots in the judicial elections; because partisanship is such a strong cue in any type of election—including nonpartisan elections—elites can rest easy that even the judges they do not get to initially appoint are not likely to have preferences too divergent from their own.[43]

What does any of this have to do with equality? To this point in our analysis, we have discussed the cases involving political, legal, economic, and social inequality, the litigants bringing these lawsuits, the judges who hear and decide the cases, and now, the courts and contexts in which the judges sit. In this chapter, we learned that the composition of state supreme courts rarely strays from the makeup of the dominant political coalition in a state. Because this coalition can exert a high level of control over the makeup of the state supreme courts, we expect that the state supreme court's composition, particularly the justices' attitudes, will predict the decisions of individual justices to promote equality while on the bench. In other words, we established in this chapter the first link in a chain: the dominant partisan regime in a state can affect the composition of the court by shaping the court's average ideology. This court capture affects equality policies if, in turn, justices' attitudes predict their behavior in these cases. Testing the second link in that chain—the relationship between attitudes and votes—is the objective of the next chapter of this book.

Appendix 6.A: Imputing State-Level Attitudes toward Inequality

Using MRP, Franko and Witko provide state-level estimates for forty-eight states (excluding Alaska and Hawaii) for the period 1987 to 2012.

For our purposes, we are of course interested in the time period from 1990 through 2015. However, because we typically lag public opinion by minus one year—under the assumption that updates to public opinion are not perceived very rapidly—we focus on the period 1989–2014. Fortunately, the Franko and Witko time series includes the year 1989; unfortunately, their time series ends in 2012.

One approach to filling in missing data would be to simply reproduce the 2012 scores for 2013 and 2014.[44] Doing so, however, would not provide estimates for any time period for Alaska and Hawaii.

Another approach is to find an "instrument" for which data are complete for the entire time series for all fifty states and use that instrument to estimate public opinion where data are missing. It turns out that per capita income is reasonably strongly correlated with public opinion on whether the rich are getting richer, and of course per capita income is available for all states for all years. Confining this analysis to the 1989 through 2012 period (because this is the period for which the public opinion variable is available), we find that a cubic equation using per capita income produces a coefficient of determination of .61, meaning that 37 percent of the variance in observed public opinion across states and time can be accounted for by the equation. Thus, as per capita income increases in a state, support for equality declines (see figure 6.A.1 for a depiction of this relationship). Using this equation, we can fill in the small number of missing data points (although all data points for Alaska and Hawaii are estimated via the equation). Specifically, the measure of public opinion we use consists of the original public opinion score, if it is available, supplemented by the predicted score for the cases (state-years) for which the original public opinion score is not available. The public opinion measures for Alaska and Hawaii are therefore estimated for the entire period and estimates for the other forty-eight states are created for 2013 through 2015. Based on this methodology, there are no missing data on public opinion for the fifty states for the period from 1989 through 2015. However, because our model assumes a one-year lag between public opinion and court decisions, predicted scores are used only in our analysis for the forty-eight states for 2013 and 2014 and for Hawaii and Alaska for the entire time period.

Figure 6.A.2 reports the trends in public attitudes toward equality in each of the states over the period 1990 to 2015. We note that there is little variability across the states in change in attitudes toward inequality: each state reproduces, to at least some degree, the decline in support for equality.

Figure 6.A.1 The Instrument Used to Impute State-Year Public Opinion

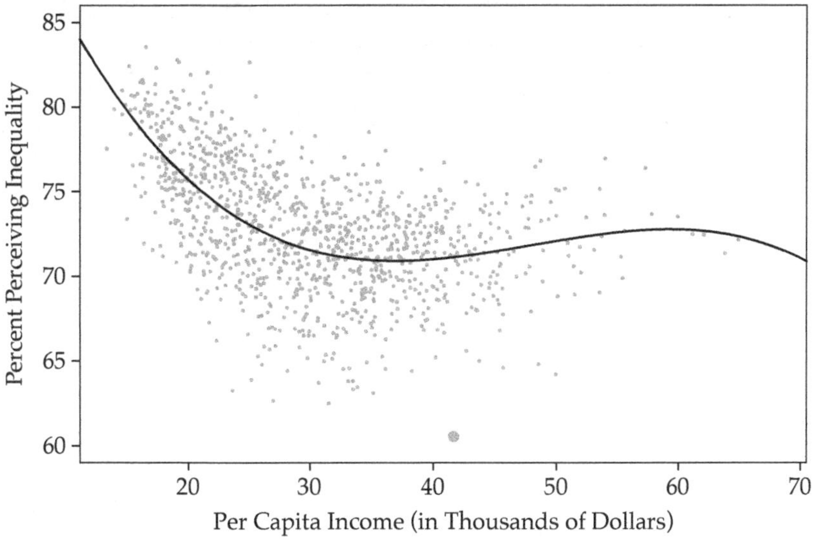

Source: Authors' compilation.
Notes: The dots show the observed relationship between state-level per capita income and the Franko and Witko measure of perceived inequality. Higher values of the measure indicate that a greater proportion of the population believe that "the rich are getting richer and the poor are getting poorer." The line shows the best fit through the data using a cubic equation.

We reiterate that, according to this measure, in every state in every year, a majority of the people see the gap between the rich and the poor as increasing. This is similar to the Canes-Wrone, Clark, and Kelly analysis in which a majority of the people in every state supported the use of the death penalty.[45]

Figure 6.A.2 State Trends in Attitudes toward Equality

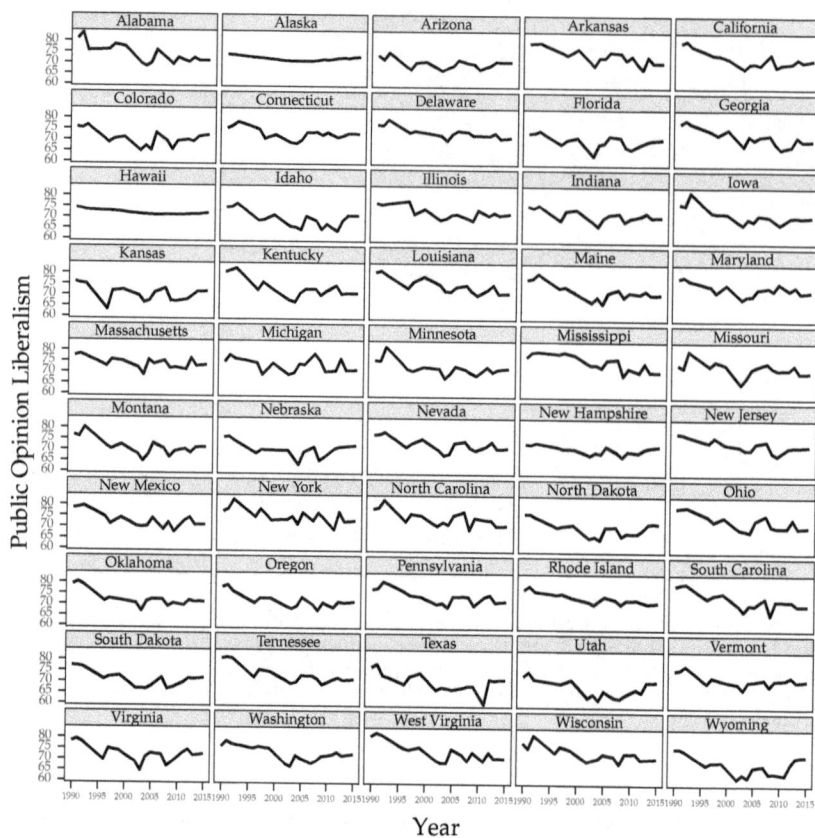

Source: Authors' compilation updating Franko and Witko 2018.
Notes: This figure plots the Franko and Witko measure of inequality beliefs by state over time. Higher values of the measure indicate that a greater proportion of the population believe that "the rich are getting richer and the poor are getting poorer." The smoother trend lines for Alaska and Hawaii reflect the fact that public opinion scores for these two states were imputed.

Appendix 6.B: Supplementary Statistical Analysis

Table 6.B.1 Distributions of Variables in Tables 6.1 and 6.2

	Mean	Standard Deviation	Minimum	Maximum	N
Court's ideology	.49	.20	0	1.00	1,300
Proportion Republican	.44	.29	0	1.00	1,300
Public beliefs about inequality	.54	.15	0	1.00	1,300
Economic liberalism	.62	.15	0	1.00	1,300
Social liberalism	.39	.17	0	1.00	1,300
Democratic dominance of state government	.50	.22	0	1.00	1,300
Whether Confederate state	.22	.41	0	1.00	1,300
Partisan elections	.13	.33	0	1.00	1,300
Nonpartisan elections	.26	.44	0	1.00	1,300
Retention elections	.38	.48	0	1.00	1,300

Source: Authors' compilation.

Table 6.B.2 Pairwise Comparisons: Marginal Effect of Democratic Dominance

	No Election	Partisan Election	Nonpartisan Election	Retention Election
No election				
Partisan election	< .001			
Nonpartisan election	.009	.065		
Retention election	.133	.002	.130	

Source: Authors' compilation.

Notes: The cell entries are *p*-values for a hypothesis test comparing the equality of the marginal effects of Democratic dominance (Ranney index) on the average ideology of a state high court in a given state-year. Small *p*-values indicate that the marginal effect of Democratic dominance (in the model reported in table 6.2) differs across the two retention methods.

CHAPTER 7

Accounting for the Voting Behavior of State Supreme Court Justices on Cases Pertinent to Inequality

OUR PURPOSE IN this chapter is to determine why some justices vote in favor of political, legal, economic, and social inequality and others do not. Although seemingly a relatively simple task, justices' votes (as we suggested in figure 4.1) are in fact a function of myriad factors, from their attitudes and values to the preferences of their constituents to the institutional and cultural context in which they do their jobs.

In this chapter, we add to the formidable literature on decision-making in state supreme courts by linking the data on cases, judges, and states that we have analyzed throughout this book into a rich new data set comprising the votes of individual state supreme court justices on issues relating to inequality. Using this data set, we test a variety of hypotheses about how these factors affect the likelihood that a particular justice will vote to advance equality in a given case.

The theoretical motivation for this chapter harkens back to the theory of political regimes, majoritarianism, and political, legal, economic, and social inequality that we introduced in chapter 1. To reiterate, there are several major elements of this theory.

Privileged upperdogs have long sought to control political institutions to their advantage. Historically, the judiciary was an easy target for these elites; their goal was to empower judicial institutions with theories and powers of minority rights, to insulate them from accountability to the majority, and to encourage them, to the extent possible, to operate in obscurity, with the smallest possible visibility and salience to their constituents.

As the dominance of the Democratic Party in the South began to fray in the 1980s, the national Republicans saw an opportunity to capture state supreme courts that had long been under the control of the Democrats. Just as Shugerman might have predicted (based on his analysis of institutional changes in nineteenth-century courts), one method of breaking elite dominance was to increase accountability to the majority in the state.[1] In the twentieth century, however, institutional reform was not necessary in many states because popular elections for judges, though flaccid, were already in place. Those seeking to break elite dominance assumed that the state supreme courts were out of step with their constituents, and that change could be brought about by raising the salience of judicial elections, thus creating a new congruence between the policies that judges promulgated and the preferences of the people of the state.

It is important to note, however, that greater majority influence on policymakers does not necessarily reduce political, legal, economic, and social inequality. Instead, where there is greater accountability to the majority, *the people's preferences*, whatever they may be, will be better reflected in the policy outputs of judicial institutions. In a given place and time, the majority may or may not favor greater equality.[2] In the 1980s in Alabama and Texas, greater majority influence (at least the majority of the voting public) resulted in more conservative Republican lawyers being elected to the state supreme courts. The Republican strategy largely succeeded in reshaping the state supreme courts in many, but certainly not all, states, and one likely consequence was a rise in pro-inequality votes in the high courts.

Dominant elites (Dahl's "governing coalitions") developed different ways of coping with threats to their dominance. By law, Minnesota elects its state supreme court justices via nonpartisan elections. In practice, as we saw in chapter 5, nearly all justices first join the court via gubernatorial appointments after strategic retirements. This system, we suspect, may be an effort by the governing coalition not to allow the people of Minnesota too much influence over the supreme court.[3] The strategies that elites pursue to maintain their dominance over the state supreme courts vary by state and are a function of both institutional arrangements (for example, the degree of popular accountability of the state supreme court) and the ideological preferences of the mass public in the state. Put simply, governing coalitions must "play the hand they are dealt" in order to gain (and maintain) control of their state supreme court.[4]

Therefore, it is not at all clear to us that efforts to empower the majorities in each of the American states will necessarily help reduce political, legal, economic, and social inequality (as Page and Gilens propose). Instead, a state's policy outputs are contingent upon the ideological predispositions of those who serve as state supreme court justices; the nature of the accountability produced (in other words, to whom and by how much); the methods, both formal and informal, of selecting and retaining justices; and the opinions and preferences of the mass public in the state.

Testing empirically for the effects of these factors is the purpose of this chapter. In general, we consider four types of influences over the votes of justices in political, legal, economic, and social inequality cases: the justices' ideologies and values; the preferences of the courts' constituents; the incentives produced by institutional structures; and some important control variables (including case characteristics). It is to a more detailed consideration of our hypotheses that we now turn.

Ideological Determinants of State Supreme Court Justices' Votes

While it is generally accepted that the justices of the U.S. Supreme Court tend to cast votes that align with their ideologies, those judges work in a unique institutional setting that provides an ideal setting for judges' attitudes to influence judicial behavior. They have life tenure, can aspire to no higher judicial office, are assisted by a large number of clerks, handle a caseload composed of highly technical, "close call" legal questions, and have almost entirely discretionary jurisdiction.[5] By contrast, in lower courts like state supreme courts, whose decisions (on at least some issues) can be reviewed by a higher court and whose justices may aspire to higher office, the relationship between judicial attitudes and judicial behavior is likely to be somewhat attenuated.[6]

Still, there is a good deal of evidence that ideological predispositions affect the decisions of state supreme court justices (although, of necessity, most of this research directly equates judges' ideologies with their party affiliations). For instance, Melinda Gann Hall and Paul Brace find that Democratic justices are less likely to impose the death penalty, although they also conclude that the extent to which judges are able to vote in accordance with their partisanship is tied to the length of their term.[7] Democratic justices who serve on courts with shorter terms are more likely to vote to impose the death penalty.[8] Similarly, Carol Ann Traut and Craig Emmert find that more conservative California justices are less likely to vote to reverse death sentences.[9] Adam Bonica and Michael Woodruff develop measures of judicial ideology based on campaign contributions, and Paul Brace, Laura Langer, and Melinda Gann Hall do the same based on the political climate of a state. Both measures succeed in demonstrating that liberal and conservative judges exhibit different decisional tendencies.[10] As one substantive example, Brace, Hall, and Langer discover that more liberal state supreme court justices are more willing, all else equal, to vote to invalidate restrictive abortion statutes.[11]

Importantly, however, not all studies find such a significant relationship between judicial attitudes and judicial choice. Brace, Hall, and Langer, for example, find no connection between judges' political party affiliations and their propensity to use their power of judicial review in abortion disputes; they argue that "partisan preferences and other personal attributes are relatively unimportant in explaining judicial choices on the abortion issue once variables capturing strategic situations are controlled."[12] In other words, the institutional context in which judges work can overshadow the ability of judges to vote their policy preferences.

Nevertheless, the bulk of the evidence suggests that state high court judges' ideologies play an important role in state supreme court decision-making. Therefore, we hypothesize:

> H_1: *Ideological Voting.* Justices with more conservative ideologies tend to vote in favor of greater political, legal, economic, and social inequality. Conversely, justices with more liberal ideologies tend to vote in favor of greater equality.

An important caveat to this hypothesis, however, is necessary. As we address empirically later in the chapter, most state supreme court decisions are unanimous, reflecting most likely powerful institutional norms that discourage dissents unless they are essential.[13] One consequence is that dissenting votes are cast only when justices feel strongly enough about the issue to act contrary to unanimity norms. Below that threshold, liberals and conservatives may well often vote similarly, which of course will weaken the statistical effect of justices' ideologies on their public votes. So there is certainly more to voting behavior than ideology.

The Influence of Institutional Structures

Beyond the roles played by judicial ideologies, scholars of state judicial behavior have leveraged the unique institutional rules that govern the state high courts to untangle the relationship between institutional characteristics and policy outputs. Institutional structures matter, existing studies suggest, because they direct the attention of judges to particular audiences.[14] These institutions—especially those related to judicial retention—constrain judges' ability to implement their preferences by encouraging them to make decisions that reflect the sentiments of those who will decide whether or not they will be retained as a judge on the state supreme court.

In one of the earliest modern studies of judicial behavior on state supreme courts, Hall combined qualitative and quantitative data on the Louisiana Supreme Court to examine the effects of judicial elections on the behavior of that high court's judges.[15] Hall found that elected judges who perceive their policy preferences on the death penalty to be out of step with the public suppress their dissents in order to appear congruent with public opinion so as to increase their chances of remaining on the bench. In this way, judicial elections constrain judges from voting their preferences and encourage them to vote in accordance with popular opinion.

Or consider the historical analysis of Shugerman, who sought to explain the rise of judicial elections.[16] Shugerman hypothesized that judicial elections were adopted, in part, to encourage judges (who had been appointed by state legislatures) to use their powers of judicial review to pare down legislative excesses. Shugerman found that the adoption of judicial elections had exactly their intended effect: where judges were no longer dependent on the legislature for their continued service on the bench, they were more likely to invalidate statutes passed by that legislature.[17]

Joanna Shepherd shows that the partisan politics of judges' retention constituencies relates to their rulings; when the retention constituency is primarily Republican, judges tend to make more conservative rulings (and vice versa for judges facing a Democratic retention constituency).[18] Moreover, as Michael Kang and Shepherd observe, this effect is particularly strong when parties donate large sums of money to a judge's reelection campaign.[19]

Judicial elections are not unique in their ability to affect the behavior of judges. Reappointments matter as well.[20] Shepherd, examining state supreme court decisions from 1995 to 1998, found that judges facing elite reappointment (rather than popular elections) were particularly likely to vote in favor of government litigants.[21] Thomas Gray comes to a similar conclusion in a study of criminal appeals from 1995 to 2010: judges who face gubernatorial reappointment tend to reflect executive preferences in their decisions more faithfully than those justices who do not face reappointment by the chief executive.[22] Legislative reappointment has similar effects: Gray shows that justices who face legislative reappointment tend to adjust their voting behavior to reflect the preferences of the legislative body responsible for reappointing them to office.[23]

Finally, retention systems matter because they encourage judges to engage in behavior that raises or lowers the salience of their court in an attempt to build their name recognition and assist with their retention efforts. In particular, a large body of literature has explored the extent to which the use of judicial elections is associated with an increase in the amount of dissensus on state supreme courts; elected judges may dissent more than appointed judges as a means of attracting attention that may contribute to their reelection. The conclusion of these studies is reasonably robust: the use of judicial elections is associated with an increase in the amount of dissenting behavior on a state supreme court.[24]

Thus, this large body of literature has taught us that retention institutions matter primarily because they focus judges' attention on their retention constituencies, encouraging ambitious judges who wish to keep their job to pay attention to the views of those who hold the power to keep them in office. To this end, judicial retention methods operate primarily to condition the effects of other factors, like public opinion, on the behavior of state high court justices. As a result, we do not expect that the nature of the retention system, by itself, is associated with different baseline levels of pro-equality voting. Thus:

H_2: *Judicial Retention Systems.* There is no relationship between the judicial retention method and the probability that a judge will cast a pro-equality vote, all else equal.

Put differently, these institutions are important not so much in and of themselves but rather because of their conditional effects: they encourage judges to pay more or less attention to the preferences of particular audiences.

Connecting Courts to Public Opinion

Our discussion of judicial retention systems suggests that public opinion plays a particularly important role in structuring the behavior of state supreme court justices. As we have noted earlier, if ever there were an argument in favor of "American exceptionalism" it would be the highly unusual (but not entirely unique) method by which judges are selected in the United States. Because so many judges and courts are elected, the question of whether public opinion influences judicial policymaking naturally arises (and if so, how it varies based on methods of judicial retention). Systematic inquiries into this question go back decades, with analyses taking many shapes and forms.[25]

The predominant answer to this question has been mixed.[26] Lee Epstein and Andrew Martin summarize the evidence in the title to a systematic review of the relationship between public opinion and judicial decision-making on the U.S. Supreme Court: "Does Public Opinion Influence the Supreme Court? Possibly Yes (but We're Not Sure Why)."[27] Even though justices have no retention constituency they must please in order to keep their position on the nation's high court, the U.S. Supreme Court's outputs tend to be more liberal during periods when the U.S. citizenry is more liberal.[28] The nature of the causal connection, however, is disputed.

Over the past two decades, scholars have turned their attention to the U.S. states, seeking to determine the extent to which public opinion affects the decisions of state supreme court justices, especially on hot-button issues. With regard to abortion policy, Caldarone, Canes-Wrone, and Clark find that the decisions of state supreme courts generally track issue-specific public opinion, although justices elected in nonpartisan elections tend to reflect public sentiment better in their voting behavior than justices elected in partisan elections.[29]

Several of these analyses have focused on what has traditionally been one of the most contentious issues to come before state supreme courts: the death penalty. Paul Brace and Brent Boyea, for example, find that judges who face elections tend to reflect public opinion more faithfully in their death penalty decisions than judges who do not face popular elections.[30] Canes-Wrone, Clark, and Kelly provide the most comprehensive analysis of the relationship between public opinion, judicial retention, and judicial behavior; they find that the extent to which public opinion affects the behavior of state supreme courts is further conditioned by methods of judicial selection and retention.[31] Again, the decisions of judges who run in elections without party labels on the ballot tend to reflect public opinion to a greater extent than judges who face partisan elections.[32] And Hall found some evidence that this public opinion effect is, in fact, reflective of retention methods: when justices are in their "terminal term," the link between public opinion and judicial behavior in death penalty cases is severed.[33]

Some argue that state courts and their decisions are rarely salient and interesting to ordinary people and that these courts therefore operate in near-total obscurity. For example, Canes-Wrone, Clark, and Amy Semet make this claim with respect to environmental policy, demonstrating that public opinion on environmental matters has practically no effect on state supreme court policymaking.[34] When it comes to matters of political, legal, economic, and social inequality, however, at least some of the issues adjudicated most likely have caught the public's attention (for example, gay rights cases).

Additionally, contested (and expensive) partisan and nonpartisan elections tend to attract the greatest amount of voter interest and participation.[35] Missouri-plan retention elections tend to receive less attention from the public, especially in the absence of a concerted effort to oust one or more judges. Not all such elections, however, fly under the radar.[36] Indeed, Canes-Wrone, Clark, and Park write that the pressure to cater to public preferences in retention elections "can be as great as that in contestable elections."[37] In the U.S. states, three examples of public opinion influence on retention-elected courts are often cited: the removal of Chief Justice Rose Bird and her colleagues from the California Supreme Court in 1986 because the justices were irrevocably opposed to the death penalty; the removal of Penny White from the Tennessee Supreme Court in 1996; and the removal of three Iowa judges in 2010 because they found constitutional protection for same-sex marriages in Iowa.[38] In all these instances, the outcome was "blamed" by some on conservative public opinion (as mobilized by interest groups). Still, despite these high-profile examples, judges who face retention elections are *much* less likely to be removed from the bench by the electorate than those state judges who face partisan and nonpartisan elections.[39]

Moreover, many of these studies of public opinion influence on state supreme courts have focused on abortion and the death penalty, two issues that often capture the public's imagination. By contrast, civil decisions do not commonly draw the attention of the mass public (although sensational criminal rulings are often likely to be reported upon and used in television advertisements).[40] Nevertheless, many state supreme court races of late have been big-money contests, with interest groups and candidates running memorable and powerful television advertisements that discuss rulings made by incumbent justices that might otherwise have fallen under the radar.[41] As a result, even those decisions that may initially go unnoticed can present sizable electoral hurdles for incumbent justices.

In short, there is good reason to believe that public opinion influences the decisions made by state supreme court justices. The evidence for this relationship is particularly strong for the sorts of decisions that frequently capture the public's attention, such as the death penalty and abortion. Beyond these super-salient issue domains, there is less evidence of public opinion influence in other types of cases, although it is hard to know whether this lacuna is robust because few studies have examined the relationship between public opinion and state supreme court behavior in issue areas that are less likely to capture the public's imagination. A major contribution of our analysis in this book, then, is to test this proposition on a much larger and more diverse data set than any existing investigation of the relationship between state supreme court justices' behavior and public opinion has done. We hypothesize:

H_3: *Public Opinion.* To the extent that their constituents favor greater equality, state supreme court judges' decisions are more likely to favor equality.

Where the public is more liberal, justices are expected to vote in favor of greater political, legal, economic, and social equality.

Once more, however, this hypothesis is perhaps not as straightforward as it seems, largely because the impact of public opinion should vary as a function of the institutional structure of the state judiciary. Different institutional structures provide different incentives for judges to pay attention to public opinion. Obviously, lifetime appointments (as in Rhode Island) provide no incentive to "pander" to public opinion. Similarly, elite reappointment systems (for example, South Carolina) redirect incentives away from public opinion per se to the opinions of the legislators who represent the public. This leads us to the final hypothesis of our research:

> H_4: *Conditional Effects of Public Opinion.* In light of the variation in the degree to which retention systems encourage judges to tend to public opinion when making their decisions, judges in courts with stronger accountability retention methods (for example, partisan and nonpartisan elections) rely more heavily on public opinion than judges in courts with weaker accountability methods (such as retention elections and reappointment systems).

Data and Methods

Analytical Preliminaries: Unanimity in State Supreme Courts

Before we discuss the research design that we use to test our hypotheses, we first explore an important aspect of state supreme court behavior that is necessary to understand our methodological approach and the issues that we face when testing our hypotheses: most state supreme court decisions are unanimous, limiting precious within-case variability in judicial behavior. This simple fact of the work of the state supreme courts has important implications for our analyses.

We return to our nearly six thousand cases pertinent to various aspects of political, legal, economic, and social inequality to illustrate an important point about the nature of state supreme court decisions: only about 30 percent of our cases involved a dissent; the remainder were unanimous decisions. The percentages of unanimously decided cases do not vary across decades; nor do they vary by issue domain. Perhaps most importantly, 31 percent of the cases favoring equality included dissenting votes, in comparison to 30 percent of the cases not favoring equality.

Across the entire twenty-six-year period, the states do vary considerably, however, in the proportion of these decisions that are unanimous. The rates by state are reported in figure 7.1. In Delaware, forty-five of the forty-eight decisions were unanimous, as were forty-nine out of fifty-two cases in Kansas. On the other hand, only one-third (twenty-four out of seventy-three) of the Michigan Supreme Court's cases were unanimous. Obviously, states with very low dissent rates are states in which neither the justices' ideologies nor

Figure 7.1 Rates of Unanimous Decisions by State High Courts in Equality Cases, 1990–2015

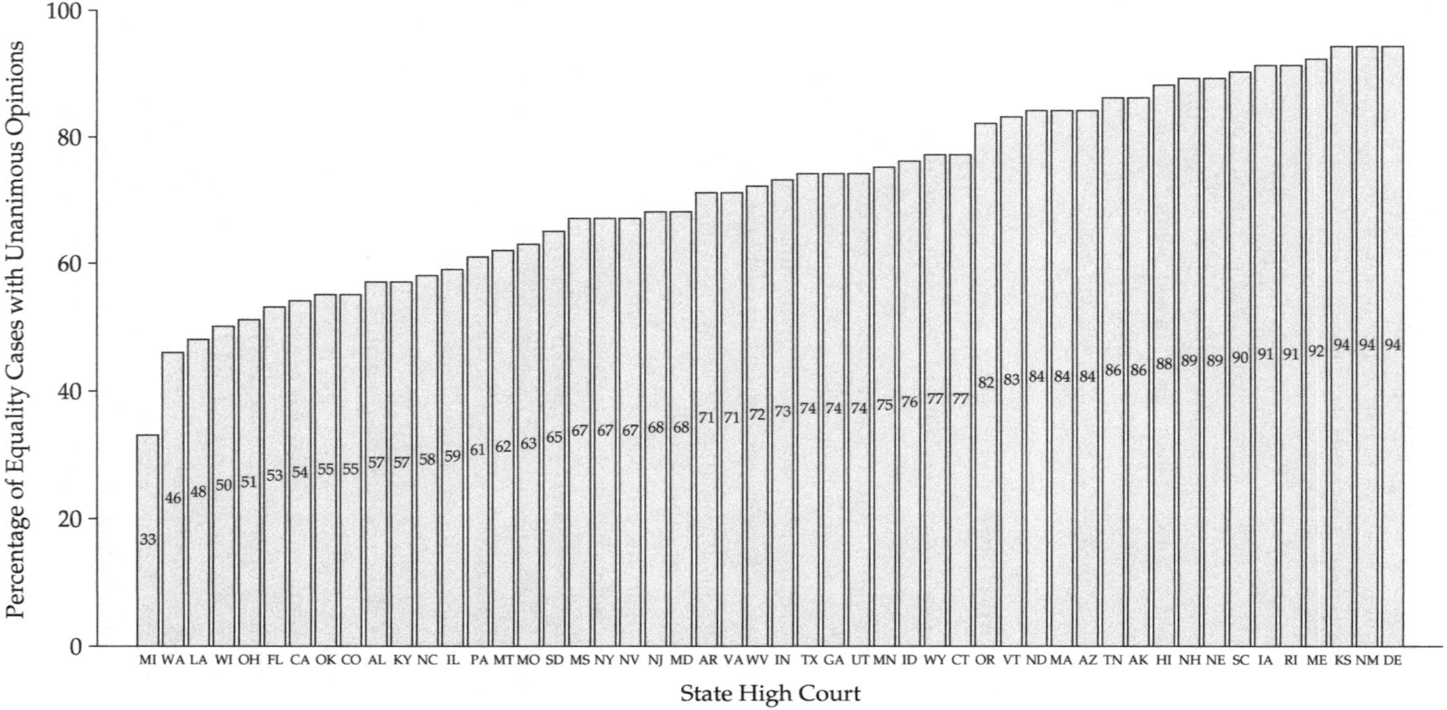

State High Court (left to right): MI 33, WA 46, LA 48, WI 50, OH 51, FL 53, CA 54, OK 55, CO 55, AL 57, KY 57, NC 58, CO 59, PA 61, MT 62, MO 63, IL 65, SD 67, MS 67, NY 68, NV 68, NJ 71, MD 71, AR 72, VA 73, WV 74, IN 74, TX 75, GA 76, UT 77, MN 77, ID 82, WY 83, CT 84, OR 84, VT 86, ND 86, MA 88, AZ 89, TN 90, AK 91, HI 91, NH 92, NE 94, SC 94, IA 94, RI, ME, KS, NM, DE

Percentage of Equality Cases with Unanimous Opinions (y-axis: 0–100)

Source: Gibson and Nelson, State High Court Inequality Database, 1990–2015.
Notes: The bars show the percentage of equality-related cases in the data set that were decided without dissent, by state.

their partisan affiliations (or nearly anything else) have much to do with how they vote: when so many decisions are unanimous, Democrats and Republicans, liberals and conservatives, are voting the same way.[42] Neither ideology nor party matters much (as confirmed in chapter 6), at least for the results that are publicly released by the courts.[43] This must be borne in mind in the analysis that follows.

Research Design

We turn to a final data set to assess our hypotheses. The unit of analysis in this data set is the judge-vote, meaning that the data set contains one observation for each judge's vote in each case. Every case in our data set therefore contains multiple rows, one for each participating judge. This enables us to include variables about cases, judges, and states in a single regression equation.

The outcome variable in the analysis is whether or not the judge casts a vote in favor of equality. For judges who sided with the majority opinion in the case, we coded their votes as following the direction of the majority opinion, using the coding rules outlined in chapter 2. For judges who dissented (in whole or in part), our coders read each dissenting opinion to determine whether, on the equality issue in the case, the dissenting judge(s) agreed with the majority opinion. Of the 36,835 judge-votes in our sample, 47 percent were pro-equality votes and 53 percent were anti-equality.[44]

Modeling Strategy

Because our outcome variable is binary (a vote for or against equality), we employ a logistic regression model with random effects for judges and states. Our modeling approach is similar to one used by Canes-Wrone, Clark, and Kelly.[45] Formally, we estimate the following model for each judge j deciding case i in state s.

$$\begin{aligned} &\Pr(\text{Pro-Equality Vote}_{jis} = 1) \\ &= \Lambda(\beta_0 + \beta_1 \text{ Judge's Ideology}_j \\ &\quad + \beta_2 \text{ Partisan Election}_{jis} \\ &\quad + \beta_3 \text{ Nonpartisan Election}_{jis} \\ &\quad + \beta_4 \text{ Retention Election}_{jis} \\ &\quad + \beta_5 \text{ Public Opinion}_{jis} \\ &\quad + \psi \text{ Controls}_{jis} + \mu_j + \lambda_s) \end{aligned}$$

Λ is the cumulative standard logistic distribution; Ψ is a vector of coefficients; and μ_j and λ_s, respectively, are the judge- and state-specific error terms.[46] We also estimate a second model that includes multiplicative interaction terms between public opinion and each of the retention system dummy variables. The judge- and state-specific error terms in our model allow for the possibility of variances in decisions across states and judges.[47] This partial pooling approach enables the models to include time-invariant state-level controls (such as whether a state was a member of the Confederacy). Moreover, since so few states switched judicial retention methods over the period of time we study, the random effects approach may also be preferable to a fixed effects approach, which would need to rely on rare within-state retention method switches to identify the conditional effects of public opinion and retention method.[48]

Public Opinion in the American States

Our primary measure of public opinion blends the two public opinion estimates provided by Caughey and Warshaw.[49] We focus on the public's economic and social liberalism for several reasons. First, unlike the inequality opinion measure, these indices reflect citizens' general ideological preferences rather than their specific understanding of the character of inequality in a state at a given point in time. It is to citizens' general orientations that we expect justices to respond; therefore, the Caughey and Warshaw measure is a better indicator of public opinion for our purposes. Second, compared to the more ambiguous inequality opinion metric, it is reasonable to expect that the judges know something about the public's general sentiments relating to social and economic liberalism. Moreover, judges are likely to recognize that, in many states, economic and social opinions are far from being the same. As a result, the Caughey and Warshaw measure fits the bill better than the Franko and Witko measure.[50]

Because Caughey and Warshaw separately estimate public sentiment on issues related to social and economic policy, we are able to assign to each case the indicator of public opinion that corresponds to that case's issue area. The two measures of public opinion liberalism map reasonably well onto our case-level issue domains. That is, cases involving gay rights, school finance, and election law (rulings pertaining to the rights of minorities, including poor people) are most relevant to public opinion on social liberalism, whereas rulings pertaining to the rights of workers and employees and pertaining to access to the states' justice institutions are most relevant to public opinion on economic liberalism. Thus, in the analysis that follows, we employ a case-specific blend of public opinion, using social liberalism public opinion for some of the cases and economic liberalism opinion for the others. To reiterate, this strategy is particularly useful inasmuch as the two indicators of public opinion in the states are essentially unrelated to one another; thus, the mass publics in some states might be characterized, for instance, as socially liberal but economically conservative. Higher values of this variable indicate more liberal publics.

Still, while our hypothesis points to an effect of the general ideological preferences of the mass public in the state, we acknowledge that the public's specific view about inequality could also affect judicial behavior. We therefore include the Franko and Witko variable in our analysis as well. We expect that the probability of a pro-equality vote increases as citizens perceive the gap between the rich and the poor to be increasing.

Control Variables: Ceteris Paribus

Note that the equation outlined in the previous section includes a vector of control variables; these are important state-year and case-level variables that we include to account for within-state, over-time variability as well as cross-case variability that might be related to both a judge's propensity to cast a vote in favor of equality and our independent variables of more theoretical interest.

To account for differences across states and over time, we include three variables. First, as we have done routinely throughout this book, we include a variable signifying whether the state was a member of the Confederacy.[51]

Second, on the theory that higher-paying judgeships are more desirable and therefore may make well-paid judges particularly attuned to retention concerns, we control for the associate justices' salary for that court in the year the case was decided.[52] Compared to what they could make in private practice, state supreme court justices receive relatively meager salaries; many interest groups and law professors have argued that increasing judicial salaries is necessary to attract high-quality judges. As one law professor explains: "Comparative salaries are crucial to the recruitment and retention of a high-quality judiciary. When states have allowed judicial salaries to become inadequate, the number of lawyers who will seek judicial positions decreases, and the number of sitting judges who leave the judiciary increases."[53] The median court-year in our data set paid its justices $119,388 a year, although the standard deviation of the variable is quite large at $31,438. Salaries significantly increased over our time period, with the median nearly doubling from $83,440 in 1990 to $161,862 in 2015. The lowest-paid courts in our data were the Montana, South Dakota, and North Dakota supreme courts in 1990; the justices of the Hawaii, Illinois, and California supreme courts in 2015 were the most highly compensated.

Finally, one of the major arguments of this book is that the state supreme courts are typically part of the state's governing coalition (see chapter 6), with the result that the high bench is usually not too out of step with the political party that controls the other organs of state government. When a state leans in a Democratic direction, liberal judges may be unlikely to want to challenge the dominant political regime by issuing rulings contrary to that regime's preferences.[54] We therefore expect a higher probability of a pro-equality vote in states that have a higher level of Democratic Party dominance.

At the level of the individual justice, we include two control variables to account for differences in judges' backgrounds: whether the judge graduated from an in-state undergraduate school, and whether the judge graduated from an in-state law school. As we argued in chapter 4, educational background provides powerful socializing experiences that might affect judges' tendency to support a pro-equality position in a given case. We therefore include these variables in the models as control variables.[55]

We also include a handful of case-level controls. Unlike the U.S. Supreme Court, which tends to use its discretionary jurisdiction to overturn lower court decisions, some state supreme courts do not always have wide discretion to choose their cases.[56] Consequently, the lower court's decision in a case may be a good starting point for an otherwise-ambivalent judge as to how a case should be decided. We therefore control for whether the lower court ruled in favor of equality, expecting that a lower court decision in a pro-equality direction will be associated with a judge-vote in favor of equality.[57]

Harkening back to chapter 3, we also hypothesize that a litigant's resources matter; consequently, we control for whether the more powerful ("upperdog") party sought equality in the litigation, expecting that judges will be more likely to vote in favor of equality when this is the case. We put forth this hypothesis for all the reasons we discussed in chapter 3 (for example, the greater resources and experiences of "repeat players").

Because courts may try to "duck" controversial rulings by using procedural rather than substantive grounds, and because conservative courts often use procedural grounds to stall liberal outcomes, we control for whether the majority or plurality opinion in the case decided the equality issue on procedural grounds.[58] When this is the case, we expect judges to be less inclined to vote in favor of equality. Finally, to account for any remaining cross-issue differences, we include dummy variables for the issue categories.[59]

Empirical Results

Table 7.1 provides the model estimates for our random effects model. The model's performance is modest but not trivial, predicting slightly more than 60 percent of the judge-votes correctly. This is an improvement over a null model that would classify 53 percent of judge-votes accurately simply by assuming that the predicted value of every vote cast is the modal category (a vote against equality).

We begin our analysis of the model's results by considering the role of justices' ideologies. Recall that H_1 suggests that liberal judges are more likely to cast pro-equality votes, all else equal. The model supports this hypothesis. As figure 7.2 shows, the probability of a pro-equality vote across the observed range of judicial ideology decreases from .52 to .34 as we compare the most liberal and the most conservative state supreme court justices.[60] Put slightly differently, there is about a fifty-fifty chance that a very liberal judge will vote in favor of political, legal, economic, and social equality but a one-third chance that a very conservative judge will cast a pro-equality vote, all else equal. As reported in the final column of table 7.1—which shows the change in predicted probability for each variable as it varies from 0 to 1—the justice's ideology is the variable with the largest substantive effect of any of the factors we consider.

Turning to H_2, there is little direct effect of retention methods on the probability that a judge will cast a pro-equality vote. All else equal, the predicted probability of a pro-equality vote is .40 for a judge who does not face the electorate, .40 for a judge who faces partisan elections, .44 for a judge

Table 7.1 Random Effects Logistic Regression Results: Pro-Equality State High Court Votes

	b	s.e.	Marginal Effect
Justice's ideology	−.75***	.08	−.18
Partisan election	.01	.12	.00
Nonpartisan election	.17	.11	.04
Retention election	.22*	.11	.05
Public opinion liberalism	.42***	.09	.10
Public beliefs about inequality	−.04	.11	−.01
In-state undergraduate school	−.05	.04	−.01
In-state law school	.02	.04	.00
Whether Confederate state	.07	.10	.02
Judicial compensation	.37***	.10	.09
Democratic Party dominance of state government	.10	.09	.02
Lower court pro-equality	.26***	.02	.06
Upperdog party sought equality	.34***	.03	.08
Decided on procedural grounds	−.09**	.03	−.02
Rights of workers and employees	−.28***	.04	−.07
Access to justice institutions	−.55***	.04	−.13
Intercept	−.17	.14	
Random effects			
State	.25***	.03	
Judge	.23***	.02	
Log likelihood	−246,189.00		
N	36,835		

Source: Authors' compilation.

Notes: All variables are scored to range from 0 to 1. The excluded category in the regression for the issue domain variable is cases relating to the rights of minorities. For method of retaining judges, it is no election (appointments). The entries reported for the random effects are the standard deviation and standard error of those estimated effects. Significance of unstandardized regression coefficients (b): ***$p \leq .001$; **$p \leq .01$; *$p \leq .05$. See appendix table 7.A.1 for the distributions of the individual variables.

who faces nonpartisan elections, and .45 for a judge who faces a Missouri plan–style retention election. Only one of these coefficients attains statistical significance (the comparison between no elections and Missouri plan–style retention elections), and only one other pairwise difference between the coefficients (between partisan elections and retention elections) reaches statistical significance.[61]

This finding is noteworthy inasmuch as most of the judges who face retention elections, like judges who do not face elections, are initially appointed to their seats, and the judges in these two retention regimes are those who face the lowest de facto probability that their retention attempt

Figure 7.2 Predicted Probability of a State High Court Justice's Pro-Equality Vote, by Judicial Ideology

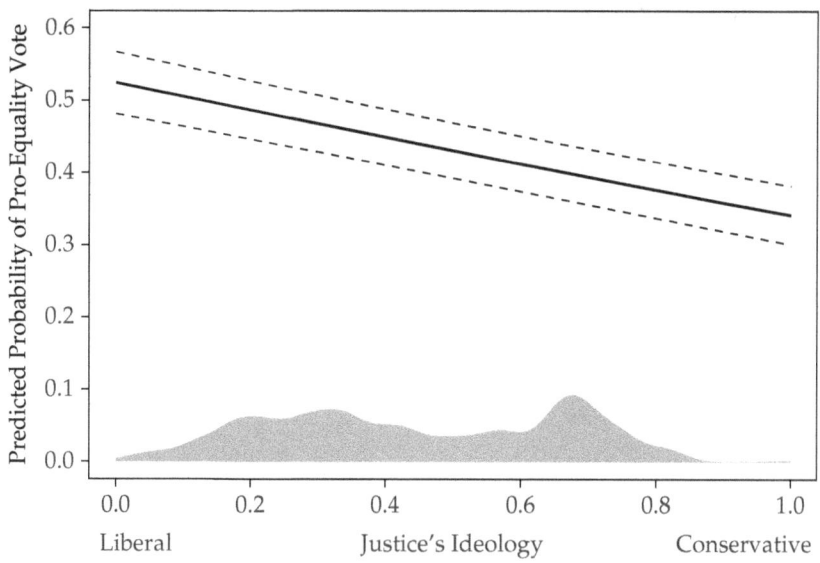

Source: Authors' compilation.
Notes: This figure shows the predicted probability of a pro-equality vote as judicial ideology varies. Higher values of the *x*-axis represent more conservative judicial ideologies. The dotted lines provide a 95 percent confidence interval around the estimated predicted probability. The predicted probabilities are calculated holding all other independent variables at their mean (for continuous variables) or modal values (for categorical variables). These estimates are derived from the model in table 7.1. The "rug" above the *x*-axis shows the frequency distribution of the justice's ideologies.

will be unsuccessful. Instead, it seems that the two groups of judges who face explicitly partisan retention methods are slightly less likely to support equality in their votes than those judges (the retention election judges) who are virtually guaranteed that they will be retained. Still, although these differences among selection systems may be statistically significant, their substantive effects are trivial, in line with our hypothesis. This, of course, does not rule out the possibility that these systems of retention condition the effect of other variables, such as public opinion; we return to that possibility later.

H_3 deals with the direct effect of public opinion, suggesting that judges are more likely to vote in a pro-equality direction in states with more liberal mass publics. As shown in table 7.1, the coefficient for public opinion liberalism

Figure 7.3 Predicted Probability of a State High Court Justice's Pro-Equality Vote, by Public Opinion

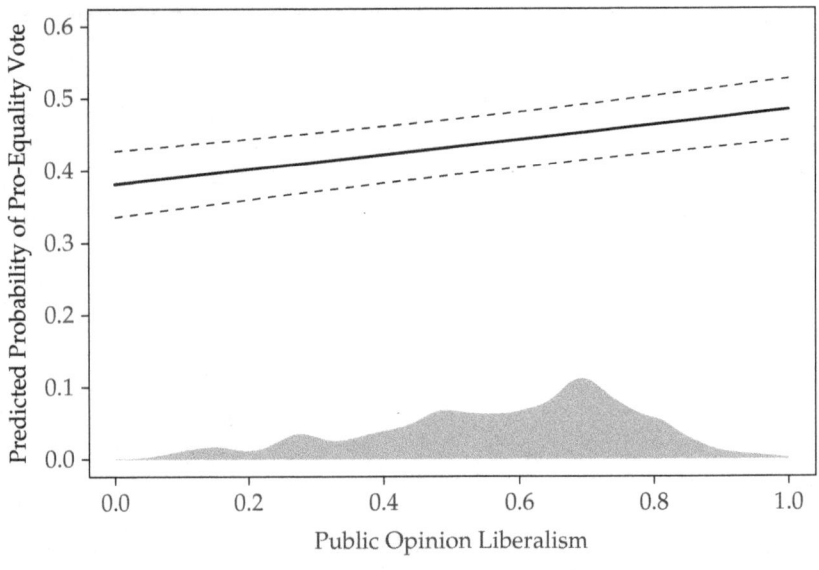

Source: Authors' compilation.
Notes: This figure shows the predicted probability of a state high court justice's pro-equality vote as public opinion liberalism varies. Higher values of the *x*-axis represent more liberal public opinion. The dotted lines provide a 95 percent confidence interval around the estimated predicted probability. The predicted probabilities are calculated holding all other independent variables at their mean (for continuous variables) or modal values (for categorical variables). These estimates are derived from the model in table 7.1. The "rug" above the *x*-axis shows the frequency distribution of public opinion liberalism.

is statistically distinguishable from zero, in line with our hypothesis. Recall that our measure of public opinion liberalism is a mixture of social liberalism for minority rights cases and economic liberalism for both rights of workers and employees and access to justice institution cases.

Figure 7.3 illustrates the substantive effect of this variable. The figure reveals that the probability that a judge will vote in a pro-equality direction increases from .38 when public opinion is at its most conservative value to a .48 probability when a judge is facing the most liberal public found in the data. Like ideology, the effect of public opinion liberalism is one of the strongest relationships we observe. Nevertheless, in line with our earlier findings on justices' ideologies, in even the most liberal public observed, New York in 2004, the probability of a justice in that state voting for greater political, legal, economic, and social equality registers about .50, all else equal. In states where public opinion leans conservative, judges decidedly tend to vote against equality. In states with liberal public opinion, the votes of the judges are a toss-up. We have more to say later about the relationship between ideology and public opinion.

Finally, our most compelling interest in public opinion concerns its conditional relationship with retention methods. Pro-equality judicial outcomes, we hypothesize, require not just that the public support equality, but that the method of reselecting judges provide an avenue for the mass public to have some influence on its judges. To assess this relationship, we estimated a second model that allows the effect of public opinion to vary based on the retention mechanism in use in the state at the time the decision was issued. The results of this model are shown in table 7.2.[62]

We begin by examining the coefficients for public opinion. Because public opinion is interacted with the three retention system dummy variables, the coefficient for public opinion liberalism in table 7.2 represents the effect of public opinion on the probability of a pro-equality vote in a no-election system (the excluded category). That the variable is not statistically significant indicates that the model provides no evidence whatsoever that public opinion liberalism affects judicial behavior in states without judicial elections, a finding consistent with Brace and Boyea's findings on the death penalty.[63]

However, the coefficients on two of the three multiplicative terms do attain statistical significance, meaning that the effect of public opinion liberalism in courts that use those two types of retention systems, partisan election and nonpartisan election systems, differs from no-election states. The easiest way to grasp these differences is to examine the predicted probability of a pro-equality vote as public opinion varies *within* each retention system. Figure 7.4 plots these probabilities.

The virtually flat lines for no-election and retention election systems (the upper-left and lower-right panels) provide visual confirmation of the statistical results just discussed: for these two systems, the probability of a pro-equality vote does not vary at all based on the level of public opinion liberalism in the state. On the other hand, the probability of a pro-equality vote increases with public opinion in both partisan election and nonpartisan election systems. Moreover, as shown by the steeper slope, the effect of public opinion is greater in nonpartisan election systems than in partisan election systems.

Table 7.2 Random Effects Logistic Regression Results: Pro-Equality State High Court Votes, with Conditional Effects for Public Opinion

	b	s.e.	Marginal Effect
Justice's ideology	−.75***	.08	−.18
Partisan election	−.33	.19	−.01
Nonpartisan election	−.35	.18	−.04
Retention election	.14	.19	.04
Public opinion liberalism	−.06	.21	.10
Partisan election × public opinion liberalism	.48*	.23	.10
Nonpartisan election × public opinion liberalism	.87***	.23	.20
Retention election × public opinion liberalism	.01	.25	−.01
Public beliefs about inequality	−.05	.11	−.01
In-state undergraduate school	−.05	.04	−.01
In-state law school	.01	.04	.00
Whether Confederate state	.07	.10	.02
Judicial compensation	.35***	.10	.08
Democratic Party dominance of state government	.10	.09	.04
Lower court pro-equality	.26***	.02	.07
Upperdog party sought equality	.34***	.03	.09
Decided on procedural grounds	−.09**	.03	−.02
Rights of workers and employees	−.27***	.04	−.07
Access to justice institutions	−.54***	.04	−.13
Intercept	.16	.20	
Random effects			
State	.25***	.03	
Judge	.23***	.02	
Log likelihood	−24,605.76		
N	36,835		

Source: Authors' compilation.

Notes: All variables are scored to range from 0 to 1. The excluded category in the regression for the issue domain variable is cases relating to the rights of minorities. For method of retaining judges, it is no election (appointments). The entries reported for the random effects are the standard deviation and the standard error of those estimated effects. Significance of unstandardized regression coefficients (*b*): ***$p \leq .001$; **$p \leq .01$; *$p \leq .05$. See appendix table 7.A.1 for the distributions of the individual variables.

We can get a clearer idea of the effect of public opinion liberalism across retention regimes by examining the size of that variable's influence under each retention regime. We do this by examining the marginal effect of public opinion for each retention method, shown in figure 7.5. As expected, the coefficient for public opinion liberalism is not statistically significant for no-election or retention election systems. However, the effects of public opinion in partisan and nonpartisan election systems are positive and

Figure 7.4 Predicted Probabilities of Pro-Equality Votes by State High Court Justices, by Retention Method

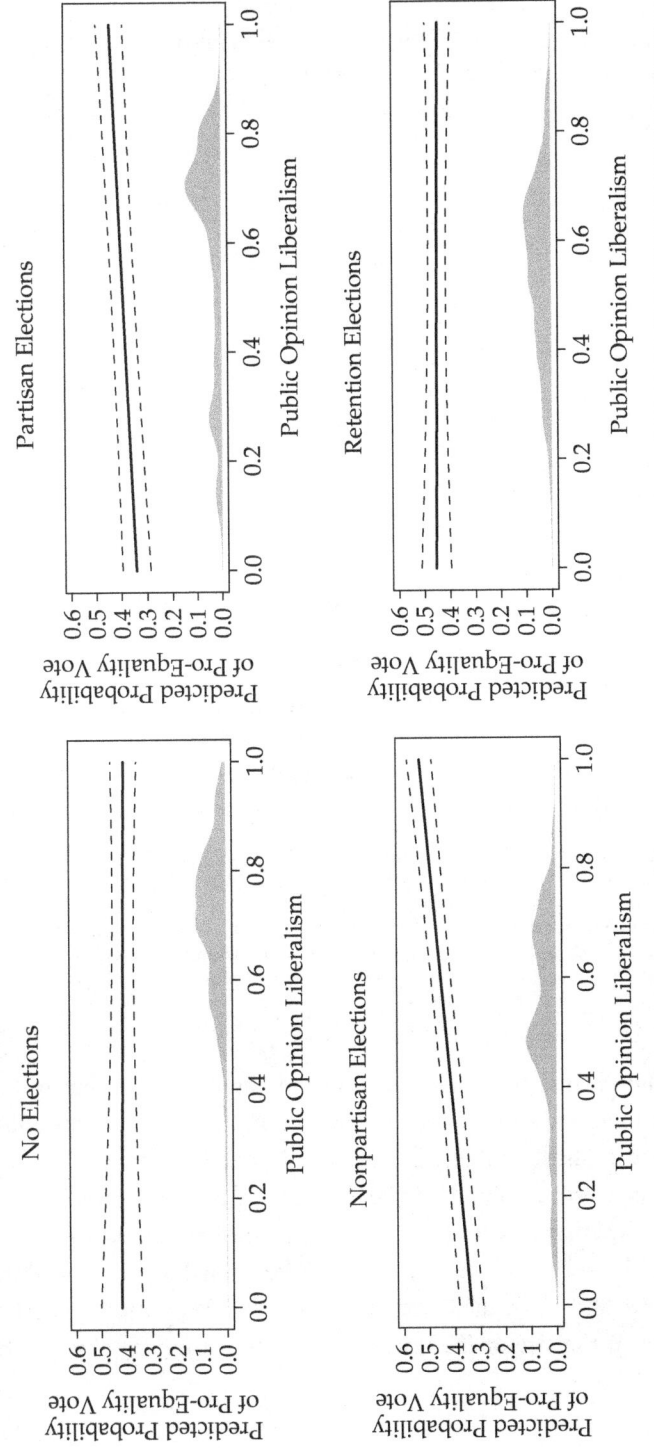

Source: Authors' compilation.
Notes: This figure shows the predicted probability of a pro-equality vote as public opinion liberalism varies, by retention mechanism. Higher values of the x-axis represent more liberal public opinion. The dotted lines provide a 95 percent confidence interval around the estimated predicted probability. The predicted probabilities are calculated holding all other independent variables at their mean (for continuous variables) or modal values (for categorical variables). These estimates are derived from the model in table 7.2. The "rugs" above each x-axis show the frequency distributions of public opinion liberalism.

Figure 7.5 Marginal Effect of Public Opinion on the Probabilities of Pro-Equality Votes by State High Court Justices, by Retention Method

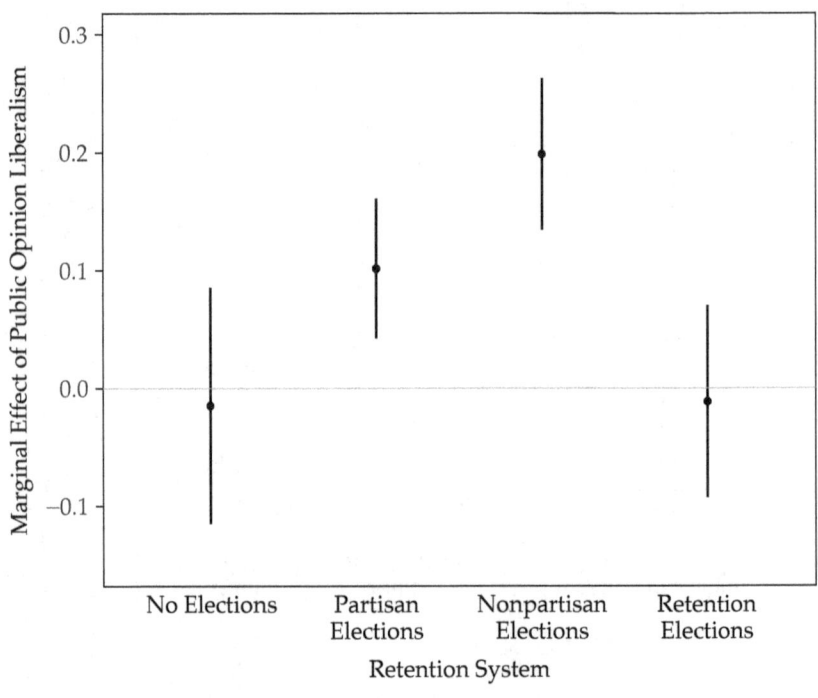

Source: Authors' compilation.
Notes: This figure shows the marginal effect of public opinion on the probability that a state supreme court justice casts a pro-equality vote, by retention system. The whiskers provide 95 percent confidence intervals around the estimates. These marginal effects are calculated holding all other independent variables at their mean (for continuous variables) or modal values (for categorical variables). These estimates are derived from the model in table 7.2.

statistically significant: as the public is more liberal in states that utilize these retention methods, the individual justices on the state supreme court in those states are a little more likely to cast pro-equality votes.

Finally, we can formally compare the influence of public opinion liberalism by testing whether or not the effect of mass opinion in each pairwise combination of retention methods differs. The probabilities from these comparisons are shown in table 7.3; these probabilities indicate whether the differences in the size of the opinion effect between each pair can be attributed to chance.

Table 7.3 The Effect of Public Opinion on the Probability of Pro-Equality Votes by State High Court Justices, by Retention Method

	No Election	Partisan Election	Nonpartisan Election	Retention Election
No election				
Partisan election	.036			
Nonpartisan election	<.001	.012		
Retention election	.956	.012	<.001	

Source: Authors' compilation.

Notes: The cell entries are probabilities for a null hypothesis test comparing the equality of marginal effects for each pair of retention methods. Small probabilities indicate that the effect of public opinion (shown in figures 7.4 and 7.5) differs across the two retention methods.

The major conclusion from this table is that the differences observed in figure 7.5 are nearly all statistically significant (even when the confidence intervals in that figure slightly overlap). Indeed, the two retention methods with statistically indistinguishable differences in the effects of public opinion are states that do not use elections and those that use Missouri plan–style retention elections. The effect of public opinion liberalism is statistically distinguishable in each of the other pairwise combinations of retention methods. Mirroring the pattern we saw in figure 7.4, these tests reveal that the effect of public opinion is somewhat greater in nonpartisan election states than in partisan election states; the difference in the effect of public opinion liberalism between partisan election and nonpartisan election states is statistically significant (p = .012). This finding fits well with previous research, including the results of Caldarone, Canes-Wrone, and Clark and of Canes-Wrone, Clark, and Kelly, and shows that the influence of public opinion is magnified in nonpartisan election settings.[64]

In summary, our analysis of the consequences of public opinion for judges' behavior in cases implicating inequality entitles us to conclude that public opinion *does* have the expected positive effect on judicial behavior, although this effect is relatively small and is only found, as expected, in states that use partisan or nonpartisan elections to retain their state high court judges. Where judges do not face the electorate, or where they face only a minuscule probability of defeat (for example, in Missouri-plan retention elections), there is no evidence of a relationship between the liberalism of the public and the probability that a judge will cast a pro-equality vote.

Finally, we turn to the effects of our control variables.[65] We observe some notable nonrelationships; for instance, there is no evidence that judges in the former Confederacy are more likely, all else equal, to cast anti-equality votes. Similarly, we observe no relationship between Democratic control of state government, as measured through the index of interparty competition, and the probability that a judge will cast a pro-equality vote. Similarly, the model provides no evidence of a linkage between the location of judges' postsecondary education—either undergraduate or law school—and their voting behavior, all else equal. And finally, the model provides no evidence that states in which the public perceives a greater level of inequality between the rich and the poor are states in which judges are any more or less likely to vote in favor of equality.

However, we do observe a relationship between the level of judicial compensation and pro-equality voting. As figure 7.6 shows, judges who are more highly compensated are, all else equal, more likely to cast pro-equality votes. As that variable moves across its range, it has an effect that rivals that of ideology, increasing from a .40 chance of a pro-equality vote by judges on state supreme courts with the lowest salaries to a .50 chance with the most highly paid judges. This effect size is particularly noteworthy when we recall that these estimates come from a model that controls for the effects of judicial ideology and public opinion. It appears that, just as more elite schooling can lead some justices to have more liberal (and, by extension, more pro-equality) policy views (see chapter 4), so too do higher-compensated judges rule more often in favor of equality.

Additionally, case characteristics play a statistically significant role in the model. Judges deciding a case in which the lower court ruled in favor of equality are .06 more likely to cast a pro-equality vote. And the grounds of the decision have a statistically significant relationship with the probability of a pro-equality vote, although the effect size is minuscule. Judges are .02 less likely to cast a pro-equality vote when a decision is made on procedural rather than substantive grounds.

The model also demonstrates some heterogeneity in the probability that a justice will vote in a pro-equality direction based on the issue area under consideration. A justice voting in a case relating to the rights of minorities will cast a pro-equality vote with .58 probability. That probability falls to .51 for cases relating to the rights of workers and employers, and to .44 for cases relating to access to justice institutions. We have no clear theoretical

Figure 7.6 Predicted Probabilities of Pro-Equality Votes by State High Court Justices, by Judicial Compensation

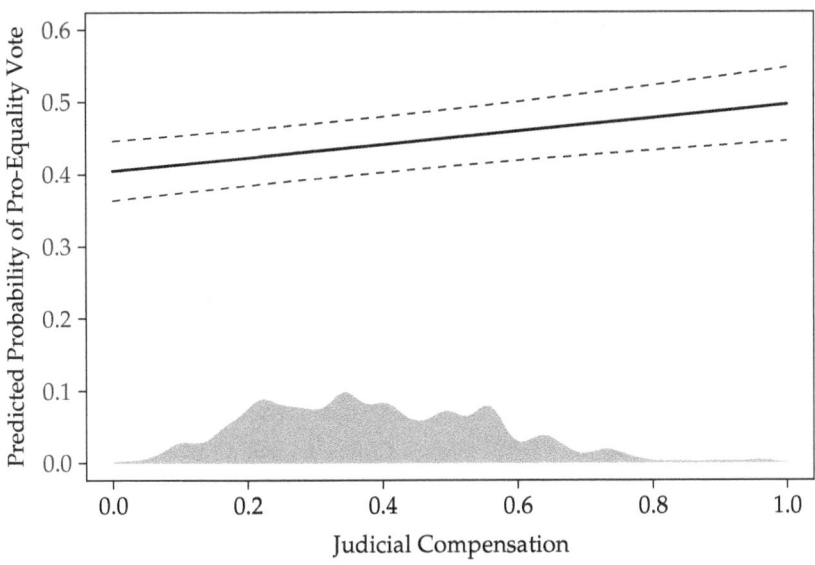

Source: Authors' compilation.
Notes: This figure shows the predicted probabilities of a pro-equality vote as judicial salary varies. Higher values of the *x*-axis represent higher judicial salaries. The dotted lines provide a 95 percent confidence interval around the estimated predicted probability. The predicted probabilities are calculated holding all other independent variables at their mean (for continuous variables) or modal values (for categorical variables). These estimates are derived from the model in table 7.1. The "rug" above the *x*-axis shows the frequency distribution of judicial compensation.

expectation for these cross-issue differences, although they demonstrate that the baseline probability of a pro-equality vote differs substantially across our three broad issue categories.

Finally, returning to a variable we discussed in some detail in chapter 3, the model also provides some evidence that litigants' resources affect the probability that a judge will cast a pro-equality vote. In cases in which the more powerful (the have) party is seeking equality, a state supreme court justice is .08 more likely to cast a pro-equality vote, all else equal. In other words, judges' votes tend to follow the preferences of litigants with more resources. When that upperdog party supports equality, judges tend to vote in favor of equality; when that upperdog supports inequality, so too does the typical state supreme court judge. The size of this effect is about half the size of the ideology effect and is relatively similar in size to the direct effect of public opinion, suggesting that resource inequalities before the court affect the broader policies that courts endorse in substantively meaningful ways. We will have more to say about this relationship in the next chapter.

The Interplay of Judicial Ideology and Public Opinion Liberalism

One major conclusion from this analysis has been that judicial ideology and public opinion liberalism are two factors that have at least some effects on judicial behavior. To this point in our discussion, we have presented the results of our model by isolating each of these concepts of interest. Yet, as we saw in chapter 5, there is a substantial relationship between public opinion and judicial ideology: generally, liberal judges often serve in liberal states. As a result, when we try to understand the circumstances under which a judge is more likely than not to vote in favor of equality, it is helpful to consider predictions while varying *both* of these concepts.

Figure 7.7 reports the predicted probability of a pro-equality vote as judicial ideology varies on the x-axis. The estimates are again drawn from the coefficients reported in table 7.2. The two lines in the figure plot the probability of a pro-equality vote with public opinion liberalism set at its minimum (the darker line) and maximum (the lighter line) values. Again, we hold all other variables at their mean or modal values. Recall that higher values of judicial ideology represent *more conservative* justices and higher values of public opinion represent *more liberal* publics. The figure demonstrates that the probability of a pro-equality vote declines as judicial ideology becomes more conservative. That there is a gap between the two lines illustrates the effect of public opinion: regardless of judicial ideology, judges in more liberal states are more likely to cast pro-equality votes.

Taken together, these two concepts have strong additive effects. A liberal justice in a liberal state is predicted to cast a pro-equality vote with .62 probability—approaching two-thirds of the time!—while that same liberal justice, transported to a very conservative state, will cast a pro-equality vote with only .42 probability. Similarly, were that judge in the highly liberal state to be one of the most conservative justices we observe, the model predicts that the judge will cast a pro-equality vote with only .43 probability.

Figure 7.7 Predicted Probabilities of Pro-Equality Votes by State High Court Justices, by Public Opinion Liberalism and Judicial Ideology

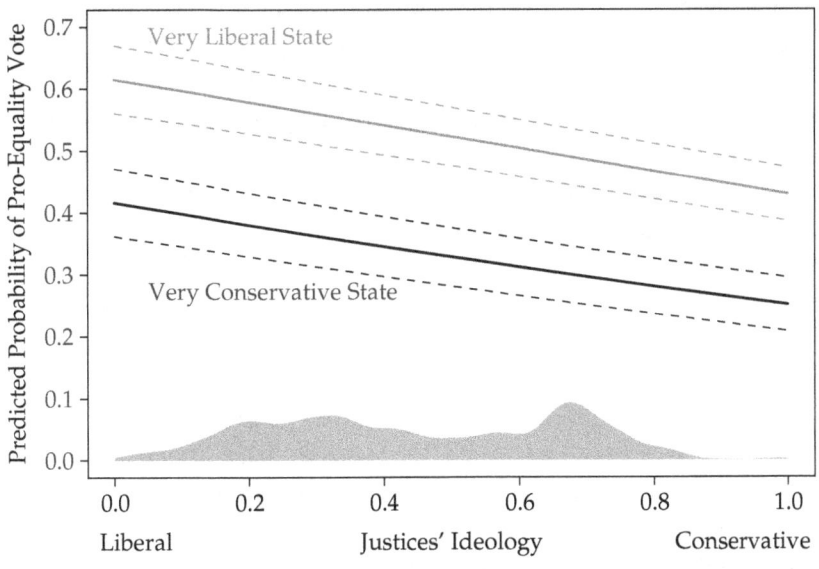

Source: Authors' compilation.
Notes: This figure shows the predicted probabilities of a state supreme court justice's pro-equality vote as judicial ideology varies for minimum and maximum values of public opinion liberalism. Higher values of the *x*-axis represent more conservative judicial ideologies. The dotted lines provide a 95 percent confidence interval around the estimated predicted probability. The predicted probabilities are calculated holding all other independent variables at their mean (for continuous variables) or modal values (for categorical variables). These estimates are derived from the model in table 7.2. The "rug" above the *x*-axis shows the frequency distribution of the justice's ideologies.

In other words, the probabilities that a liberal justice in a conservative state and a conservative justice in a liberal state will cast a pro-equality vote are nearly the same.

But a conservative justice in a conservative state will cast a pro-equality vote in only about one-quarter of the cases (a .25 probability). Thus, there is a .36 difference in the probability of a pro-equality vote between the two "aligned" types of justices (a liberal judge in a liberal state and a conservative judge in a conservative state). Of course, because we compare the effects of public opinion at the minimum and maximum values of that variable, the effect sizes we plot in this figure are the largest we could observe given the data at hand; these probabilities draw upon the most liberal and most conservative judges and states in the database. But these effect sizes are nevertheless useful to appreciate the full scope of the effects of these two concepts on the probability that a justice will support equality on the bench.

Still, recall that one of our major conclusions was that the effect of public opinion varies according to a state's judicial retention system. Because the estimates in figure 7.7 hold all other variables at their central tendencies, that figure illustrates the predicted probabilities in the modal retention system we observe: nonpartisan elections. It seems likely that these estimates could vary substantially by retention system. To that end, figure 7.8 shows the probability of a pro-equality vote as judicial ideology varies across the x-axis, and public opinion is set to its minimum and maximum values. The panels in the figure report the probabilities for each judicial retention system. Once more, we hold all the other independent variables to their mean or modal values.

The striking pattern in figure 7.8 is that the two lines in each panel vary in their distance from each other. The lower-left panel (nonpartisan elections) shows two lines whose confidence intervals do not overlap at all. (Recall that this panel is the same as that reported in figure 7.7.) On the other hand, the predicted probabilities in no-election and retention election states are basically identical regardless of the level of public opinion in the state. The lines in both panels have a negative slope, indicating that the effect of judicial ideology is still present. But the nearly overlapping lines provide a visual confirmation of the conclusion we reached earlier: in states that use these types of retention methods, the probability of a pro-equality vote does not vary according to the level of public opinion liberalism in the state.

Similarly, that the two lines in the partisan election panel are much closer together than the lines in the nonpartisan election panel illustrates the much weaker effect of public opinion in partisan election states than in nonpartisan election states. As noted earlier, a very liberal justice in a nonpartisan election state will vote in a pro-equality direction with .62 probability if that state is very liberal, but with .41 probability if that state is conservative—a difference of about .20 that is attributable to public opinion. On the other hand, the model predicts a pro-equality vote by a very liberal justice in a partisan election state with .53 probability if the state is liberal and .42 probability if the state is conservative—a public opinion effect that is about one-half the size of what we observed for the nonpartisan election case.

Figure 7.8 Predicted Probabilities of Pro-Equality Votes by State High Court Justices, by Retention Method, Public Opinion Liberalism, and Judicial Ideology

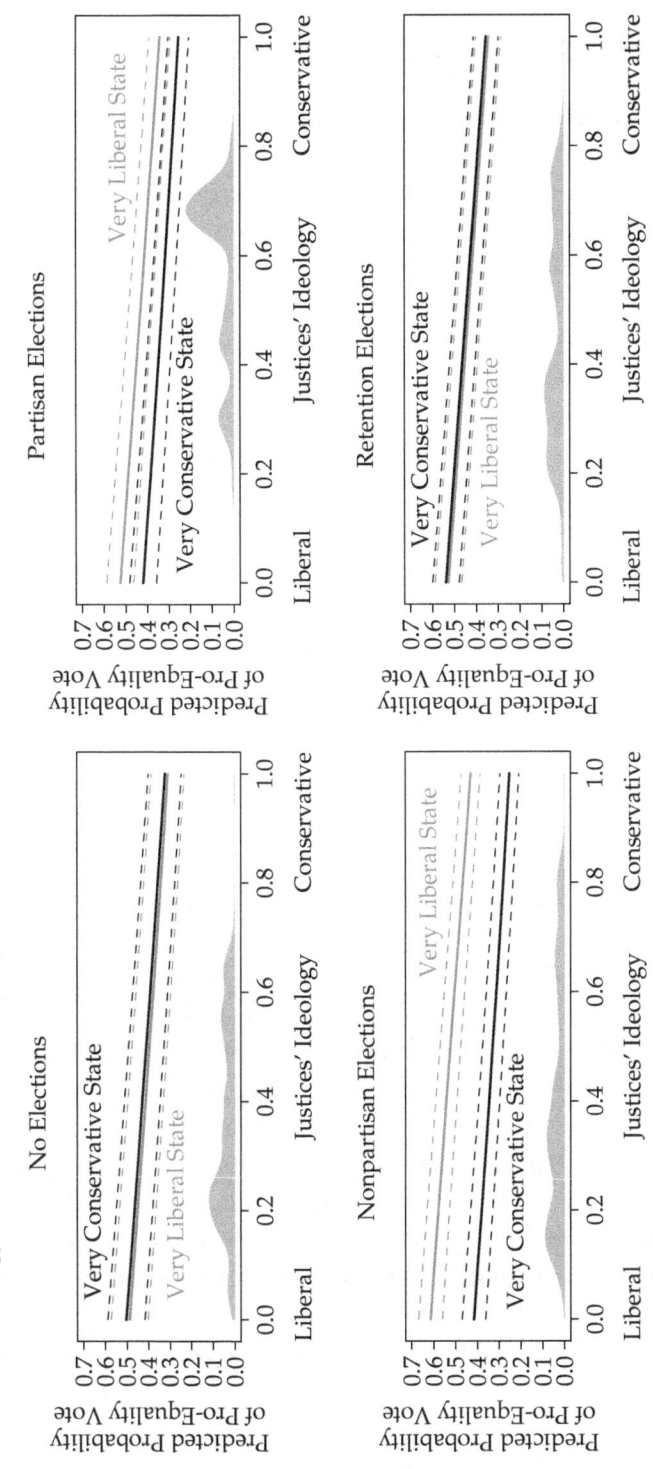

Source: Authors' compilation.
Notes: This figure shows the predicted probabilities of a pro-equality vote as judicial ideology varies, by retention mechanism and for minimum and maximum values of public opinion liberalism. Higher values of the x-axis represent more conservative judicial ideology. The dotted lines provide a 95 percent confidence interval around the estimated predicted probability. The predicted probabilities are calculated holding all other independent variables at their mean (for continuous variables) or modal values (for categorical variables). These estimates are derived from the model in table 7.2. The "rugs" above each x-axis show the frequency distributions of the justices' ideologies.

Taken together, our findings underscore the fact that neither judicial ideology nor public opinion liberalism exist in isolation from one another. Rather, especially in states that use partisan and nonpartisan elections to retain their justices, the combined effect of these two variables is noteworthy. Liberal justices in liberal states are particularly likely to favor equality in their rulings, and the predicted probability of a pro-equality vote from a conservative justice in a conservative state is quite low. Yet, in partisan and nonpartisan election states, the probability that a "mis-aligned" or "out-of-step" judge will vote in a pro-equality direction is quite similar whether the judge is a liberal judge in a conservative state or vice versa: .42 for a very liberal justice in a very conservative state, and .43 for a very conservative justice in a very liberal state. From the standpoint of the consequences for political, legal, economic, and social equality, these results suggest that the benefits of appointing judges whose policy preferences align with those of a state's citizens are particularly large in states that use partisan or nonpartisan elections, as those judges are the ones most likely to vote in ways that advance (or slow) equality through their rulings.

Summary and Concluding Thoughts

Our goal in this chapter was to marshal the data we collected on cases, judges, courts, and states to test hypotheses about the determinants of state supreme court decision-making in litigation implicating political, legal, economic, and social inequality between 1990 and 2015. Analyzing nearly thirty-seven thousand votes cast by more than nine hundred judges in nearly six thousand cases, what have we learned about the role that state supreme courts play with regard to equality in the United States?

First, and perhaps most importantly, we have seen the crucial impact of initial judicial selection on the ideological composition of state supreme courts. As we argued in chapters 5 and 6, elites dominate the process of judicial selection in the U.S. states both because many judges are initially appointed to their positions as a formal matter and because, informally, many governors have the opportunity to shape the composition of their courts through interim appointments. Our arguments in those chapters suggested that, by shaping the composition of the bench through appointments, elites can shift the policy outputs of their high courts. Until this chapter, we had not been able to confirm whether justices' ideologies (as chosen by these elites through their selection of appointees) affect the behavior of individual judges.

That has now changed. The analysis in this chapter completes the missing link between elite control of judicial appointments and the decision of individual judges to support equality in their rulings. Our analysis confirms that judicial ideology has a statistically and substantively significant relationship with the propensity of a state high court judge to cast pro-equality votes. More liberal justices are more likely to support equality.

This fact is all the more remarkable given the dramatic rates of unanimous decisions among the cases in our data set. Although this high overall level of judicial consensus threatened to wash away the relationship between judicial attitudes and judicial behavior, we observe robust and substantively meaningful relationships between these two factors.

Our second major theoretical concern with respect to inequality has two elements. First, are judges more likely to vote in favor of equality when the public in their state is liberal? Second, do differences in judicial retention—the threat of losing one's job—affect the likelihood that a judge's vote will reflect public opinion? The answers to both of these questions, our analysis suggests, is "yes."

First, with regard to the general relationship between public opinion liberalism and pro-equality voting, our results confirm that judicial decisions tend to be congruent with the mass public's preferences. That is, judges are more likely to cast pro-equality votes when the mass public in their state harbors more liberal opinions. This finding mirrors the general orientation of the U.S. Supreme Court: courts are basically reflective of and not too far out of step with public preferences in their decisions.[66]

But our analysis also revealed that the relationship between public opinion and judicial votes for equality is more complicated than it initially seems. Once we accounted for the possibility that methods of judicial retention condition the connection between public opinion and judicial behavior, we found notable differences in the relationship between public opinion liberalism and pro-equality voting. Indeed, the overall association we observed was driven mainly by those judges who face partisan or nonpartisan elections in order to keep their jobs. For judges who do not face elections, or who face only a nominal probability of defeat, our analysis indicates that there is no relationship between the liberalism of the mass public in a state and the probability that a judge will cast a pro-equality vote. On the other hand, judges who face partisan or nonpartisan elections (and especially the latter) become more likely to cast pro-equality votes as their state's public becomes more liberal.

This suggests an important difference between state high courts and the U.S. Supreme Court, and it adds to a growing consensus that nonpartisan elections are the method of judicial retention that best encourages judges to cast votes that reflect public opinion.[67] Importantly, however, this consensus has been formed largely on the basis of high-profile decisions that easily capture the public's imagination in an election campaign. Our data set, on the other hand, is composed of a set of cases that vary in their salience, from mundane workers' rights cases to high-profile gay marriage decisions. That we observe this pattern in our analysis suggests that the effects of systems of judicial accountability on judicial behavior may shape the behavior of judges much more broadly than previous research has anticipated.

We have suggested throughout this book that state supreme courts are part of an ongoing struggle for control of state government. Moreover, methods of judicial selection and retention can both impede and facilitate the ability of the governing coalition to exert control over the judicial branch of state government.

But what have we learned about these systems and the likelihood that state supreme courts will promote equality in their rulings? On the one hand, our findings in this chapter suggest that—as their original patrons hoped—judicial elections can sever the bond between political elites and high court judges by encouraging the latter to take into account public sentiment in their decision-making.[68]

However, it is not that simple. It is not just *any* type of election that provides a strong enough inducement for state supreme court justices to reflect public opinion in their rulings. Rather, judges are encouraged to incorporate public opinion into their rulings only when they face partisan and nonpartisan elections—which present them with a reasonable chance of defeat in a typical retention campaign. In Missouri plan–style retention elections, where defeats (or non-reappointments) are extraordinarily rare, or in systems with no elections at all, the "threat" of an electoral defeat is mainly an empty one, and judges' decisions do not vary with the liberalism of the public. Instead, it is only in partisan and nonpartisan election systems that the public's preferences with respect to equality are reflected in the behavior of their state high court justices. And of course, one implication of this finding is that should the mass public not prefer greater political, legal, economic, and social inequality, any important pro-equality inducement for judges would be neutralized. We will have much more to say about the implications of these findings in the next chapter.

Appendix 7.A: Supplementary Statistical Analyses

Table 7.A.1 Summary Statistics

	Mean	Standard Deviation
Justice's ideology	.45	.21
Partisan election	.28	.45
Nonpartisan election	.28	.45
Retention election	.27	.44
Public opinion liberalism	.58	.19
Beliefs about inequality	.56	.15
In-state undergraduate school	.58	.49
In-state law school	.63	.48
Whether Confederate state	.33	.47
Judicial compensation	.39	.17
Democratic Party dominance of state government	.53	.21
Lower court pro-equality	.53	.46
Upperdog party sought equality	.27	.40
Decided on procedural grounds	.17	.38
Rights of workers and employees	.22	.41
Access to justice institutions	.50	.50

Source: Authors' compilation.

Table 7.A.2 Pairwise Comparisons: Direct Effect of Retention Method

	No Election	Partisan Election	Nonpartisan Election	Retention Election
No election				
Partisan election	.932			
Nonpartisan election	.118	.055		
Retention election	.032	.047	.564	

Source: Authors' compilation.
Notes: The cell entries are probabilities for a null hypothesis test comparing the equality coefficients for each pair of retention methods. Small probabilities indicate that the effect of retention method (in the model reported in table 7.1) differs across the two retention methods.

CHAPTER 8

When Do Courts Advance Equality?

OUR PRIMARY GOAL in this book is to explain the role played by state supreme courts in creating public policies relevant to political, legal, economic, and social inequality in the U.S. states. At this point, we have waded through an ocean's worth of data, probing whether the haves come out ahead in state supreme court litigation (chapter 3), the relationship between judges' background characteristics and their attitudes (chapter 4), the role of mechanisms of judicial selection in shaping the composition of the bench (chapter 5), the extent to which the partisan composition of state supreme courts reflects a state's governing coalition and thereby limits judicial independence (chapter 6), and the determinants of a state supreme court justice's decision to support a pro-equality position in a given case (chapter 7).

Each of these analyses has offered a distinct window into the policymaking of state supreme courts. What we have not provided to this point, however, is a full accounting of *case outcomes* in state supreme courts. Courts, like legislatures and other collegial bodies, are majority-rule institutions in the sense that policy is typically made according to the vote of the majority. That is, litigants win their cases only if they capture a majority of the votes on the judicial panel that hears their case. While litigants surely would like to win the votes of as many justices as they can, they care particularly about *winning their case*. There is an enormous difference between winning the fourth vote on a seven-member court and winning the fifth or sixth vote; the pivotal fourth vote is necessary to win the case; those additional votes are just icing on the cake. Simply put, courts make case decisions by majority rule, and case outcomes are important because they stand as public policies (for example, as precedents).

In this chapter, we therefore turn our attention away from the votes of individual justices and instead focus on understanding the outcomes of individual cases. In the process, we make explicit a distinction that has been largely implicit to this point in the book: courts can contribute to inequality in two different ways.

First, as we have just seen, courts make pro-inequality policies through the judicial decisions they render: Do the decisions that command a majority of votes in the cases of the state supreme courts tend to further or inhibit political, legal, economic, and social inequality? We saw in chapter 2 that the outcomes in the six thousand decisions in our database were pro- and anti-equality in roughly equal numbers. When we analyzed the votes of individual justices in chapter 7, we saw substantial differences in judicial behavior according to judicial ideologies, public opinion, and methods of judicial retention, suggesting that these explanations might also be useful to account for the variation in the propensity of *courts*, rather than *judges*, to advance equality through the cases they decide.

This possibility requires us to revisit the analysis in the previous chapter at the level of the individual court decision, rather than at the level of the individual judge-vote. As we explained earlier, there is a meaningful difference between winning a justice's vote and winning a case, especially in state supreme courts where so many decisions are decided by unanimous votes. Because so many of the judge-votes in our data set are the "icing" that cements a policy win rather than the pivotal vote, there may be substantively important differences between the factors associated with a pro-equality case outcome and a justice's pro-equality vote.

Second, by reinforcing the resource advantages that litigants bring to the courtroom, courts may make pro-inequality policy decisions. This is the normative concern that animated Galanter's study of whether the haves come out ahead in litigation. Indeed, Galanter states in that essay that his purpose was to determine "under what conditions can litigation be redistributive."[1] In a sense, Galanter's study and the innumerable studies that have sought to examine the effects of litigant resources on judicial behavior and policymaking fit within a broader literature on inequality in the United States concerned with determining whether overprivileged upperdogs are successful in getting their way with governmental policymaking institutions. Both these studies and others, like Gilens's, examine *unequal responsiveness*: to what extent are the mechanisms of government more responsive to some interests—especially those of means—than others?

We discovered in chapter 3 a slight advantage for more powerful litigants in the outcomes of state supreme court cases dealing with inequality. However, the analyses in that chapter were incomplete: they did not address differences across courts and time in judicial ideology, public opinion, and methods of judicial retention. Another of our goals in this chapter, therefore, is to revisit Galanter's classic question with the lessons we have learned from the analyses reported in the previous chapters, examining in particular whether more powerful litigants are especially likely to win their cases in states with certain types of institutional arrangements, types of public preferences, and mixtures of judicial ideologies.

Thus, in this chapter, we analyze the outcomes of cases related to inequality in state supreme courts. We address two different outcome variables: whether cases are decided in a pro-equality direction, and whether haves are more likely to come out ahead in these cases. With regard to the former concept, we again find robust evidence that judicial ideology is the driving force behind court decisions related to inequality. And examining the latter, we uncover a striking relationship between litigant objectives and court ideology, such that upperdog litigants who seek *equality* in their litigation are more likely to win when facing liberal courts, and those who would advance *inequality* in court cases are favored by conservative courts. We conclude this chapter by connecting our empirical findings with an understanding of how state supreme courts make policy relevant to political, legal, economic, and social inequality in the U.S. states.

Hypotheses Concerning the Conditions under Which Pro-Equality Litigants Win

As we have just discussed, courts can affect inequality if better-resourced litigants are more successful at prevailing in their cases and also if state supreme court decisions, regardless of the resources of the litigants, favor equality. Later in this chapter, we examine the outcomes of these cases with an eye toward the resources of litigants. Now we address the question of the factors that determine the equality-related policy content of state supreme court decisions. We therefore pick up our analysis where we left off in the previous chapter.

There we justified and tested a series of hypotheses about the relationship between judicial ideology, methods of judicial retention, and public opinion. Our goal in the previous chapter was to explain how these factors are associated with judges' decisions to vote in favor of equality on the cases that come before them. We found that judicial ideology has a robust and substantively important effect on the behavior of state supreme court justices: more liberal justices are more likely to cast pro-equality votes. Moreover, we found that judges who face partisan or nonpartisan elections are more likely to cast pro-equality votes when the citizens of the state hold more liberal policy views; there is no evidence of a relationship between public opinion and the judicial behavior of judges who run in retention elections or have no electoral connection with their state's citizens.

Here we essentially reproduce those hypotheses (with slight updates to focus on the outcome of a particular *case* rather than a judge's *vote*):

H_1: *Judicial Ideology.* Courts with justices whose ideologies are more conservative tend to decide cases in favor of greater political, legal, economic, and social inequality. Conversely, courts staffed by justices with more liberal ideologies tend to decide cases in favor of greater equality.

H_2: *Judicial Retention Systems.* We expect to see no relationship between the judicial retention method and the probability that a case is decided in a pro-equality direction.

H_3: *Public Opinion.* To the extent that their constituents are more liberal and favor greater equality, state supreme courts' decisions are more likely to favor equality.

H_4: *Conditional Effects of Public Opinion.* Judicial systems vary in the degree to which they encourage judges to heed public opinion when making their decisions. In particular, courts with stronger accountability retention methods (for example, partisan and nonpartisan elections) rely more heavily on public opinion than courts with weaker accountability methods (such as retention elections and reappointment systems).

While we put forth the same hypotheses in this chapter that we tested in chapter 7, we recognize that there is a very important difference between the dependent variables of the two chapters. In chapter 7, we focused on the votes of the judges and found, for example, that, on average, the judges' votes seemed to be congruent with the content of public opinion in their state in the year of the vote, especially if they faced partisan or nonpartisan elections. We understood that relationship to be due to the motivation of some judges, perhaps many, to take public opinion into consideration in their decision-making, either because they thought that doing so would help their chances of keeping their seat on the court or because they thought that listening to public opinion was the right thing for judges to do. The average relationship probably was not stronger, however, because some judges were no doubt oblivious to or uninformed about the public's preferences, some judges normatively rejected public opinion influence on courts, or some judges (although in light of our findings in chapter 6, not many) were ideologically out of step with public opinion and therefore refused to be swayed by it. Still, on average, these state supreme court justices seemed to find a way to incorporate public opinion into their decisional calculus.

Our expectations are weaker, however, when we aggregate individual judge-votes to the case level, as we do in this chapter. The dependent variable for the analyses in this chapter is the case outcome. That outcome aggregates the votes of the various judges participating in the cases and is determined by majority rule. Furthermore, in the majority of these cases, the vote was unanimous. In this chapter, we are primarily interested in who wins: Do the haves come out ahead in litigation before the state supreme courts? And do pro-equality interests come out ahead?

Case-level analysis mixes variables drawn from different units of analysis. At the simplest level, we include a measure of the ideological leaning of the court by taking the average of the ideology scores of the justices serving on that court in the year in which the decision was rendered. We also include as a predictor the public's opinion on the aspect of conservatism or liberalism most relevant to the case, also in the year the case was decided. Thus, for a given state for a given year, the value of the public opinion independent variable is a single score. The dependent variable for that state varies, of course: some case outcomes in the state for that year are pro-equality, and others are not. At the conceptual level, this creates a great deal of within-state and within-year error in prediction because the public opinion independent variable generates the same prediction for all cases decided in the state in that year (ceteris paribus). Under these circumstances, we should not expect a variable such as state-level public opinion in the year of the decision (or any other state-level variable) to have much statistical power.

Relatedly, the judges voting in any particular case no doubt reflect a mixture of attitudes toward the role of public opinion in state supreme court decisions, as discussed earlier. Especially in light of the fairly common use of irregular judges sitting on state supreme court cases (to say nothing of recusals), the mixture of these views across cases within a state within a given year no doubt varies. In light of this variability, we should not expect a variable such as year-based state-level public opinion to demonstrate as much statistical connection to case-level outcomes as it does to the judge-vote outcomes.

At the same time, we do expect that average judicial ideology will be an influential predictor of case outcomes, under the simple hypothesis that the more conservative justices voting on a case are, the higher the likelihood of the outcome supporting greater inequality. Still, as with all cross-level relationships, we do not expect this connection to be particularly strong.

When Are Cases Decided in Favor of Equality?

Given that our analysis in this chapter is about the outcomes of *cases* rather than the votes of *judges*, we return to the database explained in chapters 2 and 3. The outcome variable in the model is the outcome of the case, coded 1 if the case was resolved in a pro-equality direction and 0 otherwise. About 47 percent of the 5,875 cases in the analysis were decided in a pro-equality direction.

In specifying our independent variables, we rely on our model specification from chapter 7 as much as possible. Of course, we do require a court-level (rather than justice-level) measure of judicial ideology. Thus, instead of measuring judicial ideology as an individual judge's ideology score, our measure of judicial ideology is the average of the ideology scores of the justices who served on the state supreme court in the year the case was decided. (This is the same measure explained at length in chapter 4; higher values represent more conservative courts.)[2] Following the analysis in chapter 7, we include a full suite of control variables, controlling for party control of state government, judicial compensation, public opinion, method of judicial retention, whether the state was a member of the Confederacy, and the case issue area.[3]

There are only two significant changes to our model specification. First, because our analysis is now at the level of the case rather than the judge-vote, we cannot control for any additional judge-specific factors. We therefore do not include the judge's educational background in the equation. Second, along those same lines, we can no longer include random effects for individual judges; instead, the only random effects in our logistic regression model are for the individual states. Thus, we estimate logistic regression models with random effects for states.

The results of the regression model are shown in table 8.1. The fit of this model is comparable to the judge-vote-level model presented in chapter 7: the equation predicts 59 percent of outcomes correctly, an improvement over a null model that classified 53 percent of outcomes correctly.

We begin our analysis of the model's estimates with our first hypothesis, about the relationship between court ideology and case outcomes. The coefficient is statistically significant; figure 8.1 plots estimated predicted probabilities from the model. Moving from the most liberal state supreme court in our data (the early 1990s Vermont Supreme Court) to the most conservative court (the mid-2000s South Dakota Supreme Court), the predicted probability of a pro-equality outcome declines significantly by .18, from .53 to .35. Thus, the model provides support for our first hypothesis.

Our second hypothesis relates to the effects of judicial retention methods; again, our data provide support for our hypothesis. There is no evidence that any judicial retention system is associated, on average, with more pro-equality case outcomes. Moreover, none of the pairwise comparisons among retention method types reaches statistical significance (see table 8.A.2), providing us with no evidence that the probability of a pro-equality case outcome differs in any way—favoring more or less equality—based on a state's method of judicial retention.

Third, we turn to the relationship between public opinion and case outcomes. Because the interaction terms in table 8.1 complicate our conclusions about the role of public opinion, we first test this hypothesis using a simplified model that does not allow the effect of public opinion to vary according to judicial retention method (not shown). In that model, there is no support for our hypothesis; the relationship is not statistically significant ($p = .209$). We conclude that public opinion has no direct effect on case outcomes.

Table 8.1 Random Effects Logistic Regression Results: Pro-Equality Case Outcome, with Conditional Effects for Public Opinion

	b	s.e.	Marginal Effect
Justice's ideology	−.74***	.22	−.18
Partisan election	−.41	.37	−.01
Nonpartisan election	−.25	.36	.04
Retention election	.31	.37	.04
Public opinion liberalism	−.11	.46	−.10
Partisan election × public opinion liberalism	.64	.52	.13
Nonpartisan election × public opinion liberalism	.71	.52	.15
Retention election × public opinion liberalism	−.28	.55	−.01
Public beliefs about inequality	−.06	.24	−.01
Whether Confederate state	.07	.11	.02
Judicial compensation	.31	.20	.08
Democratic Party dominance of state government	.04	.09	.01
Lower court pro-equality	.30***	.06	.07
Upperdog party sought equality	.36***	.07	.09
Decided on procedural grounds	−.05	.07	−.01
Rights of workers and employees	−.27***	.10	−.07
Access to justice institutions	−.61***	.09	−.15
Intercept	.23	.38	
Random effects			
State	.21***	.04	
Log likelihood	−3,951.80		
N	5,875		

Source: Authors' compilation.

Notes: The dependent variable in this analysis is whether the case outcome favors greater political, legal, economic, and social equality. All variables are scored to range from 0 to 1. The excluded category in the regression for the issue domain variable is cases relating to the rights of minorities, and for the method of retaining judges, it is no election. The entries reported for the random effects are the standard deviation and the standard error of those estimated effects. Significance of unstandardized regression coefficients (*b*): ***$p \leq .001$; **$p \leq .01$; *$p \leq .05$. See appendix table 8.A.1 for the distributions of the individual variables.

But perhaps the effect of public opinion appears to be indistinguishable from zero because the effect of public opinion varies according to method of judicial retention (H₄). However, as table 8.1 makes clear, none of the interaction terms is statistically significant. Indeed, in no retention regime does public opinion have a statistically significant relationship with the probability that a court will decide a given case in a pro-equality direction. Thus, the model provides support for neither of our public opinion hypotheses.

Figure 8.1 Predicted Probability of a State High Court Pro-Equality Case Outcome, by Judicial Ideology

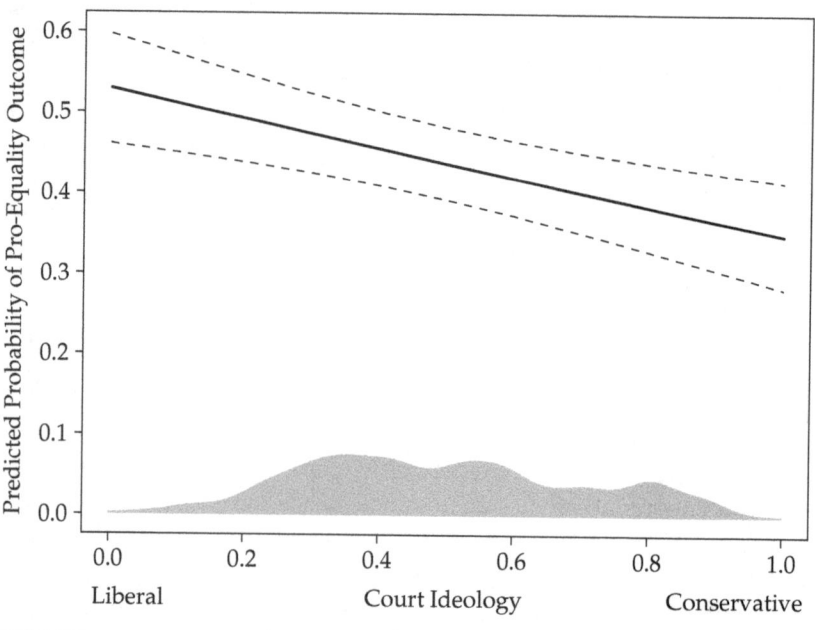

Source: Authors' compilation.
Notes: This figure shows the predicted probability of a pro-equality outcome as average court ideologies vary from their minimum to maximum values. Higher values of the x-axis represent more conservative courts. The dashed lines provide a 95 percent confidence interval around the estimated predicted probability. The predicted probabilities are calculated holding all other independent variables at their mean (for continuous variables) or modal values (for categorical variables). This figure is based on the model estimated in table 8.1. The "rug" above the x-axis shows the frequency distribution of court ideology.

Again, we observe statistically significant effects among the case-level control variables. When a case is decided in a pro-equality direction in the lower court, there is a .07 increase in the probability that the pro-equality litigant will win its case in the state supreme court. Similarly, when the better-resourced party seeks equality, the probability that its position will prevail increases significantly, by .09, from .44 to .53. Finally, we observe differences in the baseline probability of a pro-equality decision across issue areas. Cases involving minority rights have a .59 probability of a pro-equality outcome, those involving workers' rights have a .52 probability of a pro-equality outcome, and those involving access to justice are decided in a pro-equality direction with .44 probability.

The major conclusion we draw from this analysis concerns the overriding effect of judicial ideology on pro-equality case outcomes: courts with more conservative judges make more anti-equality decisions. For the reasons outlined here, we are not particularly surprised that the effect of public opinion on the outcomes of cases is not statistically distinguishable from zero in this analysis, even though we found an analogous relationship between public opinion and the judge-vote in chapter 7. There is a great deal of noise—unanimous decisions, temporary judges, and aggregation—that clouds a relationship at the case level in comparison to the analysis at the level of the judge-vote. Rather, what seems important in these results is the dominant role of judicial ideology. As we have argued throughout this book, it seems that the pro-equality positions of courts are most powerfully shaped through a calculated process of judge selection in which justices who mirror the preferences of their selectors are placed on state supreme courts.

Hypotheses Concerning the Conditions under Which Upperdog Litigants Win

Having discussed the first way in which courts can contribute to equality through case outcomes—by deciding cases in a pro-equality direction—we now turn to the second process by which courts could affect equality: by favoring in their decisions litigants with more resources. As we noted in chapter 3, extant research on the question of whether the haves come out ahead is not altogether consistent in its findings; for example, whether haves come out ahead or not has been found to vary over time. Indeed, instead of drawing a general conclusion about the success of well-resourced litigants, we suggested in chapter 3 that the more appropriate question might be: *Under what conditions* do the haves come out ahead? The purpose of our final analysis is to test several hypotheses that might answer that question.

One of the most unexpected and important findings from chapter 3 was that upperdog litigants do not necessarily seek to advance inequality in their litigation. For example, figure 3.7 reported that in about 34 percent of the cases involving state governments (a very well-resourced litigant), the state government's litigation position favored greater *equality*. This was even true of 20 percent of the cases involving large businesses and corporations as litigants. Furthermore, across all types of litigants, the analysis in chapter 3 revealed that when upperdogs are pursuing greater inequality in their litigation, they are slightly less likely to win their case than when they are pursuing greater equality (55 percent versus 59 percent). Thus, in the multivariate analysis in this chapter we hypothesize that litigation objectives matter:

> H_5: *Litigant Objectives.* Upperdog litigants seeking inequality in their litigation are less likely to secure judicial outcomes that favor greater political, legal, economic, and social inequality.

We also hypothesize that the ideological orientation of the state supreme court affects whether the haves come out ahead. We would not expect, for example, that a liberal court would be as favorably predisposed to the claims of upperdogs as a conservative court (just as we found in chapter 7 that liberal judges are generally more likely to vote in favor of outcomes that advance political, legal, economic, and social equality). Consequently, we hypothesize:

> H_6: *Judicial Ideology.* Courts dominated by liberal judges are less likely to favor the side of upperdog litigants in cases in which they seek an outcome that favors greater political, legal, economic, and social inequality.

As we argued in chapter 3, this is where most inquiries about resources end. We go a step further, however, and hypothesize an interactive relationship between court ideology and the objectives of the litigants. That is, we expect that liberal courts will favor the side of upperdogs when they are litigating in support of greater *equality*, but that they will not favor upperdogs when they are litigating in support of greater *inequality*. This hypothesis suggests a conditional effect of judicial ideologies in generating advantages for upperdog litigants. Moreover, the hypothesis implies that it is perhaps not so much that the resources of upperdogs cause them to win their cases disproportionately, but that they win because conservative courts share the same policy objectives when upperdog litigants seek to advance inequality. Thus:

> H_7: *Conditional Effect of Judicial Ideology.* Liberal courts are more likely to support upperdog litigants when they aim to advance equality; conservative courts are more likely to support upperdog litigants when they seek to advance inequality.

Following the discussion and findings in the first half of this chapter, we are less committed to hypotheses about the other factors found in chapter 7 to influence the votes of individual justices. For example, we suspect that in more liberal states courts tend to favor underdogs in their rulings, although in a multivariate analysis it seems likely that the direct effect of public opinion is not very significant. That is, if public preferences affect the ideological propensity of the state high courts, and if those propensities then structure the policy outputs of those courts, we see no reason why public opinion would independently influence court policies via other processes and mechanisms. Very much the same could be said about the other factors found in chapter 7 to influence the votes of these judges. In our model, judicial ideologies and litigant objectives are the "active ingredients."

To summarize, our most important hypotheses are that litigants' objectives are related to the "win rate" of upperdog litigants, just as are the ideological propensities of the state supreme court, and that court ideology is expected to interact with litigant objectives in predicting the outcomes in cases associated with policies regarding political, legal, economic, and social inequality.

Analysis

We continue our exploration of the outcome of cases by testing these hypotheses at the level of the individual case. We return to the case data set and again estimate a logistic regression model with random effects for states that mirrors the model presented in table 8.1. The dependent variable in our analysis is dichotomous, indicating whether the better-resourced litigant prevails in the litigation in our cases. This measure was constructed in chapter 3. We should remind the reader that excluded from this analysis is litigation in which both sides of the lawsuit are equally powerful (13 percent of the six thousand cases; see figure 3.2). In cases involving litigants of unequal resources, the upperdog won 55 percent of the time (irrespective of the upperdog's litigation objectives).

The most important independent variable of note indicates whether the better-resourced litigant in the litigation sought greater equality in the case. The variable is dichotomous, coded 1 for the 24 percent of cases in which the upperdog party sought greater equality. We include this variable both by itself and as part of a multiplicative interaction with the ideology of the court, using the same court-level ideology measure we employed in table 8.1.

One other change to the model specification for this analysis should be noted. While the analysis in table 8.1 includes a variable to indicate whether the lower court decided in favor of equality (to square with the coding of that analysis's outcome variable), this analysis uses a similar variable that indicates whether the lower court decided in favor of the better-resourced litigant.

When Are Cases Decided in Favor of Upperdog Litigants?

Recall that our hypotheses concern the objectives of litigants, the ideology of the court, and the conditional effects of those two concepts. We therefore estimate two logistic regression models. The first model considers only the direct effects of these two variables; the second model allows for the conditional relationship. We begin our analysis with table 8.2, which does not include an interaction between litigant objectives and court ideology.

The model classifies 59 percent of observations correctly, a slight improvement over a null model that would classify 55 percent of observations correctly by predicting every outcome to be in favor of the upperdog litigant. Contrary to our first hypothesis, table 8.2 provides no indication that, all else equal, powerful litigants are more likely to prevail when they seek inequality than when they seek equality. The coefficient is not statistically significant, and the substantive size of the effect is small: a less than .01 difference in the probability that the better-resourced litigant will win the case when it seeks equality compared to when it seeks inequality (holding all other variables at their mean or modal values).

More notable are the effects of judicial ideology, illustrated in figure 8.2. As hypothesized—and as shown in the figure—there is a positive relationship between the conservatism of the court and the probability that the better-resourced litigant will prevail in cases before the state supreme court. Those upperdog litigants facing the most liberal state supreme court (the Vermont Supreme Court in the early 1990s) would have a .34 probability of winning their case; were they to litigate before the most conservative court in our data (the South Dakota Supreme Court in the mid-2000s), they would have a .53 probability of prevailing—a .19 difference in predicted probabilities across the range of observed average court ideologies. Thus, figure 8.2 provides strong support for our second hypothesis.

Table 8.2 Random Effects Logistic Regression Results: Pro-Upperdog Case Outcome

	b	s.e.	Marginal Effect
Upperdog party sought equality	.01	.23	.00
Court's ideology	−.77***	.23	−.19
Partisan election	.07	.16	.02
Nonpartisan election	−.12	.13	−.03
Retention election	−.14	.12	−.04
Public opinion liberalism	−.08	.24	−.02
Public beliefs about inequality	−.26	.25	−.06
Whether Confederate state	.04	.12	.01
Judicial compensation	.20	.22	.05
Democratic Party dominance of state government	.39	.21	.09
Lower court pro-upperdog	.26***	.07	.06
Decided on procedural grounds	.20*	.08	−.05
Rights of workers and employees	−.16	.10	−.04
Access to justice institutions	−.46***	.10	−.11
Intercept	−.13	.29	
Random effects			
State	.20***	.05	
Log likelihood	−3,343.32		
N	4,945		

Source: Authors' compilation.

Notes: The dependent variable in this analysis is whether the case outcome favors the position in the litigation of the upperdog litigant. Cases with equal litigant resources are excluded from this analysis. All variables are scored to range from 0 to 1. The excluded category in the regression for the issue domain variable is cases relating to the rights of minorities, and for the method of retaining judges, it is no election. The entries reported for the random effects are the standard deviation and the standard error of those estimated effects. Significance of unstandardized regression coefficients (*b*): ***$p \leq .001$; **$p \leq .01$; *$p \leq .05$. See appendix table 8.A.1 for the distributions of the individual variables.

Perhaps interestingly, we find no relationship between our other contextual independent variables and the probability that the better-resourced litigant comes out ahead. We do not see, for example, that the haves are advantaged in places and times in which a state's public is more liberal, state supreme court judges are better compensated, Democratic dominance of state government is higher, or the justices face popular elections.

Indeed, the only other factors that table 8.2 indicates have a statistically significant relationship with litigation outcomes are the case-level control variables. All else equal, the better-resourced litigant has a .06 higher probability of winning its case before the state supreme court when it prevailed

Figure 8.2 Predicted Probability of a State High Court Pro-Upperdog Case Outcome, by Judicial Ideology

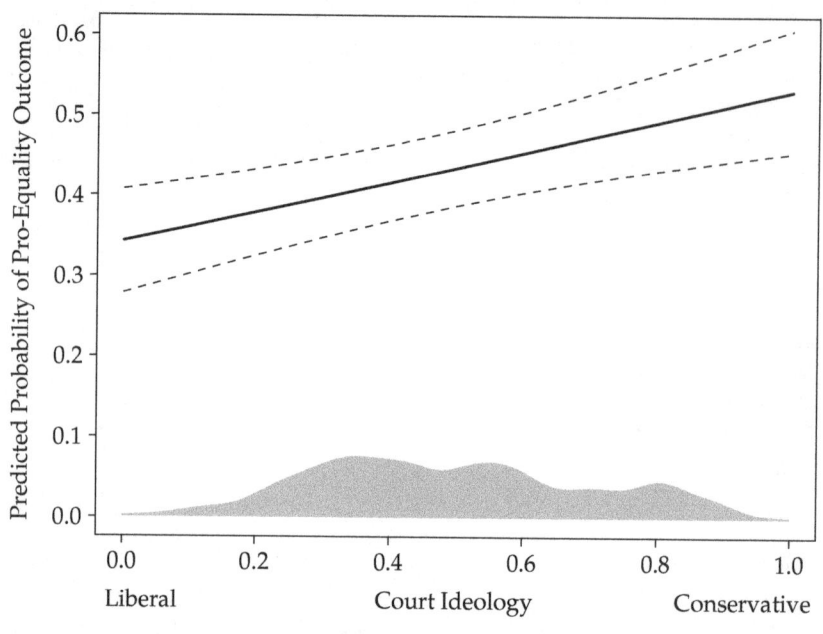

Source: Authors' compilation.
Notes: This figure shows the predicted probabilities of a case outcome favoring the upperdog litigant as average court ideologies vary from their minimum to maximum values. Higher values of the x-axis represent more conservative judicial ideologies. The dashed lines provide a 95 percent confidence interval around the estimated predicted probability. The predicted probabilities are calculated holding all other independent variables at their mean (for continuous variables) or modal values (for categorical variables). These estimates are derived from the model estimated in table 8.2. The "rug" above the x-axis shows the frequency distribution of court ideology.

at the lower court and has a .05 higher probability of victory in decisions that rest on procedural, rather than substantive, grounds. Likewise, the probability of victory for an upperdog litigant in a minority rights case is .11 higher than in cases involving access to justice institutions.

But recall our expectation that the effect of litigant objectives would vary according to the ideology of the court. To explore this possibility, table 8.3 presents the results of a second logistic regression model that includes a multiplicative interaction term between judicial ideology and litigant objectives. This model provides a slight improvement in predictive

Table 8.3 Random Effects Logistic Regression Results: Pro-Upperdog Case Outcome, with Conditional Effects for Litigant Objectives

	b	s.e.	Marginal Effect
Upperdog party sought equality	.69***	.19	.26
Court's ideology	1.09***	.24	26
Upperdog party sought equality × justice's ideology	−1.39*	.36	−.07
Partisan election	.07	.15	.02
Nonpartisan election	−.11	.13	−.03
Retention election	−.13	.12	−.03
Public opinion liberalism	−.09	.24	−.02
Public beliefs about inequality	−.27	.25	−.07
Whether Confederate state	.03	.12	.01
Judicial compensation	.21	.22	.05
Democratic Party dominance of state government	.39	.21	.10
Lower court pro-upperdog	.26***	.07	.00
Decided on procedural grounds	.22**	.08	.05
Rights of workers and employees	−.16	.10	−.04
Access to justice institutions	−.47***	.10	−.12
Intercept	−.29	.29	
Random effects			
State	.19***	.05	
Log likelihood	−3,335.91		
N	4,945		

Source: Authors' compilation.

Notes: The dependent variable in this analysis is whether the case outcome favors the position in the litigation of the upperdog litigant. Cases with equal litigant resources are excluded from this analysis. All variables are scored to range from 0 to 1. The excluded category in the regression for the issue domain variable is cases relating to the rights of minorities, and for the method of retaining judges, it is no election. The entries reported for the random effects are the standard deviation and the standard error of those estimated effects. Significance of unstandardized regression coefficients (b): ***$p \leq .001$; **$p \leq .01$; *$p \leq .05$. See appendix table 8.A.1 for the distributions of the individual variables.

power over the model shown in table 8.2, classifying about 60 percent of case outcomes correctly.

The most important conclusion we draw from table 8.3 is the statistically significant coefficient on the interaction term, which provides clear evidence supporting our seventh hypothesis—that the effect of litigant objectives varies according to judicial ideologies. To examine this effect more closely, we turn to figure 8.3, which plots the marginal effect of an upperdog's pro-equality litigation objective across the range of judicial ideology. For those values of

Figure 8.3 The Marginal Effect of Litigant Motives, by Judicial Ideology

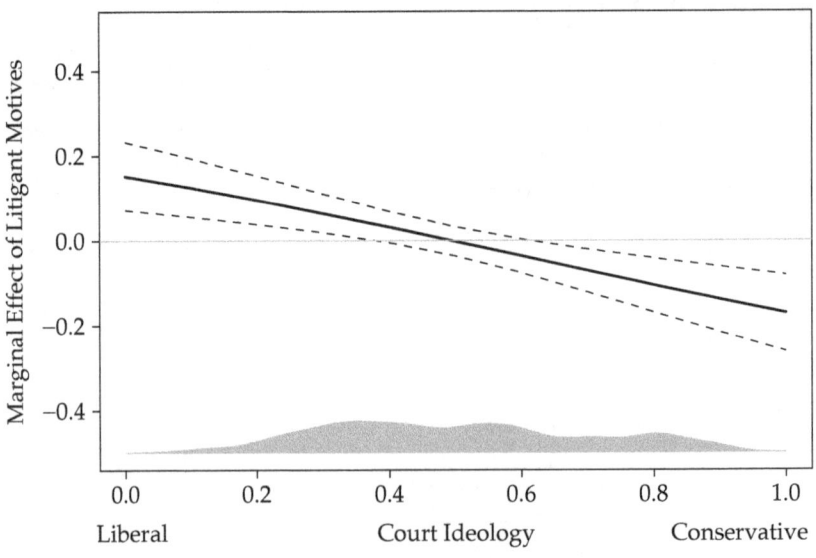

Source: Authors' compilation.
Notes: This figure shows the marginal effect of a litigant's decision to seek equality before a state supreme court on the probability that the have party will win the case as average court ideologies vary from their minimum to maximum values. Higher values of the *x*-axis represent more conservative judicial ideologies. The dashed lines depict a 95 percent confidence interval around the estimated predicted probability. The predicted probabilities are calculated holding all other independent variables at their mean (for continuous variables) or modal values (for categorical variables). These estimates are derived from the model estimated in table 8.3. The "rug" above the *x*-axis shows the frequency distribution of court ideology.

judicial ideology below about .40, the marginal effect is positive and statistically significant: when facing a liberal court, upperdogs seeking equality are, all else equal, more likely to prevail. The opposite is true for upperdog litigants who seek equality before conservative courts: when facing a court with an average ideology of about .65 or greater, an upperdog litigant seeking equality is *less* likely to win its case. Clearly, the litigant's objectives in the case matter for the outcomes, though they matter quite differently depending on whether the litigant is facing a liberal or conservative court.

To put these results into more easily understandable terms, we look to figure 8.4, which plots the predicted probability of an upperdog litigant winning as judicial ideology and litigation objectives both vary. The difference in slope between the two lines is stark, clearly illustrating the key conclusion

Figure 8.4 Predicted Probability of a State High Court Pro-Upperdog Case Outcome, by Judicial Ideology and Litigant Objectives

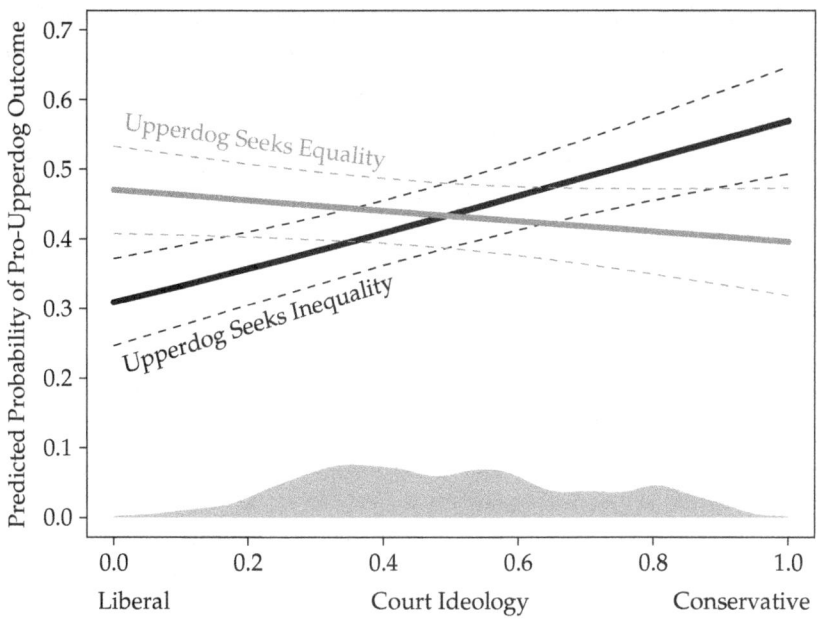

Source: Authors' compilation.
Notes: This figure shows the predicted probabilities of a case outcome in favor of the have as average court ideologies vary from their minimum to maximum values for litigants who seek equality and for those who seek inequality. Higher values of the x-axis represent more conservative judicial ideologies. The dashed lines provide a 95 percent confidence interval around the estimated predicted probability. The predicted probabilities are calculated holding all other independent variables at their mean (for continuous variables) or modal values (for categorical variables). These estimates are derived from the model estimated in table 8.3. The "rug" above the x-axis shows the frequency distribution of court ideology.

we draw from this model—when more resourced litigants seek *inequality*, they are more likely to prevail where a court's ideology is more conservative. The exact opposite is true for those upperdog litigants who seek to advance equality: their odds increase with the liberalism of the state supreme court. For an upperdog litigant seeking to advance inequality, the probability of winning increases by .26, from .31 to .56, as average court ideology changes from its most liberal to its most conservative score. On the other hand, the probability of an upperdog litigant seeking to advance equality decreases by .07, from .47 to .40, as judicial ideology changes from a level seen in the early 1990s in Vermont to that observed in South Dakota in the mid-2000s.

These findings have stark implications for studies of inequality. Were we to not account for the objectives of litigants, our analysis would end with the results provided in table 8.2 and shown in figure 8.2: upperdogs do unambiguously and uniformly better in more conservative courts. But because some haves seek to advance equality, and because more liberal courts are, on average, more receptive to cases that seek to advance equality, that finding is misleading. Objectives matter. It seems the haves do come out ahead, but they are most likely to win before courts whose ideological makeup is favorable to their claims.

Case Outcomes across States and Time

Having analyzed the correlates of upperdog and pro-equality victories in state supreme court cases, we take a step back to consider where and when—in the real world, not the statistical world—our models would predict actual state courts to be most likely to advance or slow the march of inequality. Toward this end, we selected four states whose stories have been particularly important to the narrative in this book—Alabama, Iowa, Kansas, and Texas. These four states vary widely on both outcome variables. For the pro-equality outcome, the rank ordering of the four states is Texas (27 percent), Alabama (36 percent), Iowa (46 percent), and Kansas (54 percent). The rank ordering for the states reverses, as it should, when we look at the percentage of pro-upperdog outcomes: Texas (70 percent), Alabama (66 percent), Iowa (65 percent), and Kansas (40 percent).

For each of the four states, we used the models in tables 8.1 and 8.3 to estimate the probability of an upperdog victory and a pro-equality case outcome in each of them over time. In other words, we considered the probability of a pro-equality outcome for the modal case in the data set: an access to justice case in which the lower court ruled in favor of equality (or against the upperdog), the upperdog party sought inequality in the litigation, and the state supreme court decided the case on substantive grounds. We then used the observed values of the state-specific factors for each state to compute the predicted probability of a pro-equality (figure 8.5) and pro-upperdog (figure 8.6) outcome for each state-year. The logic here is that we keep everything except the factors that vary by state the same across time and states to make comparisons as close to "all else equal"—with the exception of state-specific effects—as possible.

Figure 8.5 Predicted Probability of a State High Court Pro-Equality Case Outcome in Four States, 1990–2015

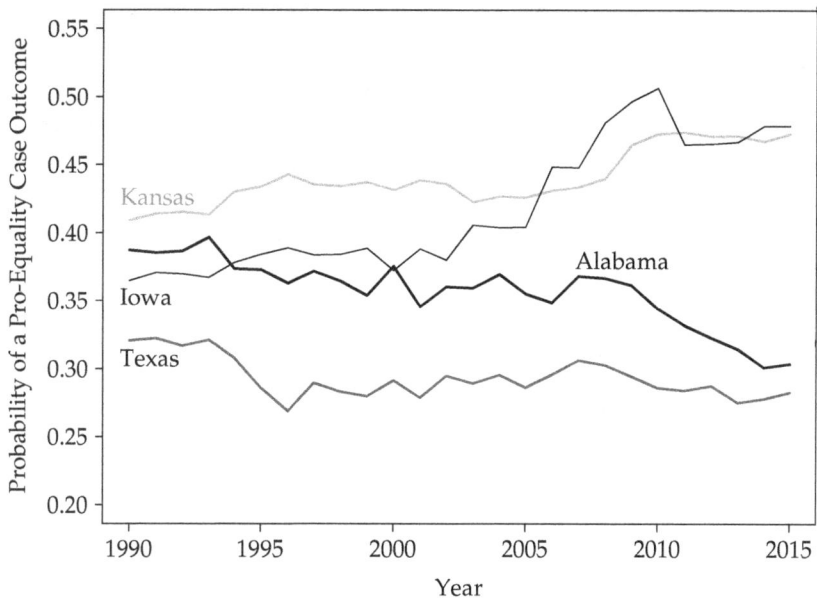

Source: Authors' compilation.
Notes: This figure shows the predicted probabilities of a pro-equality vote in selected states between 1990 and 2015. The predicted probabilities are calculated for the modal case in the data set but use the actual values of the state-specific covariates for each year. These estimates are derived from the model estimated in table 8.1.

We begin by discussing the already well-known Alabama Supreme Court. That court became substantially more conservative throughout our time period. Across the twenty-six-year period we study, the court's ideology changed from an average of .53 (on a 0–1 scale) in 1990 to .87 in 2015. This large change in the court's ideology explains why we observe a steady decrease in the probability of a pro-equality case outcome in Alabama in figure 8.5.[4]

Similarly, figure 8.6 shows a gradual *increase* in the probability of a pro-upperdog case outcome in that state. The Alabama Supreme Court's shift in ideology was particularly rapid between 1996 and 1999; during those years, its average ideology moved from .57 to .72. These years are noticeable in figure 8.6 as the beginning of a sharp upward trend in the predicted fates of well-resourced litigants bringing claims before that court.

Figure 8.6 Predicted Probability of a State High Court Pro-Upperdog Case Outcome in Four States, 1990–2015

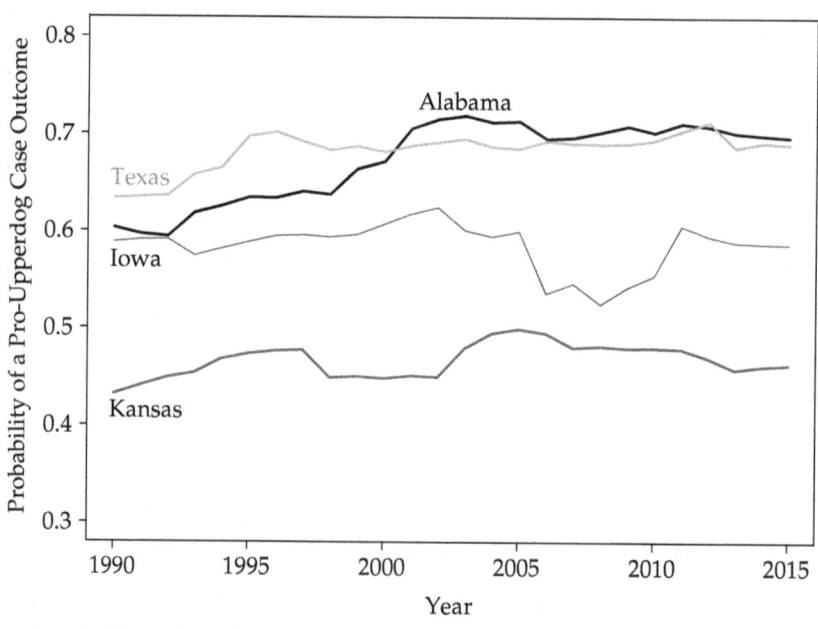

Source: Authors' compilation.
Notes: This figure shows the predicted probabilities of a pro-upperdog vote in selected states between 1990 and 2015. The predicted probabilities are calculated for the modal case in the data set but use the actual values of the state-specific covariates for each year. These estimates are derived from the model in table 8.3.

As the court's average ideology became relatively stable and conservative beginning in 2000, we observe little fluctuation in the probability of a pro-upperdog outcome. Still, the results for Alabama in both figures tell the same general story: a pro-inequality shift for that court over the course of our time period.

We now turn to the Iowa Supreme Court, beginning with a consideration of the probability of a pro-equality outcome being issued by that court (figure 8.5). The most striking pattern in the Iowa Supreme Court trend can be seen between 2005 and 2011. We observe a sharp increase in the probability of a pro-equality outcome during that period; this court's pro-equality tendencies peaked in 2009 and 2010 before sharply declining. Again, this change is suggested by a dramatic transformation of the court's ideology. The beginning of this time period is marked by a shift in the average ideology of the Iowa Supreme Court in a liberal direction; from 2005 to 2006, the court's average conservatism score swung from .71 to .49, a shift of almost 25 percent of the range of the variable. Recall that the Iowa Supreme Court ruled in favor of same-sex marriage in 2009, and that Iowa voters rejected in November 2010 three of the justices who voted in favor of equality in that case. When Iowa's Republican governor, Terry Branstad, had the opportunity to replace those three justices in early 2011, he seized it. The significant decline we observe in the predicted probability of a pro-equality outcome for that court in that year, from .51 to .46, is associated with a change in the average ideology of the Iowa Supreme Court from .38 to .61—a more than one standard deviation increase in the court's conservatism.

Figure 8.6 tells a complementary story about the probability of a pro-upperdog outcome: it began to crater in 2005 before recovering in 2011. The sharp decrease we observe in 2005 corresponds to the large leftward shift in the Iowa Supreme Court's average ideology during the end of Democrat Tom Vilsack's tenure as governor. The predicted probability returned to its equilibrium level of about .60 in 2011 after Branstad's appointees took their seats on the court. Again, the estimated Iowa trends in figures 8.5 and 8.6 suggest a similar story: as governors had the opportunity to reshape the composition of the state high court, the court's average ideology changed. With this change in average ideology came a corresponding shift in the pro-inequality tendencies of Iowa's highest judicial body.

We turn now to Kansas. One might initially be surprised to see such high pro-equality predictions in Kansas in figure 8.5. Recall, however, that this court was the home of two of the most liberal state supreme court justices in our data set. Despite this state's conservative reputation, many of the justices who served on this court during our time period were appointed by a Democratic governor. The probability of a pro-equality outcome in the Kansas Supreme Court remained relatively stable (at about .40) from 1994 to 2003, when it crept to .47 beginning in 2009. Not surprisingly, the gradual increase in the probability of a pro-equality outcome corresponded with the tenure of Governor Kathleen Sebelius, who served as that state's chief executive from 2003 to 2009. After Sam Brownback took over as governor in 2011 (following two years in which Kansas was led by Sebelius's former lieutenant governor, also a Democrat, when she transitioned to the Obama administration's cabinet), the court's pro-equality trend plateaued. The existing Democratic appointees on the court limited Brownback's attempts to manipulate the court's composition, illustrating the power of "hangover" judges to limit an ambitious politician's attempts to rein in a maverick court.

Looking at the predictions for Kansas in figure 8.6, the probability of a pro-upperdog outcome remains similarly stable during this time period. We observe a slight decrease in the probability of a pro-equality outcome at the beginning of Sebelius's tenure as governor following an increase in that court's predicted pro-upperdog tendencies toward the end of the term served by her predecessor, Republican Bill Graves. Again, both the pro-equality and pro-upperdog predictions tell the same substantive story.

Finally, there is Texas. We observe a sharp decrease in the probability of a pro-equality outcome in the first six years of our analysis. This period of time overlaps with the middle and end of efforts by the political consultant Karl Rove to steer that court in a more conservative direction through the politicization of judicial elections. Recall from chapter 1 that Rove's campaign began with the 1988 general election in Texas.[5] Indeed, the probability of a pro-equality outcome in Texas declined from .32 in 1990 to .27 in 1996 and then remained relatively stable throughout the rest of our time period. By 1998, Rove's campaign had been successful: every Texas Supreme Court justice was a Republican. This shift in the early years of our data accompanies a large change in the conservatism of the Texas Supreme Court, with the average ideology of a justice on that court changing by .2 (on a 0–1 scale) in a more conservative direction over the course of the time period covered by our data set.

Perhaps unsurprisingly by this point, the story told by figure 8.6 mirrors that told by figure 8.5 as it pertains to the Lone Star State. We observe a sharp uptick in the probability of a pro-upperdog outcome in the first half-decade of our time period, followed by a plateau in the ability of upperdogs to build their advantage before the Texas Supreme Court. Again, partisan politics allowed interested groups to shape the composition of the bench, and their efforts are reflected in the predictions of our model.

Taken together, these estimates illustrate the divergent trends that states experienced during the quarter-century we study. Some states, like Iowa, trended in a pro-equality direction during this time period; states such as Texas and Alabama shifted in a pro-*in*equality direction during these twenty-six years. The estimates for both outcome variables tend to mirror each other, and all of these trends track well the changes in partisan control of the governorship.[6]

Discussion and Concluding Comments

The contribution this chapter makes to our thesis is its focus on how the state supreme courts create public policies relevant to political, legal, economic, and social inequality. The votes of individual judges, while important to understand, are not the same thing as public policy. Instead, policies are set by case outcomes—specifically, by outcomes that make it easier or harder to mount class action lawsuits that bring underdog litigants together as a class to challenge well-resourced upperdog institutions. These policies—such as increased state funding for poorer school districts or the protection of the right of workers to organize—are likely to have an impact on society, although assessing that impact is, as we have often said, entirely beyond the scope of this research. Thus, the analysis in this chapter has been directed toward understanding policy outcomes in three overarching issue domains that comprise nine types of issues and involve dozens and dozens of specific legal policy matters.

State supreme court policymaking can contribute to policies advancing or retarding political, legal, economic, and social inequality in two distinct ways. First, as we argued in the first half of this chapter, these courts set legal policy on a wide variety of specific issues, such as whether employers can employ employees "at will." Second, these courts may be unequally responsive to different sectors of their constituents; they may be particularly attuned to the interests of overprivileged upperdog litigants on whatever matters they seek through their litigation, but especially when these haves are seeking greater political, legal, economic, and social inequality.

The principal finding of this chapter should surprise no one who has read the earlier chapters: the ideological propensity of the state high court is an important predictor of the policies it makes. Those courts staffed by more conservative judges make more anti-equality policies; conversely, those courts in which liberals are more prevalent tend to make more pro-equality policies. If we were asked how to get these courts to make more decisions favoring political, legal, economic, and social equality, our first advice, without any doubt, would be to get more liberal judges on the state high benches.

While judicial ideologies are certainly not all there is to the story, we have adduced entirely new evidence that the so-called resource advantage of upperdog litigants may be less important to policy outcomes than ideological agreement between the litigation objections of these haves and the ideological preferences of the justices. This, we contend, is one of the most important findings of this chapter, and it calls into question a great many of the conclusions reached from previous research as to why the haves come out ahead. New research must squarely face the role of ideological congruence between judges and upperdogs as an explanation for unequal success in the state supreme courts.

No state illustrates this conclusion better than Alabama. We have discovered many things about the Alabama Supreme Court. First, it has evolved from fairly significant dominance by Democratic judges to nearly complete control by Republicans judges. Second, the policies made by the court strongly favor greater political, legal, economic, and social inequality, and there has been some change in those policy outputs over time. To put this slightly differently, as the court became more conservative, so too did its bias in favor of anti-equality policies. Finally, the court became even more responsive to the litigation of overprivileged upperdogs over time, and especially when those litigants' suits were in favor of greater inequality. The Alabama Supreme Court is neither the most conservative nor the most pro-inequality court in the country, but it is one that vividly illustrates our claim that the ideologies of high court judges matter, especially for public policy.

Not a whole lot else matters for variance in equality policies relevant to political, legal, economic, and social inequality that result from case outcomes, once judicial ideologies are taken into account and litigant resources and objectives are factored in. We find, for example, no independent role of public opinion; instead, we argue, public opinion is most potent in influencing the selection of judges and in guiding the votes of individual judges. Rather than public opinion, it is ideology that reigns supreme.

As we close this chapter, we will not rehearse our global understanding of how judges with different ideological orientations get to the state supreme courts; that story is best told (or retold) in the concluding chapter. Here we will simply reinforce our conclusion that these cases vary greatly in how much they contribute to policy favoring political, legal, economic, and social inequality, largely according to the ideologies of the judges and the litigants who pursue their cases before these courts. To make that argument forcefully and coherently, however, we need to review what we have learned throughout this book. It is therefore time to gather the strands of analysis we have spun throughout the previous pages and weave them together.

Appendix 8.A: Supplementary Statistical Analyses

Table 8.A.1 Summary Statistics

	Mean	Standard Deviation
Court's ideology	.50	.21
Partisan election	.24	.42
Nonpartisan election	.27	.45
Retention election	.28	.45
Public opinion liberalism	.58	.19
Public beliefs about inequality	.56	.15
Whether Confederate state	.29	.45
Judicial compensation	.39	.18
Democratic Party dominance of state government	.52	.21
Lower court pro-equality	.51	.46
Lower court pro-upperdog	.48	.46
Upperdog party sought equality	.28	.40
Decided on procedural grounds	.17	.38
Rights of workers and employees	.23	.42
Access to justice institutions	.48	.50

Source: Authors' compilation.
Notes: $N = 5,875$. These summary statistics are for the full case data set (the data underlying table 8.1).

Table 8.A.2 Pairwise Comparisons: Direct Effect of Retention Method

	No Election	Partisan Election	Nonpartisan Election	Retention Election
No election				
Partisan election	.764			
Nonpartisan election	.228	.124		
Retention election	.237	.157	.944	

Source: Authors' compilation.
Notes: The cell entries are probabilities for a null hypothesis test comparing the equality of coefficients for each pair of retention methods. Small probabilities indicate that the effect of retention method (in the model reported in table 8.1) differs across the two retention methods.

CHAPTER 9

State Supreme Courts and Political, Legal, Economic, and Social Inequality

IN THIS CONCLUDING CHAPTER, we take a few steps away from our data to place our research findings within the larger context of the problem of political, legal, economic, and social inequality in the United States. In the earlier chapters, we have traversed a great deal of theoretical and empirical territory, with analyses of cases, litigants, judges, courts, institutions, and states. Given the diversity of our analyses and the complexity of our various findings, it is incumbent upon us to now try to figure out how everything fits together. What have we learned about the role of state supreme courts with regard to their policies relevant to the creation, maintenance, or amelioration of inequality in the United States?

It is worth reiterating here at the beginning of the chapter that ours is not a study of every sort of governmental policy that might affect political, legal, economic, and social inequality in the U.S. states. Many matters of distribution and redistribution rarely (if ever) make it to the state supreme courts because no substantive legal or constitutional issues are at stake, such as with many (if not most) aspects of tax policies.

Instead, we focus specifically on court rulings pertaining to the rights of minorities, including poor people, the rights of workers and employees, and policies affecting access to the state's justice institutions. When we address court decisions on political, legal, economic, and social inequality, we have in mind judicial rulings such as those that:

- Determine whether state funding for public school districts must be equalized in one form or another
- Determine whether gay people should be free from discrimination and allowed the same rights as all other citizens
- Determine whether barriers to equal political participation should be loosened
- Determine whether collective bargaining rights should be strengthened
- Determine whether the rights of employees vis-à-vis their employers should be strengthened
- Determine whether citizens can take their complaints against powerful institutions to state-run justice institutions for adjudication
- Determine whether it will be easier to mount lawsuits against powerful institutions because the supply of interested attorneys is increased
- Determine whether it will be easier for citizens to win lawsuits alleging injuries by powerful private institutions

While we believe we have captured the vast majority of state high court issue domains relevant to political, legal, economic, and social inequality, there are undoubtedly some important individual cases we have overlooked. And most important, issue domains that are rarely if ever litigated are beyond the purview of this project's concern with the predominant policy outputs of the state supreme courts.

One of the most important insights of those who have studied judicial policymaking is that well-resourced litigants not only seek to win their lawsuits—no surprise there—but that they also seek to shape the rules governing future litigation.[1] Examples are easy to find: Which party has the burden of proof in employment and housing discrimination cases? Can companies and institutions be held liable for Covid-related injuries to their employees? In some instances, relevant policies may be set by courts—as pertains, for instance, to punitive damages or even to how interest on damages is calculated (simple versus compounded). In other instances, powerful interests seek advantages through legislation on which courts may or may not be asked to pass judgment (for example, voter identification laws). Judge-made law—the essence of common law—is sometimes not as "sexy" as legislatively made law because it is often created in the context of rulings in individual cases rather than debated in the state legislature and enacted at signing ceremonies. Judicial precedents, in policy domains such as employment at will, are powerful and efficacious declarations of public policy even if they are often announced "under the radar," or if their policy significance is not appreciated by the mass media. Judicial scholars have long recognized this; our hope is that the analyses in this book have gone some distance toward convincing nonjudicial observers of the importance of the decisions of the country's fifty state supreme courts.

The conventional view of courts is that they are minoritarian institutions whose main function is to keep the majority in check and ensure that it plays by the rules of the democratic game. The quintessential exemplar, perhaps in the world, is the U.S. Supreme Court, which assumed the towering power of judicial review long ago, and whose judges can serve for their lifetimes with practically no accountability to the majority. These de jure judicial independence protections provide the nation's high court with the ability, both legally and practically, to make the decisions the justices think are correct without much real fear of reprisal by the other branches of government or their constituents, the American people. As Jeffrey Segal and Harold Spaeth taught us years ago, these institutional features provide Supreme Court justices with a nearly unparalleled level of judicial independence that, in turn, creates an environment in which they can cast their votes on cases in ways that largely align with their policy preferences.[2]

But advancing the interests of overprivileged minorities does not seem to require that courts be minoritarian institutions, as so many before us have assumed. Instead, institutions accountable to the majority may contribute to political, legal, economic, and social inequality if majority preferences do not favor reducing inequality. Or if those with control of who serves in majoritarian institutions prefer inequality, they will tend to select agents who share their views. Majoritarianism, by itself, is no cure for inequality in America. Perhaps it is ironic, but the interests of overprivileged upperdogs can be (and often are) served by majority rule.

It is important to reemphasize how much the state and federal courts in the United States differ. Perhaps the interests of upperdog minorities are advanced by the federal courts' lack of accountability, but as we have just noted, increased accountability to the majority in the U.S. states does not necessarily produce pro-equality outcomes. The state courts are different, at least formally, because nearly all state supreme court judges are held to some mechanisms of accountability.[3] Of course, there are a handful of exceptions—a few state judges essentially have lifetime tenure—but most state high court judges face a channel of accountability nearly unheard of anywhere else in the world: the endorsement of the electorate.[4] To continue to serve as judges on their state high courts, most of these justices must win the votes of at least a plurality of the voting public at the end of each of their terms of service. Despite these differences, we would not be surprised to find that unaccountable federal judges in Texas are just as conservative—and pro-inequality—as are the elected judges of the Texas Supreme Court.

Some might argue that state judicial elections have traditionally been elections in name only, and that, as a consequence, they have traditionally not been a vehicle through which the majority gets its preferences represented.[5] Without a doubt, judicial electoral accountability has historically been feeble and ineffective at best; the textbook example is the rubber-stamp Missouri-plan retention elections. Nearly all state supreme court justices who face this type of election are retained by voters, suggesting that what is theoretically a type of accountability may fail to have teeth in practice.[6] Consequently, throughout most of American history the mass public has played only a passive and submissive role in selecting and removing state supreme court justices.

But things have changed. In the 1980s, state courts came under more intense political scrutiny, primarily from Republicans and mainly owing to civil justice concerns (often under the banner of so-called tort reform). The Republicans recognized these courts as important policymaking institutions that were making what they considered disagreeable, too-liberal policies, and therefore they sought to break the historical Democratic stranglehold on these institutions.[7] Generally speaking, the Republicans succeeded, although our evidence is that from 1990 to 2015 the state supreme courts as a whole changed from tilting toward Democrats and liberals to a relatively even balance between the two political parties. By 2015, the number of state supreme court justices who were Democrats was very nearly equal to the number who were Republicans.

But the state high courts vary greatly on many, many different dimensions. We have repeatedly mentioned that the Alabama and Texas courts changed markedly, but perhaps we have not emphasized enough that courts like the Maryland and South Dakota high courts changed very little. These fifty state high courts have also varied enormously in their rulings on cases involving political, legal, economic, and social inequality: courts like the Kansas and New Jersey courts frequently (even typically) make decisions that advance equality, while the Texas and Indiana supreme courts have a strong tendency to issue rulings that favor inequality. Perhaps at some level we knew that the state supreme courts were enormously varied, but we have been impressed throughout our research by the breadth and depth of that variability, from the educational backgrounds of the justices to the frequency of dissent on the high courts to how they rule on cases pertinent to inequality.

Variability is interesting, to be sure, but how do we understand how these courts have contributed (if they have) to the levels of political, legal, economic, and social inequality in the United States? After all, answering that question is what motivated this project in the first place.

Our first answer, which follows from the previous discussion, is that some courts have ruled in favor of equality while others have not, and yet a third group is fairly mixed in its decisions. But this then raises the next question: What accounts for this intercourt variability?

At the most abstract and theoretical level, our findings require us to question the assumption that the state high courts are effective minoritarian institutions that protect the interests of overprivileged minorities. Indeed, as we saw in chapter 6, the party that controls the state government at any given point of time is also typically the party that controls the state high court.[8] The state supreme courts seem to be very much a part of the governing coalition in the states, just as decades ago Dahl suggested was true of the U.S. Supreme Court.[9] Furthermore, the ideological makeup of the state supreme courts in any given year tends to align with public opinion in the state. Where public opinion, especially on social issues, is more liberal, the state supreme court tends to be more liberal. Thus, in some sense, courts that advance political, legal, economic, and social equality do so not because they are independent but because they are dependent—in the sense of being connected to the other branches of state government and to the people of their state.

We think about the processes involved in the following terms. Public opinion is closely connected to which political party holds power in a state at any given point in time.[10] Candidates for state government offices who please the people are more likely to gain power than candidates who do not please the people, so this first relationship makes good sense.

The degree of party dominance in a state is also connected to the average justice ideology on the state high court.[11] This relationship also makes a good deal of sense to us. Most obviously, some percentage of state supreme court justices are in fact directly selected by the people, so the justices recruited reflect the preferences and values of the majority of the people in the state. Far more judges (and even nearly a majority of the "elected" justices), however, are initially appointed by governors or legislatures. Obviously, both of these bodies are themselves directly elected by the people; indeed, that periodic appointment systems may help courts keep in step with public opinion was one of Dahl's themes in his essay a half-century ago.[12]

Thus, regardless of whether the effect of public opinion is direct (the people selecting their justices themselves) or indirect (elected legislators or governors selecting justices), it is fairly unsurprising that the composition of a state high court tends to track the general ideological orientation of a state's citizens. While this may not be a triangle made of iron, public preferences, party control of the state government, and the ideological orientation of the state supreme court are therefore typically in alignment with one another.

Regarding the vast influence of political elites on the initial selection of justices, our evidence on the means by which formal selection systems are subverted by strategic retirements suggests to us that state governments, and governors in particular, care greatly about who goes on the high bench in their state. They may not require a supreme court that is an active partner in policymaking (though perhaps they do), but state leaders certainly do not want a court that blocks or imposes constraints on the government's ability to secure its policy objectives (which may sometimes be little more than satisfying its main constituents, such as major employers in the state who very much want to maintain the employment-at-will doctrine). Although our evidence is circumstantial, we believe that governors (like their executive counterpart at the federal level) put some effort into shaping their supreme courts, and it seems they are reasonably successful at doing so.

In many states, the state supreme court is clearly a member of the governing regime in the state.

And once these justices are placed on a state high court, many of them must face the electorate in order to keep their seat on the bench. A truism of nearly any electoral system, however, is that incumbents have some significant advantages in elections. Sitting state supreme court justices, even those initially appointed to their positions, are burnished with the veneer of incumbency and able to face the electorate with the wind at their backs. Moreover, elites—who often play an important role in the early stages of electoral campaigns (to say nothing of providing campaign resources and funding to many candidates)—can further minimize obstacles that stand in the way of their chosen judges when it is time for them to face the electorate. So long as the dominant coalition remains in power, in other words, it can use its resources to protect its judges from electoral defeat and, by extension, secure its hold on the state supreme court.

That last clause—*so long as the dominant coalition remains in power*—is an important one. In perhaps one of our most surprising findings, reported in chapter 6, we saw that the ruling regime's influence over state supreme courts seems to be greatest *in states that use popular elections to retain judges*. This finding is surprising because we would probably intuitively suspect that appointive systems, which remove voters from the equation, provide the easiest and most direct opportunity for political elites to shape the composition of the state supreme court.

This turns out not to be the case. Instead, "hangover" justices—judges from an earlier dominant political coalition continuing to serve on a state supreme court—are more commonplace in states using Missouri plan–style retention elections than in states using more competitive partisan or nonpartisan elections. This is the case because the average length of service among judges who are formally appointed to their position is considerably longer than it is for those judges formally facing partisan or nonpartisan elections. Indeed, as we have shown, the average length of service on the state supreme courts is more than a decade. What makes this important is that public opinion can and does change, creating change in the governing coalition in the state, which in turn can make a supreme court (especially its hangover judges) out of step with the governing coalition, at least in the short term.

The shorter average length of service by state supreme court justices in states with more competitive electoral systems provides more opportunities for turnover on state supreme courts. When those vacancies can be filled by governors or legislatures, those appointing elites have a direct hand in ensuring that the composition of the court remains to their liking. *But even when elites cannot fill the vacancies*, the electorate can help to keep the courts aligned with the legislative and executive branches of government: especially in partisan elections (because partisan cues have such a powerful hold over American voter behavior and because a straight-ticket voting option is offered to voters in some states), the electorate can *also* play a role in abetting elite capture by selecting judges of the same political party as they have chosen to lead the executive and legislative branches of government.

Thus, state supreme courts, to paraphrase Dahl, tend not to stray too far from the interests of the dominant political regime, *especially in states that rely on partisan or nonpartisan elections*.[13] Indeed, the political elites in power play an important role in ensuring that the court's policy preferences rarely deviate very much from their own preferences. In other words, it is highly unlikely that state supreme courts occupy an institutional position in which they can (or even want to) fulfill the minoritarian role that so many scholars ascribe to those institutions; rather, their own policies tend to reflect those originating in the political regime of the state. As Herbert Kritzer has argued, the declining dominant coalitions in some states have sought to manipulate judicial selection to preserve the courts as a controlling element, at least for a while.[14]

But what does this mean for political, legal, economic, and social inequality? Perhaps the easiest way to answer that question is with the assistance of figure 9.1, which illustrates our expected relationship between control of state government, the ideology of the state supreme court, and policymaking relevant to political, legal, economic, and social inequality in the United States. We posit that state governments shape the ideology of state supreme courts, such that these courts act as partners in the ruling regime. This, as we have just discussed, was robustly supported in our analyses in chapter 6.

The second arrow in figure 9.1 illustrates the importance of the ruling regime for inequality: regimes put judges on courts who share their preferences. Then these judges cast votes that are consonant with those preferences

Figure 9.1 Governing Coalitions and State High Court Rulings on Political, Legal, Economic, and Social Inequality

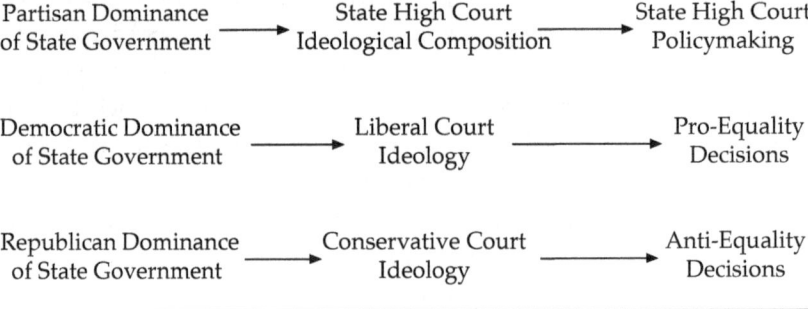

Source: Authors' compilation.

on cases relating to political, legal, economic, and social inequality. Where Democrats dominate state governments, they get liberal judges on their state supreme court, which in turn enhances greater political, legal, economic, and social equality. Conversely, Republicans select and support conservative judges, who then tend to vote against greater equality. Thus, by shaping the composition of the state supreme court, ruling regimes also affect the policymaking of courts on issues related to inequality.

This contention is also supported by our empirical evidence. In chapter 7, we tested the relationship between judges' ideologies and their voting behavior in approximately six thousand cases pertinent to inequality in the United States. The results of our analysis revealed that judges' ideologies are a substantively important predictor of judicial voting behavior: a very liberal judge is about 20 percent more likely to cast a pro-equality vote than a very conservative judge (all else equal).

When we sought in chapter 8 to explain the outcomes of equality cases heard before the state supreme courts, judicial ideology was also shown to be a powerful driving force. Across the range of average court ideology, our model estimated the most liberal state supreme court in our data (Vermont in the 1990s) to have a .18 higher probability of deciding a case in a pro-equality direction compared to the South Dakota Supreme Court in the early 2000s, the most conservative court in our data set. Looking at the propensity to decide a case in favor of the upperdog litigant, we observed a similarly sized effect, a .19 difference in the probability of a pro-upperdog case outcome between the most liberal court and the most conservative court in our data set.

But importantly, we did not stop our inquiry there: we found that upperdogs who seek to advance *inequality* are advantaged when their cases are decided by a conservative court, but that those resourced litigants who would advance *equality* fare significantly better before a more liberal court. We also found that cases are nearly 10 percent more likely to be decided in a pro-equality direction when the upperdog litigant is advocating on behalf of equality. Thus, both ideology and the objectives of litigants play a powerful role in explaining the ebb and flow of inequality in state supreme courts. When the haves come out ahead, they often have conservative courts to thank.

The influence of justices' ideologies was in no sense preordained. It is easy to rationalize our findings in retrospect given the large body of evidence documenting that U.S. Supreme Court justices' policy preferences are associated with their behavior on the bench and therefore to downplay the significance of this relationship for state supreme court justices.[15] Yet many studies have found that the influence of ideology diminishes going down the judicial hierarchy.[16] To compound the matter, some of the courts in our data set lacked the discretion to select which cases they heard; as a result, the set of cases we analyze includes many "simple" cases in which the law was relatively clear and ideology could therefore play only a negligible role in judicial decision-making. Moreover, most of the courts in our data set decided most of the cases we study unanimously. And finally, many of the decisions in our data set, though they dealt with important issues relating to inequality, were not the sort of high-profile cases, such as death penalty or abortion cases, that are likely to inspire front-page headlines (and, by extension, much more careful and considered judicial behavior). All these features stacked the deck against a finding that ideology is associated with judicial behavior in our database. Nevertheless, our results indicate that judges' attitudes play a statistically and substantively meaningful role in shaping their votes, and thus the policy outcomes these courts produce.

We should emphasize one other aspect of our data set that makes these findings at least somewhat surprising. That we find such a consistent role for ideology in the cases we analyzed—at the level of both the individual justice and the case—is noteworthy in light of the fact that most of these cases were decided by a unanimous vote. Even within this context, our analysis suggests that ideology played an important role in how these cases were decided. There are two important implications here. First, while it is easy—in an era of conflictual policymaking at both the state and federal levels—to focus on *dissensus* among state supreme court judges, the equality-related decisions we analyze (and the important public policies they promulgated) were characterized by extraordinary amounts of judicial consensus (contrived or real). Second, that we are nevertheless able to detect a significant effect for judges' ideologies even given this high rate of unanimity speaks to the importance of the process of judicial selection in shaping the composition of these courts: because conservative states tend to recruit conservative judges and conservative judges tend to vote in a pro-inequality direction, ideology is still predictive of judicial behavior in these courts even in the presence of high rates of unanimity.

Ideology does not direct judges' votes by itself; public opinion also plays a role in shaping the votes of state supreme court justices. We found in chapter 7 that state supreme court justices are more likely to cast pro-equality votes when their constituents are more liberal than when those constituents have conservative policy views. Put differently, public opinion appears to have an effect independent of judges' policy views on the probability that they will cast pro-equality votes in the cases before them.

But, as always, it is not that simple. Indeed, the role of public opinion is limited mainly to those states using partisan or nonpartisan elections to retain their judges. Under those institutions (and especially nonpartisan elections), judges' votes tend to track public opinion. Where judges face little likelihood of being removed from office—in states that forgo elections or use Missouri plan–style retention elections—we find no evidence that public opinion shapes judicial behavior. And this finding is not a mere statistical fluke. Rather, the estimated effect of public opinion under those two types of systems is incredibly close to zero.

The resources of the litigants in the cases matter as well. We saw in chapter 3 that our data set was composed of cases with dueling litigants with differential levels of power. And we also saw something not often acknowledged by those who study litigant power: a substantial number of our cases involved powerful litigants who sought to advance *equality*. In other words, contrary to a common assumption that society's upper-dogs uniformly seek to perpetuate inequality, we determined that this is simply not true. When upperdog litigants appeared before the state high courts, judges were about 10 percent more likely to vote for equality in the case when the litigant seeking equality was the upperdog party. In other words, litigants vary in the extent to which they seek to promote equality through their litigation, and parties with more resources—because they have better attorneys or more money to devote to preparation, or for any of a number of other reasons—tend to be better at attracting the votes of state high court justices.

A corollary to the relationships we illustrated in figure 8.1 is that the answer to "What is the role of state supreme courts with respect to inequality in the United States?" is not clearly "They have made it better" or "They have made it worse." Rather, the answer to that question is "It depends." At the most elemental level, state supreme courts seem not to stand in the way of state governments enacting the policies they want regarding equality, and owing to the ideological likeness and compatibility of the justices and the state government, judges will tend to vote in a fashion consonant with what the state government prefers. These courts and judges are therefore rarely a nuisance to the prevailing majority. Or as Howard Gillman coyly put it: "Most judges will have a political relationship to the regime that is evident in their decision-making."[17]

Returning to Professor Hershkoff, the possibility that state supreme courts could use positive rights and constitutional manipulation against an anti-equality state government may be a false hope.[18] When courts seek to advance equality, they do so because they are the offspring of the political branches; when they seek to advance inequality, they do so because they are the offspring of the political branches. In some sense (but see the next paragraph), courts have little independent agency.[19] If the state political regimes seek to "organize, exercise, and protect their power," they will do what they can to keep the state supreme court from getting in their way.[20] It appears to us that the state governments have been successful in this regard.

But state courts are not necessarily therefore impotent. They can (and occasionally do) defy the ruling regime in a state at a given time. Our point is simply that the state supreme courts tend to follow the lead of the political regime; they do not necessarily do so because of intimidation or retribution; they do so because they are part of the "home team," sharing the same preferences and values. States in which the governing coalition did not corral the courts would be states with different politics indeed.

Returning to Page and Gilens, empowering majority public opinion might not be the panacea they envisage. First, public opinion in the U.S. states may or may not strongly favor equality (although the Franko and Witko measure suggests that the majority nearly always believes that the gap between the rich and the poor is getting larger). Second, elections can be influenced, if not manipulated: for example, laws can be passed to designate on the general election ballot which candidate is the incumbent or to allow voters to vote a straight party ticket.[21] And third, the effect of public opinion on courts can be indirect, mediated through the institutions (political regime) that control access to the bench. These regimes do not inevitably favor greater political, legal, economic, and social equality.

Finally, perhaps one of our most important conclusions relates to something that we did *not* find: evidence that state supreme courts stand as independent counterweights against rising pro-inequality policies promulgated by the legislative and executive branches of government. Given the near-mythical status that many Americans ascribe to the judiciary, rooted in famous pro-equality decisions such as *Brown v. Board of Education* and *Obergefell v. Hodges*, we might have expected these courts to play a strong minoritarian role in state policymaking. That does not seem to be the case. Instead, our analyses lead us to conclude that state high courts are essentially majoritarian institutions whose composition reflects the ruling political regime in a state at a given point in time and whose ways of ruling follow directly from the institution's ideological composition. Indeed, it seems that, rare high-profile rulings like Iowa's *Varnum* aside, state high courts do not have a relatively independent role on questions of inequality. Instead, as Dahl implied more than sixty years ago, it seems that these institutions are closely linked with the dominant political powers in the state and rule in ways that do more to legitimate that coalition's inequality-related policies than to independently create such policies.

This is an important finding inasmuch as it teaches us something about how these institutions operate as part of the policymaking process in the states. While each of the state supreme courts reviews inequality-related cases armed with a set of positive rights that they could use to advance equality in their state, their willingness to do so differs widely. In theory, these institutions are exceptionally well positioned to resist anti-equality policies made by the legislative and executive branches of government. Yet, because these courts are staffed through the same majoritarian forces that select the legislative and executive branches, they tend to agree with the policies those branches make. The result is an institution armed with sharp arrows that are rarely taken out of their quiver.

This finding is especially noteworthy given the never-ending conversation about the "right" way to select judges for these courts. Our findings that these courts operate as majoritarian policymakers holds across appointive and elective systems of judicial selection. Contrary to claims that elected judiciaries are better situated to stand in opposition to the legislative and executive branches of government, we find that the partisanship of those institutions is *better* represented on formally elected courts than courts that use appointments to staff their bench. In short, the legitimating role of these institutions remains strong regardless of the rules used to staff them: state courts are fundamentally majoritarian institutions.

To conclude this section, we return to some very important mechanisms:

1 *Ideology*: Our theory is based on the premise that appellate court judges have a good deal of discretion in a meaningful proportion of the cases that come before them, and that this discretion creates opportunities for them to vote their ideological preferences.
2 *Public Opinion*: We have shown that justices' votes are connected to state public opinion, although we are suggesting that the influence flows from the public to the state's political regime to the court, and therefore we do not necessarily have to suggest that supreme court justices actively seek out public opinion in the state as part of their decision-making in individual cases.
3 *Selection and Retention*: In states with an appointment system, it is relatively easy for the political regime to control who goes on the state supreme court. In systems using popular elections, it theoretically is more difficult, although informal machinations allow the political regime to have more influence than observers like Shugerman would have expected. Elections can be disruptive; elites do not want the courts' constituents to have so much choice that maverick judges can be selected.[22] Insurgents certainly see elections as one means—and often the only means—of challenging the governing coalition, but governing coalitions also do what they can to protect their power. Indeed, as we found, the correlation between partisan control of the government and the composition of the court is *higher* in elected

systems than in appointive systems, in part because so many "elected" judges in fact are actually appointed.

4 *Judicial Independence*: The supreme courts of the U.S. states do not rule in favor of greater equality because they are minoritarian institutions, free from accountability to the majority. Instead, to the extent that these courts rule in favor of equality, they do so at the behest of the political coalition that governs in their state.

Some Individually Significant Findings

We opened this chapter with our best attempt at weaving our theory together with the empirical evidence we have uncovered in an effort to take a stab at explaining how state courts "work" as policymakers with respect to equality. At the same time, this project has produced quite a number of noteworthy findings and results that are important to review independent of any role they may play in our broader theoretical argument. In brief, we have discovered that:

1 State supreme courts are active participants in the making of public policy pertaining to political, legal, economic, and social inequality. We were able to identify and code approximately six thousand state supreme court cases relevant to inequality in the American states.
2 Across nearly six thousand cases spanning twenty-six years for all fifty states, we found that the state supreme courts decided about one-half of the equality-relevant cases in favor of greater equality and about one-half against greater equality.
3 Relatedly, just about half of the cases were decided in favor of upperdog litigants and half in favor of underdog litigants.
4 The state supreme courts differed enormously in how they decided cases relevant to political, legal, economic, and social inequality. About one-fourth of the decisions of the Texas Supreme Court favored equality greatly; for the Arizona Supreme Court, the figure was about two-thirds of its cases.
5 Similarly, the state supreme courts differed enormously in their partisan and ideological makeups. For instance, over the period from 1990 to 2015, a tiny fraction of the justices serving on the Maryland

Supreme Court were Republicans; for the South Dakota Supreme Court, almost none of the serving justices were Democrats.

6 Over the period from 1990 to 2015, the partisan and ideological composition of the state supreme courts shifted substantially, from, on average, Democratic and liberal dominance to relative parity between Democrats/liberals and Republicans/conservatives.

7 However, many courts, especially in the South (for example, the Alabama Supreme Court), shifted from almost complete Democratic and liberal dominance in the early part of the period to almost complete Republican and conservative dominance later in the period.

8 State supreme courts are very much a part of what Robert Dahl called "the governing coalition" in their state (although Dahl was writing not about the states but about the U.S. Supreme Court).[23] That is, the coalition that controls the other organs of state government also tends to control the state supreme court. It is relatively rare for a state supreme court to stand apart from the rest of the state government in its partisan and ideological composition.

9 The justices of the state supreme courts vary enormously in their propensity to favor greater political, legal, economic, and social inequality in their voting on cases that come before them. Some justices nearly always vote for the party favoring greater equality; others practically never vote for that side of the case.

10 State supreme court justices also differ enormously in their backgrounds and career experiences. Particularly important in terms of predicting the justices' ideological propensities are their social class origins, whether they were educated within the state in which they serve, and their career patterns. Some of our findings, however, run counter to conventional wisdom: for instance, we do not find that having served as a prosecutor predicts justices' ideologies.

11 As to diversity on the bench, our findings are mixed. While women have made significant inroads on what was once a nearly all-male fraternity of justices, we find no evidence that different selection mechanisms, formal or informal, affect the number of female justices serving on the high courts. With regard to the races of the justices, however, we find clear evidence that minority justices fare best

under appointed systems, including formally elected systems in which justices in fact first joined the state supreme court via appointment.

12. Selection systems matter for the types of justices coming to the state high courts. For example, appointed systems are considerably more likely to recruit justices trained at one of the top fourteen law schools. However, we must be very careful not to rely too heavily on formal institutional structures. For example, despite formally selecting its justices via elections, almost every single justice of the Minnesota Supreme Court first became a member of the court via a gubernatorial appointment to fill a vacated seat. These justices, of course, then ran for election enjoying all the considerable benefits of being an incumbent.

13. At the same time, across all equality-related court decisions, neither the justices' ideologies nor their partisan affiliations are as powerful predictors of their voting behavior as we expected, owing in large part to the considerable number of unanimous decisions made by these courts. Again, the state supreme courts differed enormously in the frequency of dissenting opinions. On the Delaware, New Mexico, and Kansas high courts, dissent rates were in the single digits; for the Michigan Supreme Court, dissents were filed in about two-thirds of the cases.

14. We find little systematic temporal variation across the entire database, although the trends over time in different states certainly vary.

15. Public opinion also matters. Where the public is more liberal, the state supreme court is also more liberal. The findings reinforce our conclusion that these courts are very much (on average) majoritarian institutions, fitting in well with the political climate and orientations of the state rather than standing apart as countermajoritarian institutions.

16. Finally, because these courts are not, generally speaking, in conflict with the dominant political forces in the state, they tend to favor equality in states that favor greater equality and tend to oppose greater equality in states that do not favor equality. These courts are not impotent, to be sure; they are important makers of public policy for the states. But because political forces recognize that simple fact, they simply cannot afford for the state supreme courts to become rogue

institutions. And there are a variety of important mechanisms that state elites can mobilize to keep this from happening, from methods of selecting justices to retention systems.

Additional Broader Connections and Conclusions

We have focused our attention in this book on the state supreme courts in all fifty U.S. states. These institutions are part of the subnational governments of a single country, and they are subject to selection and retention procedures that are literally unheard of elsewhere in the world. Is there anything we can learn from these institutions to help us understand political institutions and policymaking in other contexts? We hope the answer to that question is a resounding "yes."

First, scholars of many types of political institutions—courts, executive agencies, central banks, and so on—worry about "independence." A good deal of discussion about independence focuses on de jure (on paper) independence rather than on whether that independence is realized in practice (de facto independence). Our findings add to a growing consensus that de jure protections of independence may be relatively ineffective.

As we have seen in our discussion of state supreme courts, even institutions that have relatively long terms, offer generous compensation packages, benefit from high levels of public esteem, and have access to other trappings of judicial independence may not be very independent in practice. The methods by which personnel are selected to office matter. If judges or bureaucrats or central bank governors are initially selected through an explicitly political process, it stands to reason that the individuals who survive that process are themselves relatively good agents of the dominant political regime. In this sense, our conclusions fit well with Mathew McCubbins, Roger Noll, and Barry Weingast's notion of "deck stacking" in executive agencies: if "control" of an institution is set ex ante, leaders of the dominant coalition can "set it and forget it," resting easy that the institution will generally make decisions that comport with their will even without overt interference after their agents are in positions of power within the institution.[24]

Second, we are not entirely convinced that institutional "independence" is the holy grail it is often made out to be. To us, it seems that independence is nothing more than freedom for judges to make the decisions that they want to, and that they believe are right. In an idealized world, sky-high levels of judicial independence provide judges with the license to follow the law without reprisal. We do not live in that world. We do not believe that judges necessarily seek to rule arbitrarily or contrary to the law in the cases that come before them; rather, because so many of the cases they decide are not clear-cut, judges can use that zone of discretion to shade the law in ways that accord with their policy preferences. In other words, complete judicial independence creates an opportunity for unrestricted ideological policymaking. Some sort of accountability mechanisms may therefore be useful to ensure that appellate decisions are not wholly ideological, even at the cost of the loss of some degree of judicial independence.

Third, it seems to us that political scientists—especially those who study state courts—have focused much of their attention on the mechanisms through which judges (or other politicians) are retained rather than the methods by which these individuals first attain their position. We think one of the major findings of our book concerns the importance of initial selection methods. Yes, retention methods might encourage political actors to look over their shoulder—and that may be to some degree desirable—but incumbents have at their disposal an array of advantages that can help them maintain their position. Because of these advantages of incumbency, these judges often serve for long periods of time. Mobilizing to remove incumbents from office is a task fraught with collective action problems, especially when the incumbent at issue works in a relatively low-salience institution, like a state supreme court. For this reason, focusing institutional reform efforts on methods of judicial selection (rather than retention) seems to us to be the more fruitful path forward.

Finally, we cannot overstate the importance of political scientists studying institutions *as they work in practice* rather than how they are designed on paper to work. Formal rules must of course be promulgated, but when they are implemented in practice, there is often both room for discretion and slippage—even to the point that these formal rules are rarely used! As we saw with methods of judicial selection, basic facts about the human life cycle, like death and retirement, intersect with these institutions to allow nearly a majority of "elected" judges to stand for election only *after* they have the trappings of incumbency.[25] In other words, to pay attention only to formal institutional rules risks seeing only part of the picture, and a perhaps distorted part at that.

Unanswered Questions and the Limitations of Our Research

Of course, the single greatest and most glaring shortcoming of our research is its inability to assess the *impact* of the court-made policies we study. Like so many studies of policymaking, including the making of constitutional policy, this study ends with the rulings in the six thousand cases. We cannot draw any conclusions about whether these policies actually mattered for political, legal, economic, and social inequality in the U.S. states.

We know—for example, from Gerald Rosenberg's *The Hollow Hope*—that court policies often do not have their intended consequences, as has happened with public policies on the use of recreational drugs or those designed to alleviate poverty.[26] Women may have a "right" to have an abortion, but if no abortion providers are accessible, the right does indeed become a hollow hope. It is easy to overstate this argument; after all, having law on one's side most likely raises significantly the probability of having an impact as compared to not having law on one's side. But there is no question that the passage of laws—by courts, by legislatures, even by presidential or gubernatorial edict (for example, wearing masks in public)—certainly does not guarantee that political, legal, economic, and social problems will be mitigated or resolved.

Because they were beyond the original scope of our research, we have not been able to say very much about two of our most important findings: the ways in which elites circumvent formal selection systems in filling vacant seats on the state supreme courts, and the ways in which practices limiting dissent have evolved and are enforced. Regarding the former, we know little about the details of how nearly all of the justices on the Minnesota Supreme Court—and nearly half of all judges formally selected through partisan and nonpartisan elections—seemingly coordinate strategic retirements so that new justices can join the high court by appointment rather than by the formally prescribed electoral process. For the exiting justice not forced out by mandatory retirement, we wonder what sort of deals are made or incentives provided as part of the retirement bargain; for entering justices, we wonder what sort of loyalty is expected or generated by their appointment to the court. Of course, once on the court, dynamics change owing to retention practices.[27] But this attempt to manipulate the formal selection system probably has many consequences that, at present, are poorly understood.

We are not the first scholars to notice that dissent on some state supreme courts is relatively uncommon.[28] We nevertheless wonder how it is that, of fifty-two decisions by the Kansas Supreme Court on cases involving political, legal, economic, and social inequality, only three generated any dissenting opinions. We juxtapose this finding with the fact that four of the most pro-equality justices in our database have sat on the Kansas Supreme Court: Eric S. Rosen (92 percent pro-equality), Lee A. Johnson (91 percent pro-equality), Carol A. Brier (84 percent pro-equality), and William Daniel Biles (82 percent pro-equality). We realize that Kansas has been a hotbed of interbranch conflict (mainly over school finance), but we do not typically associate Kansas with strong liberalism. But the Democratic governor in that state during our time period had powerful opportunities to shape that court's composition and, by extension, its policy outputs. At the same time, a very large majority of the Kansas Supreme Court decisions were unanimous. It is not at all clear to us how this came to be.

We are also in the dark as to how the most pro-equality state supreme court in the land is found in Arizona (although it does not surprise us that the second-most pro-equality court is New Jersey's). Undoubtedly, some noise is introduced in our data by the simple fact that the distribution of types of cases assuredly varies across states; these courts are deciding cases that arise in their individual state contexts, and it would be an audacious claim to assert that the cases are strictly equivalent in any meaningful sense. We have tried to implement some case-level controls, but frankly, we are unimpressed with our own efforts on this score.[29]

We want to return to our "birds of a feather" findings. Scholars of law and courts have spent enormous intellectual energy on discussing and analyzing the countermajoritarian role of courts in the American system of separation of powers. While we have not been able to offer any empirical evidence on whether these political, legal, economic, and social inequality rulings support or oppose the laws adopted by state governments, we do report evidence that the state supreme courts are closely aligned with the dominant ideological and partisan forces in their state.[30] It is difficult to imagine, therefore, that these courts serve as a counterbalance to most state governments, although we do recognize, as we noted earlier, that ideology and partisanship are only imperfect predictors of how justices will cast their votes. And especially with systems that elect their judges, we recognize that "mavericks" do in fact come along from time to time.

Finally, another matter on which this book is entirely silent is the impact of our findings on public support for state high courts. A large literature has investigated the consequences of judicial elections for the public's support for state supreme courts and their willingness to extend legitimacy to those institutions.[31] Relatedly, studies of the U.S. Supreme Court have examined the implications of judicial politicization—especially partisan politicization—on judicial legitimacy.[32] These studies have generally concluded that politicization is a grave threat to the Court's public support.[33] Our findings have direct implications for these studies. If partisanship is the Achilles' heel of the U.S. Supreme Court's public support and state supreme courts are captured by political parties, would educating citizens about partisan capture undermine the legitimacy of state high courts? Likewise, would citizens think less of state supreme courts if they learned that many "elected" justices were, in fact, chosen by political elites rather than the people? Given the important role these courts play in policymaking in the states, understanding how our findings square with public support for these important institutions is a vital next step.

Data Resources for Studying the State Supreme Courts

Because we have immersed ourselves for several years now in collecting data on the decisions and judges of the state supreme courts, we consider ourselves in a position to offer some observations and recommendations about how information about these courts and judges can be more transparent and more readily accessible to scholars and policymakers.

We were frustrated to learn that many state supreme courts actually fail to report in their opinions the names of the justices who ruled on particular cases. Courts nearly always report the name of the majority opinion author (except in a per curium opinion, of course), and they also report the names of the justices who authored or signed dissenting and concurring opinions. But in many states the names of the other justices are not listed, making it virtually impossible to be certain about the vote count in the case, especially when justices joined (or left) the court between oral argument and the date of the decision. (Informal practices strike again!) Some states, too, decide cases in panels but are inconsistent in reporting whether or not the decision was heard en banc or by a panel. In one particularly egregious experience, one of our intrepid research assistants called the court to learn the identities of the justices who decided a case and was told by court staff that they were not sure who was on that panel and were not aware of a way that we could track it down. As far as we can tell, Lexis as well as Westlaw and Bloomberg simply repackage the information they are provided by the state courts; it is the courts that need to be more transparent in their reporting of opinions. It seems to us that a minimal condition of judicial accountability is to be able to know how each judge on a court voted in each case decided by that court.[34]

On a similar note, state supreme courts provide comprehensive biographies of their justices while they are on the bench. Then, when justices leave the high court, those biographies typically disappear, remaining hidden in the depths of archive.org for our research assistants to eventually stumble upon. State supreme court justices are important public servants, and the courts do a disservice to their constituents—and to their former justices—by not continuing to make those biographies accessible to the public, a task as easy as making a "Former Justices" page on their website. This is a simple and virtually free (the biographies already exist!) reform that state supreme courts could make that would both educate the public and acknowledge the important service that their former justices provided to their state (and this nation).[35]

Though it is rote to mention this in any study of state supreme courts, data availability remains an enormous hurdle to understanding how these institutions operate. We were privileged to receive support from the National Science Foundation and the Russell Sage Foundation to collect our data, and we have paid this debt forward by making all of our data available to other scholars. But collecting these data was demanding and difficult work that was made more trying by the opaque methods through which these courts report their decisions. We hope that our data, as well as other forthcoming databases on state supreme courts in the United States, spur additional research and systematic data collection on these institutions.

Final Thoughts

Political, legal, economic, and social inequality continues to be a pressing issue in American politics, even while the particular aspects of inequality may change from moment to moment. Unfortunately, there is nothing in this book that offers a panacea for this malady. And we fully recognize that the rulings of the state supreme courts are only a very small part of the problem or the solution. Indeed, were we to have found that all six thousand of the decisions we examined favored greater equality, we are not certain that the reality of upperdog-underdog politics would have been much different over the twenty-six-year period on which we are reporting in this book.

The simple truth of the matter is that conservative and Republican judges tend to vote in favor of inequality while liberal and Democratic judges tend to vote in favor of greater equality. Which ideology and party is in control of the state governments determines to a significant degree what type of judges go on the state supreme court. And it is impossible for us to imagine orchestrating any sort of bipartisan, cross-ideology agreement on the problems of inequality. Indeed, it seems to us that divisions over political, legal, economic, and social inequality may actually be increasing in the country.

We are nearly certain, however, that the state supreme courts cannot effectively serve to protect the interests of the underprivileged underdogs in the equality struggles. To put faith in the judiciary, even with its arsenal of positive state constitutional rights, is indeed a hollow hope. The myth that somehow courts will have both the political power and the motivation to act independently of the other organs of state government should be dispelled by this book. For better or for worse, courts are not the solution.

NOTES

Chapter 1: The Role of State Supreme Courts in Creating Public Policies That Affect Political, Legal, Economic, and Social Inequality

1. See, for a recent example, Gilens 2012. Other very important work on this problem includes Bartels 2008, 2016; Enns 2015; Enns and Wlezien 2011; Gilens 2005, 2009; Gilens and Page 2014; Hill and Leighley 1992; Page and Gilens 2017; Page and Jacobs 2009; and Rigby and Wright 2013. For useful literature reviews, see Erikson 2015 and Scheve and Stasavage 2017.
2. See, for a recent example, Grumbach 2018.
3. For examples of publications put forward by liberal-leaning interest groups to address judicial selection in the states, see the Brennan Center's *New Politics of Judicial Elections* series of reports (for example, Sample et al. 2010). For research funded by conservative interests to advance their favored method of judicial selection, see Bonneau 2012, 2018 and Fitzpatrick 2018. Judicial elections have been subject to intense interest by various groups since the turn of the millennium, and it has become routine for interest groups to spend hundreds of thousands of dollars (or more) to influence the outcome of a state supreme court race.
4. As Helen Hershkoff (2009–2010, 1523) asserts: "Unlike the Federal Constitution, which consistently has been interpreted as excluding affirmative claims to government assistance, every state constitution in the United States . . . contains some explicit commitment to positive rights." This article has been extremely valuable to our project.
5. Dinan 2009; Pascal 2008; Rava 1998; Usman 2010.
6. Buller 2012.

7. See Dahl 1971; Gibson and Gouws 2003.
8. 347 U.S. 483 (1954).
9. 576 U.S. 644 (2015).
10. Dahl 1957.
11. For example, Friedman 2010; Rosen 2006; and Sunstein 2009; but see Johnson and Strother 2021.
12. See also Hall and Ura 2015.
13. Douglas 1970.
14. McCloskey 1994, 129.
15. Michele Gilman (2014) provides a telling examination of the ways in which the U.S. Supreme Court has ruled in favor of political, legal, economic, and social inequality in cases involving redistribution and the social safety network; laws related to businesses, including unions; equal access to education; equal funding of public schools; and politics and power, including campaign finance.
16. Bonica et al. 2018.
17. Bonica and Sen 2017.
18. But see Cohen 2020.
19. For example, Rosenberg 2008.
20. Klarman 1998–1999, 161 (footnotes omitted).
21. Chemerinsky 2014.
22. 274 U.S. 200, 207 (1927).
23. Klarman 1998–1999, 162 (footnotes omitted).
24. 558 U.S. 310 (2010).
25. 545 U.S. 469 (2005).
26. 585 U.S. 1 (2018). For more on the contemporary Supreme Court's decisions on business issues, see Epstein, Landes, and Posner 2017.
27. Hirschl 2007.
28. Ibid., 212–13.
29. Ibid., 213–14.
30. Ibid., 216–17.
31. Ibid., 217.
32. Ibid., 218.
33. For example, Binder 1999, 2014.
34. See Grumbach 2018.
35. See Abrahamson and Gutmann 1987. While state supreme courts can utilize their constitutions to "raise the ceiling" of constitutional protections afforded to citizens, they are of course prohibited from interpreting their state constitutions to deny state citizens the protections of the federal constitution and statutes. In other words, they cannot use their constitutions to "lower the floor" of constitutional protections provided to citizens.
36. 463 U.S. 1032 (1983), 1040–41.
37. For example, when the Iowa Supreme Court ruled in *Varnum v. Brien* (2009) that the Iowa constitution protected the right of gays and lesbians to marry, its opinion

could not be appealed to the U.S. Supreme Court. For that reason, same-sex marriage was legal in Iowa—and untouched by the federal judiciary—even though the U.S. Supreme Court did not decide *Obergefell v. Hodges* until 2015.
38. O'Connor 1984, 5.
39. Tarr and Porter 1987, 10.
40. An obvious example is state and federal constitutional prohibitions on "cruel and unusual punishment." While explicating this phrase in a state constitution, a state high court need not be boxed in by the U.S. Supreme Court's understanding of the clause in the Eighth Amendment to the U.S. Constitution.
41. Hershkoff 2009–2010, 1534.
42. Ibid.
43. Ibid., 1535 (footnotes omitted).
44. We recognize that federal issues are occasionally involved in state constitutional litigation (for example, residency requirements). Nevertheless, state constitutional development has often proceeded largely unconstrained by the federal constitution and laws.
45. Rava 1998, 553.
46. Ibid. For a more expansive coding of welfare provisions that includes coding of the aspirational language often found in constitutional preambles, see Braveman 1989.
47. Hershkoff and Loffredo 2011, 924. Rava (1998, 548) agrees: "From the founding, the states were charged with providing for the poor, a state duty derived from English law and tradition." However, the "state duty remained largely discretionary and unenforceable."
48. See Nedelsky 1990.
49. Hall 2001a.
50. Baumann, Nelson, and Neumann 2021.
51. Holbrook and Van Dunk 1993, 955.
52. Barrilleaux 1997, 1462; see also Barrilleaux, Holbrook, and Langer 2002.
53. Page and Gilens 2017.
54. Shugerman 2012.
55. The literature on political intolerance is vast, ranging from Stouffer (1955) to Sullivan, Piereson, and Marcus (1982) to Gibson and Gouws (2003).
56. See Gibson, Claassen, and Barceló 2020.
57. For example, Dahl 1971; see also Gibson and Gouws 2003.
58. We do not contend that identifying different domains of rights is an easy task. Consider, for instance, the problem of the death penalty. Fortunately for us, the issue domains we address are less controversial.
59. Haltom and McCann 2004.
60. There are some important exceptions to this generalization, as, for example, in attitudes toward inheritance taxes.
61. For example, Hollis-Brusky 2015.
62. Bonneau and Hall 2009; Kritzer 2015a.
63. Bayne 2000.

64. Schotland 2001.
65. Gibson et al. 2011, 545.
66. Note that Schotland first made his widely quoted "noisier, nastier, and costlier" observation in 1985.
67. The idea that controlling the judiciary can be a powerful weapon for advancing upperdog interests is not a new one. As Adam Liptak explained in a 2010 *New York Times* article:

> Almost 40 years ago, a Virginia lawyer named Lewis F. Powell Jr. warned that the nation's free enterprise system was under attack. He urged the U.S. Chamber of Commerce to assemble "a highly competent staff of lawyers" and retain outside counsel "of national standing and reputation" to appear before the Supreme Court and advance the interests of American business.
>
> "Under our constitutional system, especially with an activist-minded Supreme Court," he wrote, "the judiciary may be the most important instrument for social, economic and political change."

68. This is a classic example of the widespread and deliberate misrepresentation of the McDonald's coffee case. For the truth of the litigation, see Haltom and McCann 2004.
69. Gwynne et al. 2005.
70. Green 2004.
71. Sample et al. 2010.
72. Bonneau and Hall 2009; Hall 2014a.
73. And in Bolivia today as well; see Driscoll and Nelson 2012.
74. See, for example, Lax and Phillips 2009b (pro-LGBT policies); Barrilleaux and Rainey 2014, Beland, Rocco, and Waddan 2016 (implementing Obamacare and expanding Medicaid); Barrilleaux, Holbrook, and Langer 2002, Dawson and Robinson 1963 (assistance to the poor); and Dye 1984, Hill and Leighley 1992, Kelly and Witko 2012 (adoption and diffusion of public policies). For an excellent review of the literature related to state politics and inequality, see Flavin 2017.
75. Walker 1969.
76. For a study that makes an analogous argument at the state level, see Flavin 2012.
77. See, for example, Hill and Leighley 1992.
78. Galanter 1974. For additional discussion of these studies, see chapter 3.
79. A great analogy can be found between Gilens's award-winning research and our project. Notably, Gilens (2012, 3) *does not* address "inequalities in the administration of policies once they are adopted." Just as our book considers the myriad factors affecting state supreme court policymaking, Gilens's book similarly addresses the many influences on Democratic responsiveness. Although Gilens acknowledges that there are more aspects of democratic responsiveness that scholars can and should study to fully understand democratic representation in America, he focuses on a key but crucial part: government responsiveness to public preference. We consider this an excellent model for our book.

80. In the field of law and politics, the classic illustration of this is Gerald Rosenberg's research, reported in *The Hollow Hope* (2008). The "hope" is that law can be an instrument of social change, especially because legal institutions are thought to be minoritarian institutions. That the hope is "hollow" is illustrated in Rosenberg's work by case studies in school desegregation, abortion rights, and several other issue domains.

Chapter 2: The Political, Legal, Economic, and Social Inequality State Supreme Court Database

1. We reiterate that the states vary in the names they give their high courts, and that we refer to the highest court in each state's judicial hierarchy as the "state high court" or the "state supreme court" despite its specific name. Both Oklahoma and Texas have two "supreme courts"—one dealing with civil matters, the other with criminal matters—bringing the number of state supreme courts to fifty-two. In general, we exclude the Oklahoma and Texas high criminal courts from our analyses.
2. Eisenberg and Miller 2009, 1469–70, table 2.
3. For another example of this sort of research that uses legalistic rather than policy categories for cases, see Kritzer et al. 2007.
4. Ware 2013; see also Gilman 2014.
5. Gilens 2012.
6. Bruch, Meyers, and Gornick 2016.
7. Spaeth et al. 2020.
8. Brace and Hall 2009; Hall and Windett 2013.
9. Canes-Wrone, Clark, and Semet (2018, 681) describe their search protocol: "for cases decided between January 1, 1990 and December 31, 2014: SY, DI(environmental or conservation or wetlands or pollution or pollutants or contamination or groundwater or 'natural resources' or 'oil #and gas' or sewage or landfill or 'hazardous waste' or mining or landfill or water or air or contaminants or 'impact assessment' or drilling or fracking or 'endangered species' or contaminants or air or water or energy or electric) or SY, DI(permit /p environmental or water or air or mining or drilling or landfill)."
10. Caldarone, Canes-Wrone, and Clark (2009, 564) used the following strategy: "First, we included all cases in the Westlaw categories for abortion and also abortion-related cases in the Westlaw category for trespass. Second, we searched the general database for cases with the term 'abortion,' excluding ones within the criminal code for 'homicide and abortion.' Because many state criminal codes still list abortion within the same classification as homicide, a pure search on the term abortion turns up thousands of homicide cases. (The Westlaw topic code for the homicide category is 110 349 350h 35 96h.) Third, to find wrongful death cases related to abortion policy, we conducted a search with the terms 'wrongful death' and 'fetus.' Finally, we searched for cases with the phrase 'wrongful birth.'"
11. LexisNexis 2005.

12. We investigated a variety of other possible approaches. For most issue areas, a keyword search returned case lists that were far too large for our team of research assistants to read. Another possible method, Lexis's "Core Terms" for each case, turned out to do a worse job classifying the known cases than did the headnote strategy.
13. We were surprised to see a headnote this specific do the best job of classifying our election law cases; in practice, it seems that cases relating to voting rights get tagged with this "Poll Tax" headnote because they generally include some reference to Jim Crow laws.
14. Specifically, we told coders: "By 'substantive or procedural ruling' we mean that the outcome of the case relates directly to the assigned issue area. It is not enough for a case to use a particular issue area as a setting; the holding of the case must have ramifications for legal doctrine in the issue area. In other words, it is not enough for a case to simply mention your issue; rather, the doctrine that flows from that decision needs to relate, either substantively or procedurally, to the issue area. Cases that relate to the issue area need to be coded, even if they do not change the state of the law (for example, they just affirm the state supreme court's prior decision in that area of law)."
15. For example, the Supreme Court Database (Spaeth et al. 2020) codes decisions that are "pro-underdog," "anti-business," "anti-employer," "pro-competition," "pro-small business vis-à-vis large business," "pro-economic underdog," "pro-trial in arbitration," and "pro-union" as liberal decisions.
16. Heise 1995. For other important studies of state high courts and school funding, see Bauries 2009; Bosworth 2001; Hill and Kiewiet 2015; Lundberg 2000; Rebell 2009; and Swenson 2000.
17. *Marrero v. Commonwealth*, 739 A.2d 110, 111 (Pa. 1999).
18. *Marrero*, 739 A.2d at 113–14.
19. *Abbeville County School District v. State*, 767 S.E.2d 157, 179–80 (S.C. 2014).
20. *Abbeville*, 767 S.E.2d at 159.
21. *Abbeville*, 767 S.E.2d at 179.
22. *Abbeville*, 767 S.E.2d at 180.
23. *Bismarck Public School District #1 v. State*, 511 N.W.2d 247, 262–63 (N.D. 1994).
24. *Bismarck*, 511 N.W.2d at 251.
25. *McCleary v. State*, 269 P.3d 227, 261 (Wash. 2012).
26. *Gannon v. State*, 298 Kan. 1107, 319 P.3d 1196 (2014); *Gannon v. State*, 308 Kan. 372, 420 P.3d 477 (2018).
27. *Goodridge v. Department of Public Health*, 798 N.E.2d 941, 969 (Mass. 2003) ("We declare that barring an individual from the protections, benefits, and obligations of civil marriage solely because that person would marry a person of the same sex violates the Massachusetts Constitution").
28. *Varnum v. Brien*, 763 N.W.2d 862, 906 (Iowa 2009).
29. *Lockyer v. City and County of San Francisco*, 95 P.3d 459, 499 (Cal. 2004). The California Supreme Court also directed officials to take all necessary remedial steps to undo the effects of their past unauthorized actions, including notifying all

affected same-sex couples that their marriages were void and a legal nullity. *Lockyer*, 95 P.3d at 499.
30. *In re Marriage Cases*, 183 P.3d 384, 453 (Cal. 2008) ("[W]e determine that the language of section 300 limiting the designation of marriage to a union 'between a man and a woman' is unconstitutional and must be stricken from the statute, and that the remaining statutory language must be understood as making the designation of marriage available both to opposite-sex and same-sex couples").
31. *Ex parte D.W.W.*, 717 So. 2d 793, 796 (Ala. 1998).
32. *Robert C. Ozer, P.C. v. Borquez*, 940 P.2d. 371 (Colo.App. 1995).
33. U.S. Const. art. I, § 4, cl. 1.
34. On alterations to election timing in favor of some groups over others, see Anzia 2014; on gerrymandering, see Ansolabehere and Palmer 2016; on moving polling places, see Haspel and Knotts 2005.
35. Feigenbaum, Palmer, and Skelton 1993, 65.
36. National Conference of State Legislatures 2019.
37. Ibid.
38. *Gentges v. Oklahoma State Election Board*, 319 P.3d 674, 679 (Okla. 2014).
39. *Holt v. 2011 Legislative Reapportionment Commission*, 67 A.3d 1211, 1242–43 (Pa. 2013).
40. "Firefighters in Alabama and Mississippi, police in Alabama, Colorado, Mississippi, and Wyoming, and teachers in Arizona all find themselves in a legal environment where no set statutes or existing case law governs collective bargaining at the state level" (Sanes and Schmitt 2014, 5; see also Slater 2013).
41. N.J. Const. art. I, para. 19.
42. Williams 1990, 46–47.
43. O'Reilly and Gath 1983 (citing the 1977 Ohio Supreme Court decision *Dayton Classroom Teachers Association v. Dayton Board of Education*, in which the court held that a school district has inherent discretionary authority to enter into collective bargaining agreements with unions).
44. Malin 2013. The state supreme court reasoned that the Virginia legislature's repeated refusal to enact legislation authorizing collective bargaining by public employees indicated that the legislature did not intend for public officials to have an implied power to enter such agreements.
45. *Indiana Education Employment Relations Board v. Benton Community School Corporation*, 266 Ind. 491 (1977) (holding that the act violated article 1, section 12, of the Indiana constitution because it precluded judicial review of EERB preelection decisions).
46. Malin 2013.
47. *Parkway School District v. Parkway Association of Education, etc., Local 902/MNEA*, 807 S.W.2d 63, 67 (Mo. 1991).
48. *Independence-National Education Association v. Independence School District*, 223 S.W.3d 131, 134 (Mo. 2007).
49. *Independence-National Education Association v. Independence School District*, 223 S.W.3d at 141.

50. *Eastern Missouri Coalition of Police v. City of Chesterfield*, 386 S.W.3d 755, 762 (Mo. 2012); *American Federation of Teachers v. Ledbetter*, 387 S.W.3d 360, 367 (Mo. 2012).
51. *Appeal of East Derry Fire Precinct*, 631 A.2d 918, 920 (N.H. 1993).
52. Muhl 2001.
53. Lemley 1987.
54. Muhl 2001, 4.
55. Ibid., 10.
56. Ibid.
57. *Rooney v. Tyson*, 91 N.Y.2d 685, 687 (N.Y. 1998).
58. *Talley v. Flathead Valley Community College*, 857 P.2d 701, 706 (Mont. 1993).
59. *White v. State*, 540 N.W.2d 354, 356 (Neb. 1995).
60. *White v. State*, 540 N.W.2d at 356.
61. *White v. State*, 540 N.W.2d at 358.
62. *Ryan v. Dan's Food Stores, Inc.*, 972 P.2d 395, 399 (Utah 1998).
63. *Ryan v. Dan's Food Stores, Inc.*, 972 P.2d at 402–4: "In determining whether a contract is unconscionable, we use a two-pronged analysis. . . . The first prong—substantive unconscionability—focuses on the agreement's contents. The second prong—procedural unconscionability—focuses on the formation of the agreement."
64. *Ryan v. Dan's Food Stores, Inc.*, 972 P.2d at 409–10.
65. *Nelson v. James H. Knight DDS, P.C.*, 834 N.W.2d 64 (Iowa 2013).
66. Buller 2012; Harris 2019.
67. For example, Galanter 2004.
68. Sternlight 2003.
69. Gutman 2018.
70. Demaine and Hensler 2004.
71. Sternlight 2003.
72. *State ex rel. Hewitt v. Kerr*, 461 S.W.3d 798, 803 (Mo. 2015).
73. *State ex rel. Hewitt*, 461 S.W.3d at 815.
74. *State v. Philip Morris USA, Inc.*, 927 A.2d 503 (N.H. 2007).
75. *Paulson v. Flathead Conservation Dist.*, 91 P.3d 569, 574 (Mont. 2004).
76. *Appeal of Town of Durham*, 821 A.2d 1097 (N.H. 2003).
77. See Fitzpatrick 2019.
78. *Ex parte Equity National Life Insurance Company*, 715 So. 2d 192, 195–96 (Ala. 1997).
79. *Ex parte Water Works & Sewer Board*, 738 So. 2d 783, 797 (Ala. 1998); *Disch v. Hicks*, 900 So. 2d 399, 408–9 (Ala. 2004).
80. See *American Abstract & Title Company v. Rice*, 186 S.W.3d 705, 706 (Ark. 2004). See also *Lenders Title Company v. Chandler*, 186 S.W.3d 695, 697 (Ark. 2004).
81. *American Abstract & Title Company*, 186 S.W.3d at 707.
82. *American Abstract & Title Company*, 186 S.W.3d at 707.
83. *American Abstract & Title Company*, 186 S.W.3d at 712.
84. *Wilkes v. Phoenix Home Life Mutual Insurance Company*, 902 A.2d 366, 368 (Pa. 2006).

85. *Wilkes v. Phoenix Home Life Mutual Insurance Company*, 902 A.2d at 369.
86. *Wilkes v. Phoenix Home Life Mutual Insurance Company*, 902 A.2d at 370.
87. *Wilkes v. Phoenix Home Life Mutual Insurance Company*, 902 A.2d at 372.
88. *Wilkes v. Phoenix Home Life Mutual Insurance Company*, 902 A.2d at 373.
89. *Wilkes v. Phoenix Home Life Mutual Insurance Company*, 902 A.2d at 374.
90. *Wilkes v. Phoenix Home Life Mutual Insurance Company*, 902 A.2d at 388.
91. Alaska is generally treated as an exception. See Di Pietro and Carns 1996.
92. Tunney 1974, 637.
93. *Alyeska Pipeline Service Company v. Wilderness Society*, 421 U.S. 240, 247 (1975).
94. Tunney 1974.
95. Eisenberg and Miller 2013. Note that the "American Rule" has been superseded by statute (as stated in 493 F.3d 110 at 114) with the enactment of the Civil Rights Attorney's Fees Awards Act of 1976.
96. *In re Corral-Lerma*, 451 S.W.3d 385, 387–88 (Tex. 2014).
97. *Broadwater v. Old Republic Surety*, 854 P.2d 527, 528 (Utah 1993).
98. *Broadwater v. Old Republic Surety*, 854 P.2d at 534–35.
99. *Pribble v. State Farm Mutual Automobile Insurance Company*, 933 P.2d 1108, 1114 (Wyo. 1997).
100. *Roberts v. Dudley*, 993 P.2d 901, 911 (Wash. 2000).
101. *In re Estate of Lash*, 776 A.2d 765, 769 (N.J. 2001).
102. Light 2001, 317.
103. *Jenkins v. Patel*, 684 N.W.2d 346, 348 (Mich. 2004).
104. *Jenkins v. Patel*, 684 N.W.2d at 348.
105. *Jenkins v. Patel*, 684 N.W.2d at 354–55.
106. *Mobile Infirmary Medical Center v. Hodgen*, 884 So. 2d 801, 818–19 (Ala. 2003).
107. *Stone v. Williamson*, 753 N.W.2d 106, 108 (Mich. 2008).
108. *Stone v. Williamson*, 753 N.W.2d at 116.
109. However, we do acknowledge that, like U.S. Supreme Court cases, these state supreme court rulings are not of equal substantive significance. In describing the issue areas, we have tried not to focus on blockbuster decisions but to instead document the mundane nature of many of these rulings. One limitation of our analysis is that a case is a case. We know of no reasonable way to weight the database by the policy significance of the outcome of each individual case.
110. Appendix 2.C reports the details of how we have weighted the analyses in this book to account for the unequal distribution of cases by major issue domains.
111. For example, some class action lawsuits are rejected on procedural rather than substantive grounds. The bottom-line effect when this happens, however, is that the lawsuit does not go forward.
112. Obviously, we did not read and code the lower court decision, so our analysis of whether the pro-equality litigant won in the lower court is based on the outcome at the level of the state supreme court and whether the earlier decision was affirmed or reversed.
113. In 12 percent of the cases, either there was no lower court decision or the decision could not be scored as either pro- or anti-equality.

114. As we have noted, there are no systematic patterns of over-time variability in these data, so we are warranted in aggregating across the entire time span for each state.
115. This analysis, which we treat as entirely preliminary, does not (and cannot easily) control for differences in the types of equality cases that come before these courts. Still, because we are analyzing the population of equality-relevant cases, we are comfortable with descriptive conclusions such as the following: the Texas Supreme Court, given the mix of equality cases that it considered between 1990 and 2015, issues the fewest pro-equality decisions of any state supreme court in the country.
116. As an analogy, people vary in the degree to which they care about being on time (sometimes referred to as "timeousness"). This is a generalized behavioral propensity that individuals attempt to implement within discrete events. Idiosyncratic factors may cause timeous people to not be on time for an appointment, just as chance can cause non-timeous people to be on time. It is nevertheless useful to determine the correlates of this sort of behavioral tendency as a central tendency (as well as conducting case-level analysis to understand deviations from the central tendency). There is a considerable history in judicial behavior studies of using an aggregated behavioral outcome measure such as this (for example, percent liberal). Moreover, for fixed attributes of judges (for example, ideology, an invariant attribute in our study), variation across cases in voting is understood statistically as within-group variance, which is error variance, which, of course, weakens relationships. (In other words, for justice X the prediction from ideology is for every single case the same; deviation from that prediction is error variance.)
117. Justice Malone was appointed to fill a vacancy on the Alabama Supreme Court in 2011. In the subsequent Republican primary, he lost the nomination to the infamous Roy Moore, garnering only 24.5 percent of the vote. He subsequently won an election to the Alabama intermediate appellate court.
118. According to the Kansas Supreme Court website: "Justice Eric Rosen is a Topeka native. After earning a bachelor's degree and a master's degree with honors at the University of Kansas, he received a law degree from Washburn University School of Law. He was in private practice and worked as an assistant district attorney and as associate general counsel for the Kansas Securities Commissioner before being named a district court judge for the 3rd Judicial District. He served 12 years before being named to the Supreme Court." See Kansas Supreme Court, https://www.kscourts.org/About-the-Courts/Supreme-Court/Supreme-Court-Justices/Supreme-Court-Justices/Eric-S-Rosen (accessed August 10, 2020).
119. For more details on this process, see Nelson and Gibson 2018.
120. The policy outcome questions were idiosyncratic to issue area. For the questions asked, see table 2.1.
121. One of these six cases was also judged in the ICR coding not to have passed the filter.
122. We reiterate that analyses within each domain do not raise any concerns and do not require any weighting.

Chapter 3: Do the Haves Come Out Ahead in the State High Courts?

1. Following existing research, we distinguish between litigants with great resources (the haves, or upperdogs) and litigants with limited resources (the have-nots, or underdogs). We offer a more complete discussion of this concept later in the chapter.
2. Google reports that this article has been cited over five thousand times. For more on this article and its legacy, see Epp 1999; Grossman, Kritzer, and Macaulay 1999; and Lempert 1999. For an outstanding accounting of the literature, see Kritzer 2003.
3. See, for example, Black and Boyd 2012, McGuire 1995, Sheehan 1992, Sheehan, Mishler, and Songer 1992, Ulmer 1985 (U.S. Supreme Court); Haire, Lindquist, and Hartley 1999, Songer and Sheehan 1992, Songer, Sheehan, and Haire 1999, Szmer, Songer, and Bowie 2016 (U.S. courts of appeals); Boyd 2015 (U.S. district courts); and Brace and Hall 2001, Songer, Kuersten, and Kaheny 2000, Wheeler et al. 1987 (U.S. state supreme courts).
4. See Atkins 1991 (England); Chen, Huang, and Lin 2014 (Taiwan); Dotan 1999 (Israel); Haynie 1994 (the Philippines); He and Su 2013 (China); and Sheehan and Randazzo 2012 (Australia).
5. Dahl 1957.
6. See also Wanner 1975.
7. On interest within academia, see Epstein, Landes, and Posner 2013a; Kang and Shepherd 2011. On interest outside of academia, see Cohen 2020; Liptak 2010, 2013; Shepherd 2013.
8. Epstein, Landes, and Posner 2013a.
9. See also Emmert 1991 and Farole 1999.
10. Wheeler et al. 1987.
11. Ibid., 438.
12. Ibid., 443.
13. Brace and Hall 2001, 414.
14. Ibid., 409.
15. Sample et al. 2010.
16. Kang and Shepherd 2011.
17. Wheeler et al. 1987.
18. Following all extant literature about whether the haves come out ahead in the courts, we are at this point in the chapter implicitly assuming that upperdog litigants always litigate in favor of greater political, legal, economic, and social *inequality*. The assumption is implicit in earlier research because the authors of those studies did not have independent measures of the policy direction of the outcomes in the cases and therefore had to assume that upperdogs always seek inequality. In our research, having the conventional measures of litigant resources (haves versus have-nots) *and* measures of policy outcomes allows us to test the hypothesis that upperdogs always seek greater inequality. In fact, our analysis will show that in a very substantial

number of cases upperdogs actually seek greater *equality*. Nevertheless, at this point we simply accept the existing framework for analyzing the success of upperdog litigants, thereby allowing readers to compare our findings with the findings of earlier research. Later in the chapter, we reconsider the implicit assumption of this theory and present evidence that upperdogs do not always seek inequality in their litigation. As we note, the implications of this empirical finding for the upperdog theory are quite substantial and may require that all earlier empirical findings be reconsidered.

19. The first-listed litigants are the petitioners in about two-thirds of the cases. As an implication, cross-filing is relatively common in these cases, meaning that a party is simultaneously a respondent and a petitioner. Additionally, states differ in how case captions list the parties to the case. We therefore had coders examine the "first-listed parties" (those listed before the "*v.*" in the case caption) and the "second-listed parties" (typically those listed after the "*v.*"). Then the coders indicated whether those parties were the petitioner, the respondent, cross-filers, and so on. The combination of these variables enables us to determine the relative power of the parties on each side of the case.

20. For example, see the gay rights case: *Advisory Opinion to the Attorney General Re: Florida Marriage Protection Amendment*, 926 So. 2d 1229 (2006).

21. Songer and Sheehan 1992.

22. Black and Owens 2012. See also Black and Boyd 2012; and Collins 2004, 2008. By examining a broad set of power differentials, our approach differs from that taken by Brace and Hall (2001), whose "interest centers on cases in which natural persons confront private organizations or businesses." They acknowledge that "this approach falls short of a comprehensive assessment of power asymmetric cases but serves as a reasonable and practical beginning for attacking the issue at the state level" (400).

23. A very large majority of our cases follow the convention of one party (typically the "petitioner") against another (the "respondent"). However, because our issue domains include public law litigation (for example, gay rights), the specific mixture of parties in the cases varies quite a lot.

24. Galanter 1974.

25. See *State ex rel. Hunter v. Purdue Pharma L.P.*, No. CJ-2017-816, 2019 WL 4019929 (Okl. Dist. August 26, 2019).

26. See Kritzer 2003.

27. The word "listed" is important. States often truncate the parties to a case when they report the opinion to Lexis. Typically, they do so when a large group of similar people is on one side of a case (for example, a group of parents suing a state to challenge educational funding). About 20 percent of first-listed parties and about 25 percent of second-listed parties contain a phrase like "and others" or "et al." in the case caption, leading us to believe that there were other parties to the case not listed in the caption. We suspect (though cannot verify) that it is unlikely that additional litigant *types* were obscured by this truncation.

28. In other words, given the case caption *Hunter Smith, Robert Jones, and the American Civil Liberties Union v. Clayton, MO School District*, research assistants coded litigant

status for Smith (other natural person) and Clayton School District (educational institution), because they are the first-listed party on each side of the case. Then, in a separate question, RAs coded the litigant status of all parties on each side of the case: other natural persons and private organization for the first-listed parties and educational institution for the second-listed parties. Given our specific coding scheme, we know the status of the first "petitioner" and the first "respondent," as well as the categories of additional listed litigants, via checklist coding. As we have noted, our analysis of litigant status or power focuses on the most powerful litigant type on the petitioner and respondent sides of the cases.

29. The "relative power" of parties is, in many senses, a more useful concept than that of a "have" or an "upperdog" because so many cases have equally matched parties, as figure 3.2 shows. In analyses discussing whether a have or an upperdog wins a case, generally we exclude equally matched cases. An alternative approach would be to include equally matched cases in the analysis, but there is no clear method for doing so in a way that does not artificially inflate or deflate the number of cases in which haves come out ahead. This approach is analogous to those that exclude unanimous decisions from analyses of the voting behavior of U.S. Supreme Court justices. Still, it is noteworthy and potentially theoretically important to acknowledge that upperdogs frequently are involved in litigation with other upperdogs.
30. For example, Black and Owens 2012.
31. Because the data revealed twenty-eight cases at the extreme negative and positive ends, the outliers were recoded. The resulting index varies from –6 to +6. This also has the advantage of making the power differential variable symmetrical.
32. For example, Segal and Spaeth 2002; Epstein, Landes, and Posner 2013b.
33. As we have noted, this analysis excludes those cases in which the power of the litigants on both sides of the case is equal according to our measurement scheme. $N = 5,030$.
34. Songer and Sheehan 1992, table 2; Wheeler et al. 1987, table 2.
35. Songer and Sheehan 1992, table 3.
36. Ibid.
37. There are only 26 cases with litigants who are "poor individuals," and only 46 cases in which a "minority person" is a litigant. There are 4,586 litigants, however, in the "other natural person" category.
38. 763 N.W.2d 862 (Iowa 2009).
39. 698 N.W.2d 858 (Iowa 2005).
40. 317 Or. 406 (Or. 1993).
41. Litigants' success rates vary somewhat by whether they seek inequality, just as it depends on whether they are the more powerful party. In our data, upperdogs tend to win slightly less when they seek inequality: in 55 percent of the instances in which the haves pursue greater inequality they win, compared to 59 percent when their litigation position favors equality. Thus, we have discovered two conflicting trends in these data: we find a tendency for the haves to come out ahead, but we also find a similarly small but statistically significant tendency for the party seeking equality to come out ahead.

42. In the aggregate, upperdog success does not vary by time. Within each state, however, court decisions often exhibit temporal trends. Unfortunately, some are negative and others are positive. The range of the standardized regression coefficients (equivalent to Pearson's r) from regressing the percentages of cases favoring inequality-seeking upperdogs on the year of the decisions is from $-.45$ to $+.26$. Because 56 percent of the states have negative relationships and the remainder are positive relationships, the mean is $-.02$ (standard deviation = .15; $N = 50$). In only six states is the coefficient of determination less than $-.20$ or greater than $+.20$. The most general conclusion we draw is that there is some temporal variability in these data, but it is not strong and the data exhibit heterogeneous trends, that is, trends that are idiosyncratic to each state and most likely heavily affected by the specific mix of cases in any given year.

Chapter 4: The Backgrounds and Ideologies of State Supreme Court Justices

1. See, for example, Segal 1984, Epstein and George 1992 (case attributes); Grossman 1966, 1967, Segal and Spaeth 2002, Tate 1981 (judge characteristics); Maltzman, Spriggs, and Wahlbeck 2000, Epstein and Knight 1998 (bargaining among judges); Hall 1987, 1992, 1995, 2014b, Brace and Hall 1997, Kritzer 2016 (institutional structure of the judiciary); Brace and Boyea 2008, Traut and Emmert 1998 (public opinion); and Canes-Wrone, Clark, and Kelly 2014, Shugerman 2010, 2012 (temporal differences).
2. The attitudinal model is the dominant approach to decision-making at the level of the U.S. Supreme Court (for example, Segal and Spaeth 2002), so we refer to judges' attitudes as a key determinant of their behaviors. We do not, however, have a strict view of what an "attitude" is and is not. Instead, we are content with equating "attitudes" with "values," with "ideologies," and even with "judicial philosophies" and "senses of justice." "Senses of justice" is particularly attractive to us because these cases so often pit one theory of justice against another (especially in a common law system). However, "attitudes" and "ideologies" are so firmly ensconced in the literature that we tend to default to these terms.
3. In frequently defining liberal outcomes as those favoring the underdog, the codebook to the U.S. Supreme Court Database makes clear the connection between upperdogs/underdogs and liberalism/conservatism. See Spaeth et al. 2020.
4. This is, of course, analogous to the common practice of treating "pro-defendant" decisions in criminal cases as liberal decisions and "anti-defendant" decisions as conservative decisions (for example, Spaeth et al. 2020).
5. Segal and Spaeth 2002.
6. Zorn and Bowie 2010.
7. Perry 1991.
8. Segal and Spaeth 1996.
9. Klein and Hume 2003.

10. Epstein, Landes, and Posner 2013a.
11. National Center for State Courts, State Court Organization/Court Statistics Project, https://www.ncsc.org/sco (accessed August 19, 2020).
12. Hall 2001a; National Center for State Courts 2020.
13. Emmert and Traut 1992.
14. Spaeth et al. 2020.
15. Hall and Windett 2016; see also chapter 7.
16. Vining and Wilhelm 2010; Cann and Wilhelm 2011.
17. See, for example, Segal and Cover 1989.
18. On the federal judiciary, see, for example, Martin and Quinn 2002; Epstein et al. 2007. But on state courts, see Windett, Harden, and Hall 2015.
19. Brace, Langer, and Hall 2000.
20. Bonica and Woodruff 2015; Windett, Harden, and Hall 2015.
21. See, for example, Nagel 1961; Pinello 1999.
22. See, for example, Bonica and Woodruff 2015; Windett, Harden, and Hall 2015.
23. Canes-Wrone, Clark, and Kelly 2014; Caldarone, Canes-Wrone, and Clark 2009.
24. Watson and Downing 1969; Goelzhauser 2016, 2019.
25. Grumbach 2018; Masket and Shor 2014; La Raja and Schaffner 2015.
26. See, for example, Campbell et al. 1960; Jennings and Markus 1984. But see Baum 2017.
27. See, for example, Segal and Spaeth 2002 (party affiliation or ideology); Boyd, Epstein, and Martin 2010, Kastellec 2013, Glynn and Sen 2015 (demographic characteristics); and Grossman 1966, 1967, Tate 1981, George 2008 (judges' background characteristics). For a review of this literature, see Harris and Sen 2019.
28. See, for example, Campbell et al. 1960.
29. Epstein, Knight, and Martin 2003.
30. Ibid.
31. Carnes 2013, 3–4, internal citations omitted.
32. Matthews 1954b, 18. See also Matthews 1954a.
33. Carnes 2013.
34. Gilens 2012; see also Page and Gilens 2017.
35. Carnes 2012; see also Carnes and Lupu 2016. Social class origins also color other parts of the democratic process as diverse as the narratives that structure candidates' campaigns to the issues that legislators choose to champion once they reach office (Carnes 2013). While few members of Congress or state legislators identify as members of the working class, those who hail from that background exhibit voting patterns that are strikingly different from the voting patterns of their upper-class counterparts. In short, social class is a defining feature of the American political system.
36. Carnes 2016, 85. See, for example, Galanter 1974.
37. Aliotta 1988, 279.
38. See also Carnes 2016; Wright 1997; Burden 2007.
39. Keely and Tan 2008.
40. Burden 2007.

41. Meltzer and Richard 1981; Rehm 2011.
42. Sullivan et al. 1993.
43. We recognize, of course, the diversity of types of private practice of law, ranging from solo practitioners to plaintiffs' attorneys to corporate lawyers. Unfortunately, biographical sources rarely distinguish among the types of private legal practices where judges were employed before coming to the bench, so we lack detailed information on this aspect of their legal experiences.
44. This process of social reinforcement may continue once a judge is on the bench. Because judges' votes are public, judges may risk social sanction for ruling in a way that is unacceptable to their peers. There is no better illustration of this than the ostracization of federal judges in the American South in the school desegregation era following *Brown v. Board of Education* (as documented by Peltason 1961).
45. Bonica and Sen 2017; See also Bonica, Chilton, and Sen 2016.
46. Langer 2006; Bratton and Spill 2006; Goelzhauser 2016, 2019.
47. With a tiny number of exceptions noted later, we exclude judges who served on a state supreme court in an irregular capacity.
48. Note that we have excluded the judges of the Oklahoma and Texas high criminal courts.
49. We have slightly different objectives in our various analyses that ought to be acknowledged. For our analysis of judges, we seek to define a population of judges who sat on the fifty state high courts during the period 1990 to 2015. For our analysis of individual judge voting behavior in cases, we seek to include *all* judges who cast a vote in one of our cases. These two objectives do not perfectly overlap, even if they almost completely overlap.
50. See, for example, Schmidhauser 1959, 1961.
51. We focus on the major approaches to measuring judicial social class origins, acknowledging that others exist. For example, James Brudney, Sara Schiavoni, and Deborah Merritt (1999, 1754) posit a relationship between religion and social class: "It seems plausible to infer that Catholic or Jewish affiliation is a rough proxy for social class."
52. Wold 1974; Gibson 1978, 1980.
53. According to Gallup, for example, between 2016 and 2018 only 2 percent of American adults considered themselves "upper class," while 9 percent said that they were "lower class." The remaining 89 percent of Americans described themselves as "middle class" (Newport 2018).
54. Schmidhauser 1959, 1961.
55. Marshall 1993, 143–44.
56. Epstein et al. 2021.
57. See, for example, Barber 1970.
58. Matthews 1954a, 7.
59. Carnes (2016, 100), for example, defines "state lawmakers as working class if they were listed in the NCSL's Labor Unions category or in its Business (non-manager) category, a category that was defined as 'blue collar; other white collar (clerical, sales etc.) and personal services (barbers, hairdressers, cashiers, etc.)' in the first study

of the occupational profiles of state legislatures." By this measure, no judge in our data set would be from the working class.
60. See, for example, Ewing 1938; Schmidhauser 1959; Hall 1976.
61. Cohen 2005.
62. Sen 2014.
63. Ideally, we would also gather data about the quality of the judges' secondary school educations as well. However, finding this information for a large proportion of state high court judges is impossible. Luckily, late adolescent and early career socialization have been found to be reliable predictors of legislative behavior. Using prior occupational status as a measure of social class, Carnes (2012) finds that legislators from the working class are more liberal on economic policy. At the same time, Carnes and Sadin (2015) find no evidence that *childhood* social class—measured as whether a legislator was raised in a working-class household—is associated with a significant difference in legislative behavior. This suggests that the effect of social class, especially for elites, is felt through political learning and socialization after childhood.
64. Brudney, Schiavoni, and Merritt 1999, 1752.
65. Aliotta 1988, 279.
66. This presumption of a causal effect of adolescence and early adulthood experiences has certainly been widespread with regard to some recent nominees to the U.S. Supreme Court (and to other elected officials who may have done offensive things in the early periods of their lives).
67. See, for example, Aliotta 1988.
68. These arguments land with greater weight in this analysis owing to the fact that we are typically considering educational institution choices made many, many decades ago. Today, with programs such as Pell Grants available and tuition grants at private institutions now commonplace, we suspect that institutional choices are likely somewhat less constrained by social class origins than in the past.
69. We do not know the state in which each judge was born and/or grew up, so the only data we can consider is the state in which the judge attended undergraduate school and the state in which he or she served on the state supreme court.
70. See National Center for Education Statistics, "Integrated Postsecondary Education Data System: Institutional Characteristics," https://nces.ed.gov/ipeds/use-the-data/survey-components/4/institutional-characteristics (accessed April 20, 2021).
71. At Duke and Vanderbilt, for instance.
72. Note that these figures pertain to the four hundred or so institutions that the judges attended, not to the universe of public, private, and religious schools. And the unit of analysis is the judge, not the school.
73. And, we might add, public out-of-state tuition, at an average of $2,149 (median = $2,034), was considerably less expensive than private tuition.
74. The University of Houston might be a classic illustration of how this measurement strategy overreaches. There are four flagship schools in Texas: the University of Texas, Texas A&M, the University of Houston, and Texas Tech University. A more restrictive measure might include only UT and A&M. However, the other undergraduate

school indicators pick up variance that is not captured by this flagship variable. (And of course, the flagship variable scores all private institutions—for example, Rice University—as not-flagship.)

75. Gibson 1983, 21.
76. Sisk, Heise, and Morriss 1998, 1463.
77. Bonica et al. 2018.
78. Bonica and Sen 2017.
79. This uncertainty is evident in the large number of studies that have examined the relationship between educational background and judicial behavior. Some studies find that judges who went to more prestigious law schools tend to vote more liberally, while other studies find no evidence of a relationship between educational background and judicial behavior (Brudney, Schiavoni, and Merritt 1999; Giles and Walker 1975; Nagel 1974; Sisk, Heise, and Morriss 1998; Tate 1981; George 2008). However, these studies tend to look at a broad swath of appellate courts' dockets and typically focus only on the prestige of the institution. We, by contrast, view educational background as a window into a judge's social class origins, and our measures of educational backgrounds therefore differ from those used in most previous studies, which estimate the relationship between educational backgrounds and political behavior.
80. Gibson 1983, 36. We acknowledge that self-selection is also a likely mechanism here. As Gibson puts it: "Prestigious law schools may not change the values of their students, making them more liberal, but rather more liberal undergraduates self-select prestigious law schools."
81. Although we admit to not knowing how enduring and widespread the practice has been, the conventional wisdom is that in-state law schools tend to teach the "nuts-and-bolts" of law, often focused on the state's bar exam, while national law schools are more likely to address larger topics and theories of law, politics, and society.
82. The "Top 14" ("T14") law schools are Berkeley, Chicago, Columbia, Cornell, Duke, Georgetown, Harvard, Michigan, New York University, Northwestern, Pennsylvania, Stanford, Virginia, and Yale. These law schools have consistently been at the top of the *U.S. News & World Report* rankings for law school quality and are routinely used by social scientists as measures of "elite" law school status. See, for example, Boyd et al. 2021; Hinkle et al. 2012; Hinkle and Nelson 2018; Sen 2014.
83. Nor have we attempted to adjust these cost figures for the years in which the fees were actually paid. All educational costs are reported in 1980 dollars.
84. In his autobiography, Moore (2005, 9) noted that his father was a farmer, a construction worker, and a jackhammer operator.
85. We have tried to be careful about our use of causal language in this chapter because, apart from temporal sequences, our analysis supports only the weakest of causal inferences. Even when an experience predates service on a state supreme court, selection effects are likely to be quite significant. Essentially what we establish in this chapter is little more than "what goes with what"—and perhaps just as important, "what does *not* go with what."

86. For a useful discussion about the effects of prior judicial experience on the quality of the bench, see Epstein et al. 2009.
87. Bonica et al. 2018.
88. See, for example, Segal and Spaeth 2002; Sunstein et al. 2006; Epstein, Landes, and Posner 2013b.
89. See, for example, Pinello 1999.
90. Where a judge had run for office on a partisan ballot, we used that party designation as the judge's party affiliation. We searched through newspaper accounts, biographies, and other sources to find information on the remaining judges. If we could find no information about a judge's party affiliation but that judge was initially appointed to the bench by a governor or legislator, we took the party affiliation of that appointing authority as the judge's.
91. We ultimately were able to classify every judge as being either more likely to be a Republican or more likely to be a Democrat, although we acknowledge that some judges were difficult to score. Charles Levin of the Michigan Supreme Court, for example, clearly distanced himself from both the Republican and Democratic Parties when he ran for office. Nevertheless, we classified him as a Democrat because he is a member of the powerful Michigan Levin dynasty. As another example, we scored former professional football player Alan Page as a Democratic justice of the Minnesota Supreme Court even though the only partisan information we could find came from a single source that discussed Page's postjudicial experiences. For other justices, we were forced to rely on partisan information contained in obituaries. Thus, while we were able to eventually assign a partisan label to each judge, we acknowledge that some measurement error might still exist in the construction of this variable, both because some of the information is based on only a handful of sources and because some information comes from postjudicial sources. Ultimately, we opted to force each judge into this binary coding scheme rather than omit justices from the analysis who were difficult to classify, in large part because the ease of classification is directly related to method of judicial selection: judges who run in partisan elections or who were appointed to the bench are easy to classify, while judges who were initially selected through nonpartisan elections are much more difficult.
92. Bonica and Woodruff 2015; see also Bonica 2013, 2014. There is no perfect way to measure the ideological proclivities of state supreme court justices. Of the two most widely used indicators—partisan attachment and the Bonica-Woodruff ideology measure—we consider the ideology scores the most useful. Our decision on this matter is based in part on the considerable amount of within-group heterogeneity among both Democrats (for example, the South) and Republicans (for example, the Northeast); in part on the performance of the two measures for various analytical purposes (discussed later); and even in part on the simple fact that the latter is a continuous measure while the former is merely a dichotomy. Finally, although we (and nearly all state politics scholars) often write about *partisan* control of the institutions of state government, we actually believe that, when it comes to courts, *ideology* is more important than partisanship. In any event, we utilize both measures

in many of the analyses that follow, only discarding partisanship when we reach our final multivariate models. Still, we recognize that all measures of state high court judges contain considerable measurement error, which, of course, works against the rejection of null hypotheses concerning the role of ideology in judicial decision-making.

93. Justice Alan M. Wilner earned AB and MLA degrees from the John Hopkins University and a JD from the University of Maryland School of Law. He worked in private practice after law school for three years before becoming assistant attorney general of Maryland for three years. He then returned to private practice before becoming a staff assistant for the Office of the Governor. He began his judicial career as a judge for the Court of Special Appeals of Maryland. He then became the chief judge for the Court of Special Appeals of Maryland before moving to the Court of Appeals of Maryland. See Maryland Manual On-Line, "Court of Appeals: Former Judges: Alan M. Wilner," updated May 5, 2017, https://msa.maryland.gov/msa/mdmanual/29ap/former/html/msa11679.html; and Bloomberg, "Alan M. Wilner: Former Judge, Court of Appeals of Maryland," https://www.bloomberg.com/profile/person/6358188 (accessed August 3, 2020).

94. Justice Dale V. Sandstrom received a BA degree from North Dakota State University and a JD from the University of North Dakota Law School. He worked for the U.S. Senate and served as an assistant attorney general. He also served on the staff of the North Dakota Criminal Justice Commission before being appointed state securities commissioner in 1981. In 1983, he was appointed to the Public Service Commission, where he served until 1992, when he was elected justice of the Supreme Court of North Dakota. See State of North Dakota Courts, "Dale V. Sandstrom," https://www.ndcourts.gov/dale-v-sandstrom (accessed August 3, 2020); and Nowatzki 2015.

95. Justice Frederic W. Allen enlisted in the Navy following his graduation from high school. He then graduated from Miami University of Ohio, as part of the V-12 officer training program, before attending Boston University School of Law. He next worked in private practice for more than thirty years before being appointed to the Supreme Court. Throughout his life, he was an avid sailor and a member of the Malletts Bay Boat Club. See "Frederick W. Allen: 1926–2016," *Burlington Free Press*, April 13, 2016, https://www.legacy.com/obituaries/burlingtonfreepress/obituary.aspx?n=frederic-w-allen&pid=179592227&fhid=19659 (accessed August 3, 2020).

96. Justice Larry Lehman was born in Iowa City, Iowa. He graduated from the University of Wyoming College of Law and then worked in private practice with the firm of Vehar, Lehman, Beppler, and Jacobson, PC. He first served as a Unita County judge for three years before becoming a state district judge serving Albany and Carbon Counties. He was appointed to the Supreme Court of Wyoming by Governor Mike Sullivan. See "Justice Lehman Dies at 59," *Casper Star Tribune*, December 10, 2004, https://trib.com/news/state-and-regional/justice-lehman-dies-at/article_2a350f25-8b74-54b8-8d4a-3da828339145.html; and "Justice Larry L. Lehman," *Albany Democrat-Herald*, December 18, 2004, https://democratherald.com/news/local/obituaries/justice-larry-l-lehman/article_720fef50-92c7-51a5-88b2-02a2ad88d68f.html (accessed August 3, 2020).

97. Because there was a single extreme outlier at both the liberal and conservative ends of the scores, we have rescored those two judges as just a little bit more liberal/conservative than the next most liberal/conservative judge.
98. There is substantial heterogeneity in the state-level correlations between these two variables. Within each state, these correlations vary from .031 (South Carolina) to .997 (Utah), with an average correlation of .66.
99. Our data set covers a longer period of time than the Bonica and Woodruff data set. In our data, the average state is missing ideology scores for three judges. We have used the equation in each state linking party affiliation to the ideology score to impute ideology scores for the judges for whom no score is available from Bonica and Woodruff. Where a Bonica and Woodruff score exists, we use it; where it does not, we use the predicted score from the ideology-party regression. Because there are no missing data for the party affiliation variable, we are able to score all judges on the ideology measure. In four states (Florida, Iowa, Idaho, and Rhode Island), ideology scores are available for all judges in our database. The state with the most missing data on judges' ideologies is Delaware, which is perhaps not surprising owing to the unique system of bipartisan appointments to the Delaware Supreme Court. In South Dakota, only two Democrats have served on the state supreme court, and neither has a Bonica-Woodruff ideology score. We have therefore used the North Dakota equation to estimate the scores for the missing data. As we noted earlier, the correlation of party affiliation with ideology among the large majority of judges for whom both scores are available is .63 ($N = 823$). For the ideology measure with the imputed scores, the correlation with party affiliation is .64 ($N = 981$). So the strength of the relationship remains unchanged, but the number of judges scored on ideology is about 20 percent higher. At the level of the court, the correlations of the percentage of judges who are Democrats with the average ideology scores, observed and imputed, respectively, are −.53 and −.49 ($N = 50$). Thus, again, the basic nature of the correlation of these two variables has not changed as a consequence of the imputation process.
100. See, for example, Grossmann 2019.
101. Indeed, when educational costs are regressed on the other independent variables reported in table 4.1, a remarkable 68 percent of the variance can be explained. However, when the variable indicating a religious undergraduate institution is omitted from the equation in table 4.1, the effect of educational costs on ideology is still not statistically significant.
102. Neither our data nor our theory is strong enough to analyze the complex causal pathways connecting backgrounds to experiences to attitudes. We note, however, the following relationships:

   Cost of education: −.45 → in-state law school: .16 → conservatism

103. Our coders coded these positions based on job titles, since finding reliable information about the types of cases handled by an attorney is nearly impossible for many of those who later served as judges. Some people with the title "county attorney" or "assistant attorney general" spend nearly all of their time prosecuting criminal cases;

others may handle an entirely civil caseload. We note, however, that this is the same classification system used by many states. Iowa, for example, defines by statute any "assistant attorney general," "county attorney," "assistant county attorney," "city attorney," or "assistant city attorney" as a prosecutor (Iowa Code §801.4[12]).
104. Bonica and Woodruff 2015.
105. Goelzhauser 2016, 2019.
106. To provide a sense of raw numbers, consider prior clerkship experience. Out of about one thousand judges, our coders indicated that only forty-seven had prior clerkship experience, but Goelzhauser found no evidence of that experience; for eleven judges, our coders found no evidence of prior clerkship experience, but Goelzhauser indicated that these judges did have prior clerkship experience.

Chapter 5: The Institutions

1. Savchak and Barghothi 2007.
2. Shugerman 2012; Kritzer 2020.
3. Hall 2001a; Geyh 2019.
4. Driscoll and Nelson 2012, 2013, 2015, 2019. A handful of other countries, such as Switzerland, use judicial elections to select judges on local courts with limited policy-making authority.
5. Shugerman 2010, 2012; Kritzer 2015a.
6. Shugerman 2010, 2012.
7. Ibid.
8. Ibid.
9. Kales 1914, 1917.
10. See Watson and Downing 1969; Caufield 2009; Goelzhauser 2016, 2019.
11. We have struggled with the nomenclature for describing various types of electoral systems. For example, "retention systems" might be used to refer to the methods by which incumbent judges are given another term and would, of course, be distinguishable from "retention elections," which are the elections based on the Missouri plan ("Shall Judge X be retained?"). The problem with the term "retention systems" is that these systems may not in fact retain an incumbent judge, and in many instances no one is being retained because the seat is open (because there is no incumbent). Some scholars have solved this problem by referring to partisan and nonpartisan elections that allow for the possibility of multiple candidates as "contestable elections" and juxtaposing them to "retention elections," equating the latter with "noncontestable" elections. Of course, while these elections cannot be contested by candidates, interest groups can and do contest them (Canes-Wrone, Clark, and Park 2012; Hughes 2019). Moreover, we cannot refer to partisan and nonpartisan elections as "reelection systems" not only because of open seats but also, and more importantly, because so many incumbent judges in elected systems get to the high court via appointment and therefore are facing their *first* election for the seat when it comes time for them to ask

voters to "reelect" them. Nevertheless, by referring to these as "retention systems," we are stressing the fact that these institutions establish incentives for those who hold a judgeship and who want to keep their job to cater to the wishes of those who determine whether they in fact get to keep their jobs.

12. Caufield 2009; Goelzhauser 2016, 2019.
13. This was also true in Rhode Island until a constitutional amendment was passed in 1994. The legislature sat as a "grand committee" to choose judges (Kritzer 2020).
14. Baum, Klein, and Streb 2017.
15. Arizona also used this method of judicial selection prior to adopting the Missouri plan (Kritzer 2020).
16. Bonneau and Hall 2009 (nonpartisan elections); Nelson, Caufield, and Martin 2013 (partisan elections); Kritzer 2015a, 2015b (hybrid elections).
17. Nelson, Caufield, and Martin 2013. We note that we have investigated various classification rules for these two states for the analyses we employ in this book; the conclusion of those tests is that whether Ohio and Michigan are treated as partisan or nonpartisan election states results in no changes to the substantive conclusions we draw.
18. Illinois requires a supermajority (60 percent) vote for a judge to remain on the bench. New Mexico requires justices to receive 57 percent of the vote to keep their seat (Kritzer 2020).
19. Savchak and Barghothi 2007.
20. By contrast, many states changed their methods of judicial selection and retention in the decades prior to our analysis. In our analysis, we account for the actual method by which the judges in our data reached the bench, even if that state no longer used that method of selection during the period of our analysis. For a spectacular history of recent attempts at changing judicial selection in the United States, both successful and unsuccessful, see Kritzer 2020.
21. See, for example, Shugerman 2012; Kritzer 2020.
22. Illinois allows the Illinois Supreme Court to fill a vacancy. Arkansas and Louisiana require a special election to be held to fill a vacancy.
23. National Center for State Courts 2020. Interim judges in Arkansas and Louisiana cannot seek election (Holmes and Emrey 2006; Berry and Lisk 2017), and interim appointments in Louisiana are made by the Supreme Court, rather than the governor.
24. Holmes and Emrey 2006.
25. Herndon 1962; Berry and Lisk 2017.
26. Aspin et al. 2000; Bonneau and Hall 2009; Hall 2001a.
27. Nelson 2011, 2017.
28. Pérez-Peña 2010.
29. See, for example, McCubbins, Noll, and Weingast 1989.
30. See Cohen et al. 2008; Hassell 2017.
31. Kales 1917, 425.
32. See Bonneau and Hall 2009.
33. See, for example, Aldrich 1995.

34. See, for example, Canes-Wrone, Clark, and Kelly 2014.
35. See, for example, Hall 2001a.
36. Bonneau and Hall 2009; Hall 2007, 2014a.
37. See Campbell et al. 1960.
38. Kales 1917, 425.
39. Nelson 2011; Berry and Lisk 2017.
40. For example, in 1949 Minnesota passed a law requiring that the ballots for the state's supreme court identify which candidate was the incumbent, if one existed (Bonneau and Cann 2015b; Bonneau and Loepp 2014; Kritzer 2020).
41. Hall 2014a.
42. See, for example, Jacob 1964; Bratton and Spill 2002; Reddick, Caufield, and Nelson 2009; Alozie 1996; Hurwitz and Lanier 2008; Goelzhauser 2016, 2019.
43. Shugerman 2012.
44. Hall and Bonneau 2006; Bonneau and Hall 2009; Gill, Lazos, and Waters 2011; Gill 2013, 2014; Goelzhauser 2019.
45. Geyh 2008, 2019.
46. Hanssen 2002; National Center for State Courts 2020.
47. Note that we coded the judicial selection mechanism that was in effect when the judge took office, which may differ from the method in use during the 1990–2015 period (Hanssen 2002).
48. See, for example, Holmes and Emrey 2006; Herndon 1962.
49. One research design point is important to emphasize before we go further: our analysis, by necessity, examines only those judges who actually became state supreme court judges. Thus, we can compare whether elective or appointive methods of judicial selection are more or less likely to put a particular type of judge on the bench; our sample of individuals includes only those who were successful at attaining a judgeship. We can say nothing about those candidates who were unsuccessful.
50. See, for example, Bratton and Spill 2002.
51. Ibid.
52. See, for example, Reddick, Caufield, and Nelson 2009.
53. This same pattern holds when we examine the relationship between social class background and selection system for Democratic justices and also for Republican justices.
54. See Key 1949; Baumann, Nelson, and Neumann 2021.
55. See, for example, Holmes and Emrey 2006; Herndon 1962.

Chapter 6: The Capture of State Supreme Courts by State Political Regimes

1. Throughout this chapter, we use the terms "elites" and "governing coalition" and even "political regime" more or less synonymously. The "elites" to whom we refer are those who make up the "governing coalition" in a state, and the nature of the "governing

coalition" defines the "political regime" in that state. Most important to our use of these terms is that they are entirely distinct from (even if connected to) the "mass public" in the state.
2. Gibson and Nelson 2017a.
3. See, for example, Rosenberg 2008.
4. Dahl 1957, 285.
5. Ibid., 294.
6. See, for example, Slotnick, Schiavoni, and Goldman 2017.
7. See, for example, Johnson 2020.
8. On the increase in attention to ideology in judicial selection, see, for example, Epstein, Segal, and Westerland 2008.
9. Dinan 2018.
10. The court-year is the unit of analysis rather than the court-year-judge; thus, there are twenty-six years for each state and fifty states for each year, for a total N of 1,300 (with no missing data of course).
11. In some years, the turnover is quite considerable. See, for example, the Kentucky Supreme Court in 2006.
12. Obviously, all judges who neither joined nor left the court are scored at 365 days. But joiners and leavers are assigned the actual numbers of days that year that they spent on the court. We then selected the X judges—with X being defined as the number of authorized judges on the court (5, 7, or 9)—who served for the greatest number of days that year. In some years, one or more seats were vacant for the entire year, so the number of judges defining a court in a given year may not be the same as the number of authorized judges. In no instance, however, is the number of judges we select to define the court greater than the number of authorized judges. This methodology has the effect of reducing the number of justices for analysis from 981 to 941, so the practical consequence for any given substantive conclusion is most likely trivial.
13. Note that because our measures of partisan affiliation and ideology characterize individual judges and do not change over time, it is reasonable to aggregate the sitting justices by court without regard to time.
14. Care must be taken with this analysis because it does not describe the composition of the courts during any given year but rather during the entire twenty-six-year period.
15. Perhaps no one has illustrated the consequences of party competition better than V. O. Key (1949).
16. Ranney 1976.
17. Klarner 2013. We used the version of Klarner's data found in Jordan and Grossmann 2020.
18. For a useful review of this literature, see Gillman 2008; see also Gillman 2002.
19. In this analysis, we focus on the sitting judges, as defined earlier. In a handful of court-years (six out of 1,300), a court was divided fifty-fifty, which we scored as "divided" control.
20. Dahl 1957.

21. There is a large and important literature on measuring state-level public opinion. For important examples, see Erikson, Wright, and McIver 1993; Berry et al. 1998, 2007; Berry et al. 2010; Brace et al. 2002; and Lax and Phillips 2009a.
22. Romer et al. 2006; Vavreck and Rivers 2008.
23. Erikson, Wright, and McIver 1993.
24. Gibson 1988, 1989.
25. Brace et al. 2002. When the sample of one poll is divided by the states, we follow Lax and Phillips (2009a) and Warshaw and Rodden (2012) in referring to this method as "disaggregation"; we refer to it as "aggregation" when multiple polls are added together before being divided by the states.
26. Brace et al. 2002.
27. Lax and Phillips 2009a; Pacheco 2011.
28. Gelman and Little 1997; Park, Gelman, and Bafumi 2004, 2006. See also Gelman et al. 2016.
29. Lax and Phillips 2009a, 2012. See also Leerman and Wasserfallen 2017; and Enns and Koch 2013.
30. Park, Gelman, and Bafumi 2004; Warshaw and Rodden 2012 (election results); Lax and Phillips 2009a; Pacheco 2011; Kastellec 2016, 2018 (large aggregated polls). For a cautious response, see Buttice and Highton 2013.
31. Caughey and Warshaw 2016, 2018; Franko and Witko 2018.
32. Caughey and Warshaw 2018. Christopher Warshaw was kind enough to provide us with updated public opinion and policy liberalism scores for our entire period from 1990 to 2015. We very much appreciate his generous and prompt help on our project. See also Caughey and Warshaw 2016.
33. Caughey and Warshaw 2018, 255.
34. Franko and Witko 2018.
35. Some missing data exist for individual states; at the beginning and end of the time series, the authors simply reproduced the public opinion score for the state from the most recent available time point.
36. Note that the correlation of the inequality opinion measure and social liberalism is very weakly in the *wrong* direction ($r = -.10$). More socially liberal publics tend to believe that "the rich are getting richer and the poor are getting poorer" at lower rates.
37. Our measure of Confederate status is our attempt to account for the often unique behavior of southern states (see, for example, Springer 2019).
38. Appendix table 6.B.2 provides information on the pairwise differences in effect sizes across retention methods. The three pairs that are significantly different from one another are no election and partisan election ($p < .001$), no election and nonpartisan election ($p = .009$), and partisan election and retention election ($p = .002$).
39. Looking at the actual rather than the formal method of selection, there is no substantive difference between initial election and appointment. Judges who were initially elected to their position served about one year longer on the bench, on average, than those who were initially appointed (twelve years compared to thirteen years). This difference is due, in part, to the fact that some initially appointed elected judges were

defeated in their first election; these very short terms of service pull down the average term length for initially appointed judges below that for the initially elected justices. Formal selection is the better metric to use for this analysis, however, inasmuch as these formal methods are closer to the retention method: judges in a nonpartisan election state may be initially elected, but they must face the electorate regardless of their actual method of selection in order to keep their job.

40. National Center for State Courts 2020; Ash and MacLeod 2020.
41. Hall 2001a; Bonneau and Hall 2009.
42. Geyh 2019, 161.
43. Bonneau and Cann 2015a, 2015b. For comparisons of the effect of partisan and nonpartisan ballots on voter behavior, see Klein and Baum 2001; Rock and Baum 2010; Schaffner and Streb 2002; Schaffner, Streb, and Wright 2001; and Kirkland and Coppock 2018.
44. A commonplace (but little discussed) strategy for imputing missing data is to simply reproduce the latest score in a time series for subsequent years, which is what Franko and Witko do. Kastellec (2018, 39) uses the same method.
45. Canes-Wrone, Clark, and Kelly 2014.

Chapter 7: Accounting for the Voting Behavior of State Supreme Court Justices on Cases Pertinent to Inequality

1. Shugerman 2012.
2. Rigby and Wright 2013.
3. It is therefore not surprising that Minnesota is the state that gave us the U.S. Supreme Court ruling in *Republican Party of Minnesota v. White*. That case overturned Minnesota's prohibitions on certain types of campaign speech in races for its state supreme court. For more on strategic retirements from state supreme courts, see Hall 2001b and Curry and Hurwitz 2016.
4. Efforts are sometimes made to restructure the state supreme courts, but they are contentious, expensive, and time-consuming, and they often fail (Shugerman 2012; Kritzer 2020). As a result, a much safer approach for elites is to develop and implement informal practices for maintaining control of the state supreme courts; public fights rarely produce much of value.
5. Segal and Spaeth 2002.
6. Zorn and Bowie 2010; Epstein, Landes, and Posner 2013a.
7. Hall and Brace 1992; see also Brace and Hall 1995.
8. Brace and Hall 1997.
9. Traut and Emmert 1998.
10. Bonica and Woodruff 2015; Brace, Langer, and Hall 2000; see also Nagel 1974.
11. Brace, Hall, and Langer 2001.
12. Brace, Hall, and Langer 1999, 1296.

13. Hall and Windett 2016; Dubois 1988; Hall 1987.
14. See, for example, Hall 1987; Baum 2006; Romano and Curry 2020.
15. Hall 1987.
16. Shugerman 2010.
17. Interestingly, there is some evidence that Shugerman's finding could be time-bound. Brace, Hall, and Langer (2001) find that elected justices are *less* willing to invalidate laws than their appointed counterparts; Langer (2002) finds that this willingness is contingent on the salience of the issue area.
18. Shepherd 2009b; Kritzer 2016.
19. Kang and Shepherd 2015. Kang and Shepherd (2011) show that elected judges who receive more money from business interests are more likely to vote in favor of those interests when those issues come before their court; moreover, this effect is particularly prominent for judges elected in partisan (rather than nonpartisan) elections, and the connection is stronger for Republican judges than for Democratic judges.
20. Blake 2018.
21. Shepherd 2009a.
22. Gray 2019.
23. Gray 2017.
24. Hall and Brace 1989; Shepherd 2010; Hall and Windett 2016.
25. See, for example, Cook 1977; Gibson 1980; Giles, Blackstone, and Vining 2008; Kritzer 1979; Kuklinski and Stanga 1979; Marshall 1989, 2008; McGuire and Stimson 2004; Nelson 2014; and Norpoth and Segal 1994.
26. Most scholars seem to oppose public influence over courts; see, for example, Benesh 2013; Epstein 2013; Hume 2013; and Streb 2013. However, there are some spirited dissents; see Gibson 2013; and Gibson and Nelson 2019.
27. Epstein and Martin 2010.
28. But see Johnson and Strother 2021.
29. Caldarone, Canes-Wrone, and Clark 2009; see also Canes-Wrone, Clark, and Park 2012.
30. Brace and Boyea 2008.
31. Canes-Wrone, Clark, and Kelly 2014.
32. Canes-Wrone and Clark 2009.
33. Hall 2014b. These studies are not unanimous, however. Traut and Emmert (1998) find that the justices of the California Supreme Court, who face retention elections, are responsive to elite, rather than popular, opinion in their death penalty decisions.
34. Canes-Wrone, Clark, and Semet 2018.
35. Bonneau and Hall 2009.
36. Hughes 2019; Harris 2019.
37. Canes-Wrone, Clark, and Park 2012, 211.
38. On Chief Justice Bird's removal, see, for example, Canes-Wrone, Clark, and Kelly 2014; Wold and Culver 1987. On the removal of Penn White, see Kritzer 2020. On the removal of three Iowa judges in 2010, see Buller 2012; Harris 2019. Many additional examples could be provided, as in the removal of Judge Aaron Persky in

California after his sentencing decision regarding a man who raped a Stanford undergraduate; see Gibson and Nelson 2019; Gersen 2016.
39. See, for example, Aspin et al. 2000; Hall 2001a.
40. See, for example, Hall 2015.
41. See, for example, Hall 2014a, 2015.
42. On the correlates of dissent rates, see Hall and Windett 2016.
43. Perhaps what matters most is the willingness of private dissenters to keep their dissents private; see, for example, Hall 1987; Epstein, Landes, and Posner 2011, 2012.
44. Analyzing such a large number of units (judge-votes) makes reliance on statistical significance to test hypotheses a particularly ineffective methodological approach. To illustrate this point, we have taken what everyone would regard as very weak Pearson correlation coefficients and examined their levels of statistical significance with various numbers of cases.

$$\begin{array}{llll}
\text{Judge-votes, } N = 36{,}835 & r = -.046, p < .001 & r = -.097, p < .001 \\
\text{Cases, } N = 5{,}861 & r = -.046, p < .001 & r = -.097, p < .001 \\
\text{Judges, } N = 946 & r = -.046, p = .160 & r = -.097, p = .003 \\
\text{States, } N = 50 & r = -.046, p = .753 & r = -.097, p = .504
\end{array}$$

Indeed, with 36,835 cases, a Pearson correlation coefficient of .014 is significant at .003.
45. Canes-Wrone, Clark, and Kelly 2014.
46. We generally follow the notation used by Canes-Wrone, Clark, and Kelly (2014). Note that judicial ideology is constant within each judge in our data set.
47. Ibid.; Gelman and Hill 2007.
48. There are other possible ways to model the data. Hall (2014a) uses a fully pooled model that does not account for unobserved heterogeneity by state. This approach is appropriate only under the assumption that the control variables included fully account for cross-state and cross-judge differences. Our approach, by contrast, includes controls for state and judge that account for any unobserved heterogeneity across judges or states. Second, we considered a model with fixed effects for judges and states, as Canes-Wrone, Clark, and Kelly (2014) did for some of their analyses. In a fixed effects model, the state dummy variables account for any time-invariant, cross-sectional differences across states. However, because some of our covariates—such as the judge's educational background or ideology—do not change within judge over time, fixed effects are an inappropriate method to model the data. As a result, we deploy the random effects approach.
49. Caughey and Warshaw 2018.
50. Because we rely on the measure constructed by Caughey and Warshaw, we cannot control for public opinion by party, as Kastellec (2018) does. That is, their measures of public opinion are measures of opinion in the states as a whole.
51. We control for this variable owing to the findings in chapter 6. However, none of the substantive results we report in this chapter depends on the inclusion of this variable.

52. See, for example, Epstein, Landes, and Posner 2013b; Squire 2008. Some have found that judges' responsiveness to public opinion dissipates at the end of their time on the bench; see, for example, Hall 2014b. We investigated this possibility in several ways, estimating models that control for the judge's age at the time of the decision or including variables that indicate whether the judge was at least sixty-five (or seventy) years of age. We further estimated models that tested for a conditional effect on public opinion. In no case did any of these variables reach statistical significance. We therefore do not pursue this line of analysis further.
53. Averill 1995, 286.
54. We have reestimated the model with a modified Democratic Party dominance index coded such that higher scores indicate dominance by the justice's political party; the results are identical regardless of the measure we include in the model.
55. We have reestimated the model to allow the effect of public opinion liberalism to vary according to the geographic location of a justice's educational background. There is no evidence that the effect of public opinion liberalism differs based on whether a judge attended an undergraduate or law school in the state in which he or she serves.
56. Perry 1991. We have reestimated the model with a control variable for whether or not the state has an intermediate appellate court, an institutional feature that is linked to a court's ability to exercise discretionary jurisdiction. Including this variable does not change the substantive results we report.
57. We examine the decision of the most previous lower court, that is, the court whose decision is being appealed to the state supreme court.
58. See, for example, Fallon 2002.
59. Note that we have not included a control variable for the year of the decision. Various preliminary analyses provided no evidence of an overall time trend in support for equality. Still, including a time trend in the model does not change any of the substantive results we report.
60. For figure 7.2 (and all similar statistical quantities in this chapter), we hold all interval-level variables at their mean values and categorical variables at their modes. All variables in the model are scored from 0 to 1. We report the frequency distribution of the predictor variable via "rugs" at the bottom of the figures.
61. For more information on the pairwise comparisons, see table 7.A.2.
62. In predicting 61 percent of judge-votes correctly, this model fits the data about as well as the model in table 7.1.
63. Brace and Boyea 2008.
64. Caldarone, Canes-Wrone, and Clark 2009; Canes-Wrone, Clark, and Kelly 2014.
65. We summarize the results of the control variables using the estimates from table 7.1, although we would reach identical conclusions were we to use the estimates from table 7.2.
66. See, for example, Epstein and Martin 2010.
67. See, for example, Caldarone, Canes-Wrone, and Clark 2009; Canes-Wrone, Clark, and Kelly 2014.
68. Shugerman 2012.

Chapter 8: When Do Courts Advance Equality?

1. Galanter 1974, 95.
2. We use the makeup of the court in the year the case was decided, owing to the large number of temporary judges who sit on the cases we analyze. Because irregular judges are not formal members of the court, we lack information about their ideologies. Temporary judges are chosen by the court, which has broad discretion over whom it will recruit to sit on a case. For this reason, our expectation that irregular judges reflect the composition of the court in the year the case was decided makes our measure appropriate for this analysis.
3. We control for a state's Confederacy status because of the findings in chapter 6. However, none of the substantive results we report in this chapter depends on the inclusion of this variable.
4. We also observe a rather sharp decline in the probability of a pro-equality outcome in Alabama at the end of our time period. Between 2009 and 2014, the average ideology of the court's justices changed by less than .10, yet our measure of public opinion indicates that the Alabama public's liberalism fell by a whopping .45 during this time. Although the effects of public opinion are not statistically significant in table 8.1, they do have relatively large estimated substantive effects in some states that are incorporated into the predicted probabilities in figure 8.5. For this reason, the predicted probability of a pro-equality outcome falls noticeably, from .37 in 2008 to .30 in 2015.
5. Gwynne et al. 2005.
6. A corollary to this conclusion is that there is no uniform time trend across the states. Some states changed in a more pro-equality direction during these twenty-six years; others moved in the opposite direction; and some stayed relatively stable. These varying trends help to explain why we observe no overall pro- or anti-equality temporal movement in our data, and also further justify our decision to not include a linear time variable in our model specification.

Chapter 9: State Supreme Courts and Political, Legal, Economic, and Social Inequality

1. See, for example, Galanter 1974.
2. Segal and Spaeth 2002.
3. Hall 2001a.
4. Driscoll and Nelson 2012.
5. For a forceful argument against this position, see Bonneau and Hall 2009.
6. Aspin et al. 2000; Bonneau and Hall 2009; Hall 2001a.
7. Gwynne et al. 2005.
8. We lay out this theory in terms of party control of state governments, but we could just as well call this ideological control of the government, as in "when liberals

dominate a state's political institutions, they also tend to dominate the state's judicial institutions." Because ideology and partisanship are moderately to strongly correlated, and because state politics research traditionally examines "party" control and dominance (for example, one-party-dominant states), we tend to cast our argument in terms of partisanship, not ideology.
9. Dahl 1957.
10. Using the state-year database, the three public opinion variables can account for one-third of the variance in party dominance in the state, with the best predictor being public opinion liberalism on economic issues, closely followed by public opinion on equality and inequality issues (the Franko and Witko "the rich are getting richer . . ." measure).
11. Although the relationship is weaker, the three public opinion indicators account for about one-fourth of the variance in court ideology. Note that even when the opinion measures are included in the equation, the interparty competition variable accounts for additional significant variance in court ideology, raising the explained variance to more than one-third.
12. Dahl 1957.
13. Ibid.
14. Kritzer 2020.
15. See, for example, Segal and Spaeth 2002.
16. See, for example, Zorn and Bowie 2010.
17. Gillman 2008, 655.
18. Hershkoff 2009–2010; Hershkoff and Loffredo 2011.
19. This is very much like Theunis Roux's (2013) argument that the South African Constitutional Court has judicial independence because the government gives it to them. A court whose independence is dependent on government cannot truly be independent. See Gibson 2016.
20. Gillman 2008, 644.
21. Kritzer 2020.
22. A great example can be found in Alabama, where the governor appointed a replacement for a justice who left the supreme court. Former state supreme court justice Roy Moore then challenged the appointed replacement judge in the next Republican Party primary. Even with the advantages of incumbency, the incumbent won only 25 percent of the vote. After defeating his Democratic opponent, Roy Moore, a maverick judge if ever there was one, then began his second stint on the Alabama Supreme Court.
23. Dahl 1957.
24. McCubbins, Noll, and Weingast 1989.
25. We are not in a position to offer very many specific policy prescriptions based on our empirical analysis. However, for anyone interested in reducing the influence of the political regime over the state supreme courts (a position we do not necessarily endorse), a simple reform would be to allow vacated seats to remain unfilled until the next election, or to appoint interim judges, as Louisiana does, and prohibit them from serving a full term on the court.

26. Rosenberg 2008.
27. As Justice Malone on the Alabama Supreme Court well knows (see chapter 2, note 117).
28. See, for example, Hall and Windett 2016.
29. We recognize that "all else equal" may very well be a hollow hope.
30. Using a limited number of cases from the 1990s, Stefanie Lindquist (2017) reports that the supreme courts in Maine and New Mexico invalidated none of the statutes challenged in litigation before their courts, while the Oregon Supreme Court invalidated almost half of the statutes challenged in cases before it.
31. See, for example, Benesh 2006; Cann and Yates 2008, 2016; Gibson 2008a, 2008b, 2009, 2011, 2012, 2013; Gibson and Caldeira 2012, 2013; Gibson et al. 2011; Gibson and Nelson 2017b; Nelson 2016; Salamone 2014, 2018; Woodson 2015, 2017; Zilis 2015, 2018.
32. See, for example, Bartels and Johnston 2013, 2020; Gibson and Nelson 2014, 2015a, 2015b, 2016; Nelson and Gibson 2020; Nelson and Tucker 2021.
33. See, for example, Christenson and Glick 2015; Gibson and Caldeira 2009a, 2009b; Gibson and Nelson 2017a; Nelson and Gibson 2019.
34. We also note the problem of irregular judges serving on the state supreme courts, a more widespread practice than some might realize. Irregular judges, obviously, are subject to different accountability pressures (especially those who would like to receive new assignments in the future). But it is not always clear in official court records which judges are serving temporarily and why irregular judges were assigned to certain cases.
35. We realize that it is perhaps too much to ask to have a standardized set of biographical items to report on each justice serving on a state supreme court (for example, the date of birth should always be reported). But it seems to us that, going forward, it might be a useful exercise for law libraries (or some other institution) to collect standardized biographical information for every newly recruited judge (and other public officials, for that matter). Collecting the information when the person joins the court would generate more reliable data, especially compared to harvesting data from newspaper obituaries when the judge dies.

REFERENCES

Abrahamson, Shirley S., and Diane S. Gutmann. 1987. "The New Federalism: State Constitutions." *Judicature* 71(2, August/September): 88–99.
Aldrich, John H. 1995. *Why Parties? The Origin and Transformation of Political Parties in America.* Chicago: University of Chicago Press.
Aliotta, Jilda M. 1988. "Social Backgrounds, Social Motives, and Participation on the U.S. Supreme Court." *Political Behavior* 10(3): 267–84.
Alozie, Nicholas O. 1996. "Selection Methods and the Recruitment of Women to State Courts of Last Resort." *Social Science Quarterly* 77(1): 110–26.
Ansolabehere, Stephen, and Maxwell Palmer. 2016. "A Two-Hundred Year Statistical History of the Gerrymander." *Ohio State Law Journal* 77(4): 741–62.
Anzia, Sarah. 2014. *Timing and Turnout: How Off-Cycle Elections Favor Organized Groups.* Chicago: University of Chicago Press.
Ash, Elliott, and W. Bentley MacLeod. 2020. "Mandatory Retirement for Judges: Improved Performance on U.S. State Supreme Courts." Working Paper 28025. Cambridge, Mass.: National Bureau of Economic Research.
Aspin, Larry, William K. Hall, Jean Bax, and Celeste Montoya. 2000. "Thirty Years of Judicial Retention Elections: An Update." *Social Science Journal* 37(1): 1–17.
Atkins, Burton M. 1991. "Party Capability Theory as an Explanation for Intervention Behavior in the English Court of Appeal." *American Journal of Political Science* 35(4): 881–903.
Averill, Lawrence H., Jr. 1995. "The Arkansas Courts: Observations on the Wyoming Experience with Merit Selection of Judges." *University of Arkansas at Little Rock Law Journal* 17(Winter): 281–328.
Barber, James Alden, Jr. 1970. *Social Mobility and Voting Behavior.* Chicago: Rand McNally and Company.

Barrilleaux, Charles. 1997. "A Test of the Independent Influences of Electoral Competition and Party Strength in a Model of State Policy-Making." *American Journal of Political Science* 41(4): 1462–66.

Barrilleaux, Charles, Thomas Holbrook, and Laura Langer. 2002. "Electoral Competition, Legislative Balance, and American State Welfare Policy." *American Journal of Political Science* 46(2): 415–27.

Barrilleaux, Charles, and Carlisle Rainey. 2014. "The Politics of Need: Examining Governors' Decisions to Oppose the 'Obamacare' Medicaid Expansion." *State Politics and Policy Quarterly* 14(4): 437–60.

Bartels, Brandon L., and Christopher D. Johnston. 2013. "On the Ideological Foundations of Supreme Court Legitimacy in the American Public." *American Journal of Political Science* 57(1): 184–99.

———. 2020. *Curbing the Court: Why the Public Constrains Judicial Independence.* New York: Cambridge University Press.

Bartels, Larry M. 2008. *Unequal Democracy: The Political Economy of the New Gilded Age.* New York and Princeton, N.J.: Russell Sage Foundation and Princeton University Press.

———. 2016. *Unequal Democracy: The Political Economy of the New Gilded Age*, 2nd ed. New York and Princeton, N.J.: Russell Sage Foundation and Princeton University Press.

Baum, Lawrence. 2006. *Judges and Their Audiences: A Perspective on Judicial Behavior.* Princeton, N.J.: Princeton University Press.

———. 2017. *Ideology in the Supreme Court.* Princeton, N.J.: Princeton University Press.

Baum, Lawrence, David Klein, and Matthew J. Streb. 2017. *The Battle for the Court: Interest Groups, Judicial Elections, and Public Policy.* Charlottesville: University of Virginia Press.

Baumann, Zachary, Michael J. Nelson, and Markus Neumann. 2021. "Party Competition and Policy Liberalism." *State Politics and Policy Quarterly*. Forthcoming, doi:10.1017/spq.2020.2.

Bauries, Scott R. 2009. "Is There an Elephant in the Room? Judicial Review of Educational Adequacy and the Separations of Powers in State Constitutions." *Albany Law Review* 61(4): 701–73.

Bayne, William C. 2000. "Lynchard's Candidacy, Ads Putting Spice into Justice Race." *Commercial Appeal*, October 29.

Beland, Daniel, Philip Rocco, and Alex Waddan. 2016. *Obamacare Wars: Federalism, State Politics, and the Affordable Care Act.* Lawrence: University of Kansas Press.

Benesh, Sara C. 2006. "Understanding Public Confidence in American Courts." *Journal of Politics* 68(3): 697–707.

———. 2013. "Judicial Elections: Directions in the Study of Institutional Legitimacy." *Judicature* 96(5): 204–8.

Berry, Kate, and Cathleen Lisk. 2017. *Appointed and Advantaged: How Interim Vacancies Shape State Courts.* New York: Brennan Center for Justice.

Berry, William D., Richard C. Fording, Evan J. Ringquist, Russell L. Hanson, and Carl E. Klarner. 2010. "Measuring Citizen and Government Ideology in the U.S. States: A Reappraisal." *State Politics and Policy Quarterly* 10(2): 117–35.

Berry, William D., Evan J. Ringquist, Richard C. Fording, and Russell Hanson. 1998. "Measuring Citizen and Government Ideology in the American States, 1960–1993." *American Journal of Political Science* 42(1): 327–48.

———. 2007. "The Measurement and Stability of State Citizen Ideology." *State Politics and Policy Quarterly* 7(2): 111–32.

Binder, Sarah A. 1999. "The Dynamics of Legislative Gridlock, 1947–96." *American Political Science Review* 93(3): 519–33.

———. 2014. "Polarized We Govern?" Brookings Institution (May). https://www.brookings.edu/research/polarized-we-govern/ (accessed August 18, 2020).

Black, Ryan C., and Christina L. Boyd. 2012. "U.S. Supreme Court Agenda Setting and the Role of Litigant Status." *Journal of Law, Economics, and Organization* 28(2): 286–312.

Black, Ryan C., and Ryan J. Owens. 2012. *The Solicitor General and the United States Supreme Court.* New York: Cambridge University Press.

Blake, William D. 2018. "Judicial Independence on Unelected State Supreme Courts." *Justice System Journal* 39(1): 21–38.

Bonica, Adam. 2013. "Ideology and Interests in the Political Marketplace." *American Journal of Political Science* 57(2): 294–311.

———. 2014. "Mapping the Ideological Marketplace." *American Journal of Political Science* 58(2): 367–86.

Bonica, Adam, Adam Chilton, Kyle Rozema, and Maya Sen. 2018. "The Legal Academy's Ideological Uniformity." *Journal of Legal Studies* 47(1): 1–43.

Bonica, Adam, Adam Chilton, and Maya Sen. 2016. "The Political Ideologies of American Lawyers." *Journal of Legal Analysis* 8(2): 277–335.

Bonica, Adam, and Maya Sen. 2017. "A Common-Space Scaling of the American Judiciary and Legal Profession." *Political Analysis* 21(5): 114–21.

Bonica, Adam, and Michael Woodruff. 2015. "A Common-Space Measure of State Supreme Court Ideology." *Journal of Law, Economics, and Organization* 31(3): 472–98.

Bonneau, Chris W. 2012. "A Survey of Empirical Evidence Concerning Judicial Elections." Federalist Society (March). http://www.fed-soc.org/library/doclib/20120719_Bonneau2012WP.pdf (accessed August 18, 2020).

———. 2018. "The Case for Partisan Judicial Elections." Federalist Society White Paper (January 8). https://fedsoc.org/commentary/publications/the-case-for-partisan-judicial-elections-1 (accessed August 18, 2020).

Bonneau, Chris W., and Damon M. Cann. 2015a. *Voters' Verdicts: Citizens, Campaigns, and Institutions in State Supreme Court Elections.* Charlottesville: University of Virginia Press.

———. 2015b. "Party Identification and Vote Choice in Partisan and Nonpartisan Elections." *Political Behavior* 37(March): 43–66.

Bonneau, Chris W., and Melinda Gann Hall. 2009. *In Defense of Judicial Elections.* New York: Routledge Press.

Bonneau, Chris W., and Eric Loepp. 2014. "Getting Things Straight: The Effects of Ballot Design and Electoral Structure on Voter Participation." *Electoral Studies* 34(June): 119–30.

Bosworth, Matthew. 2001. *Courts as Catalysts: State Supreme Courts and Public School Finance Equity.* Albany: State University of New York Press.

Boyd, Christina L. 2015. "Litigant Status and Trial Court Appeal Mobilization." *Law and Policy* 37(4): 294–323.

Boyd, Christina L., Lee Epstein, and Andrew D. Martin. 2010. "Untangling the Causal Effect of Sex on Judging." *American Journal of Political Science* 54(2): 389–411.

Boyd, Christina L., Michael J. Nelson, Ian Ostrander, and Ethan D. Boldt. 2021. *The Politics of Federal Prosecution*. Oxford: Oxford University Press.

Brace, Paul, and Brent D. Boyea. 2008. "State Public Opinion, the Death Penalty, and the Practice of Electing Judges." *American Journal of Political Science* 52(2): 360–72.

Brace, Paul, and Melinda Gann Hall. 1995. "Studying Courts Comparatively: The View from the American States." *Political Research Quarterly* 48(1): 5–29.

———. 1997. "The Interplay of Preferences, Case Facts, Context, and Rules in the Politics of Judicial Choice." *Journal of Politics* 59(4): 1206–31.

———. 2001. "'Haves' Versus 'Have Nots' in State Supreme Courts: Allocating Docket Space and Wins in Power Asymmetric Cases." *Law and Society Review* 35(2): 393–417.

———. 2009. State Supreme Court Data Project. https://www.ruf.rice.edu/~pbrace/statecourt/ (accessed August 19, 2020).

Brace, Paul, Melinda Gann Hall, and Laura Langer. 1999. "Judicial Choice and the Politics of Abortion: Institutions, Context, and the Autonomy of Courts." *Albany Law Review* 62(4): 1265–303.

———. 2001. "Placing State Supreme Courts in State Politics." *State Politics and Policy Quarterly* 1(1): 81–108.

Brace, Paul, Laura Langer, and Melinda Gann Hall. 2000. "Measuring the Preferences of State Supreme Court Judges." *Journal of Politics* 62(2): 387–413.

Brace, Paul, Kellie Sims-Butler, Kevin Arceneaux, and Martin Johnson. 2002. "Public Opinion in the American States: New Perspectives Using National Survey Data." *American Journal of Political Science* 46(1): 173–89.

Bratton, Kathleen A., and Rorie Spill. 2002. "Existing Diversity and Judicial Selection: The Role of the Appointment Method in Establishing Gender Diversity in State Supreme Courts." *Social Science Quarterly* 83(2): 504–18.

———. 2006. "State Legislative and Judicial Data and Research." https://www.lsu.edu/faculty/bratton/research.htm (accessed August 18, 2020).

Braveman, Daan. 1989. "Children, Poverty, and State Constitutions." *Emory Law Journal* 38(3): 577–614.

Bruch, Sarah K., Marcia K. Meyers, and Janet C. Gornick. 2016. "Separate and Unequal: The Dimensions and Consequences of Safety Net Decentralization in the U.S., 1994–2014." IRP Discussion Paper 1432-16. Institute for Research on Poverty (August). https://www.irp.wisc.edu/publications/dps/pdfs/dp143216.pdf (accessed April 28, 2021).

Brudney, James J., Sara Schiavoni, and Deborah J. Merritt. 1999. "Judicial Hostility toward Labor Unions? Applying the Social Background Model to a Celebrated Concern." *Ohio State Law Journal* 60(5): 1675–771.

Buller, Tyler J. 2012. "Framing the Debate: Understanding Iowa's 2010 Judicial Retention Election through a Content Analysis of Letters to the Editor." *Iowa Law Review* 97(5): 1745–86.

Burden, Barry C. 2007. *Personal Roots of Representation*. Princeton, N.J.: Princeton University Press.

Buttice, Matthew K., and Benjamin Highton. 2013. "How Does Multilevel Regression and Poststratification Perform with Conventional National Surveys?" *Political Analysis* 21(4): 449–67.

Caldarone, Richard P., Brandice Canes-Wrone, and Tom S. Clark. 2009. "Partisan Labels and Democratic Accountability: An Analysis of State Supreme Court Abortion Decisions." *Journal of Politics* 71(2): 560–73.

Campbell, Angus, Phillip E. Converse, Warren E. Miller, and Donald E. Stokes. 1960. *The American Voter*. Chicago: University of Chicago Press.

Canes-Wrone, Brandice, and Tom S. Clark. 2009. "Judicial Independence and Nonpartisan Elections." *Wisconsin Law Review* 2009(1): 21–66.

Canes-Wrone, Brandice, Tom S. Clark, and Jason P. Kelly. 2014. "Judicial Selection and Death Penalty Decisions." *American Political Science Review* 108(1): 23–29.

Canes-Wrone, Brandice, Tom S. Clark, and Jee-Kwang Park. 2012. "Judicial Independence and Retention Elections." *Journal of Law, Economics, and Organization* 28(2): 211–34.

Canes-Wrone, Brandice, Tom S. Clark, and Amy Semet. 2018. "Judicial Elections, Public Opinion, and Decisions on Lower Salience Issues." *Journal of Empirical Legal Studies* 15(4): 672–707.

Cann, Damon M., and Teena Wilhelm. 2011. "Case Visibility and the Electoral Connection in State Supreme Courts." *American Politics Research* 39(3): 557–81.

Cann, Damon M., and Jeff Yates. 2008. "Homegrown Institutional Legitimacy: Assessing Citizens' Diffuse Support for State Courts." *American Politics Research* 36(2): 297–329.

———. 2016. *These Estimable Courts: Understanding Public Perceptions of State Judicial Institutions and Legal Policy-Making*. New York: Oxford University Press.

Carnes, Nicholas. 2012. "Does the Numerical Underrepresentation of the Working Class in Congress Matter?" *Legislative Studies Quarterly* 37(1): 5–34.

———. 2013. *White-Collar Government: The Hidden Role of Class in Economic Policy Making*. Chicago: University of Chicago Press.

———. 2016. "Why Are There So Few Working-Class People in Political Office? Evidence from State Legislatures." *Politics, Groups, and Identities* 4(1): 84–109.

Carnes, Nicholas, and Noam Lupu. 2016. "Do Voters Dislike Working-Class Candidates? Voter Biases and the Descriptive Underrepresentation of the Working Class." *American Political Science Review* 110(4): 832–44.

Carnes, Nicholas, and Meredith L. Sadin. 2015. "The 'Mill Worker's Son' Heuristic: How Voters Perceive Politicians from Working-Class Families—and How They Really Behave in Office." *Journal of Politics* 77(1): 285–98.

Caufield, Rachel Paine. 2009. "Reconciling the Judicial Ideal and the Democratic Impulse in Judicial Retention Election." *Missouri Law Review* 74(3): 573–604.

Caughey, Devin, and Christopher Warshaw. 2016. "The Dynamics of State Policy Liberalism." *American Journal of Political Science* 60(4): 899–913.

———. 2018. "Policy Preferences and Policy Change: Dynamic Responsiveness in the American States, 1936–2014." *American Political Science Review* 112(2): 249–66.

Chemerinsky, Erwin. 2014. *The Case against the Supreme Court.* London: Penguin Books.
Chen, Kong-Pin, Kuo-Chang Huang, and Chang-Ching Lin. 2014. "Party Capability versus Court Preference: Why Do the 'Haves' Come Out Ahead?—An Empirical Lesson from the Taiwan Supreme Court." *Journal of Law, Economics, and Organization* 31(1): 93–126.
Christenson, Dino P., and David M. Glick. 2015. "Chief Justice Roberts's Health Care Decision Disrobed: The Microfoundations of the Supreme Court's Legitimacy." *American Journal of Political Science* 59(2): 403–18.
Cohen, Adam. 2020. *Supreme Inequality: The Supreme Court's Fifty-Year Battle for a More Unjust America.* New York: Penguin Press.
Cohen, Marty, David Karol, Hans Noel, and John Zaller. 2008. *The Party Decides: Presidential Nominations before and after Reform.* Chicago: University of Chicago Press.
Cohen, Richard. 2005. "Ivy-Covered Court." *Washington Post*, November 15, p. A21.
Collins, Paul M., Jr. 2004. "Friends of the Court: Examining the Influence of Amicus Curiae Participation in U.S. Supreme Court Litigation." *Law and Society Review* 38(4): 807–32.
———. 2008. *Friends of the Supreme Court: Interest Groups and Judicial Decision Making.* New York: Oxford University Press.
Cook, Beverly B. 1977. "Public Opinion and Federal Judicial Policy." *American Journal of Political Science* 21(3): 567–600.
Curry, Todd A., and Mark S. Hurwitz. 2016. "Strategic Retirements of Elected and Appointed Justices: A Hazard Model Approach." *Journal of Politics* 78(4): 1061–75.
Dahl, Robert. 1957. "Decision-Making in a Democracy: The Supreme Court as National Policy-Maker." *Journal of Public Law* 6(2): 279–95.
———. 1971. *Polyarchy: Participation and Opposition.* New Haven, Conn.: Yale University Press.
Dawson, Richard E., and James A. Robinson. 1963. "Inter-Party Competition, Economic Variables, and Welfare Policies in the American States." *Journal of Politics* 25(2): 265–89.
Demaine, Linda J., and Deborah R. Hensler. 2004. "'Volunteering' to Arbitrate through Predispute Arbitration Clauses: The Average Consumer's Experience." *Law and Contemporary Problems* (67)1: 55–74.
Dinan, John J. 2009. *The American State Constitutional Tradition.* Lawrence: University Press of Kansas.
———. 2018. "Obama-Appointed Judges Undercut Trump on Immigration." *Associated Press*, November 20.
Di Pietro, Susanne, and Teresa W. Carns. 1996. "Alaska's English Rule: Attorney's Fee Shifting in Civil Cases." *Alaska Law Review* 13(1): 33–94.
Dotan, Yoav. 1999. "Do the 'Haves' Still Come Out Ahead? Resource Inequalities in Ideological Courts: The Case of the Israeli High Court of Justice." *Law and Society Review* 33(4): 1059–80.
Douglas, William O. 1970. *Points of Rebellion.* New York: Random House.
Driscoll, Amanda, and Michael J. Nelson. 2012. "The 2011 Judicial Elections in Bolivia." *Electoral Studies* 31(3): 628–39.

———. 2013. "The Political Origins of Judicial Elections: Evidence from the United States and Bolivia." *Judicature* 96(4): 151–60.

———. 2015. "Judicial Selection and the Democratization of Justice: Lessons from the Bolivian Judicial Elections." *Journal of Law and Courts* 3(1): 115–48.

———. 2019. "Chronicle of an Election Foretold: The 2017 Bolivian Judicial Elections." *Politica y Gobierno* 26(1): 41–64.

Dubois, Philip L. 1988. "The Illusion of Judicial Consensus Revisited: Partisan Conflict on an Intermediate State Court of Appeals." *American Journal of Political Science* 32(4): 946–67.

Dye, Thomas R. 1984. "Party and Policy in the States." *Journal of Politics* 46(4): 1097–116.

Eisenberg, Theodore, and Geoffrey P. Miller. 2009. "Reversal, Dissent, and Variability in State Supreme Courts: The Centrality of Jurisdictional Source." *Boston University Law Review* 89: 1451–504.

———. 2013. "The English versus the American Rule on Attorney Fees: An Empirical Study of Public Company Contracts." *Cornell Law Review* 98(3): 327–81.

Emmert, Craig F. 1991. "Litigants in State Supreme Court Judicial Review Cases: Participation and Success." *Justice System Journal* 15(1): 486–93.

Emmert, Craig F., and Carol Ann Traut. 1992. "State Supreme Courts, State Constitutions, and Judicial Policy-Making." *Justice System Journal* 16(1): 37–48.

Enns, Peter K. 2015. "Reconsidering the Middle: A Reply to Gilens." *Perspectives on Politics* 13(4): 1072–74.

Enns, Peter K., and Julianna Koch. 2013. "Public Opinion in the U.S. States: 1956–2010." *State Politics and Policy Quarterly* 13(3): 349–72.

Enns, Peter K., and Christopher Wlezien, eds. 2011. *Who Gets Represented?* New York: Russell Sage Foundation.

Epp, Charles R. 1999. "The Two Motifs of 'Why the "Haves" Come Out Ahead' and Its Heirs." *Law and Society Review* 33(4): 1089–98.

Epstein, Lee. 2013. "The Assault on the Assaulters of Judicial Elections." *Judicature* 96(5): 218–22.

Epstein, Lee, and Tracey E. George. 1992. "On the Nature of Supreme Court Decision Making." *American Political Science Review* 86(2): 323–37.

Epstein, Lee, and Jack Knight. 1998. *The Choices Justices Make.* Washington, D.C.: Congressional Quarterly Press.

Epstein, Lee, Jack Knight, and Andrew D. Martin. 2003. "The Norm of Prior Judicial Experience and Its Consequences for Career Diversity on the U.S. Supreme Court." *California Law Review* 91(4): 903–65.

Epstein, Lee, William M. Landes, and Richard A. Posner. 2011. "Why (and When) Judges Dissent." *Journal of Legal Analysis* 3(1): 101–37.

———. 2012. "Are Even Unanimous Decisions in the United States Supreme Court Ideological?" *Northwestern University Law Review* 106(2): 699–713.

———. 2013a. "How Business Fares in the Supreme Court." *Minnesota Law Review* 97(4): 1431–72.

———. 2013b. *The Behavior of Federal Judges: A Theoretical and Empirical Study of Rational Choice.* Cambridge, Mass.: Harvard University Press.

———. 2017. "When It Comes to Business, the Right and Left Sides of the Court Agree." *Washington University Journal of Law and Policy* 54: 33–55.

Epstein, Lee, and Andrew D. Martin. 2010. "Does Public Opinion Influence the Supreme Court? Possibly Yes (but We're Not Sure Why)." *University of Pennsylvania Journal of Constitutional Law* 13(2): 263–81.

Epstein, Lee, Andrew D. Martin, Kevin M. Quinn, and Jeffrey A. Segal. 2009. "Circuit Effects: How the Norm of Federal Judicial Experience Biases the U.S. Supreme Court." *University of Pennsylvania Law Review* 157(3): 101–46.

Epstein, Lee, Andrew D. Martin, Jeffrey A. Segal, and Chad Westerland. 2007. "The Judicial Common Space." *Journal of Law, Economics, and Organization* 23(2): 303–25.

Epstein, Lee, Jeffrey A. Segal, and Chad Westerland. 2008. "The Increasing Importance of Ideology in the Nomination and Confirmation of Supreme Court Justices." *Drake Law Review* 56(3): 609–35.

Epstein, Lee, Thomas G. Walker, Nancy Staudt, Scott Hendrickson, and Jason Roberts. 2021. The U.S. Supreme Court Justices Database. Updated January 17. http://epstein.wustl.edu/research/justicesdata.html (accessed April 28, 2021).

Erikson, Robert S. 2015. "Income Inequality and Policy Responsiveness." *Annual Review of Political Science* 18(1): 11–29.

Erikson, Robert S., Gerald C. Wright, and John P. McIver. 1993. *Statehouse Democracy: Public Opinion and Policy in the American States.* Cambridge: Cambridge University Press.

Ewing, Cortez A. M. 1938. *The Judges of the Supreme Court, 1789–1937: A Study of Their Qualifications.* Minneapolis: University of Minnesota Press.

Fallon, Richard H. 2002. "The 'Conservative' Paths of the Rehnquist Court's Federalism Decisions." *University of Chicago Law Review* 69(2): 429–94.

Farole, Donald J., Jr. 1999. "Reexamining Litigant Success in State Supreme Courts." *Law and Society Review* 33(4): 1043–58.

Feigenbaum, Edward D., James A. Palmer, and David T. Skelton. 1993. *Election Case Law.* Washington, D.C.: National Clearinghouse on Election Administration.

Fitzpatrick, Brian. 2018. "The Case for Political Appointment of Judges." Federalist Society (April). https://fedsoc-cms-public.s3.amazonaws.com/update/pdf/iVB4QbtuZK9bPoycPybs0f8wcrxa8XJ2DIDpYtGu.pdf (accessed April 28, 2021).

———. 2019. *The Conservative Case for Class Actions.* Chicago: University of Chicago Press.

Flavin, Patrick. 2012. "Income Inequality and Policy Representation in the American States." *American Politics Research* 40(1): 29–59.

———. 2017. "Political Equality in the American States: What We Know and What We Still Need to Learn." *State and Local Government Review* 49(1): 60–69.

Franko, William, and Christopher Witko. 2018. *The New Economic Populism: How States Respond to Economic Inequality.* Oxford: Oxford University Press.

Friedman, Barry. 2010. *The Will of the People: How Public Opinion Has Influenced the Supreme Court and Shaped the Meaning of the Constitution.* New York: Farrar, Straus and Giroux.

Galanter, Marc. 1974. "Why the 'Haves' Come Out Ahead: Speculations on the Limits of Legal Change." *Law and Society Review* 9(1): 95–160.

———. 2004. "The Vanishing Trial: An Examination of Trials and Related Matters in Federal and State Courts." *Journal of Empirical Legal Studies* 1(3): 459–570.

Gelman, Andrew, and Jennifer Hill. 2007. *Data Analysis Using Regression and Multilevel-Hierarchical Models*. Cambridge: Cambridge University Press.

Gelman, Andrew, Jeffrey Lax, Justin Phillips, Jonah Gabry, and Robert Trangucci. 2016. "Using Multilevel Regression and Poststratification to Estimate Dynamic Public Opinion." Working paper.

Gelman, Andrew, and Thomas C. Little. 1997. "Poststratification into Many Categories Using Hierarchical Logistic Regression." *Survey Methodology* 23(2): 127–35.

George, Tracey E. 2008. "From Judge to Justice: Social Background Theory and the Supreme Court." *North Carolina Law Review* 86(5): 1333–67.

Gersen, Jeannie Suk. 2016. "The Unintended Consequences of the Stanford Rape-Case Recall." *New Yorker*, June 17. https://www.newyorker.com/news/news-desk/the-unintended-consequences-of-the-stanford-rape-case-recall (accessed August 18, 2020).

Geyh, Charles Gardner. 2008. "The Endless Judicial Selection Debate and Why It Matters for Judicial Independence." *Georgetown Journal of Legal Ethics* 21(4): 1259–82.

———. 2019. *Who Is to Judge? The Perennial Debate over Whether to Elect or Appoint America's Judges*. New York: Oxford University Press.

Gibson, James L. 1978. "Judges' Role Orientations, Attitudes, and Decisions: An Interactive Model." *American Political Science Review* 72(3): 911–24.

———. 1980. "Environmental Constraints on the Behavior of Judges: A Representational Model of Judicial Decision Making." *Law and Society Review* 14(2): 343–70.

———. 1983. "From Simplicity to Complexity: The Development of Theory in the Study of Judicial Behavior." *Political Behavior* 5(1): 7–49.

———. 1988. "Political Intolerance and Political Repression during the McCarthy Red Scare." *American Political Science Review* 82(2): 511–29.

———. 1989. "The Policy Consequences of Political Intolerance: Political Repression during the Vietnam War Era." *Journal of Politics* 51(1): 13–35.

———. 2008a. "Challenges to the Impartiality of State Supreme Courts: Legitimacy Theory and 'New-Style' Judicial Campaigns." *American Political Science Review* 102(1): 59–75.

———. 2008b. "Campaigning for the Bench: The Corrosive Effects of Campaign Speech?" *Law and Society Review* 42(4): 899–928.

———. 2009. "'New-Style' Judicial Campaigns and the Legitimacy of State High Courts." *Journal of Politics* 71(4): 1285–304.

———. 2011. "Judging the Politics of Judging: Are Politicians in Robes Inevitably Illegitimate?" In *What's Law Got to Do with It? What Judges Do, Why They Do It, and What's at Stake*, edited by Charles Gardner Geyh. Palo Alto, Calif.: Stanford University Press.

———. 2012. *Electing Judges: The Surprising Effects of Campaigning on Judicial Legitimacy*. Chicago: University of Chicago Press.

———. 2013. "Electing Judges: Future Research and the Normative Debate about Judicial Elections." *Judicature* 96(5): 223–31.

———. 2016. "Reassessing the Institutional Legitimacy of the South African Constitutional Court: New Evidence, Revised Theory." *Politikon* 43(1): 53–77.

Gibson, James L., and Gregory A. Caldeira. 2009a. *Citizens, Courts, and Confirmations: Positivity Theory and the Judgments of the American People.* Princeton, N.J.: Princeton University Press.

———. 2009b. "Confirmation Politics and the Legitimacy of the U.S. Supreme Court: Institutional Loyalty, Positivity Bias, and the Alito Nomination." *American Journal of Political Science* 53(1): 139–55.

———. 2012. "Campaign Support, Conflicts of Interest, and Judicial Impartiality: Can the Legitimacy of Courts Be Rescued by Recusals?" *Journal of Politics* 74(1): 1–17.

———. 2013. "Judicial Impartiality, Campaign Contributions, and Recusals: Results from a National Survey." *Journal of Empirical Legal Studies* 10(1): 76–103.

Gibson, James L., Christopher Claassen, and Joan Barceló. 2020. "Deplorables: Emotions, Political Sophistication, and Political Intolerance." *American Politics Research* 48(2): 252–62.

Gibson, James L., Jeffrey A. Gottfried, Michael X. Delli Carpini, and Kathleen Hall Jamieson. 2011. "The Effects of Judicial Campaign Activity on the Legitimacy of Courts: A Survey-Based Experiment." *Political Research Quarterly* 64(3): 545–58.

Gibson, James L., and Amanda Gouws. 2003. *Overcoming Intolerance in South Africa: Experiments in Democratic Persuasion.* Cambridge: Cambridge University Press.

Gibson, James L., and Michael J. Nelson. 2014. "The Legitimacy of the U.S. Supreme Court: Conventional Wisdoms and Recent Challenges Thereto." *Annual Review of Law and Social Science* 10: 201–19.

———. 2015a. "Can the U.S. Supreme Court Have Too Much Legitimacy?" In *Making Law and Courts Research Relevant: The Normative Implications of Empirical Research*, edited by Brandon L. Bartels and Chris W. Bonneau. New York: Routledge.

———. 2015b. "Is the U.S. Supreme Court's Legitimacy Grounded in Performance Satisfaction and Ideology?" *American Journal of Political Science* 59(1, January): 162–74.

———. 2016. "Change in Institutional Support for the U.S. Supreme Court: Is the Court's Legitimacy Imperiled by the Decisions It Makes?" *Public Opinion Quarterly* 80(3, Fall): 622–41.

———. 2017a. "Reconsidering Positivity Theory: What Roles Do Politicization, Ideological Disagreement, and Legal Realism Play in Shaping U.S. Supreme Court Legitimacy?" *Journal of Empirical Legal Studies* 14(3, September): 592–617.

———. 2017b. "Judicial Elections: Judges and Their New-Style Constituencies." In *The Oxford Handbook of U.S. Judicial Behavior*, edited by Lee Epstein and Stefanie A. Lindquist. New York: Oxford University Press.

———. 2019. "The Least Accountable Branch?" *Judge's Journal* 55(1): 30–35.

Gilens, Martin. 2005. "Inequality and Democratic Responsiveness." *Public Opinion Quarterly* 69(5): 778–896.

———. 2009. "Preference Gaps and Inequality in Representation." *PS: Political Science and Politics* 42(2): 335–41.

———. 2012. *Affluence and Influence: Economic Inequality and Political Power in America.* New York and Princeton, N.J.: Russell Sage Foundation and Princeton University Press.

Gilens, Martin, and Benjamin I. Page. 2014. "Testing Theories of American Politics: Elites, Interest Groups, and Average Citizens." *Perspectives on Politics* 12(3): 564–81.

Giles, Micheal W., Bethany Blackstone, and Richard L. Vining. 2008. "The Supreme Court in American Democracy: Unraveling the Linkages between Public Opinion and Judicial Decision Making." *Journal of Politics* 70(2): 293–306.

Giles, Micheal W., and Thomas G. Walker. 1975. "Judicial Policy-Making and Southern School Segregation." *Journal of Politics* 37(4): 917–36.

Gill, Rebecca D. 2013. "Beyond High Hopes and Unmet Expectations: Judicial Selection Reforms in the States." *Judicature* 96(6): 278–93.

———. 2014. "Implicit Bias in Judicial Performance Evaluations: We Must Do Better Than This." *Justice System Journal* 35(3): 271–94.

Gill, Rebecca D., Sylvia Lazos, and Mallory M. Waters. 2011. "Are Judicial Performance Evaluations Fair to Women and Minorities? A Cautionary Tale from Clark County, Nevada." *Law and Society Review* 45(3): 731–60.

Gillman, Howard. 2002. "How Political Parties Can Use the Courts to Advance Their Agendas: Federal Courts in the United States, 1875–1891." *American Political Science Review* 96(3): 511–24.

———. 2008. "Courts and the Politics of Partisan Coalitions." In *The Oxford Handbook of Law and Politics*, edited by Keith E. Whittington, Daniel R. Keleman, and Gregory A. Caldeira. Oxford: Oxford University Press.

Gilman, Michele. 2014. "A Court for the One Percent: How the Supreme Court Contributes to Economic Inequality." *Utah Law Review* 1(3): 389–463.

Glynn, Adam N., and May Sen. 2015. "Identifying Judicial Empathy: Does Having Daughters Cause Judges to Rule for Women's Issues?" *American Journal of Political Science* 59(1): 37–54.

Goelzhauser, Greg. 2016. *Choosing State Supreme Court Justices: Merit Selection and the Consequences of Institutional Reform.* Philadelphia: Temple University Press.

———. 2019. *Judicial Merit Selection: Institutional Design and Performance for State Courts.* Philadelphia: Temple University Press.

Gray, Thomas. 2017. "The Influence of Legislative Reappointment on State Supreme Court Decision-Making." *State Politics and Policy Quarterly* 17(3): 275–98.

———. 2019. "Executive Influence on State Supreme Court Justices: Strategic Deference in Reappointment States." *Journal of Law, Economics, and Organization* 35(2): 422–53.

Green, Joshua. 2004. "Karl Rove in a Corner." *Atlantic* (November). https://www.theatlantic.com/magazine/archive/2004/11/karl-rove-in-a-corner/303537/ (accessed August 18, 2020).

Grossman, Joel B. 1966. "Social Backgrounds and Judicial Decision-Making." *Harvard Law Review* 79(8): 1551–64.

———. 1967. "Social Backgrounds and Judicial Decisions: Notes for a Theory." *Journal of Politics* 29(2): 334–51.

Grossman, Joel B., Herbert M. Kritzer, and Stewart Macaulay. 1999. "Do the 'Haves' Still Come Out Ahead?" *Law and Society Review* 33(4): 803–10.

Grossmann, Matt. 2019. *Red State Blues: How the Conservative Revolution Stalled in the States.* New York: Cambridge University Press.

Grumbach, Jacob M. 2018. "From Backwaters to Major Policymakers: Policy Polarization in the States, 1970–2014." *Perspectives on Politics* 16(2): 416–35.

Gutman, David. 2018. "Did You Read the Fine Print? We Did. These Are the Rights You Give Up by Renting a Limebike or Ofo." *Seattle Times*, July 11. https://www.seattletimes.com/seattle-news/transportation/bike-share-user-agreements-the-rights-you-give-up-by-renting-a-limebike-or-ofo/ (accessed August 18, 2020).

Gwynne, Sam, Bill Miller, Kim Ross, and Tom Phillips. 2005. "Tort Reform in Texas: Rove's Genius at Work." PBS *Frontline*, April 12, 2005. https://www.pbs.org/wgbh/pages/frontline/shows/architect/interviews/gwynne.html (accessed August 18, 2020).

Haire, Susan Brodie, Stefanie A. Lindquist, and Roger Hartley. 1999. "Attorney Expertise, Litigant Success, and Judicial Decisionmaking in the U.S. Courts of Appeals." *Law and Society Review* 33(3): 667–85.

Hall, Kermit L. 1976. "Social Backgrounds and Judicial Recruitment: A Nineteenth-Century Perspective on the Lower Federal Judiciary." *Western Political Quarterly* 29(2): 243–57.

Hall, Matthew E. K., and Joseph Daniel Ura. 2015. "Judicial Majoritarianism." *Journal of Politics* 77(3): 818–32.

Hall, Matthew E. K., and Jason Harold Windett. 2013. "New Data on State Supreme Court Cases." *State Politics and Policy Quarterly* 13(4): 427–45.

———. 2016. "Discouraging Dissent: The Chief Judge's Influence in State Supreme Courts." *American Politics Research* 44(4): 682–709.

Hall, Melinda Gann. 1987. "Constituent Influence in State Supreme Courts: Conceptual Notes and a Case Study." *Journal of Politics* 49(4): 1117–24.

———. 1992. "Electoral Politics and Strategic Voting in State Supreme Courts." *Journal of Politics* 54(2): 427–46.

———. 1995. "Justices as Representatives: Elections and Judicial Politics in the American States." *American Politics Research* 23(4): 485–503.

———. 2001a. "State Supreme Courts in American Democracy: Probing the Mythos of Judicial Reform." *American Political Science Review* 95(2): 315–30.

———. 2001b. "Voluntary Retirements from State Supreme Courts: Assessing Democratic Pressures to Relinquish the Bench." *Journal of Politics* 63(4): 1112–40.

———. 2007. "Voting in State Supreme Court Elections: Competition and Context as Democratic Incentives." *Journal of Politics* 69(4): 1147–59.

———. 2014a. "Televised Attacks and the Incumbency Advantage in State Supreme Courts." *Journal of Law, Economics, and Organization* 30(March): 138–64.

———. 2014b. "Representation in State Supreme Courts: Evidence from the Terminal Term." *Political Research Quarterly* 67(2): 335–46.

———. 2015. *Attacking Judges: How Campaign Advertising Influences State Supreme Court Elections*. Palo Alto, Calif.: Stanford University Press.

Hall, Melinda Gann, and Chris W. Bonneau. 2006. "Does Quality Matter? Challengers in State Supreme Court Elections." *American Journal of Political Science* 50(1): 20–33.

Hall, Melinda Gann, and Paul Brace. 1989. "Order in the Courts: A Neo-Institutional Approach to Judicial Consensus." *Western Political Quarterly* 42(3): 391–407.

———. 1992. "Toward an Integrated Model of Judicial Voting Behavior." *American Politics Quarterly* 20(2): 147–68.

Haltom, William, and Michael McCann. 2004. *Distorting the Law: Politics, Media, and the Litigation Crisis.* Chicago: University of Chicago Press.

Hanssen, Andrew F. 2002. "On the Politics of Judicial Selection: Lawyers and State Campaigns for the Merit Plan." *Public Choice* 110(1/2): 79–97.

Harris, Allison P. 2019. "Voter Response to Salient Judicial Decisions in Retention Elections." *Law and Social Inquiry* 44(1): 170–91.

Harris, Allison P., and Maya Sen. 2019. "Bias and Judging." *Annual Review of Political Science* 22(1): 241–59.

Haspel, Moshe, and H. Gibbs Knotts. 2005. "Location, Location, Location: Precinct Placement and the Costs of Voting." *Journal of Politics* 67(2): 560–73.

Hassell, Hans J. G. 2017. *The Party's Primary: Control of Congressional Nominations.* Cambridge: Cambridge University Press.

Haynie, Stacia L. 1994. "Resource Inequalities and Litigation Outcomes in the Philippine Supreme Court." *Journal of Politics* 56(3): 752–72.

He, Xin, and Yang Su. 2013. "Do the 'Haves' Come Out Ahead in Shanghai Courts?" *Journal of Empirical Legal Studies* 10(1): 120–45.

Heise, Michael. 1995. "The Court vs. Educational Standards." *The Public Interest* 120(1): 55–63.

Herndon, James. 1962. "Appointment as a Means of Initial Accession to Elective State Courts of Last Resort." *North Dakota Law Review* 38(1): 60–74.

Hershkoff, Helen. 2009–2010. "'Just Words': Common Law and the Enforcement of State Constitutional Social and Economic Rights." *Stanford Law Review* 62(5): 1521–82.

Hershkoff, Helen, and Stephen Loffredo. 2011. "State Courts and Constitutional Socio-Economic Rights: Exploring the Underutilization Thesis." *Penn State Law Review* 115(4): 923–82.

Hill, Kim Quaile, and Jan E. Leighley. 1992. "The Policy Consequences of Class Bias in State Electorates." *American Journal of Political Science* 36(2): 351–65.

Hill, Sarah A., and D. Roderick Kiewiet. 2015. "The Impact of State Supreme Court Decisions on Public School Finance." *Journal of Law, Economics, and Organization* 31(1): 61–92.

Hinkle, Rachael K., Andrew D. Martin, Jonathan David Shaub, and Emerson H. Tiller. 2012. "A Positive Theory and Empirical Analysis of Strategic Word Choice in District Court Opinions." *Journal of Legal Analysis* 4(2): 407–44.

Hinkle, Rachael K., and Michael J. Nelson. 2018. "The Intergroup Foundations of Policy Influence." *Political Research Quarterly* 71(4): 729–42.

Hirschl, Ran. 2007. *Towards Juristocracy: The Origins and Consequences of the New Constitutionalism.* Cambridge, Mass.: Harvard University Press.

Holbrook, Thomas, and Emily Van Dunk. 1993. "Electoral Competition in the American States." *American Political Science Review* 87(4): 955–62.

Hollis-Brusky, Amanda. 2015. *Ideas with Consequences: The Federalist Society and the Conservative Counterrevolution.* Oxford: Oxford University Press.

Holmes, Lisa M., and Jolly A. Emrey. 2006. "Court Diversification: Staffing the State Courts of Last Resort through Interim Appointments." *Justice System Journal* 27(1): 1–13.

Hughes, David. 2019. "New-Style Campaigns in State Supreme Court Retention Elections." *State Politics and Policy Quarterly* 19(2): 127–54.

Hume, Robert J. 2013. "Legitimacy, Yes but at What Cost?" *Judicature* 96(5): 209–12.

Hurwitz, Mark S., and Drew Noble Lanier. 2008. "Diversity in State and Federal Appellate Courts: Change and Continuity across 20 Years." *Justice System Journal* 29(1): 47–70.

Jacob, Herbert. 1964. "The Effect of Institutional Differences in the Recruitment Process: The Case of State Judges." *Journal of Public Law* 13(1): 104–19.

Jennings, Kent M., and Gregory B. Markus. 1984. "Partisan Orientations over the Long Haul: Results from the Three-Wave Political Socialization Panel Study." *American Political Science Review* 78(4): 1000–18.

Johnson, Ben, and Logan Strother. 2021. "The Supreme Court's (Surprising?) Indifference to Public Opinion." *Political Research Quarterly* 74(1): 18–34.

Johnson, Carrie. 2020. "Wave of Young Judges Pushed by McConnell Will Be 'Ruling for Decades to Come.'" National Public Radio, *All Things Considered*, July 2. https://www.npr.org/2020/07/02/886285772/trump-and-mcconnell-via-swath-of-judges-will-affect-u-s-law-for-decades (accessed August 19, 2020).

Jordan, Marty P., and Matt Grossmann. 2020. "The Correlates of State Policy Project," version 2.1. East Lansing, Mich.: Institute for Public Policy and Social Research (IPPSR).

Kales, Albert M. 1914. *Unpopular Government in the United States*. Chicago: University of Chicago Press.

———. 1917. "Methods of Selecting Judges." *Central Law Journal* 70(6): 1729–54.

Kang, Michael S., and Joanna M. Shepherd. 2011. "The Partisan Price of Justice: An Empirical Analysis of Campaign Contributions and Judicial Decisions." *New York University Law Review* 86(1): 69–130.

———. 2015. "Partisanship in State Supreme Courts: The Empirical Relationship between Party Campaign Contributions and Judicial Decision Making." *Journal of Legal Studies* 44(1): 161–85.

Kastellec, Jonathan P. 2013. "Racial Diversity and Judicial Influence on Appellate Courts." *American Journal of Political Science* 57(1): 167–83.

———. 2016. "Empirically Evaluating the Countermajoritarian Difficulty: Public Opinion, State Policy, and Judicial Review before *Roe v. Wade*." *Journal of Law and Courts* 4(1): 1–42.

———. 2018. "How Courts Structure State-Level Representation." *State Politics and Policy Quarterly* 18(1): 27–60.

Keely, Louise C., and Chih Ming Tan. 2008. "Understanding Preferences for Income Redistribution." *Journal of Public Economics* 92(5): 944–61.

Kelly, Nathan J., and Christopher Witko. 2012. "Federalism and American Inequality." *Journal of Politics* 74(2): 414–26.

Key, V. O., Jr. 1949. *Southern Politics in State and Nation*. New York: Alfred A. Knopf.

Kirkland, Patricia, and Alexander Coppock. 2018. "Candidate Choice without Party Labels: New Insights from U.S. Mayoral Elections 1945–2007 and Conjoint Survey Experiments." *Political Behavior* 40(3): 571–91.

Klarman, Michael. 1998–1999. "What's So Great about Constitutionalism?" *Northwestern University Law Review* 93(1): 145–94.

Klarner, Carl. 2013. "Other Scholars' Competitiveness Measures." Harvard Dataverse, version 1. https://dataverse.harvard.edu/dataset.xhtml?persistentId=doi:10.7910/DVN/QSDYLH (accessed August 18, 2020).

Klein, David, and Lawrence Baum. 2001. "Ballot Information and Voting Decisions in Judicial Elections." *Political Research Quarterly* 54(4): 709–28.

Klein, David E., and Robert J. Hume. 2003. "Fear of Reversal as an Explanation of Lower Court Compliance." *Law and Society Review* 37(3): 579–606.

Kritzer, Herbert M. 1979. "Federal Judges and Their Political Environments: The Influence of Public Opinion." *American Journal of Political Science* 23(1): 194–207.

———. 2003. "The Government Gorilla: Why Does Government Come Out Ahead in Appellate Courts?" In *In Litigation: Do the "Haves" Still Come Out Ahead?*, edited by Herbert M. Kritzer and Susan S. Silbey. Palo Alto, Calif.: Stanford University Press.

———. 2015a. *Justices on the Ballot: Continuity and Change in State Supreme Court Elections.* New York: Cambridge University Press.

———. 2015b. "State Supreme Court Election Data." Harvard Dataverse, V20, doi: 10.7910/DVN/1P1JFG.

———. 2016. "Impact of Judicial Elections on Judicial Decisions." *Annual Review of Law and Social Science* 12(1): 353–71.

———. 2020. *Judicial Selection in the States: Politics and the Struggle for Reform.* Cambridge: Cambridge University Press.

Kritzer, Herbert M., Paul Brace, Melinda Gann Hall, and Brent T. Boyea. 2007. "The Business of State Supreme Courts, Revisited." *Journal of Empirical Legal Studies* 4(2, July): 427–39.

Kuklinski, James H., and John E. Stanga. 1979. "Political Participation and Government Responsiveness: The Behavior of California Superior Courts." *American Political Science Review* 73(4): 1090–99.

La Raja, Raymond J., and Brian F. Schaffner. 2015. *Campaign Finance and Political Polarization: When Purists Prevail.* Ann Arbor: University of Michigan Press.

Langer, Laura. 2002. *Judicial Review in State Supreme Courts: A Comparative Study.* Albany: State University of New York Press.

———. 2006. *State Supreme Court Chief Justice Database.* Tempe: Arizona State University.

Lax, Jeffrey R., and Justin H. Phillips. 2009a. "How Should We Estimate Public Opinion in the States?" *American Journal of Political Science* 53(1): 107–21.

———. 2009b. "Gay Rights in the States: Public Opinion and Policy Responsiveness." *American Political Science Review* 103(3): 367–86.

———. 2012. "The Democratic Deficit in the States." *American Journal of Political Science* 56(1): 148–66.

Leerman, Lucas, and Fabio Wasserfallen. 2017. "Extending the Use and Precision of Subnational Public Opinion Estimation." *American Journal of Political Science* 61(4): 1003–22.

Lemley, Thomas G. 1987. "Employment at Will: Missouri Recognizes the Public Policy Exception." *Missouri Law Review* 52(3): 677–96.

Lempert, Richard. 1999. "A Classic at 25: Reflections on Galanter's 'Haves' Article and Work It Has Inspired." *Law and Society Review* 33(4): 1099–112.

LexisNexis. 2005. "LexisNexis Headnotes: How to Use the *More Like This Headnote* and *Retrieve All Headnotes* Features." http://www.lexisnexis.com/documents/LawSchool Tutorials/20070430111658_small.pdf (accessed August 18, 2020).

Light, Matthew W. 2001. "Who's the Boss? Statutory Damage Caps, Courts, and State Constitutional Law." *Washington and Lee Law Review* 58(1): 316–65.

Lindquist, Stefanie A. 2017. "Judicial Activism and State Supreme Courts: Institutional Design and Judicial Behavior." *Stanford Law and Policy Review* 28(1): 61–108.

Liptak, Adam. 2010. "Justices Offer Receptive Ear to Business Interests." *New York Times*, December 18, p. A1.

———. 2013. "Corporations Find a Friend in the Supreme Court." *New York Times*, May 4, p. BU1.

Lundberg, Paula J. 2000. "State Courts and School Funding: A Fifty-State Analysis." *Albany Law Review* 63(4): 1101–46.

Malin, Martin H. 2013. "Does Public Employee Collective Bargaining Distort Democracy? A Perspective from the United States." *Comparative Labor Law and Policy Journal* 34(2): 277–306.

Maltzman, Forrest, James F. Spriggs II, and Paul J. Wahlbeck. 2000. *Crafting Law on the Supreme Court*. New York: Cambridge University Press.

Marshall, Thomas R. 1989. *Public Opinion and the Supreme Court*. Boston: Unwin Hyman.

———. 1993. "Symbolic versus Policy Representation on the U.S. Supreme Court." *Journal of Politics* 55(1): 140–50.

———. 2008. *Public Opinion and the Rehnquist Court*. Albany: State University of New York Press.

Martin, Andrew D., and Kevin M. Quinn. 2002. "Dynamic Ideal Point Estimation via Markov Chain Monte Carlo for the U.S. Supreme Court." *Political Analysis* 10(2): 134–53.

Masket, Seth, and Boris Shor. 2014. "Polarization without Parties: Term Limits and Legislative Partisanship in Nebraska's Unicameral Legislature." *State Politics and Policy Quarterly* 15(1): 67–90.

Matthews, Donald R. 1954a. *The Social Background of Political Decision-Makers*. New York: Random House.

———. 1954b. "United States Senators and the Class Structure." *Public Opinion Quarterly* 18(1): 5–22.

McCloskey, Robert G. 1994. *The American Supreme Court*. Chicago: University of Chicago Press.

McCubbins, Mathew D., Roger G. Noll, and Barry R. Weingast. 1989. "Structure and Process, Politics, and Policy: Administrative Arrangements and the Political Control of Agencies." *Virginia Law Review* 75(2): 431–82.

McGuire, Kevin T. 1995. "Repeat Players in the Supreme Court: The Role of Experienced Lawyers in Litigation Success." *Journal of Politics* 57(1): 187–96.

McGuire, Kevin T., and James A. Stimson. 2004. "The Least Dangerous Branch Revisited: New Evidence on Supreme Court Responsiveness to Public Preferences." *Journal of Politics* 66(4): 1018–35.

Meltzer, Allan H., and Scott F. Richard. 1981. "A Rational Theory of the Size of Government." *Journal of Political Economy* 89(5): 914–27.

Moore, Roy. 2005. *So Help Me God: The Ten Commandments, Judicial Tyranny, and the Battle for Religious Freedom.* Nashville: Broadman & Holman.

Muhl, Charles J. 2001. "The Employment-at-Will Doctrine: Three Major Exceptions." *Monthly Labor Review* 124(1): 3–11.

Nagel, Stuart S. 1961. "Political Party Affiliations and Judges' Decisions." *American Political Science Review* 55(4): 843–50.

———. 1974. "Multiple Correlation of Judicial Background and Decisions." *Florida State University Law Review* 2(2): 258–80.

National Center for State Courts. 2020. "Judicial Selection in the States." NCSC. http://www.judicialselection.us (accessed August 19, 2020).

National Conference of State Legislatures. 2019. "Free and Equal Election Clauses in State Constitutions." NCSL (November 4). https://www.ncsl.org/research/redistricting/free-equal-election-clauses-in-state-constitutions.aspx (accessed August 18, 2020).

Nedelsky, Jennifer. 1990. *Private Property and the Limits of American Constitutionalism: The Madisonian Framework and Its Legacy.* Chicago: University of Chicago Press.

Nelson, Michael J. 2011. "Uncontested and Unaccountable: Rates of Contestation in Trial Court Elections." *Judicature* 94(5): 208–17.

———. 2014. "Responsive Justice? Retention Elections, Prosecutors, and Public Opinion." *Journal of Law and Courts* 2(1): 117–52.

———. 2016. "Judicial Elections and Support for State Courts." In *Judicial Elections in the 21st Century*, edited by Chris W. Bonneau and Melinda Gann Hall. New York: Routledge.

———. 2017. "The Effect of Electoral Competition on Judicial Decisionmaking." Paper presented at the annual meeting of the Southern Political Science Association. New Orleans, January 12–14.

Nelson, Michael J., Rachel Paine Caufield, and Andrew D. Martin. 2013. "OH, MI: A Note on Empirical Examinations of Judicial Elections." *State Politics and Policy Quarterly* 13(4): 495–511.

Nelson, Michael J., and James L. Gibson. 2018. "Using Survey Technology for Data Collection." *Law and Courts Newsletter* 28(1): 9–11.

———. 2019. "How Does Hyper-Politicized Rhetoric Affect the U.S. Supreme Court's Legitimacy?" *Journal of Politics* 81(4): 1512–16.

———. 2020. "Measuring Subjective Ideological Disagreement with the U.S. Supreme Court." *Journal of Law and Courts* 8(1): 75–94.

Nelson, Michael J., and Patrick Tucker. 2021. "The Dynamics of U.S. Supreme Court Legitimacy." *Journal of Politics* 83(2): 767–71.

Newport, Frank. 2018. "Looking into What Americans Mean by 'Working Class.'" *Gallup*, August 3. https://news.gallup.com/opinion/polling-matters/239195/looking-americans-mean-working-class.aspx (accessed August 18, 2020).

Norpoth, Helmut, and Jeffrey Segal. 1994. "Popular Influence on Supreme Court Decisions." *American Political Science Review* 88(3): 711–16.

Nowatzki, Mike. 2015. "Justice Sandstrom to Step Down after 24 Years on ND Supreme Court." *Jamestown Sun*, last modified December 30, 2015. https://www.jamestownsun.com/news/3913919-justice-sandstrom-step-down-after-24-years-nd-supreme-court (accessed August 18, 2020).

O'Connor, Sandra Day. 1984. "Our Judicial Federalism." *Case Western Law Review* 35(1): 1–12.

O'Reilly, James T., and Neil Gath. 1983. "Structures and Conflicts: Ohio's Collective Bargaining Law for Public Employees." *Ohio State Law Journal* 44(4): 891–942.

Pacheco, Julianna. 2011. "Using National Surveys to Measure Dynamic U.S. State Public Opinion: A Guide for Scholars and an Application." *State Politics and Policy Quarterly* 11(4): 415–39.

Page, Benjamin I., and Martin Gilens. 2017. *Democracy in America? What Has Gone Wrong and What We Can Do about It*. Chicago: University of Chicago Press.

Page, Benjamin I., and Lawrence R. Jacobs. 2009. *Class War? What Americans Really Think about Economic Inequality*. Chicago: University of Chicago Press.

Park, David K., Andrew Gelman, and Joseph Bafumi. 2004. "Bayesian Multilevel Estimation with Poststratification: State-Level Estimates from National Polls." *Political Analysis* 12(4): 375–85.

———. 2006. "State Level Opinions from National Surveys: Poststratification Using Multilevel Logistic Regression." In *Public Opinion in State Politics*, edited by Jeffrey E. Cohen, 209–28. Palo Alto, Calif.: Stanford University Press.

Pascal, Elizabeth. 2008. "Welfare Rights in State Constitutions." *Rutgers Law Journal* 39(4): 863–901.

Peltason, Jack W. 1961. *Fifty-Eight Lonely Men: Southern Federal Judges and School Desegregation*. New York: Harcourt, Brace & World.

Pérez-Peña, Richard. 2010. "Christie, Shunning Precedent, Drops Justice from Court." *New York Times*, May 3, p. A22.

Perry, H. W., Jr. 1991. *Deciding to Decide: Agenda Setting in the United States Supreme Court*. Cambridge, Mass.: Harvard University Press.

Pinello, Daniel R. 1999. "Linking Party to Judicial Ideology in American Courts: A Meta-analysis." *Justice System Journal* 20(3): 219–54.

Ranney, Austin. 1976. "Parties in State Politics." In *Politics in the American States*, 3rd ed., edited by Herbert Jacob and Kenneth Vines. Boston: Little, Brown & Co.

Rava, William C. 1998. "State Constitutional Protections for the Poor." *Temple Law Review* 71(3): 543–78.

Rebell, Michael A. 2009. *Courts and Kids: Pursing Educational Equity through the State Courts.* Chicago: University of Chicago Press.

Reddick, Malia, Rachel Paine Caufield, and Michael J. Nelson. 2009. "Racial and Gender Diversity on State Courts: An AJS Study." *Judges' Journal* 48(3): 28–32.

Rehm, Phillip. 2011. "Social Policy by Popular Demand." *World Politics* 63(2): 271–99.

Rigby, Elizabeth, and Gerald C. Wright. 2013. "Political Parties and Representation of the Poor in the American States." *American Journal of Political Science* 57(3): 552–65.

Rock, Emily, and Lawrence Baum. 2010. "The Impact of High-Visibility Contests for U.S. State Court Judgeships: Partisan Voting in Nonpartisan Elections." *State Politics and Policy Quarterly* 10(4): 368–96.

Romano, Michael K., and Todd A. Curry. 2020. *Creating the Law: State Supreme Court Opinions and the Effect of Audiences.* New York: Routledge.

Romer, Daniel, Kate Kenski, Kenneth Winneg, Christopher Adasiewicz, and Kathleen Hall Jamieson. 2006. *Capturing Campaign Dynamics, 2000 and 2004: The National Annenberg Election Survey.* Philadelphia: University of Pennsylvania Press.

Rosen, Jeffrey. 2006. *The Most Democratic Branch: How the Courts Serve America.* New York: Oxford University Press.

Rosenberg, Gerald N. 2008. *The Hollow Hope: Can Courts Bring about Social Change?*, 2nd ed. Chicago: University of Chicago Press.

Roux, Theunis. 2013. *The Politics of Principle: The First South African Constitutional Court, 1995–2005.* New York: Cambridge University Press.

Salamone, Michael F. 2014. "Judicial Consensus and Public Opinion: Conditional Response to Supreme Court Majority Size." *Political Research Quarterly* 67(2): 320–34.

———. 2018. *Perceptions of a Polarized Court: How Division among Justices Shapes the Supreme Court's Public Image.* Philadelphia: Temple University Press.

Sample, James, Adam Skaggs, Jonathan Blitzer, and Linda Casey. 2010. *The New Politics of Judicial Elections 2000–2009: Decade of Change.* New York: Brennan Center for Justice.

Sanes, Milla, and John Schmitt. 2014. *Regulation of Public Sector Collective Bargaining in the States.* Washington, D.C.: Center for Economic and Policy Research.

Savchak, Elisha Carol, and A. J. Barghothi. 2007. "The Influence of Appointment and Retention Constituencies: Testing Strategies of Judicial Decisionmaking." *State Politics and Policy Quarterly* 7(4): 394–415.

Schaffner, Brian F., and Matthew Streb. 2002. "The Partisan Heuristic in Low-Information Elections." *Public Opinion Quarterly* 66(4): 559–81.

Schaffner, Brian F., Matthew Streb, and Gerald Wright. 2001. "Teams without Uniforms: The Nonpartisan Ballot in State and Local Elections." *Political Research Quarterly* 54(1): 7–30.

Scheve, Kenneth, and David Stasavage. 2017. "Wealth Inequality and Democracy." *Annual Review of Political Science* 20: 451–68.

Schmidhauser, John R. 1959. "The Justices of the Supreme Court: A Collective Portrait." *Midwest Journal of Political Science* 3(1): 1–57.

———. 1961. "Judicial Behavior and the Sectional Crisis of 1837–1860." *Journal of Politics* 23(4): 615–40.

Schotland, Roy A. 1985. "Elective Judges' Campaign Financing: Are State Judges' Robes the Emperor's Clothes of American Democracy?" *Journal of Law and Politics* 2: 57–167.

———. 2001. "Campaign Finance in Judicial Elections." *Loyola of Los Angeles Law Review* 34(4): 1489–512.

Segal, Jeffrey A. 1984. "Predicting Supreme Court Cases Probabilistically: The Search and Seizure Cases, 1962–1981." *American Political Science Review* 78(4): 891–900.

Segal, Jeffrey A., and Albert D. Cover. 1989. "Ideological Values and the Votes of U.S. Supreme Court Justices." *American Political Science Review* 83(2): 557–65.

Segal, Jeffrey A., and Harold J. Spaeth. 1996. "The Influence of Stare Decisis on the Votes of United States Supreme Court Justices." *American Journal of Political Science* 40(4): 971–1003.

———. 2002. *The Supreme Court and the Attitudinal Model Revisited.* New York: Cambridge University Press.

Sen, Maya. 2014. "How Judicial Qualification Ratings May Disadvantage Minority and Female Candidates." *Journal of Law and Courts* 2(1): 33–65.

Sheehan, Reginald S. 1992. "Governmental Litigants, Underdogs, and Civil Liberties: A Reassessment of a Trend in Supreme Court Decisionmaking." *Western Political Quarterly* 45(1): 27–39.

Sheehan, Reginald S., William Mishler, and Donald R. Songer. 1992. "Ideology, Status, and the Differential Success of Direct Parties before the Supreme Court." *American Political Science Review* 86(2): 464–71.

Sheehan, Reginald S., and Kirk A. Randazzo. 2012. "Explaining Litigant Success in the High Court of Australia." *Australian Journal of Political Science* 47(2): 239–55.

Shepherd, Joanna M. 2009a. "Are Appointed Judges Strategic Too?" *Duke Law Journal* 58(7): 1589–626.

———. 2009b. "The Influence of Retention Politics on Judges' Voting." *Journal of Legal Studies* 38(1): 169–206.

———. 2010. "The Politics of Judicial Opposition." *Journal of Institutional Economics* 166(1): 88–107.

———. 2013. *Justice at Risk: An Empirical Analysis of Campaign Contributions and Judicial Decisions.* Washington, D.C.: American Constitution Society.

Shugerman, Jed Handelsman. 2010. "Economic Crisis and the Rise of Judicial Elections and Judicial Review." *Harvard Law Review* 123(5): 1061–150.

———. 2012. *The People's Courts: Pursuing Judicial Independence in America.* Cambridge, Mass.: Harvard University Press.

Sisk, Gregory C., Michael Heise, and Andrew P. Morriss. 1998. "Charting the Influences on the Judicial Mind: An Empirical Study of Judicial Reasoning." *New York University Law Review* 73(5): 1377–500.

Slater, Joseph E. 2013. "Teaching Private-Sector Labor Law and Public-Sector Labor Law Together." *Saint Louis University Law Journal* 58(1): 209–22.

Slotnick, Elliot, Sara Schiavoni, and Sheldon Goldman. 2017. "Obama's Judicial Legacy: The Final Chapter." *Journal of Law and Courts* 5(2): 363–422.

Songer, Donald, Ashlyn Kuersten, and Erin Kaheny. 2000. "Why the Haves Don't Always Come Out Ahead: Repeat Players Meet Amici Curiae for the Disadvantaged." *Political Research Quarterly* 53(3): 537–56.

Songer, Donald R., and Reginald S. Sheehan. 1992. "Who Wins on Appeal? Upperdogs and Underdogs in the United States Courts of Appeals." *American Journal of Political Science* 36(1): 235–58.

Songer, Donald R., Reginald S. Sheehan, and Susan Brodie Haire. 1999. "Do the 'Haves' Come Out Ahead over Time? Applying Galanter's Framework to Decisions of the U.S. Courts of Appeals, 1925–1988." *Law and Society Review* 33(4): 811–32.

Spaeth, Harold J., Lee Epstein, Andrew D. Martin, Jeffrey A. Segal, Theodore J. Ruger, and Sara C. Benesh. 2020. Supreme Court Database. http://supremecourtdatabase.org (accessed August 18, 2020).

Springer, Melanie J. 2019. "Where Is 'the South'? Assessing the Meaning of Geography in Politics." *American Politics Research* 47(5): 1100–34.

Squire, Peverill. 2008. "Measuring the Professionalization of U.S. State Courts of Last Resort." *State Politics and Policy Quarterly* 8(3): 223–38.

Sternlight, Jean R. 2003. "The Rise and Spread of Mandatory Arbitration as a Substitute for the Jury Trial." *University of San Francisco Law Review* 38(1): 17–38.

Stouffer, Samuel A. 1955. *Communism, Conformity, and Civil Liberties: A Cross-Section of the Nation Speaks Its Mind.* New York: J. Wiley.

Streb, Matthew J. 2013. "Gibson's *Electing Judges*: What We Know and What We Need to Know about the Effects of Politicized Judicial Campaigns." *Judicature* 96(5): 213–17.

Sullivan, John L., James Pierson, and George E. Marcus. 1982. *Political Tolerance and American Democracy.* Chicago: University of Chicago Press.

Sullivan, John L., Pat Walsh, Michal Shamir, David G. Barnum, and James L. Gibson. 1993. "Why Politicians Are More Tolerant: Selective Recruitment and Socialization among Political Elites in Britain, Israel, New Zealand, and the United States." *British Journal of Political Science* 23(1): 51–76.

Sunstein, Cass R. 2009. *A Constitution of Many Minds: Why the Founding Document Doesn't Mean What It Meant Before.* Princeton, N.J.: Princeton University Press.

Sunstein, Cass R., David Schkade, Lisa M. Ellman, and Andres Sawicki. 2006. *Are Judges Political? An Empirical Analysis of the Federal Judiciary.* Washington, D.C.: Brookings Institution Press.

Swenson, Karen. 2000. "School Finance Reform Litigation: Why Are Some State Supreme Courts Activist and Others Restrained?" *Albany Law Review* 63(4): 1147–82.

Szmer, John, Donald R. Songer, and Jennifer Bowie. 2016. "Party Capability and the U.S. Courts of Appeals: Understanding Why the 'Haves' Win." *Journal of Law and Courts* 4(1): 65–102.

Tarr, Alan G., and Mary Cornelia Porter. 1987. "Introduction: State Constitutionalism and State Constitutional Law." *Publius* 17(1): 1–12.

Tate, Neal C. 1981. "Personal Attribute Models of the Voting Behavior of U.S. Supreme Court Justices: Liberalism in Civil Liberties and Economics Decisions, 1946–1978." *American Political Science Review* 75(2): 355–67.

Traut, Carol Ann, and Craig F. Emmert. 1998. "Expanding the Integrated Model of Judicial Decision Making: The California Justices and Capital Punishment." *Journal of Politics* 60(4): 1166–80.

Tunney, John. 1974. "Court Awarded Attorney's Fees and Equal Access to the Courts." *University of Pennsylvania Law Review* 122(3): 636–713.

Ulmer, Sidney S. 1985. "Governmental Litigants, Underdogs, and Civil Liberties in the Supreme Court: 1903–1968 Terms." *Journal of Politics* 47(3): 899–909.

Usman, Jeffrey Omar. 2010. "Good Enough for Government Work: The Interpretation of Positive Constitutional Rights in State Constitutions." *Albany Law Review* 73(4): 1459–534.

Vavreck, Lynn, and Douglas Rivers. 2008. "The 2006 Cooperative Congressional Election Study." *Journal of Elections, Public Opinion, and Parties* 18(4): 355–66.

Vining, Richard L., Jr., and Teena Wilhelm. 2010. "Explaining High-Profile Coverage of State Supreme Court Decisions." *Social Science Quarterly* 91(3): 704–23.

Walker, Jack L. 1969. "The Diffusion of Innovations among the American States." *American Political Science Review* 63(3): 880–99.

Wanner, Craig. 1975. "The Public Ordering of Private Relations: Part I: Initiating Civil Cases in Urban Trial Courts." *Law and Society Review* 8(3): 421–40.

Ware, Stephen J. 2013. "Originalism, Balanced Legal Realism and Judicial Selection: A Case Study." *Kansas Journal of Law and Public Policy* 22(2): 165–204.

Warshaw, Christopher, and Jonathan Rodden. 2012. "How Should We Measure District-Level Public Opinion on Individual Issues?" *Journal of Politics* 74(1): 203–19.

Watson, Richard Abernathy, and Rondal G. Downing. 1969. *The Politics of the Bench and the Bar: Judicial Selection under the Missouri Nonpartisan Court Plan*. New York: Wiley.

Wheeler, Stanton, Bliss Cartwright, Robert A. Kagan, and Lawrence M. Friedman. 1987. "Do the 'Haves' Come Out Ahead? Winning and Losing in State Supreme Courts, 1870–1970." *Law and Society Review* 21(3): 403–45.

Williams, Robert F. 1990. *The New Jersey State Constitution: A Reference Guide*. New York: Greenwood Press.

Windett, Jason H., Jeffrey J. Harden, and Matthew E. K. Hall. 2015. "Estimating Dynamic Ideal Points for State Supreme Courts." *Political Analysis* 23(3): 461–69.

Wold, John T. 1974. "Political Orientations, Social Backgrounds, and Role Perceptions of State Supreme Court Judges." *Western Political Quarterly* 27(2): 239–48.

Wold, John T., and John H. Culver. 1987. "The Defeat of the California Justices: The Campaign, the Electorate, and the Issue of Judicial Accountability." *Judicature* 70(6): 348–55.

Woodson, Benjamin. 2015. "Politicization and the Two Modes of Evaluating Judicial Decisions." *Journal of Law and Courts* 3(2): 193–221.

———. 2017. "The Two Opposing Effects of Judicial Elections on Legitimacy Perceptions." *State Politics and Policy Quarterly* 17(1): 24–46.

Wright, Erik Olin. 1997. *Class Counts: Comparative Studies in Class Analysis.* New York: Cambridge University Press.

Zilis, Michael A. 2015. *The Limits of Legitimacy: Dissenting Opinions, Media Coverage, and Public Responses to Supreme Court Decisions.* Ann Arbor: University of Michigan Press.

———. 2018. "Minority Groups and Judicial Legitimacy: Group Affect and the Incentives for Judicial Responsiveness." *Political Research Quarterly* 71(2): 270–83.

Zorn, Christopher, and Jennifer Barnes Bowie. 2010. "Ideological Influences on Decision Making in the Federal Judicial Hierarchy: An Empirical Assessment." *Journal of Politics* 72(4): 1212–21.

INDEX

Boldface numbers refer to figures and tables.

Abbeville County School District v. State (South Carolina), 44
access to a state's justice institutions: background to as an issue domain, 53–59; coding court rulings as supporting or undermining equality, **42–43**; issue of, 261; litigant power differential and, **81**; litigant status and goals in litigation before state high courts, **90**; rulings pertaining to as an issue domain, 33–34 (*see also* attorneys' fees, payment of; class action policies; damage caps in civil litigation; mandatory arbitration policies); upperdog wins in state high court cases, percentage of, **83**
Alabama: class action litigation in, 55; defeat of appointed replacement judge by Roy Moore, 316n22; greater majority influence produced election of more conservative judges, 201; high court flip from conservative Democrats to conservative Republicans, 193; ideological polarization of the state high court, 172; judicial ideology and public policy in, 258; partisan makeup of state supreme court, 168; predicted probability of a state high court pro-equality outcome, **253**; predicted probability of a state high court pro-upperdog outcome, **254**; probability of pro-equality or upperdog case outcomes over time, 252–54; pro-equality outcome, decline in probability of, 315n4; Rove's strategy to elect Republicans to the Supreme Court, 17–18
Alaska: percentage of high court justices educated in both in-state undergraduate and legal institutions, 117, **118**; state high court justices' undergraduate institutions, 113, **114**
Aliotta, Jilda, 105, 111–12
Alons et al. v. Iowa District Court (Iowa), 91
American Abstract & Title Co. v. Rice (Arkansas), 55

American Federation of Teachers v. Ledbetter (Missouri), 49
Appeal of East Derry Fire Precinct (New Hampshire), 49
Appeal of Town of Durham (New Hampshire), 54
Arizona: pro-equality decisions in, 62, 274, 280; success rate of haves in the high court when seeking inequality, 93, 96
Arkansas: class action litigation in, 55; judicial retention in, 142; partisan affiliation and ideology of high court justices in, 193
Ash, Elliott, 191
attorneys' fees, payment of: the American rule, 56–57; coding court rulings as supporting or undermining equality, **43**; issue of, 33–34; issue of, background to, 56–57; LexisNexis headnotes used for case identification, 38; pro-equality outcomes, percentage of cases with, **60**

Bafumi, Joseph, 180
Barret, Amy Coney, 110
Barrilleaux, Charles, 14
Berry, Kate, 143
Biles, William Daniel, 280
Bird, Rose, 207
Bismarck Public School District #1 v. State (North Dakota), 45
Black, Ryan, 76
Bolivia, 136
Bonica, Adam, 5, 101, 107, 116, 123, 203
Bonica-Woodruff ideology score, 123, 129, 131, 303*n*92, 305*n*99
Boyea, Brent, 206–7, 219
Brace, Paul: cases focused on by, 296*n*22; death penalty votes by state supreme court justices, 202–3, 206–7, 219; invalidate laws, relative willingness of elected and appointed justices to, 312*n*17; partisan affiliation/judicial ideology and state supreme court justices' voting behavior, 202–3; party-adjusted surrogate judge ideology measure (PAJID), 101; public opinion, creating state-level measures of, 179; State Supreme Court Data Project, 36, 66; variability in the treatment of underdog/upperdog litigants by state courts, 74, 93; voting behavior of judges facing elections, 206–7
Branstad, Terry, 255
Bratton, Kathleen A., 108, 152
Brier, Carol A., 280
Broadwater v. Old Republic Surety (Utah), 57
Brown, Linda, 96
Brownback, Sam, 45, 190, 255–56
Brown v. Board of Education, 3–5, 96, 272
Bruch, Sarah, 30
Brudney, James, 111, 300*n*51
Buck v. Bell, 6
Bush, George H. W., 57
business interests, 73–74

Caldarone, Richard, 36, 206, 223, 289*n*10
California: mandatory arbitration in Los Angeles, 53; partisan control of government in, 175; pay of supreme court justices in, 214; Republican governor in a "liberal" state, 183
Canes-Wrone, Brandice: death penalty, majority support for, 197; keyword search used by, 36; methodology used by, 211, 289*n*9–10, 313*n*48; public opinion, state supreme court decisions and, 206–7, 223
capture of state supreme courts by state political regimes, 159–61, 192–95, 264–68, 271–72, 274; change in Democratic Party dominance in the fifty states, 1990-2015, **174**; courts and dominant political coalitions, relations between, 161–64; governing coalitions and

state high court rulings on inequality, **268**; the ideological and partisan composition of state supreme courts, 164–72; ideological polarization of state supreme courts, 172; interconnection of state supreme court ideology and partisanship with state public opinion and partisan control of state government, 182–86; judicial elections, role of, 186–92 (*see also* judicial selection); partisan "trifectas" and state supreme courts, 175–78; party control of the branches of state governments, 1990-2015, **176**; party dominance in state political regimes, 173–75; public opinion, role of, 178–86, 264–65 (*see also* public opinion); state high court alignment with other state political institutions, **178**

Carnes, Nicholas, 103–5, 110, 300–301n59, 301n63

Carrico, Harry L., 191

case outcomes, equality/inequality and, 234–36, 257–59; across states and time, 252–57; hypotheses concerning the conditions under which pro-equality litigants win, 236–39; hypotheses concerning the conditions under which upperdog litigants win, 243–45; pro-equality outcomes (*see* pro-equality case outcomes); pro-upperdog outcomes (*see* pro-upperdog case outcomes); supplementary statistical analyses, **259**

Caughey, Devin, 180, 212, 313n50

Chemerinsky, Erwin, 6

Christie, Chris, 144

Citizens United v. Federal Election Commission, 7, 59

Clark, Tom S.: death penalty, majority support for, 197; keyword search used by, 36; methodology used by, 211, 289n9–10, 313n48; public opinion, state supreme court decisions and, 206–7, 223

class action policies: coding court rulings as supporting or undermining equality, **42**; issue of, 33; issue of, background to, 54–56; LexisNexis headnotes used for case identification, 38; pro-equality outcomes, percentage of cases with, **60**

Clinton, Hillary, 15

collective bargaining rights: coding court rulings as supporting or undermining equality, **41**; issue of, 32, 261; issue of, background to, 48–49; LexisNexis headnotes used for case identification, 38; pro-equality outcomes, percentage of cases with, **60**

Colorado, partisan control of government in, 175

Commonwealth v. County Board of Arlington County (Virginia), 48–49

Constitution, U.S., Fifth Amendment, takings clause, 7

"Contract with America" (1994), 57

Cooperative Congressional Election Study, 179

criminal cases, exclusion of, 29–30

Dahl, Robert: capture of the Supreme Court by a governing coalition, 4, 21, 160, 162–63, 175, 264, 267, 272, 275; composition of the U.S. Supreme Court, public sentiment and, 178–79; interests of minorities advanced by the U.S. Supreme Court, 72–73; periodic appointment systems, public opinion and, 265

damage caps in civil litigation: coding court rulings as supporting or undermining equality, **43**; issue of, 34; issue of, background to, 58–59; LexisNexis headnotes used for case identification, 38; pro-equality outcomes, percentage of cases with, **60**

Delaware: dissent rate of the state supreme court, 276; election law in, 47;

partisan control of government in, 175; percentage of high court justices educated in both in-state undergraduate and legal institutions, 117, **118**; unanimity in state supreme court decisions in, 209

Disch v. Hicks (Alabama), 55

Douglas, William O., 4

Eastern Missouri Coalition of Police v. City of Chesterfield (Missouri), 49

education: social class background and, 111–19; state high court justices' undergraduate institution, in-state versus out-of-state, by state, **114**; state high court justices who attended both in-state undergraduate and law school, percentage of, **118**

Eisenberg, Theodore, 29

election law: coding court rulings as supporting or undermining equality, **41**; issue of, 32, 261; issue of, background on, 47–48; LexisNexis headnotes used for case identification, 38; pro-equality outcomes, percentage of cases with, **60**

election of judges. *See* judicial selection

Emmert, Craig, 203, 312*n*33

employment-at-will policies: coding court rulings as supporting or undermining equality, **42**; exceptions to, 50–51; issue of, 32, 261; issue of, background to, 50–52; LexisNexis headnotes used for case identification, 37; *Nelson v. Knight* (Iowa), 52–53; pro-equality outcomes, percentage of cases with, **60**

Emrey, Jolly, 143

Epstein, Lee, 73, 110, 206

equality/inequality: accountability to the majority and, 13–14; case outcomes across states and time, 252–57; case outcomes and (*see* case outcomes, equality/inequality and; pro-equality case outcomes; pro-upperdog case outcomes); changes in public opinion regarding, 1990-2015, **182**; coding court rulings for, 39, **40–43**; contribution of this book to the literature on, 25–27; courts are not the solution to issues of, 282–83; data on (*see* State High Court Inequality Database); equality sought in litigation by type of litigant, **89**; goals of haves/upperdog litigants regarding, 88–95; governing coalitions and state high court rulings, **268** (*see also* capture of state supreme courts by state political regimes); hungover courts and, 194; litigants and (*see* have nots/underdogs; haves/upperdogs; litigants); majoritarian state supreme courts and, overview of findings regarding, 261–74; pro-equality outcomes in state high courts across different policy subdomains, **60**; public opinion regarding, 180–82, 196–97, **197–99**; public policy and, 75; voting behavior of state supreme court justices pertinent to (*see* voting behavior of state supreme court justices on cases pertinent to inequality)

Erikson, Robert, 179

Ex parte D.W.W. (Alabama), 46

Ex parte Equity National Life Insurance Company (Alabama), 55

Ex parte Water Works & Sewer Board (Alabama), 55

Federal Arbitration Act (1925), 53

Federal Election Commission, 47

Franko, William, 180–81, 195–96, 212–13, 272

Frederic, Allen, 123

Galanter, Marc, 26, 71–73, 81–84, 86, 235–36

Gannon I–VI (Kansas), 45

gay rights: coding court rulings as supporting or undermining equality,

40; issue of, 31, 261; issue of, background on, 45–46; LexisNexis headnotes used for case identification, 38; litigant status and goals in litigation before state high courts, 90–91; pro-equality outcomes, percentage of cases with, **60**

Gelman, Andrew, 180

Gentges v. Oklahoma State Election Board (Oklahoma), 47–48

Georgia, ideological makeup of state supreme court, 168

Geyh, Charles, 193

Gibson, James, 16, 109, 115–16, 179, 302*n*80

Gilens, Martin: analogy between this book and research by, 288*n*79; class origins as determinant of attitudes and values, 104; empowering majorities in each of the states, anticipated result of, 202, 272; policy preferences, identification of policy domains based on, 30; political inequality translates to economic inequality thesis, 1, 26; shift to greater majority rule, argument for, 14–15; unequal responsiveness, study of, 236

Gillman, Howard, 271

Gilman, Michele, 286*n*15

Goelzhauser, Greg, 108, 133, 306*n*106

Goodridge v. Department of Public Health (Massachusetts), 46, 290*n*27

Gornick, Janet, 30

Graves, Bill, 256

Gray, Thomas, 205

Gwynne, Sam, 17

Hall, Matthew, 36, 101

Hall, Melinda Gann: cases focused on by, 296*n*22; invalidate laws, relative willingness of elected and appointed justices to, 312*n*17; modeling approach used by, 313*n*48; partisan affiliation/ judicial ideology and state supreme court justices' voting behavior, 202–3; party-adjusted surrogate judge ideology measure (PAJID), 101; State Supreme Court Data Project, 36, 66; variability in the treatment of underdog/upperdog litigants by state courts, 74, 93; voting behavior of elected judges in Louisiana, study of, 204

Haltom, William, 15

Hamilton, Alexander, 14

hangover judges. *See* judicial hangover

Hanssen, Andrew, 148

Harden, Jeffrey, 101

Harris, Kamala, 128

have nots/underdogs: case outcomes favoring (*see* pro-equality case outcomes); policy objectives of, 75 (*see also* equality/inequality). *See also* haves/upperdogs

haves/upperdogs: case outcomes favoring (*see* pro-upperdog case outcomes); hypotheses concerning wins by, 243–45; inequality sought in litigation by, question of, 88–95; interstate variability in differential win rates by whether or not seeking inequality, **95**; interstate variability in support for when seeking inequality, **94**; policy objectives as factor influencing litigation success of, 244, 246, 248–52, **249**, 269; policy objectives of, 75; relative power and success of, 71–72, 96; relative power and success of, previous research regarding, 72–75; results showing the success of, 82–88; sources of the variability in litigation success of, 93; win rates of, 92–93

Hawaii: judicial retention in, 141; partisan affiliation and ideology of high court justices in, 193; pay of supreme court justices in, 214

Heise, Michael, 116

348 Index

Herndon, James, 143
Hershkoff, Helen, 11–12, 271, 285n4
Hirschl, Ran, 8–9, 12–14, 18
Holbrook, Thomas, 13
Holmes, Lisa, 143
Holt v. 2011 Legislative Reapportionment Commission (Pennsylvania), 48
Hunter, Mike, 77

ideology: of judges (*see* judicial ideology); of law professors and judges, 5; public beliefs (*see* public opinion)
Illinois: election law in, 47; judicial selection and retention in, 142; partisan control of government in, 175; pay of supreme court justices in, 214; success rate of haves in the high court when seeking inequality, 96
independence: de jure versus in practice, 277; judicial (*see* judicial independence)
Independence National Education Association v. Independence School District (Missouri), 49
Indiana: anti-equality decisions in, 62; election law in, 47; ideological polarization of the state high court in, 172; partisan affiliation and ideology of high court justices in, 193; Public Employee Labor Relations Act, 49; success rate of haves in the high court when seeking inequality, 96
inequality. *See* equality/inequality
In re Corral-Lerma (Texas), 57
In re Estate of Lash (New Jersey), 57
In re Marriage Cases (California), 46, 291n30
Iowa: gay rights litigation in the state supreme court, 46, 91; *Nelson v. Knight*, 52–53; predicted probability of a state high court pro-equality outcome, **253**; predicted probability of a state high court pro-upperdog outcome, **254**; probability of pro-equality or upperdog case outcomes over time, 252, 254–55
issue domains: focus on, 260–61; identifying, 29–34, 37–38; levels of inequality and, 75; rulings pertaining to access to a state's justice institutions, 33–34, 75; rulings pertaining to the rights of minorities, including poor people, 31–32, 75; rulings pertaining to the rights of workers and employees, 32, 75

Janus v. American Federation of State, County, and Municipal Employees, 7
Jenkens v. Patel (Michigan), 58
Johnson, Lee A., 280
Johnson & Johnson, 77
judges/judicial behavior, 97–99; attitudinal model for state compared to U.S. supreme court justices, 99–101; backgrounds: decision-making and, 102–3; backgrounds: professional experience and career path, 106–7, 119, **120,** 121–23; backgrounds: social class origins, 103–5, 109–19, 132; campaign contributions and, 74, 101; data on the attributes of state supreme court justices, 107–8 (*see also* State High Court Justices Database); gender of, 152–53; model connecting backgrounds with attitudes and behavior, **98**; partisanship and, 101–2; partisanship/ideology and, 123–31; race and ethnicity of, 153–54
judicial accountability: advocacy for, 13–16; politics of, 16–19. *See also* judicial retention; judicial selection
judicial empowerment, 8
judicial hangover, 20–21, 161–63, 190–92, 194, 256, 266
judicial ideology, 98–99, 268–70, 273; average ideological conservatism score of state high courts, 1990-2015, **167**; background characteristics and attitudes of state high court justices,

INDEX 349

by initial selection, **151**; distribution of state high court justices' ideologies, by party affiliation, **124**; haves/ upperdog litigation success and, 244, 246, **248**, 249–52, **250–51**; ideological polarization of state high courts, 172; interconnection of state supreme court ideology and partisanship with state public opinion and partisan control of state government, 182–86; judicial selection and, 156–57; models of judicial behavior and, 99–102; operationalizing, 123–31; predictors of a state high court justices' ideology, by political party, **130**; predictors of a state high court justices' ideology and political party, **125**; predictors of average state high court ideology, 1990-2015, **185**; predictors of average state high court ideology by retention method, **188**; pro-equality case outcomes and, 237, 239–40, **242**, **243**; professional experience/career path and, 106–7, 119–23; public opinion liberalism, measure of, 218; public opinion liberalism and, 218–19, 226–30; relationship between partisanship and ideology on state high courts, 1990-2015, **171**; relationship between public opinion liberalism, Democratic Party dominance, and state high court ideology, **186**; relationship between year of birth and conservative ideology, **127**; social class origins and, 105, 109–19; on state supreme courts, 165, 168, 171–72; variability in the ideological composition of state high courts, 1990-2015, **170**; voting behavior of state supreme court justices and, 202–4
judicial independence, 161, 262, 274, 277–78. *See also* capture of state supreme courts by state political regimes
judicial policymaking, 35
judicial precedents, 35, 262

judicial retention, 134–35, 273–74, 278; capture of state high courts and, 187–92; contemporary systems of, 141–42; informal methods of, 143–44; key points to keep in mind, 142–43; marginal effect of Democratic dominance, by retention method, **189**; predictors of average state high court ideology and, **188**; pro-equality case outcomes and, 237, 240; voting behavior of state supreme court justices and, 204–6, 215–17
judicial selection, 134–36, 157–58, 273–74, 278–79; appointed interim state high court justices in states with formal judicial elections, percentage of, **150**; background characteristics and attitudes of state high court justices, by initial selection, **151**; capture of state high courts and, 186–92; composition of the bench and, 147–57; contemporary systems of, 138–41; demographic attributes and method of initial selection, 151–54; elections and elites in contemporary, 145–46; elections and partisanship in contemporary, 16–18; elite control of state courts and, 144–47; female state high court justices serving under different selection systems, percentage of, **152**; formal and informal selection of judges in the database, 148–49; history of in the United States, 136–38; ideology/partisan attachments and method of initial selection, 156–57; informal methods of, 143; interim appointments, 146–47; judicial election ballot types, **140**; "Kales plan"/"Missouri plan"/"merit selection," 138, 148; key points to keep in mind, 142–43; methods of judicial selection and retention for state high courts, 2015, **139**; minority state high court justices serving under different selection systems, percentage of, **153**; prior professional

experience and method of initial selection, 156; social class background and method of initial selection, 154–55; tenure length and, 190–92
judicial voting behavior. *See* voting behavior of state supreme court justices on cases pertinent to inequality
judiciary, the: courts as minoritarian institutions, 3–8; elite capture of, 8–9, 22 (*see also* capture of state supreme courts by state political regimes); selection effect, ideologically homogenous and conservative resulting from, 4–5; state high/supreme courts (*see* state supreme courts); U.S. Supreme Court (*see* Supreme Court, United States)

Kales, Albert, 138, 145–46
Kang, Michael S., 74, 205, 312*n*19
Kansas: dissent rate of the state supreme court, 276, 280; percentage of high court justices educated in both in-state undergraduate and legal institutions, 117, **118**; predicted probability of a state high court pro-equality outcome, **253**; predicted probability of a state high court pro-upperdog outcome, **254**; probability of pro-equality or upperdog case outcomes over time, 252, 255–56; school finance, "poster child" for battle over, 45; state supreme court as policymaking institution, study of, 29; unanimity in state supreme court decisions in, 209
Kastellec, Jonathan P., 313*n*50
Kelly, Jason P., 197, 207, 211, 223, 313*n*48
Kelo v. City of New London, 7
Kentucky: election law in, 47; pro-equality decisions in, 62
Key, V. O., 13, 309*n*15
Klarman, Michael, 5–7
Klarner, Carl, 173

Klobuchar, Amy, 128
Kritzer, Herbert M., 267

Landes, William, 73
Langer, Laura, 101, 108, 203, 312*n*17
Lavender, Robert E., 191
Lax, Jeffrey R., 179–80, 310*n*25
legal policy liberalism, 39
Lehman, Larry L., 123
Levin, Charles, 303*n*91
LexisNexis: headnotes, 37–38; use of, 36
LexisNexis case categorization scheme, 30
LGBT rights. *See* gay rights
Lindquist, Stefanie, 317*n*30
Liptak, Adam, 288*n*67
Lisk, Cathleen, 143
litigants: distribution of types across state high courts, **79**; effect of litigant status differentials on petitioner success before state high courts, **87**; effect of petitioner status differential on petitioner success before state high courts, **86**; equality/inequality and relative power of, 71–72, 96; equality sought in state high court litigation, by type of litigant, **89**; measuring litigant status, 76–78; measuring power differentials, 78, 80, **80**; measuring power differentials by issue domain, **81**; measuring the outcome of a case, 80–81; petitioner wins in state high courts, percentage of, **85**; probability of petitioner win in state high courts, by petitioner status differential, **87**; pro-equality, factors leading to win for, 236–39; as "repeat player," 73; resources of, 270–71 (*see also* haves/upperdogs); status and goals in litigation before state high courts, **90**; success rates in state high courts by litigant status, **84**; upperdog, factors leading to win for, 243–45. *See also* have nots/underdogs; haves/upperdogs
Little, Thomas C., 180

Lockyer v. City and County of San Francisco (California), 46
Loffredo, Stephen, 12
Louisiana: common law systems, partial exception to, 35; percentage of high court justices educated in both in-state undergraduate and legal institutions, 117, **118**; state high court justices' undergraduate institutions, 113, **114**

MacLeod, Bentley, 191
Mahon v. Keisling et al. (Oregon), 91
majority empowerment thesis, 14–16, 21
Malone, Charles R., 64
mandatory arbitration policies: coding court rulings as supporting or undermining equality, **42**; issue of, 33; issue of, background to, 53–54; LexisNexis headnotes used for case identification, 38; pro-equality outcomes, percentage of cases with, **60**
Mansfield, Edward M., 119
Marrero v. Commonwealth (Pennsylvania), 44
Marshall, Thomas, 109–10
Martin, Andrew, 206
Maryland, partisan makeup of state supreme court, 168, 274–75
Massachusetts: judicial retention in, 141; pro-equality decisions in, 62; Republican governor in a "liberal" state, 183
Matthews, Donald, 104, 110
McCann, Michael, 15
McCleary v. State (Washington), 45
McCloskey, Robert, 4
McCubbins, Mathew, 277
McIver, John, 179
Merritt, Deborah, 111, 300n51
methodology: case identification, 35–38; for case-level analysis, 238–39; coding as pro- or anti-equality, 39, **40–43**; coding cases, 38, 65–67; coding judge attributes, 132–33; filtering cases, 39, 69; measurement of social class origins, 109–19; measuring litigant status, 76–78; measuring power differentials, 78, 80, **80**; measuring power differentials by issue domain, **81**; measuring state-level public opinion, 179–82, 195–97, **197,** 212–13; measuring the outcome of a case, 80–81; validity and reliability of coders' judgments, 59, 67–69; weighting the case data, 69–70
Meyers, Marcia, 30
Michigan: dissent rate of the state supreme court, 276; judicial selection in, 140–41; pro-equality decisions in, 62; unanimity in state supreme court decisions in, 209
Michigan v. Long, 10
Miller, Geoffrey, 29
Minnesota: coordination of retirements from the Supreme Court to thwart formal selection process, 279; partisan control of government, 175; percentage of interim appointments on state high court, 149, **150,** 201
minorities: less privileged (*see* have nots/ underdogs); privileged (*see* haves/ upperdogs); rights of (*see* rights of minorities, including poor people)
Mississippi: judicial retention in, 142; percentage of the public believing that the rich are getting richer, 181
Missouri, collective bargaining litigation in, 49
Mobile Infirmary Medical Center v. Hodgen (Alabama), 58
Montana, pay of supreme court justices in, 214
Moore, Roy, 108, 119, 145, 294n117, 302n84, 316n22
Morriss, Andrew, 116

National Annenberg Election Survey, 179
National Center for Education Statistics, Integrated Postsecondary Education Data System, 113, 115

National Center for State Courts, 191
National Council on State Legislatures, 47
Nebraska, computing partisanship in, 173–74
Nelson v. Knight (Iowa), 52–53
Nevada, percentage of high court justices educated in both in-state undergraduate and legal institutions, 117, **118**
New Hampshire: ideological polarization of the state high court in, 172; judicial retention in, 141; percentage of high court justices educated in both in-state undergraduate and legal institutions, 117, **118**
New Jersey: judicial retention in, 141–42, 144; partisan affiliation and ideology of high court justices in, 193; partisan makeup of state supreme court, 168; pro-equality decisions in, 62, 280; Republican governor in a "liberal" state, 183; right to collective bargaining in, 48; success rate of haves in the high court when seeking inequality, 96
New Mexico: dissent rate of the state supreme court, 276; ideological makeup of state supreme court, 168; ideological polarization of the state high court in, 172; judicial selection and retention in, 142; partisan affiliation and ideology of high court justices in, 193
New York, pro-equality decisions in, 62
Noll, Roger, 277
North Carolina, judicial retention in, 142
North Dakota, pay of supreme court justices in, 214

Obama, Barack, 162
Obergefell v. Hodges, 4, 272, 287*n*37
O'Connor, Sandra Day, 10–11
Ohio: evolution of collective bargaining in, 48; judicial selection in, 140–41; state high court justices' undergraduate institutions, 113, **114**

Oklahoma, litigant status versus Johnson & Johnson, question of, 77
Oregon: election law in, 47; partisan affiliation and ideology of high court justices in, 193
Owens, Ryan, 76

Pacheco, Julianna, 180
Page, Alan, 303*n*91
Page, Benjamin I., 14–15, 202, 272
Park, David, 180, 207
Parkway School District v. Parkway Association of Education, etc., Local 902/ MNEA (Missouri), 49
partisanship: attitudes/values of state supreme court justices and, 101–2; average partisan makeup of state high courts, **166**; change in Democratic Party dominance in the fifty states, 1990-2015, **174**; decisional behavior of state supreme court justices and, 123–24; distribution of state high court justices' ideologies, by party affiliation, **124**; ideology and, 123–31; interconnection of state supreme court ideology and partisanship with state public opinion and partisan control of state government, 182–86; judicial selection and, 156–57; marginal effect of Democratic dominance, by retention method, **189**; partisan "trifectas" and state supreme courts, 175–78; party dominance in state political regimes, 173–75; predictors of a state high court justices' ideology, by political party, **130**; predictors of a state high court justices' ideology and political party, **125**; relationship between partisanship and ideology on state high courts, 1990-2015, **171**; selection of judges and, 138, 140–41; of state supreme courts, 165, 168, 171–72; variability in the partisan composition of state high courts, 1990-2015, **169**

Paulson v. Flathead Conservation District (Montana), 54
Pennsylvania: class action litigation in, 56; ideological makeup of state supreme court, 168; judicial selection and retention in, 142
Persky, Aaron, 312–13*n*38
Phillips, Justin H., 180, 310*n*25
policy domains. *See* issue domains
Political, Legal, Economic, and Social Inequality State Supreme Court Database. *See* State High Court Inequality Database
poor people/the impoverished, rights of. *See* rights of minorities, including poor people
Posner, Richard, 73
Pribble v. State Farm Mutual Automobile Insurance Company (Wyoming), 57
pro-equality case outcomes: case-level control variables and, 242; model accounting for, 239–40; predicted probability of by judicial ideology, **242**; predicted probability of in four states, **253**; random effects logistic regression results with conditional effects for public opinion, **241**; results of the model accounting for, 240–43
pro-upperdog case outcomes: case-level control variables and, 247–48; marginal effect of litigant objectives by judicial ideology, **250**; model accounting for, 245–46; predicted probability of by judicial ideology, **248**; predicted probability of by judicial ideology and litigant objectives, **251**; predicted probability of in four states, **254**; random effects logistic regression results, **247**; random effects logistic regression results with conditional effects for litigant objectives, **249**; results of the model accounting for, 246–52

public opinion: attitudes toward equality in each of the states, 196–97, **197–99**; changes in attitudes toward equality and liberalism, **182**; composition of the bench and, 178–79; haves/upperdog litigation success and, 245; identification of issue domains and, 30; interconnection of state supreme court ideology and partisanship with state public opinion and partisan control of state government, 182–86; judicial ideology and, 218–19, 226–30; measuring state-level, 179–82, 195–97, 212–13; pro-equality case outcomes and, 237–41, **241**, 270; relationship between public opinion liberalism, Democratic Party dominance, and state high court ideology, **186**; voting behavior of state supreme court justices and, 206–9, 217–23, 273

Ranney, Austin, 173
Ranney index, 173
Rava, William C., 12, 287*n*47
Republican Party of Minnesota v. White, 311*n*3
Rhode Island: judicial retention in, 141; partisan makeup of state supreme court, 168; percentage of high court justices educated in both in-state undergraduate and legal institutions, 117, **118**; success rate of haves in the high court when seeking inequality, 96
rights of minorities, including poor people: background to as an issue domain, 44–48; coding court rulings as supporting or undermining equality, **40–41**; litigant power differential and, 81; litigant status and goals in litigation before state high courts, **90**; rules pertaining to as an issue domain, 31–32 (*see also* election law; gay rights; school finance); upperdog wins in state high court cases, percentage of, **83**

354   Index

Robert C. Ozer, P.C. v. Borquez (Colorado), 46
Roberts v. Dudley (Washington), 57
Rodden, Jonathan, 310*n*25
Rooney v. Tyson (New York), 51
Roosevelt, Franklin D., 162
Rosen, Eric S., 64, 280
Rosenberg, Gerald, 279, 289*n*80
Roux, Theunis, 316*n*19
Rove, Karl, 17–18, 20, 256
Ryan v. Dan's Food Stores, Inc. (Utah), 51–52, 292*n*63

Sadin, Meredith L., 301*n*63
Sandstrom, Dale V., 123
Schiavoni, Sara, 111, 300*n*51
Schmidhauser, John, 109
school finance: coding court rulings as supporting or undermining equality, 40; funding equality, background on, 44–45; funding equality, issue of, 31, 261; LexisNexis headnotes used for case identification, 38; pro-equality outcomes, percentage of cases with, **60**
Schotland, Roy A., 288*n*66
Sebelius, Kathleen, 255–56
Segal, Jeffrey, 262
Semet, Amy, 36, 207
Sen, Maya, 5, 107, 116
Sheehan, Reginald, 76, 82, 84–85
Shepherd, Joanna M., 74, 204–5, 312*n*19
Shugerman, Jed, 147, 201, 204, 273, 312*n*17
Sisk, Gregory, 116
Smith, Bill, 18
social class: background characteristics and attitudes of state high court justices, by initial selection, **151**; concept of, 103–4; judicial behavior and, 105, 132; judicial selection and, 154–55; legislative behavior and, 104–5; measuring social class origins, 109–19
Songer, Donald, 76, 82, 84–85
South Carolina, judicial selection in, 140

South Dakota: ideological makeup of state supreme court, 168, 268; partisan affiliation and ideology of high court justices in, 193; partisan makeup of state supreme court, 168, 275; pay of supreme court justices in, 214
Spaeth, Harold, 36, 39, 65, 262
Spill, Rorie, 108, 152
State ex rel. Hewitt v. Kerr (Missouri), 54
State High Court Inequality Database, 28–29, 65; case identification methodology, 35–38; coding as pro- or anti-equality, 39, **40–43**; coding cases, 38, 65–67; controlling for case-level attributes, 59, 61–62; creating, 35–44; exclusions from, 29–30; filtering cases, 39, 69; intercourt variability in supporting greater equality, 62, **63**; inter-justice variability in support for greater equality, 62, 64, **64**; introduction to, 29–35; issue/policy domains (*see* issue domains); pro-equality outcomes in state high courts across different policy subdomains, **60**; validity and reliability of coders' judgments, 59, 67–69; weighting the case data, 69–70
State High Court Justices Database: conclusions from, 131–32; creation of, 108, 132–33; inter-coder reliability, 68–69; measuring on-the-job experiences, 119–23; measuring social class origins, educational background as approach to, 111–19; measuring social class origins, previous attempts at, 109–11; operationalizing judicial ideologies, 123–31; state high court justices' undergraduate institution, in-state versus out-of-state, by state, **114**; state high court justices who attended both in-state undergraduate and law school, percentage of, **118**
state justice institutions, access to. *see* access to a state's justice institutions

State Safety Net Policy data set, 30
state supreme courts: broader connections and conclusions of research on, 277–78; capture of by elites (*see* capture of state supreme courts by state political regimes); case outcomes from (*see* case outcomes, equality/inequality and); data resources, limitations and frustrations associated with, 281–82; the ideological and partisan composition of, 164–72; as majoritarian policymakers, overview of findings, 261–74; overriding conclusions about, 26–27; politics of judicial elections, 16–19 (*see also* judicial selection); significance of in addressing issues of inequality, 2–3, 9–12; significant findings, overview of, 274–77; theory undergirding research, overview of, 19–22; unanswered questions and the limitations of the research, 279–81; underutilization thesis, 12; variability across, 12, 264
State v. Philip Morris USA, Inc. (New Hampshire), 54
Stone v. Williamson (Michigan), 58–59
substantive due process, 73
Supreme Court, United States: attitudinal model of judicial behavior applied to, 99–100; attorneys' fees, statement of the American rule regarding, 56; backgrounds of justices, 103; caseload reduction in recent years, 2, 9; dominant political coalition and, 162–63; independence/insulation of, 13; minoritarian institution, as exemplar of, 262; protection of overprivileged minorities by, 5–8; withdrawal from politics of, 2

Talley v. Flathead Valley Community College (Montana), 51
Tennessee: ideological polarization of the state high court in, 172; judicial retention in, 142

Texas: anti-equality decisions in, 62; greater majority influence produced election of more conservative judges, 201; partisan affiliation and ideology of high court justices in, 193; predicted probability of a state high court pro-equality outcome, **253**; predicted probability of a state high court pro-upperdog outcome, **254**; probability of pro-equality or upperdog case outcomes over time, 252, 256; pro-equality decisions in, 274; Rove's strategy to elect Republicans to the Supreme Court, 17; success rate of haves in the high court when seeking inequality, 93, 96
tort reform, 15
Traut, Carol Ann, 203, 312*n*33
Trump, Donald, 145, 162
Tyson, Mike, 51

underdogs. *See* have nots/underdogs
upperdogs. *See* haves/upperdogs
U.S. government as a litigant excluded from analysis, 77
U.S. Supreme Court Justices Database, 110
Utah: ideological makeup of state supreme court, 168; partisan control of government in, 175; percentage of the public believing that the rich are getting richer, 181

Van Dunk, Emily, 13
Varnum v. Brien (Iowa), 46, 91, 272, 286–87*n*37
Vilsack, Tom, 255
Virginia, judicial selection in, 140
voting behavior of state supreme court justices on cases pertinent to inequality, 200–202, 230–33; control variables in model of, 213–15, 224–26; empirical results from model of, 215–30; ideological determinants, 202–4, 215; institutional structures and, 204–6,

215–17; judicial ideology and public opinion liberalism, interplay of, 218–19, 226–30; pro-equality state high court vote, effect of public opinion on probability of by retention method, **223**; pro-equality state high court vote, predicted probability of by judicial compensation, **225**; pro-equality state high court vote, predicted probability of by judicial ideology, **217**; pro-equality state high court vote, predicted probability of by public opinion, **218**; pro-equality state high court vote, predicted probability of by public opinion liberalism and judicial ideology, **227**; pro-equality state high court vote, predicted probability of by retention method, **221**; pro-equality state high court vote, predicted probability of by retention method, public opinion liberalism, and judicial ideology, **229**; pro-equality state high court votes, random effects logistic regression results, **216**; pro-equality state high court votes with conditional effects for public opinion, random effects logistic regression results, **220**; public opinion, influence of, 206–9, 217–23; public opinion in the American states, measuring, 212–13; rates of unanimous decisions by state high courts in equality cases, **210**; research design and modeling strategy for model of, 211–12; supplementary statistical analyses, **233**; unanimity in most state supreme court decisions, 209–11

Voting Rights Act of 1965, 47

Walker, Jack L., 25
Wallace, John, 144
Ware, Stephen, 29
Warshaw, Christopher, 180, 212, 310*n*25, 310*n*32, 313*n*50
Weingast, Barry, 277
West Virginia, ideological polarization of the state high court in, 172
Wheeler, Stanton, 73–75
White, Penny, 207
White v. State (Nebraska), 51
Wilkes v. Phoenix Home Life Mutual Insurance Company (Pennsylvania), 56
Wilner, Alan M., 123
Windett, Jason, 36, 101
Witko, Christopher, 180–81, 195–96, 212–13, 272
Wold, John, 109
Woodruff, Michael, 101, 123, 203
workers and employees, rights of: background to as an issue domain, 48–53; coding court rulings as supporting or undermining equality, **41–42**; litigant power differential and, **81**; litigant status and goals in litigation before state high courts, **90**; rulings pertaining to as an issue domain, 32 (*see also* collective bargaining rights; employment-at-will policies); upperdog wins in state high court cases, percentage of, **83**
workers' compensation cases, exclusion of, 30
Wright, Gerald, 179
Wyoming: partisan affiliation and ideology of high court justices in, 193; partisan makeup of state supreme court, 168